Using
WordPerfect 6.0
for DOS

▌More Software Application Tutorials from Mitchell McGraw-Hill

For Full Term
Application Courses...

Schmitz	Practical DOS! 2nd Edition (2.0 - 5.0)
Frederick/Yasuda	Using Windows 3.0/3.1
Larsen/Hydrusko	Using WordPerfect 6.0 for Windows
Leeburg/Larsen	Using WordPerfect for Windows
Cluck	Using Word for Windows
Leeburg/Purvis	Using WordPerfect 6.0 for DOS
O'Donnell/Phillips	Beginning WordPerfect 6.0 for DOS
O'Donnell/Phillips	Advanced WordPerfect 6.0 for DOS
Pitter/Pitter	Using Lotus 1-2-3 for DOS Release 3.1+
Williams/Williams	Beginning Lotus 1-2-3 Release 2.2
Williams/Williams	Advanced Lotus 1-2-3 Release 2.2
Williams/Williams	Beginning Lotus 1-2-3 for Windows
Williams/Williams	Advanced Lotus 1-2-3 for Windows
Amoroso	Decision Making Using Lotus 1-2-3: Building Quality Applications
Shuman	Using Microsoft Excel 4.0 for Windows
Pitter/Pitter	Using Microsoft Excel 4.0 for Windows: The Basics
Grauer/Barber	Database Management Using dBASE IV and SQL
Shuman	Using dBASE IV
Reiss	Using Paradox 4.0
Reiss	Using Paradox for Windows
Eakins	Desktop Publishing on PC Compatibles and the Macintosh: Pagemaker 4X
Frederick/Yasuda	Using Microsoft Works 3.0 for DOS
Frederick/Yasuda	Using Microsoft Works 3.0 for Windows
Yasuda/Frederick	Using Microsoft Works 3.0 on the MAC

For a Quicker Pace
or Brief Introduction...

Schmitz	First Look at DOS 6.0
Schmitz	First Look at Windows 3.0/3.1
Ellis	First Look at Macintosh and System 7
Leeburg/Purvis	First Look at WordPerfect 6.0 for DOS
Cluck	First Look at Microsoft Word for Windows 2.0
Larsen/Hydrusko	First Look at WordPerfect 6.0 for Windows
Smith	First Look at Lotus Release 4 for Windows
Skinner	First Look at Lotus 1-2-3 for DOS Release 3.1+
Skinner	First Look at Harvard Graphics 3.0 for DOS
Skinner	First Look at Lotus Release 2.4
Rosner	First Look at Quattro Pro for Windows
Ellis	First Look at Paradox for Windows
Price	First Look at dBASE 1.5/2.0 for DOS
Larsen/Leeburg	First Look at NetWare 2.2
Pitter	First Look at Works 2.0 for the Mac
Pitter	First Look at Works 2.0 for the PC

Using

WordPerfect 6.0

for DOS

April 18th

Verlene Leeburg
Peggy Purvis

Mitchell McGraw-Hill
New York St. Louis San Francisco Auckland Bogota Caracas
Lisbon London Madrid Mexico Milan Montreal New Delhi Paris
San Juan Singapore Sydney Tokyo Toronto

Mitchell McGraw-Hill
San Francisco, CA 94133

Using WordPerfect 6.0 for DOS

1 2 3 4 5 6 7 8 9 0   SEM   SEM   9 0 9 8 7 6 5 4

ISBN 0-07-037625-5

Sponsoring editor: Roger Howell
Editorial assistant: Kim James
Technical reviewer: Annette Calloway
Production supervisor: Leslie Austin
Project manager: Jane Granoff
Interior designer: Wendy Calmenson
Compositors: Abby Zimberg, Rad Proctor
Cover designer: Michael Rogondino
Printer and binder: Semline, Inc.

Library of Congress Card Catalog No. 93-78734

Contents

Lesson 8 Working with Multiple Documents   175

Lesson 9 Advanced Formatting Features   198

Preface

Using WordPerfect 6.0 utilizes the same sound pedagogy and comprehensive coverage demonstrated in the author's previous WordPerfect texts, *Using WordPerfect for Windows, Using WordPerfect 5.1,* and *Using WordPerfect 5.0.* It presents the word processing concepts and WordPerfect commands in a step-by-step format so that this book can be used in a self-paced or lecture environment and later as a reference tool.

Approach and Organization

Using WordPerfect 6.0 assumes no prior knowledge. The first lesson introduces the student to the IBM PC and DOS. Students then progress into WordPerfect 6.0. Each feature is then implemented into interesting and fun real-world examples using hands-on exercises and screen displays. In addition to producing standard forms such as letters, envelopes, and contract agreements, the student will create projects with a desktop publishing flair such as newsletters, letterheads, tables, and forms.

Each lesson begins with a list of objectives. Separate sections then describe the different program features, beginning with a description and procedure of the function, followed by exercises that lead the student through a practical application. Both the pull-down menu and the shortcut function key approach are offered whenever available for each function. All exercises give both keyboard and mouse steps required to accomplish each task. "Tips" and "Caution" sections throughout the text alert the student to possible problems or errors. Each lesson concludes with a review of commands, a self-test, and additional exercises to reinforce the student's learning.

Distinguishing Features

- **Comprehensive coverage** progresses from novice to advanced word processing concepts, including desktop publishing features presented in a building-block approach.

- **Tutorial approach** guides the reader through easy to read and understand step-by-step hands-on exercises.

- **Screen displays** add clarity to the exercises and improve the comfort level of the student.

- **Mouse, keyboard, and shortcut keys** steps are given for each function and feature presented.
- **Case study** creates realism through the use of documents that might be used in a real business environment.
- **Proven author** Verlene Leeburg has co-authored *Using WordPerfect 5.0*, *Using WordPerfect 5.1*, and *Using WordPerfect for Windows*.
- **Two appendices** containing a comprehensive command summary and the WordPerfect 6.0 codes are found at the end of the text.

Supporting Materials

- **The Instructor's Manual** contains teaching tips, answers to the end-of-lesson review questions, copies of completed end-of-lesson assignments, and additional projects and tests that instructors may use as optional learning aids.
- **A data disk** containing the sample documents that correspond with the assignments in each lesson is packaged with the Instructor's Manual. The sample files may be copied to floppies and distributed to students or can be loaded onto a network that can be accessed by students.

Hardware Requirements

- Personal computer using at least a 386 processor
- 520K free conventional memory
- DOS 6.0 (or an earlier version with a memory management program)
- Hard disk with 16M free disk space for complete installation
- VGA graphics adapter and monitor

Acknowledgements

We would like to thank all the people at Mitchell McGraw-Hill Publishing for their part in orchestrating the production of this textbook, specifically our editor, Roger Howell. Special thanks to Jane Granoff and her staff for helping us get through the process. We give our appreciation to our copy editor, Mark Woodworth, for his attention to detail and sense of humor. We also want to recognize Sheri Aaberg for allowing us to model our case study after her business. We received invaluable feedback from our technical editor, Annette Callaway, and our reviewers: Sarah Baker, Ambassador College; Sallyann Hanson, Mercer County Community College; Rhea Leonard, independent software trainer and consultant.

Acknowledgements are not complete without thanking our families for their understanding and support. We are indebted to them for helping us make it through the long work days, production deadlines and endless edits. We hope to share our success with them.

Introducing the PC and Disk Operating System

Objectives

Upon completion of this lesson, you will be able to do the following:

- List the parts of a computer system
- Identify the keyboard and its various keys
- Know the proper way to handle and prepare floppy disks
- List the three types of software
- Define word processing and list standard features
- List advantages for using word processing
- Boot the computer
- Define a file
- Name files using correct DOS naming conventions
- Use various file management DOS commands
- Use wildcards
- Recognize directory and subdirectory organization
- Create directories
- Change from one directory to another
- Copy a file from one directory to another
- Remove a directory

To prepare for this lesson, you will begin using your personal computer (PC). Locate a blank floppy disk that you will use for your sample work.

The first few sections of this lesson are strictly "reading" sections to give you the necessary background information on hardware and software to enable you to begin working on your computer. Read these sections carefully. You will then proceed to a brief introduction of the Disk Operating System (DOS) that offers important details on creating and naming documents, caring for and handling storage disks, and working on hard disk systems. After completing this lesson, you will be ready to begin working with WordPerfect 6.0 in Lesson 2.

A Computer System

The four basic elements of a computer system are **input, processing, storage,** and **output.** Input comes from computer users' entering instructions or data from an input device, such as the keyboard or mouse. Once the data has been entered, it is processed in the **central processing unit (CPU).** Processing is the execution of a set of instructions given to the computer to perform logical or arithmetic calculations. Storage is divided into two types, **primary** and **secondary.**

Primary storage is data being processed in memory. Memory is like your work desk, holding the computer's executing instructions, the data currently being processed, and the calculations being created by the CPU. This memory is temporary and the data in it is erased when the computer loses power or the program is terminated.

Secondary storage, on the other hand, is data permanently stored on disk (either floppy or hard disk). Disk storage is similar to a filing cabinet. Once data is saved to disk it will not be lost when the computer's power is turned off. Output is the data after it has been converted to readable information, either displayed on the computer screen or printed on paper.

Computer Hardware

The physical elements of the computer system that we can see and touch are called **hardware.** Some of the hardware components in your computer might be the system unit, the keyboard, the monitor, disk drives, printers, and the mouse, as shown in Figure 1-1.

System Unit

The system unit is made up of several main components, including the microprocessing unit, main memory, and disk drives.

Microprocessor   The **microprocessor unit** is the "brain" of a microcomputer. The microprocessor coordinates all the computer's activities, executes the arithmetic calculations, and performs logical operations using equal-to, greater-than, and less-than comparisons. It operates by executing a program, which is a list of instructions telling the computer exactly what to do.

Memory   **Main memory** is the temporary workspace the computer uses to store information and instructions that the microprocessor needs for processing. Programs to be executed and data to be processed must first be placed into main memory. Memory is measured in bytes. A byte is essentially the equivalent of one character. Another term used for temporary memory is **RAM (random access memory).** Remember, this memory is lost when the computer power is turned off. **ROM (read only memory)** is memory that cannot be changed. This memory provides diagnostic checking for the computer's components at the time of startup to make sure each part is operable.

Figure 1-1

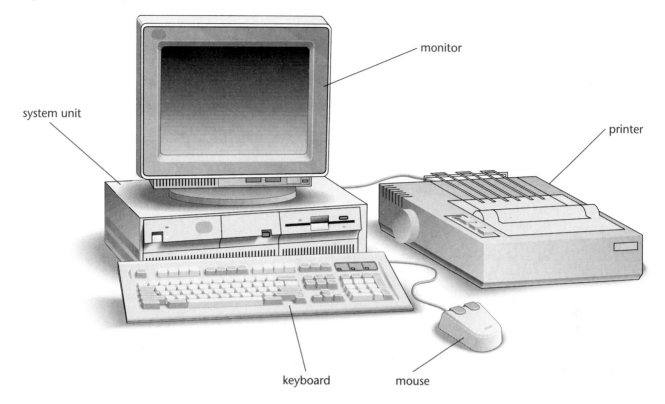

Disk Drives   The **disk drives** are the devices that read and write data from or to a permanent storage disk with a mechanism called a **read/write head,** shown in Figure 1-2. As the disk spins, the read/write head finds the location of the information something like the needle of a record player. The two types of disk drives commonly available are hard disk drives and floppy disk drives.

A **hard disk drive** is a high-speed, large-capacity, vacuum-sealed disk located on the inside of the computer system unit. A hard disk drive is designated as drive C.

A **floppy disk drive** reads removable floppy disks. The first disk drive is designated as drive A and the second is drive B. Depending upon the way your computer is configured, the disk drives may be stacked on top of each other or installed side by side.

Floppy Disks   **Floppy disks** (also called diskettes) are the magnetic storage media on which programs and data are stored. Floppies can be inserted into the floppy disk drives to access or retrieve information. Two sizes of floppy disks are available: $5\frac{1}{4}$ and $3\frac{1}{2}$ inch. The $5\frac{1}{4}$ inch disks come in two capacities: either high density, which hold 1.2 megabytes (MB) of data, or double-density, which hold up to 360 kilobytes (KB) of information. The $3\frac{1}{2}$ inch disks are also available in two capacities: high-density, which hold 1.44 MB, or double-density, holding 720 KB.

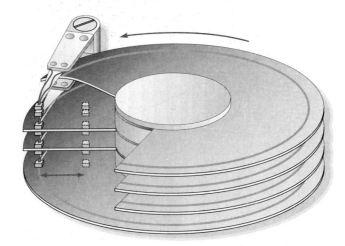

Figure 1-2

Floppy disk drives are always referred to as drive A and drive B. The placement of drives A and B in the system unit will vary depending upon the manufacturer. Figure 1-3 shows a typical system unit containing drives A, B and C.

Keep in mind the following rules for handling floppy disks:

Do:

- Keep disks away from magnetic fields (including telephones, televisions, radios, vacuum cleaners).
- Keep away from dust, food and drinks, smoke, excessive heat and cold.
- Transport in a dust-free, plastic disk storage box.
- Keep 5 ¼ inch disks in their paper jackets.
- Always make backups of the information on floppy disks.

Don't:

- Don't bend or crease disks.
- Don't touch the shiny surfaces of the inside material.
- Don't write on disk labels after they are attached to the disk unless using a soft felt-tipped pen.
- Don't use paper clips or rubber bands on disks.
- Don't force the disk into the drive.
- Don't insert or remove the disk while the drive light is on.
- Don't place your disks on top of your monitor or computer.

Monitor

The computer uses the monitor to display information, data, and commands as they are entered from the keyboard. The two basic types of monitors are black-and-white (monochrome) and color.

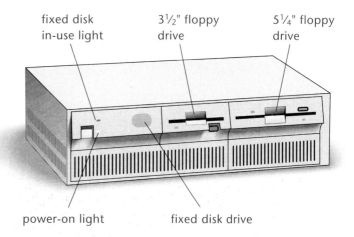

fixed disk   3½" floppy   5¼" floppy
in-use light   drive   drive

power-on light   fixed disk drive

Figure 1-3

Printers

Printers are characterized mainly by the way in which characters are formed on the page. The two categories are: impact (dot-matrix) printers, which form the characters by striking the paper through a ribbon like a typewriter; and nonimpact printers such as laser printers, which use toner like a copy machine, or inkjet printers, which use an ink spray.

Keyboard

The keyboard allows you to communicate with the computer. There are two basic types of keyboards available for the PC. The differences between the two types of keyboards lie mainly in the arrangement and the number of keys. The original keyboard designed for the first PC is called the PC/XT keyboard and contains 84 keys shown in Figure 1-4. The newer designs are called the AT, PS/2, or enhanced keyboards and usually have 101 keys, although different manufacturers vary the arrangement and number slightly. An illustration of the enhanced keyboard is shown in Figure 1-5.

▍ Computer Software

A computer can do nothing until it is given instructions. This set of written instructions is a computer **program** and is called **software** since it is in the form of codes on disk and cannot be seen or touched like computer hardware.

There are three general categories of software:

- **Programming languages** are the tools used to write software programs. Some popular programming languages are COBOL, BASIC, FORTRAN, and assembler language.

- **Application software** packages are those programs designed to perform a particular task for the user. For example, you would find the right software for the application (job). A few examples include: WordPerfect as word processing software to write text, Lotus 1-2-3 as spreadsheet software to enter and calculate numbers, and Harvard Graphics as graphics software to make graphs.

Figure 1-4

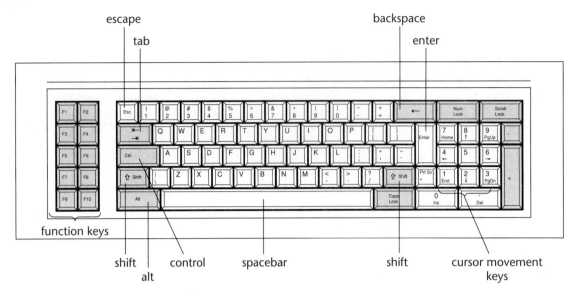

Figure 1.5

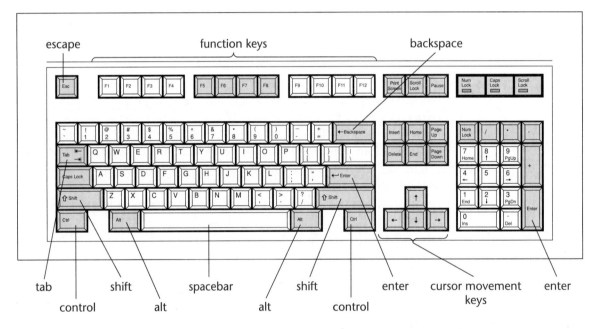

- **Operating system software** is mandatory software used to run the computer and orchestrate the communication between the user, computer, and storage. The operating system software specially designed for the IBM PC and compatible computers is called DOS, which stands for Disk Operating System.

Introducing Word Processing

Word processing means literally "to process words" with the help of a computer.

Timesaving Features

Most popular word processing programs today allow you to do the following:

- Type at rough-draft speed and make corrections later.
- Adjust paragraphs with word wrap (discussed in Lesson 2).
- Insert, delete, move, and copy text without retyping.
- Add or remove enhancements, such as boldface, underline, center, flush-right, italics.
- Search/replace specified words or phrases.
- Add headers or footers with automatic page numbering.
- Use built-in dictionaries for spell check, thesaurus, grammar check, and hyphenation.
- Save the documents for later recall.
- Print as many copies as needed.

Advanced Features

Some of the more sophisticated word processors may include a number of advanced features that enable you to do the following:

- Create footnotes, table of contents, index, glossary, bibliography, lists of illustrations, and charts (some automatically).
- Prepare columns or tables, some with math capabilities.
- Enhance forms with boxes and shading.
- Perform mail merge (blending a letter with names and addresses from a mailing list).
- Apply desktop publishing features, such as importing graphics and using fancy fonts, borders, and proportional spacing.
- Program keyboard macros to automate user keystrokes.

Uses for Word Processing

The uses of word processed documents are virtually as limitless as your imagination. Some of the most prevalent uses are as follows:

- Multidraft documents: documents written in a business environment are revised an average of three times, benefiting greatly from the ease of storage and revision offered by word processing.
- Policy and procedure manuals: extremely large documents that must be maintained for a long period of time can be written once and periodically edited and updated.
- Statistical documents: word processors can align numbers as they are typed and perform some mathematical calculations.

- Form-merge letters: one letter can be merged with a list of addresses, making "personalized" letters print to each name in the list.
- Lists: lists of clients, vendors, or parts inventory can be typed with name, address, telephone number, and any other relevant information desired. Periodically, the list can be updated, sorted, and printed.
- Term papers, reports, and books: documents can be created and their appearance embellished with the use of many advanced and technical features, then revised easily before printing.
- Newsletters, brochures, flyers, and advertisements: documents can be prepared using the desktop publishing features, such as varying font sizes, importing graphics, and adding ruling lines and boxes.

Turning on Your PC

You are now ready to power-up, which is known as **booting.** The two ways to boot the computer are a **cold boot,** starting the system when the power is off, and a **warm boot,** restarting or resetting the system when the computer is already on.

Cold Boot

When a cold boot is performed, the microprocessor executes a small program that checks the hardware and memory, and then searches the hard disk for the operating system (DOS). If the boot was successful in locating all the required boot information, part of the DOS software is loaded into memory and your computer is ready to run.

HANDS-ON ACTIVITY

In this hands-on exercise, you will cold boot your computer.

NOTE: If your computer is connected to a network, follow the directions you are given by your instructor instead of the steps shown below.

If you have a hard disk system, complete the following steps:

1. Remove any floppy disks from the drives
2. Locate the On/Off switch on your monitor and turn it on
3. Locate the On/Off switch on the system unit and flip it to the 1 (ON) position

If your computer does not have a hard disk,

1. Insert a DOS system disk into drive A
2. Latch the drive door until it snaps shut

   NOTE: If you are using a 3½ inch disk, there is no door to latch.

3. Locate the On/Off switch on your monitor and turn it on
4. Locate the On/Off switch on the system unit and flip it to the 1 (ON) position

Warm Boot

A warm boot (sometimes called **soft boot, reset,** or **restart**) reboots the computer after it is already powered up. Just as in a cold boot, the system resets memory and reloads DOS. You may need to use a warm boot to restart the computer because of a software lockup, a keyboard lockup, or the inability to properly exit a program or a game. Rebooting should be your last resort, however, since memory will be cleared and you will lose your unsaved changes to the current document.

To warm boot, press and hold the Ctrl, Alt, and Delete keys simultaneously. On some newer computers, there is a reset button on the front panel of the system unit.

▌ HANDS-ON ACTIVITY

Now you will practice a warm boot.

For hard disk systems,

1. Remove any floppy disks from the drives

2. Press and hold Ctrl, Alt, and Delete simultaneously

   or

   Press the RESET button

   The screen will go blank for a second, and then the system will begin booting.

For floppy disk systems (computers without hard disks),

1. Insert a DOS system disk into drive A

2. Latch the drive door until it snaps shut

   NOTE: If you are using a 3½ inch disk, there is no door to latch.

3. Press and hold Ctrl, Alt, and Delete simultaneously

   or

   Press the RESET button

   The screen will go blank for a second, and then the system will begin booting.

The DOS Prompt

When you power up the computer, the system performs a self-diagnostic test, then DOS automatically loads into memory from the hard disk. A screen prompt may appear, asking you to enter the date and time. If the system prompts for the current date and time, press Enter twice to accept the current date and time.

When your computer is successfully booted and the date and time settings are complete, the current drive letter appears as either C:\> or A:\>.

This combination of drive letter, colon, backslash, and greater-than symbol is called the **DOS prompt** and indicates that your computer is booted and DOS is waiting for your next command.

Giving a DOS Command

Commands given to DOS must follow specific rules of syntax as follows:

- Commands may be entered in either uppercase or lowercase characters.
- A space must follow the command word, if further information is required.
- Reference to disk drives must be followed with a colon, for instance A: or C:.
- DOS is ready to accept a command if the prompt is displayed and the blinking cursor is positioned to the right of the DOS prompt.
- [Enter] must be pressed after each command to instruct DOS to execute your request.
- When a command is successfully completed, the DOS prompt returns. If it is not successful, an error message will display.

Setting Date and Time

Many of the newer computers have an automatic clock setup, but if your system has not been equipped with such a clock or if your clock setup is faulty, you may need to manually enter the date and time.

HANDS-ON ACTIVITY

To check or change your current date and time, proceed with the following steps.

1. Type **DATE**

2. Press [Enter]

   The date message will prompt you for the current date as shown in Figure 1-6.

Figure 1-6

```
C:\>date
Current date is Fri 06-18-1993
Enter new date (mm-dd-yy):
```

NOTE: Your actual current date, of course, will be different from the date shown in Figure 1-6. The cursor is positioned after the colon.

3. Type the current date either in the format mm-dd-yy (06-18-93 for June 18, 1993) or mm/dd/yy (6/18/93)

4. Press [Enter]

5. Type **TIME**

6. Press [Enter]

The system prompts for the current time as shown in Figure 1-7.

Figure 1-7

```
C:\>time
Current time is   4:41:27.94p
Enter new time:
```

7. Type the correct time

NOTE: *You may enter the time either in the a.m. and p.m. format, such as 4:41p, or in the 24-hour-clock format, such as 16:41. Seconds and beyond are not required.*

8. Press [Enter]

Formatting Floppy Disks

The DOS **FORMAT** command is a very essential but dangerous command since it erases a disk and sets it up for new data to be stored. You must be extremely careful to specify the correct disk drive and be sure that the disk in the drive is either blank or contains data that you intend to be destroyed.

It is necessary to perform the format command on new floppy disks to prepare them for data storage.

CAUTION: *Do not format a disk that contains information that you need to keep. In addition, always perform the format command using floppy drive letters (A: or B:). Never try to format a hard disk drive letter, such as drive C:, D:, E:, and so on.*

TIP: *Floppy disks can now be purchased preformatted from the factory to avoid having to use the format command.*

HANDS-ON ACTIVITY

Perform the following steps to format your blank working disk. The instructions are designed to format the disk in drive A. If your floppy is located in drive B, please substitute B: wherever A: is shown. Refer to the earlier discussion of types of floppy disks, and make sure you have the correct type of floppy for your disk drive. Ask your instructor for clarification if you are not certain about your computer hardware.

1. Place the blank disk in drive A

At the DOS prompt,

2. Type **FORMAT A:**

3. Press [Enter]

DOS instructs you to place a new (blank) disk in drive A, and press [Enter] when ready to begin.

4. Press [Enter]

NOTE: If you are using DOS release 5.0 or higher, you will be asked if you would like to add a "volume label" to the disk. That is simply a name for the disk. Press [Enter] *to skip the naming step and continue.*

DOS will display "Format Complete" when finished and ask if you want to format another disk.

5. Type **N** for no

Your disk is now ready to store data.

Changing the Default Drive

As previously discussed, the DOS prompt is the combination of the current drive letter, colon, backslash, and greater-than symbol and indicates that your computer is booted and DOS is waiting for your next command. The current drive letter appears as either C:\> or A:\>. The drive letter shown is the active drive and is called the **default drive**, meaning that all commands given will automatically default to and perform the desired function on the drive shown. For example, a DOS prompt of A:\> tells DOS to use the disk in drive A to retrieve files or execute commands. Unless the user specifies a different drive, DOS assumes drive A.

To change the default drive, simply type the letter of the drive (either uppercase or lowercase), followed by a colon (:). DOS checks to see if there is a disk inserted in that drive; if so, the DOS prompt changes. If there is no disk in the drive, you will see an error message.

HANDS-ON ACTIVITY

Now that you have formatted your blank disk in drive A, let's change the default from C: to A:.

At the DOS prompt C:\>,

1. Type **A:**

2. Press [Enter]

   The prompt changes to A:\>.

   Now let's change back to drive C.

3. Type **C:**

4. Press [Enter]

Managing Your Files

A file is a collection of related information that can be data (data file) or instructions for manipulating data (program file). In order to store this information on disk, you give it a name. DOS is responsible for storing your file on disk when you are ready to save your work and retrieving it the next time you need to edit or print it. On each disk are two files, a directory, and the **file allocation table (FAT)** which keeps track of all the files, where they are located on the disk, the size of each file in bytes, and how much available space remains on the disk.

File Names

Each file on a disk must have a unique name to identify it. Each **file name** consists of two parts—a name and an extension. A file name can be up to eight characters long, followed by a period and an extension of up to three characters. (The period and the file extension are optional in WordPerfect.) For example:

DOS allows the following characters to be used in file names:

All alphabet letters, A through Z

All numbers, 0 through 9

The following symbols: # & $ @ ! ( ) { } - _ ^ ~ % ' `

All other characters are invalid, including spaces. If you feel that it will be difficult to remember which symbols are legal (valid) and which ones are not allowed, it would be a safe practice to avoid using symbols.

It is advisable that you develop a logical system for naming your files. File names are a personal preference, but should describe the data held in the file as accurately as possible, given the constraints. For example, the name CHARLIE.LET does a good job of describing a file that is a letter to Charlie.

The example used above is one popular naming convention—assigning the three extension characters as an abbreviation for the type of document (such as .LET for letter, .MEM for memo, .RPT for report, and so on). Examples of this naming system might be SALLY.MEM or SAFETY.RPT.

Another example: if three different people are creating documents, use the first three letters of their last names for the extension characters (such as .LEE for Leeburg or .AND for Anderson). A letter from Leeburg to the Finance Department might be named FIN-LET.LEE and a second letter to the same department might be named FIN-LET2.LEE.

Effective file naming is difficult, as you can see, because you are limited as to the number of characters you can use. The more files you create, the more difficult it is to distinguish between them. As you become more proficient in using WordPerfect, however, and observe other users' naming systems, you will be able to create conventions that match your needs.

Listing Files with DIR

The completed sample files that coincide with the exercises in this book are supplied for your convenience on a sample disk included with the book. Please ask your instructor to provide you with a copy of this disk. Insert it in the computer's floppy drive.

The DOS command used to list on the monitor the names of files stored on a disk is the directory command, which is abbreviated as DIR.

The **DIR** command displays a list of all the file names on the disk, the size of each file in bytes, and the date and time each file was created or last saved. DIR also counts how many files are stored on a disk/directory, and displays how many bytes of free space remain on the disk.

The DIR command syntax and a few of the available options are listed as follows:

DIR	Displays the directory of the current default drive. At the DOS prompt, type **DIR** and press (Enter).
DIR *x:*	The *x* stands for a specified disk drive. Use this command to list a directory of a drive other than the current default drive. To enter the command, at the DOS prompt type **DIR,** followed by a space, the letter of the desired drive, and a colon. For example, to display the directory of drive B when drive A is active, type **DIR B:** and press (Enter).
DIR/p	The /p is an option to pause after each screenful of text when viewing long directory lists. To continue, simply press any key. To xexecute this command, type **DIR/p** and press (Enter).
DIR/w	The /w is an option to display the directory list in a "wide" view (horizontally across the screen instead of vertically). This directory view only displays the file names, not the size, date, or time. To use this function, type **DIR/w** and press (Enter).

▌ HANDS-ON ACTIVITY

In this exercise, you will use the DOS directory commands to view the files on the sample disk located in your drive.

NOTE: This book will assume that you are using drive A for the sample disk and will give instructions to type A: to access the disk. If your sample disk is inserted in drive B, simply substitute B: wherever A: is shown.

NOTE: The following conventions used in this book will help you work through the Hands-On Activities.

- *All steps actually to be performed by the student are printed in color.*
- *When performing a step, the student should type only the text shown in the special* **typing font** *or press the keys as shown.*

Insert your sample disk in drive A (making sure the disk drive is latched shut). Then, to change the default to drive A,

1. Type **A:**

2. Press (Enter)

   To list a directory of the sample disk,

3. Type **DIR**

4. Press (Enter)

A listing of the files appears vertically on the screen. If you have more than 23 lines in your list, the text will scroll off the top of your monitor window.

Most DOS commands can be modified by use of options (also called switches). The proper syntax for entering options is the command, a forward slash (/), and the option. A space is optional between the DOS command and the slash.

CAUTION: Be sure to use the correct slash when entering an option command. On all keyboards the forward slash (/) is located on the bottom row of the typewriter section near the Enter *key; on enhanced keyboards there is a second forward slash in the far right-hand numeric keypad section.*

Next, use the DIR command with a pause option (/P).

5. Type `DIR/P`

6. Press Enter

    The list fills one screen, pauses, and displays the message "Press any key to continue."

7. Press any key on the keyboard

    Now, let's try the DIR command with the wide option.

8. Type `DIR/W`

9. Press Enter

    The listing displays horizontally across the screen.

Using Wildcards

Wildcard characters are also known as **global file name characters,** enabling users to group files together that have similar file names. For instance, if you had been careful to name all your memo files with a .MEM extension, you could work with those files as a group instead of one at a time.

The two DOS **wildcard characters** are ? and *. The ? represents *one* character in a file name and the * represents *any number* of characters in a file name. For example, if you wanted to list all file names beginning with the letter S, you could use the * to substitute for any number of other letters in the file name. The command would be **DIR S*.***

On the other hand, if you wanted to list all files beginning with the letter S that have no more than four characters, then you must use three question marks to allow up to three characters following the S. The command would be **DIR S???.***

▊ HANDS-ON ACTIVITY

For these exercises, make sure that your sample disk is engaged in the disk drive and the appropriate DOS prompt is displayed on the screen.

List all files on the sample disk beginning with the letter **S** followed by any other characters.

1. Type DIR S*.*

2. Press [Enter]

    CAUTION: Be sure to press the [Spacebar] *after the DOS command DIR.*

    Three files will display, all beginning with the letter S.

    Now, list all files ending with the extension .SD.

3. Type DIR *.SD

4. Press [Enter]

    Five files will display, all ending with the extension .SD.

    Let's list all files.

5. Type DIR

    or

    Type DIR *.*

6. Press [Enter]

    The entire list of files from the sample disk is too large to display on one screen. In the next section you will learn how to stop the screen from scrolling and view the whole list.

    List all files on the sample disk with no more than six characters in the file name section, followed by any extension.

7. Type DIR ??????.*

    The screen will display those files that have six or fewer characters in the file name.

Copying Files

The DOS **COPY** command is used to make a duplicate copy of a document to another file, disk, or directory. You may also use the DOS wildcard characters to copy groups of files. There are three parts to the COPY syntax:

*   Type the command **COPY** followed by a space.
*   Type the source (the name and location of the file to be copied) followed by a space.
*   Type the target (the location where the file is to be copied to) and press [Enter].

CAUTION: Be sure always to type a space between the three parts of the COPY command.

The COPY command syntax is:

COPY(space)<source>(space)<target> [Enter]

▌**HANDS-ON ACTIVITY**

In this exercise, you will copy the sample file SPEAKER.LST to a duplicate file called NEWFILE.DOC. Both the source and the target files will be located on the same disk.

First, let's display a directory of the sample disk in wide format to make sure that you have the source document SPEAKER.LST.

At the A:\> prompt,

1. Type `DIR/W`

2. Press `Enter`

Now perform the copy command.

3. Type `COPY SPEAKER.LST NEWFILE.DOC`

4. Press `Enter`

The system responds, "1 file copied." Now list the files on the disk again to look for the new file name.

5. Type `DIR/W`

6. Press `Enter`

Deleting Files

The **ERASE** or **DEL** command is used to permanently remove a file from disk. Wildcard characters can also be used to perform group deletions. Use extreme caution when deleting files. Once an important file is deleted, it may be difficult or impossible to restore it.

▌**HANDS-ON ACTIVITY**

In this exercise, you will delete the file NEWFILE.DOC that you created with the COPY command in the exercise above.

Make sure that your sample disk is in drive A and you are at the DOS prompt A:\>.

First, let's verify the file name NEWFILE.DOC.

1. Type `DIR/W`

2. Press `Enter`

To delete the file,

3. Type `DEL NEWFILE.DOC`

4. Press `Enter`

Now, look at another directory list to verify that the file has been deleted.

5. Type `DIR/W`

6. Press `Enter`

▌ Directory Management

Disks are much like a filing cabinet drawer—providing storage, but no organization. To make it easier to find files in a filing cabinet drawer, you can divide the drawer into main categories with hanging folders. Within the hanging folders, you can either file documents directly or use manila file folders to subdivide the categories further.

What Is a Directory?

A **directory** is a storage compartment in a disk for holding files. All disks have a main directory called the **root directory**. Instead of storing all your files in the root directory, similar to the filing cabinet drawer, subdivisions called **subdirectories** can be created for each topic. When you diagram your directory arrangement on paper, it may resemble a tree, similar to the one shown in Figure 1-8. Thus, the hard disk organizational structure is referred to as a **tree structure**.

The rationale behind the use of tree-structured directories is that related groups of files can be easily kept together. As you move up the tree away from the root, each directory topic becomes more specialized in what it contains. You may create unlimited levels of directories and subdirectories branching up from the root directory.

An example of a logical tree structure is that you might want to create a directory branch for each kind of program you use. You may create a WP directory for word processing, a directory called SS for your spreadsheets, and a directory for your games called GAMES. Assuming you own many game programs, you may want to make a subdirectory for each specific game, such as CHESS, PACMAN, GOLF, and so on.

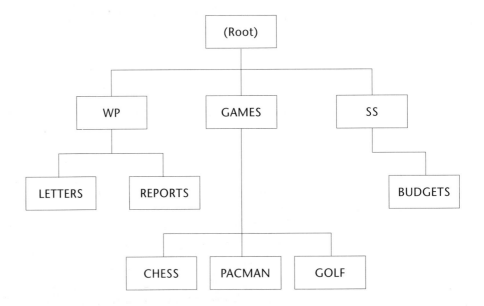

Figure 1-8

The backslash (\) is used to designate the root directory and is also used to separate the names of each level of directories and subdirectories. This directory location is called the **path.** For instance, in the example above, the path to the GAMES directory on drive C would be written as C:\GAMES. The path to the subdirectory called CHESS would be written as C:\GAMES\CHESS. WordPerfect 6.0 is usually stored in a directory called \WP60.

CAUTION: There are two different slashes on the keyboard and they are easily confused. Remember, the forward slash (/) is used for a DOS option switch, while the backslash (\) is used to designate directory names.

Creating a Directory

Directories or subdirectories are created with the Make Directory command, typed either **MD** or **MKDIR**, followed by the name of the new directory. Directory names must follow the same naming rules as file names, except that you normally want to avoid using extensions.

▌ HANDS-ON ACTIVITY

So far all the sample files on the floppy are stored at the root directory of the disk. In this exercise, you will create a subdirectory on your sample floppy disk in drive A called PLAY, then copy a file from the root directory into the new subdirectory and practice moving from one directory to another.

Make sure that you have the sample floppy in the disk drive, and if you are using drive B, substitute **B:** wherever **A:** is shown.

First, let's change the default to drive A:

1. Type **A:**

2. Press (Enter)

    Now, create a subdirectory of the root called PLAY.

3. Type **MD\PLAY**

4. Press (Enter)

    Use the DIR command to look at the contents of the disk.

5. Type **DIR/p**

6. Press (Enter)

    If the new subdirectory is not shown on the first screenful of file names, press any key to view the next screen. The new subdirectory will be listed with a creation date and time, but instead of seeing the number of bytes in the size column, you will see <DIR>, indicating that this item is not a single document, but a storage container for files.

Changing Directories

To move from one location to another in a tree-structured disk, you use the Change Directory command, typed as either **CD** or **CHDIR**. You are not changing the name of the directory, rather you are changing your location in the hard disk.

▌**HANDS-ON ACTIVITY**

You are currently positioned in the root directory of the floppy. Your DOS prompt (A:\>) indicates that you are located on drive A (A:) and you are at the root directory (\). From the root, you can see the subdirectory PLAY listed but you cannot see the contents of PLAY.

Now you will change from the root directory into the PLAY directory with the CD command.

1. Type **CD\PLAY**

2. Press ⎡Enter⎤

    The system prompt changed from A:\> to A:\PLAY>, indicating that you are now located in the PLAY directory on drive A. To view the contents of PLAY,

3. Type **DIR**

4. Press ⎡Enter⎤

    Your screen will display a dot and a double-dot marker but no data files. Therefore, the PLAY directory is empty. Compare your screen to Figure 1-9.

Figure 1-9

```
A:\PLAY>dir

Volume in drive A has no label
Directory of A:\PLAY

.            <DIR>        06-18-93     4:39p
..           <DIR>        06-18-93     4:39p
        2 file(s)              0 bytes
                        972288 bytes free

A:\PLAY>
```

Now, let's use the Change Directory command to move back to the root directory from the PLAY directory. (Remember, the backslash (\) means "root directory.")

5. Type **CD**

6. Press ⎡Enter⎤

Using the Copy Command with Directories

Now let's copy one of the sample files from the root directory of the floppy into the PLAY directory.

Make sure you are located at the root directory of the floppy drive with the sample disk, such as A:\>.

▌ HANDS ON ACTIVITY

Let's look at the contents of the disk again, this time in a wide view. Locate the sample file CONFER.SD, then copy it to the PLAY directory:

1. Type `DIR/w`

2. Press Enter

3. Type `COPY CONFER.SD \PLAY`

4. Press Enter

    Move into the PLAY directory to verify that the file was copied correctly.

5. Type `CD\PLAY`

6. Press Enter

7. Type `DIR`

8. Press Enter

    The file CONFER.SD should appear in the list following the two dot markers.

    Now delete the file and return to the root directory.

9. Type `DEL CONFER.SD`

10. Press Enter

11. On your own, verify the deletion with `DIR`

12. On your own, change directories to the root

Removing Directories

To eliminate a directory, use the Remove Directory command, typed as either **RD** or **RMDIR**. Three conditions must be met in order to successfully remove a directory:

- The directory cannot contain any files.
- There cannot be any subdirectories.
- The directory cannot be your current location.

▌ HANDS-ON ACTIVITY

You will now remove the practice directory PLAY by first changing your location to PLAY, checking to make sure that PLAY is empty, then returning to the root directory to remove PLAY.

At the A:\> prompt,

1. Type `CD\PLAY`

2. Press Enter

3. At the A:\PLAY> prompt, type `DIR`

4. Press Enter

   The only entries in the PLAY directory should be

   . <DIR>

   ..<DIR>

   Now let's return to the root directory.

5. Type `CD\`

6. Press Enter

   Verify that PLAY exists.

7. Type `DIR/p`

8. Press Enter

   Now, remove the directory PLAY.

9. Type `RD\PLAY`

10. Press Enter

    Verify that PLAY was removed.

11. Type `DIR/p`

12. Press Enter

On Your Own

▌ Review of Commands

Description	Keystrokes
List the commands to do the following: Set the computer date	_____
Format a floppy disk in drive A	_____
List files of the default drive	_____
List files with a pause	_____
List files in a wide screen	_____
List files ending in .LET	_____
Copy the file TEST.DOC from the current drive to drive B	_____
Delete the file TEST.DOC from the current drive	_____
Create a directory called C:\FILES branching off the root directory	_____

Change to the directory called
C:\FILES from the root directory   _____

Remove the directory called
C:\FILES from the root directory   _____

Lesson Review

1. What is the difference between memory and storage?

2. What is the difference between a hard disk and a floppy disk?

3. What are three of the rules regarding proper handling of floppy disks?

4. What are three of the typical features of word processing software?

5. What is an example of a date format that is acceptable to DOS?

6. What letter is usually the first hard drive letter?

7. Which of the following names is legal?
   a. CHARLES 2.LET
   b. CHARLES.LET2
   c. CHARLES2.LET

8. What are the five columns of information displayed by the DIR command?

9. If the current drive is A, how do you change to B?

10. What are two ways to remove the contents of a floppy disk?

Assignments

1.1 Directions

1. Turn the computer on and load DOS.

2. Use the Date and Time commands to see if your computer clock is set correctly. If not, enter the current date and time to update your computer clock.

3. Insert a floppy disk in drive A and change the default drive from C to A.

4. Display the directory of each drive.

5. Display the directory of drive C horizontally and print the screen.

6. Locate a blank floppy disk and format it.

7. Locate the sample disk and copy the file FEASIBLE.RPT to REPORT.FSB.

8. Locate the empty floppy disk you just formatted and create two subdirectories. Name one REPORTS and the other one LETTERS.

9. Display the directory of the disk and print the screen.

10. Remove the subdirectory called REPORTS.

2

Introducing
WordPerfect 6.0

Objectives

Upon completion of this lesson, you will be able to do the following:

- Start the WordPerfect 6.0 program
- Identify the areas of the WordPerfect window
- Use the Backspace key
- List the default settings for formatting the document
- Execute and cancel a command
- Select the text and graphics view modes
- Work with dialog boxes
- Use the scroll bars
- Use WordPerfect's Help features
- Exit WordPerfect

This lesson will familiarize you with the WordPerfect 6.0 program. It illustrates how to execute and cancel commands and how to use the Help features, which offer fast, on-line assistance on a variety of topics and operations.

Starting Point

Before beginning the lesson, make certain that your computer is turned on and the DOS prompt is displayed.

Starting WordPerfect

To start WordPerfect on a PC that is not connected to a network, at the DOS prompt you must change to the directory where WordPerfect is stored. When WordPerfect 6.0 is installed it automatically creates a directory called \WP60. Therefore, we will assume in this text that the name of the main WordPerfect directory is \WP60. Before starting WordPerfect you must type **CD\WP60** and press Enter. This will make the directory in which the Word-Perfect program resides the current directory. Then, to begin the WordPerfect 6.0 program, type **WP** and press Enter.

NOTE: If your computer is connected to a network, obtain instructions from your instructor or system administrator on how to start WordPerfect.

▎ HANDS-ON ACTIVITY

NOTE: This text assumes that the WordPerfect directory name is \WP60. If your system differs, please substitute the actual directory name where WP60 is shown.

Now let's change to the WordPerfect directory.

At the DOS prompt,

1. Type `CD\WP60` (either uppercase or lowercase alphabetic characters)

   CAUTION: Be sure to use the \ (backslash) and not the / (forward slash).

2. Press `Enter`

   Now, let's begin WordPerfect.

3. Type `WP`

4. Press `Enter`

▎ The WordPerfect Window

When WordPerfect is started, a blank screen appears with either a horizontal blinking line or a vertical blinking line at the top left of the screen, called the **cursor.** (The appearance of the cursor—horizontal or vertical—is dependent upon the active view mode, which is discussed later in this chapter.) This area is your **document window** where you will create or edit your documents. As you start to type text, it appears at the location of the cursor. The cursor indicates where you are located in your document and also shows the point of action.

At the bottom of the screen is an information line called the **status line.** The left side of the status line indicates the font (the typeface) and point size that will be used for the current document. The right side of the status line displays the current position of the cursor: the document number, the page number, line number, and position number. The line number (shown as **Ln**) indicates the vertical position of the cursor relative to the top edge of the page, and the position number (shown as **Pos**) indicates the horizontal position of the cursor relative to the left edge of the page. The line number and position number are shown in inches. The page number (**Pg**) gives the current page, while the document number (**Doc**) tells which document is active when you are working with more than one document.

Your screen should appear similar to Figure 2-1.

▎ HANDS-ON ACTIVITY

To become familiar with the status line, you are going to enter text. As you type, notice that the status line changes to reflect the current position of the cursor. Before you begin the exercise, look at the font name and point size, which are shown in the left end of the status line.

1. Type `Interoffice Memorandum`

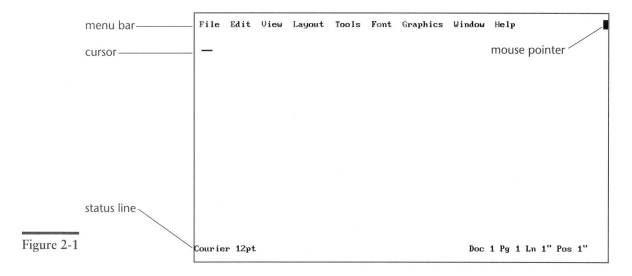

Figure 2-1

As you type the text, the status line Pos number changes to 3.2. (If your font is not Courier 12 pt, this may be different.) Remember, the Pos number indicates the position of the cursor relative to the left edge of the page.

2. Press Enter 5 times

The Enter key in word processors operates like the carriage return on a typewriter. Each time you press Enter, a new blank line is inserted into the text and the cursor moves to the left margin of the next new line.

The first time you press Enter, the cursor moves to the left margin of the next line. The next four times you press Enter, WordPerfect creates blank lines. The status line Ln number reads 1.83".

Using the Backspace Key

The Backspace key erases the character to the left of the cursor. A character, a space, or a blank line can be erased using Backspace. Remember, when Backspace is pressed it "backs up" to erase one character, space, or line.

CAUTION: If the Backspace *is held down, it will repeat very quickly, so use just a quick tap.*

▋ HANDS-ON ACTIVITY

To see how Backspace works, you are going to delete the blank lines and part of the text "Interoffice Memorandum."

1. Press Backspace 5 times

The blank lines are removed and the cursor is positioned at the end of "Memorandum."

2. Press Backspace 22 times

The text is deleted. Notice the Pos number in the status line reads 1".

Default Settings

When you first begin a WordPerfect document, all the formatting necessary to create and print a page are automatically set for you, such as top and bottom margins, left and right margins, line spacing, and tab stops. These settings are automatically preset when WordPerfect is installed on your computer and are called **default settings.** A few are listed below:

- Left margin: 1 inch
- Right margin: 1 inch
- Top margin: 1 inch
- Bottom margin: 1 inch
- Line spacing: single
- Tab stops: set every ½ inch
- Justification: Left
- Page length: 54 lines
- Paper Size: 8½ by 11 inches

Figure 2-2 shows these dimensions on an 8½-by-11-inch page.

Executing and Canceling a Command

You may select WordPerfect 6.0 commands in three ways: pull-down menus, function key menus, or shortcut keys. The pull-down menus can be executed by using either the mouse or the keyboard.

Using a Mouse

If a mouse is installed on your computer, you have the option of using it to make a selection from the menu bar.

The mouse is moved by sliding it across a flat surface such as a desktop or mouse pad. As the mouse is moved on the desktop, the mouse pointer (indicated as a nonblinking block in the text mode or an arrow in the graphics mode on the screen) moves in the same direction.

A slight movement of the mouse on the desktop will move the mouse pointer a great distance on the screen. Should you run out of space on the desktop, simply pick up the mouse, reposition it, and begin sliding it again.

Some mice come with two buttons, others with three. The left mouse button is the one you will use most. In a few instances you will need to use the right mouse button. (If your mouse has three buttons, you will not use the middle button in WordPerfect.)

To make a selection using the mouse, you slide the mouse across your desk until the mouse pointer on the screen is located on the desired item, then gently press and release the left mouse button once, quickly. This action is called **clicking,** and the entire operation is often referred to as "point-and-click." There are two additional terms that you need to know for using the mouse: **double-clicking** means rapidly pressing and releasing the left mouse button twice (the motion should be gentle). **Dragging** means to hold the mouse button down while moving the mouse.

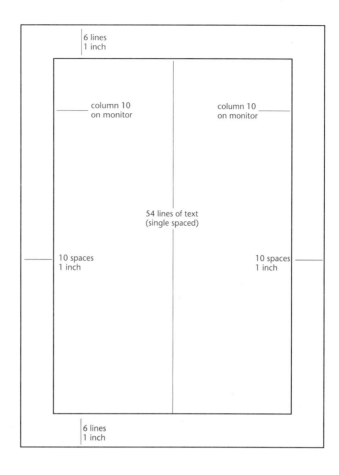

Figure 2-2

Pull-Down Menus

The main **menu bar** located on the first row at the top of the screen lists nine categories from which to select. After a category in the main menu is selected, a **pull-down menu** appears with another list of choices in that category. These submenus are called pull-down because of the way they open from the main menu, much like pulling down a window shade or projector screen.

To select a category from the menu bar with the *mouse*, position the mouse pointer on the menu option and click the left mouse button once. A pull-down menu appears for you to select the desired option. If the wrong menu option is selected, click the right mouse button to close the menu.

Ellipses (...) following any menu option indicate that additional information is required before WordPerfect can complete the task. When you select a menu option that has an ellipsis, a window called a **dialog box** appears in the form of a menu box containing more information or choices for that item.

The *keyboard* may also be used to select an option on the menu bar by using a combination of Alt and the menu letters. While holding down the Alt key, tap the underlined (or bold) letter of the desired menu option. Once the pull-down menu appears, you just type the underlined (or bold) letter of the desired option. To close a menu without making a selection, press Esc. Press Esc once again to exit the menu bar and return the cursor to the document window.

▌ HANDS-ON ACTIVITY

The following exercise shows how to issue a command from the menu bar using either mouse or keyboard. You will access the Layout Styles menu to issue a command using both methods. If you do not have a mouse attached to your system, skip steps 1 through 3. Remember, to "select" with the mouse, point to the item in the main menu and click the left mouse button.

1. Select **L**ayout

    The Layout pull-down menu shown in Figure 2-3 appears.

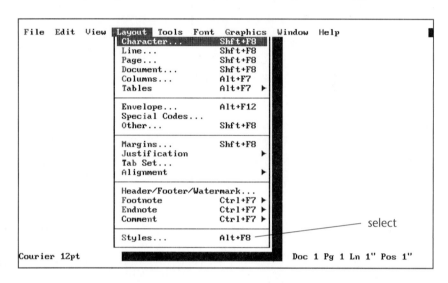

Figure 2-3

Notice that each option listed in the menu has either a bold or an underlined letter. To select an option, type the bold or underlined letter of the desired option. For instance, to activate the Styles option found at the bottom of the Layout pull-down menu screen,

2. Select **S**tyles

    The Styles List dialog box appears as shown in Figure 2-4.

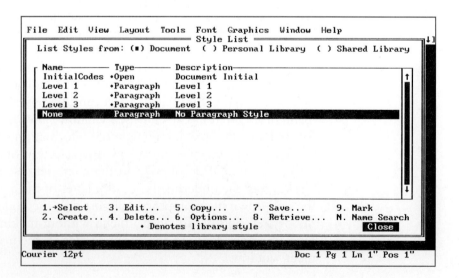

Figure 2-4

To close the menu,

3. Click the right mouse button

Now, let's try issuing a command using the keyboard.

4. Press and hold ⟨Alt⟩ and press **L** (for <u>L</u>ayout)

The Layout pull-down menu appears. To display the Styles List dialog box,

5. Type **S** (for <u>S</u>tyles)

Now, to close the menu and return to the document window,

6. Press ⟨Esc⟩

Function Key Menus

WordPerfect has also assigned the function keys as an alternative method of executing commands. Depending upon the style of keyboard attached to your system, you may have ten function keys on the left side of the keyboard labeled ⟨F1⟩ through ⟨F10⟩ or twelve function keys across the top labeled ⟨F1⟩ through ⟨F12⟩ (the **enhanced keyboard**).

Each function key will perform as many as four different features when used alone or in conjunction with the ⟨Shift⟩, ⟨Alt⟩, and ⟨Ctrl⟩ keys. The function key template for the enhanced keyboard shown in Figure 2-5 illustrates how ⟨F8⟩ when pressed alone (the bottom line in the template) is Underline; ⟨Shift⟩ + ⟨F8⟩ is Format; ⟨Alt⟩ + ⟨F8⟩ is Style; and ⟨Ctrl⟩ + ⟨F8⟩ is Font.

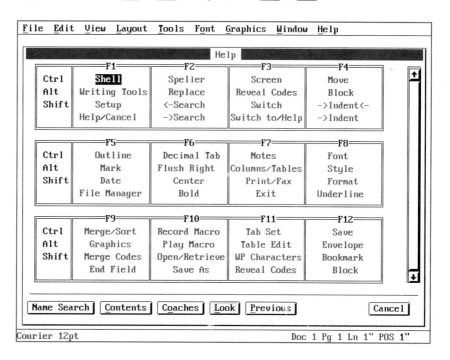

Figure 2-5

▌ HANDS-ON ACTIVITY

In this exercise, you are going to activate the Styles menu again by using the function keys.

1. Press $\boxed{\text{Alt}}$ + $\boxed{\text{F8}}$

   Notice that the Layout menu is bypassed and the Styles List dialog box displays. This is an efficient method by which to give WordPerfect a command.

   To exit the Styles List menu,

2. Press $\boxed{\text{Esc}}$

   NOTE: From this point forward, function keystrokes (if any) will follow the menu commands and will be indicated with a √ symbol.

Shortcut Keys

WordPerfect also gives you 15 shortcut keystrokes that are activated by the keystroke combination of holding the $\boxed{\text{Ctrl}}$ key and pressing one alphabet letter. Each of these shortcut keys will be addressed when the feature is discussed throughout the book.

Viewing in the Text or Graphics Mode

The WordPerfect window can be displayed in two types of screens, either the text or the graphics mode. This choice depends upon the graphics capabilities of your computer. When WordPerfect 6.0 is first installed on your computer, the text mode is automatically activated in order to be compatible with all types and ages of computer hardware. Then you have the option to select the mode that gives you the best display for your individual monitor.

Figure 2-6A illustrates the text mode and Figure 2-6B the graphics mode. As you can see (more clearly on your monitor than in the figures), the main menu at the top of the screen shows one letter in bold in the text mode whereas in the graphics mode one letter is underlined.

▌ HANDS-ON ACTIVITY

In the following exercise you will switch back and forth between the text and graphics mode to determine which mode you prefer to use on your computer. You will use the keyboard to execute the commands in this activity.

To display the View menu,

1. Hold down $\boxed{\text{Alt}}$ and press **V**

   The View pull-down menu shown in Figure 2-7 appears (page 34).

   The current mode (either Text or Graphics) will be marked with a check mark or an asterisk denoting the current view mode. Switch to the mode that is *not* marked to change the screen display.

2. Select either **T** (for Text) or **G** (for Graphics)

   Let's switch again.

3. Repeat steps 1 and 2 to observe the changes

   Decide which mode you prefer and make that mode current.

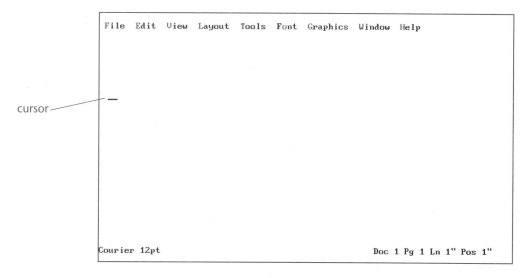

cursor

Figure 2-6A

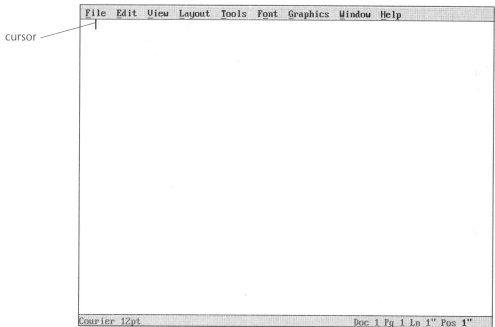

cursor

Figure 2-6B

NOTE: From this point forward in this book, the screen displays will be shown in the graphics mode. You may, however, work in the text mode since an older computer will perform slower in the graphics mode than in text mode.

Working with Dialog Boxes

As you have seen, the ellipses (...) following any menu option indicate that you will be presented with a dialog box requesting additional information to complete the task. Dialog boxes come in many varieties, depending upon the task involved, and contain different elements or components.

There are seven different elements or components that may appear in a dialog box. They are: text box, ellipses, drop-down list box, list box, check

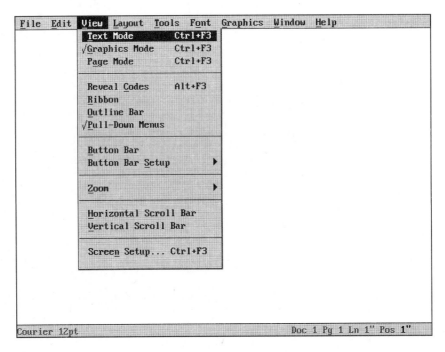

Figure 2-7

box, radio buttons, and command buttons. Dialog boxes may appear with only one component or a combination of different components.

Figure 2-8 uses the Line Format dialog box to illustrate text boxes, el-lipses, radio buttons, command buttons, and check boxes. The Font dialog box appears in Figure 2-9 in which drop-down browse buttons are used to select from a list of the Font and Size options, results of which are shown in a sample box. Figure 2-10 shows the Graphics Fill Styles dialog box, which displays a list box. Each component is described below.

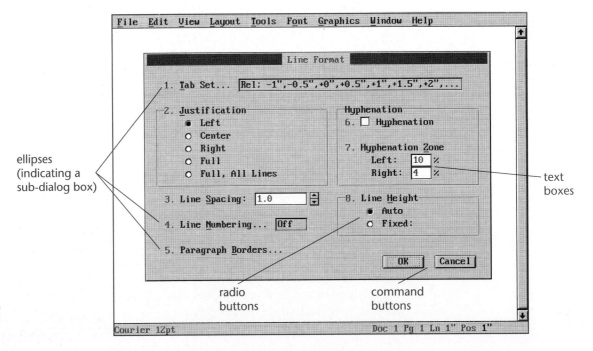

Figure 2-8

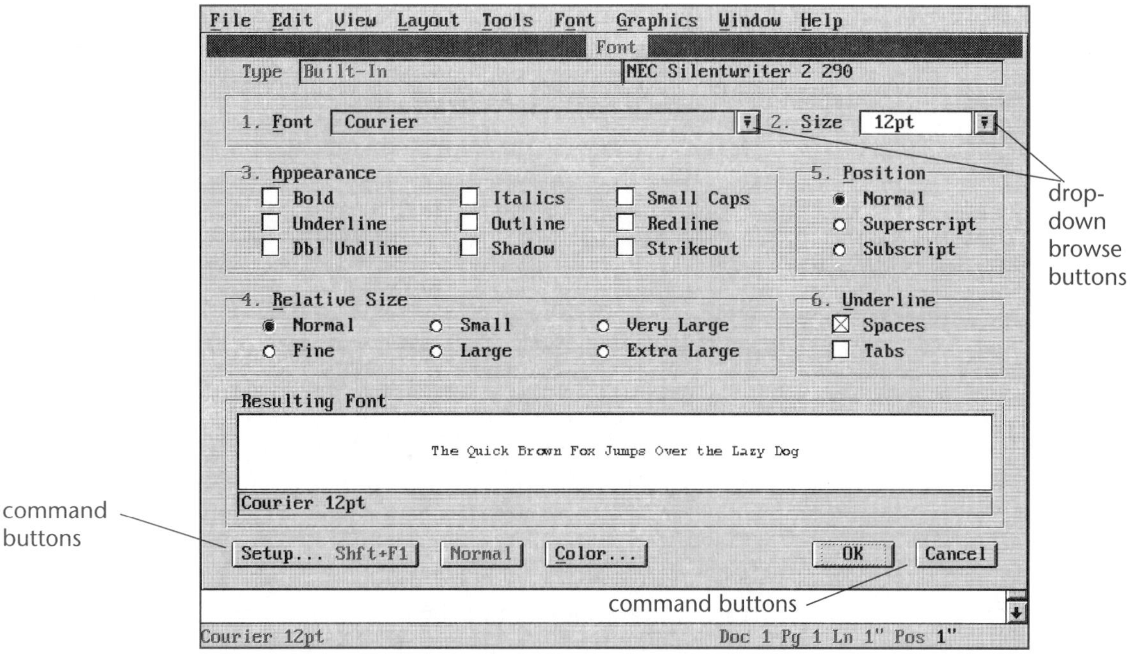

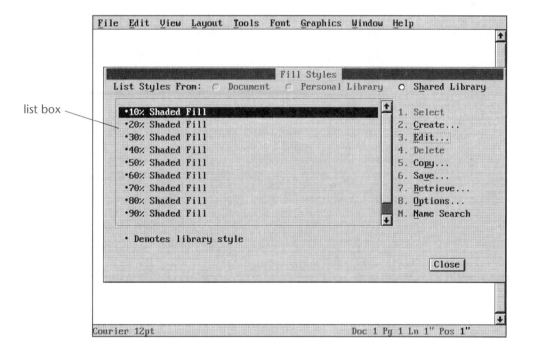

Figure 2-9

Figure 2-10

Text box   A text box may appear in one of two ways: containing text or empty. If the box is empty, the cursor is flashing in the box, so you may type the required information. If the box contains text, when the option is selected, the existing text is automatically highlighted so that as you enter new information, the highlighted or existing text is replaced. In Figure 2-8, the Hyphenation Zone option appears with two text boxes—one for the Left and the other for the Right. When you press **Z** to select the Hyphenation

Zone option, the existing text in the Left text box is automatically high-lighted, so that as you type new information the old is replaced. The Line Spacing option is also presented with a text box.

Ellipses   When ellipses (...) follow an option in a dialog box, they indicate that you will be presented with a sub-dialog box. In Figure 2-8, notice that there are several options (Tab Set, Line Numbering, Paragraph Borders) that are followed with ellipses.

Check boxes   Check boxes allow you to switch a feature on or off. If there is an X inside the box, the feature is turned on; the absence of an X indicates the feature is turned off. The Hyphenation option in Figure 2-8 is a check box and is currently turned off. To turn the option on, either select the check box or type the underlined letter representing the option. In this instance, you would type a y to turn on the Hyphenation feature.

Radio buttons   Radio buttons allow you to select one option from a set of two or more options. For example, in Figure 2-8, in the Justification section of the Line Format dialog box, five options are shown for justifying your document. However, only one option may be selected at a time. An option button is selected by clicking on the button or pressing the underlined letter of the option, in this case typing a J for Justification and then typing the highlighted or underlined letter of the desired option. The selected option is indicated by a black dot in the radio button.

Command buttons   The two most common command buttons found on the majority of the dialog boxes are OK and Cancel. Once you have filled the dialog box to your liking, select OK or press the function key [F7] to instruct WordPerfect to execute or save the selected settings. If you wish to exit the dialog box and not save the changes, select Cancel or press the [Esc] key.

Drop-down list boxes   Drop-down list boxes are indicated by a small arrow (called the **browse button**) in the box to the right of the option. The current setting is displayed in the box. To open a window listing additional options, either select the arrow or select the option by pressing the under-lined letter and then pressing the [↓]. Figure 2-9 shows two drop-down list boxes: Font and Size.

List boxes   List boxes are like menus in that they display a list of options or items from which you can choose. To make a selection from a list box, select the item by either clicking on it or using the [↑] or [↓] arrow keys. The Graphics Fill Styles dialog box shown in Figure 2-10 is composed of a list box, plus three radio buttons.

Executing a Command in a Dialog Box

To execute an option or command in a dialog box using the keyboard, either type the number preceding the option or type the underlined or bold letter indicated in the option. If an option is preceded by an arrow in the text mode or surrounded with a dotted box in the graphics mode, WordPerfect is indi-cating that that is the default option and can be executed by pressing [Enter]. If a dialog box appears with neither bold or underlined options, use the keyboard to move through the options, using ⌜Tab⌟ to move forward and ⌜Shift⌟ + ⌜Tab⌟ to move backward. Or, to select an option using the mouse, simply position the mouse pointer on the option and click the left mouse button once.

▌ **HANDS-ON ACTIVITY**

In this exercise, you will learn to execute options in a dialog box by using the *mouse*. If you do not have a mouse attached to your system, move to the next exercise.

1. Select Layout

    The Layout pull-down menu appears.

2. Select Line

    The Line Format menu appears as shown in Figure 2-11. Notice that the first option, Tab Set, is followed by ellipses indicating that a sub-dialog box will appear when this option is selected.

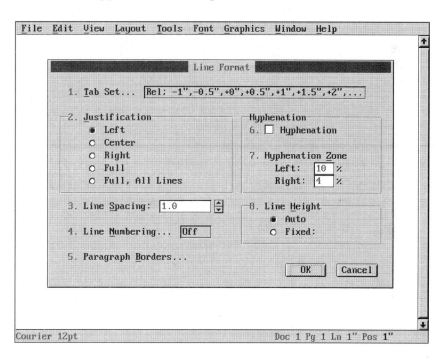

Figure 2-11

3. Select Tab Set

    A sub-dialog box called Tab Set appears. To return to the previous dialog box,

4. Select Cancel

    The Line Format dialog box reappears. Notice the second section of this dialog box, called Justification, which consists of radio buttons. Remember, only one radio button can be selected at any one time. The selected option is indicated by a black dot in the radio button.

5. Select Center

The Center option is now selected and indicated by a black dot in the radio button.

Look at the third section, called Line Spacing. A text box is presented for this option so that you can type the desired line spacing.

6. Select **Line Spacing**

The text (1.0, for single spacing) in the text box is now highlighted, so whatever text you type replaces the highlighted text.

7. Type **2** (for double spacing)

Also, notice that to the right of the text box is a double-headed arrow. If you don't wish to type text in this box, you can change the line spacing by clicking on either the up arrow, which increases the number, or the down arrow, which decreases the number.

8. Move the mouse pointer to the double-headed arrow

9. Select the up arrow

The line spacing text box now reflects 2.10. (These values may vary depending upon the base font you have selected.)

10. Select the down arrow twice and press Enter

The number in the text box now reads 1.90.

A check box is presented for the Hyphenation option. Currently, the Hyphenation option is turned off. To turn it on,

11. Select **Hyphenation**

The check box now has an X in it to indicate that the option is turned on. Remember, a check box acts as a toggle—you turn it off the same way you turn it on.

There are two command buttons in the lower right-hand corner of the dialog box—OK and Cancel. Notice that the OK button has a dotted box around the button, indicating that the option is the default and can be executed by pressing Enter instead of using the mouse to select the button. If the Cancel button is selected, none of your changes will be saved.

12. Select **Cancel**

The Line Format dialog box is closed and none of the changes made were saved.

Now, you are going to experiment with drop-down list boxes.

13. Select **Font**

The Font pull-down menu appears.

14. Select **Font**

The Font dialog box appears, as shown in Figure 2-12. Notice that the Font and Size section of this dialog box are both drop-down list boxes.

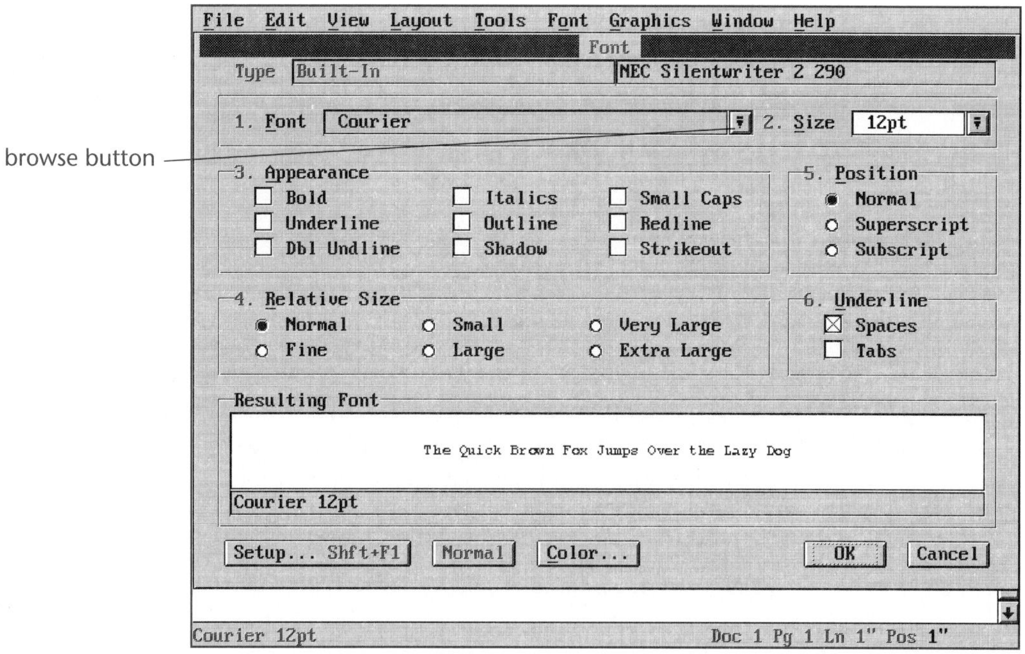

browse button

Figure 2-12

15. Select **Font**

A drop-down list box (shown in Figure 2-13) appears with a list of various options available for this feature. (The available fonts on your system may differ slightly from the ones in Figure 2-13.) Notice that the cursor is blinking in an empty text box at the top of the list, indicating that you can type the desired option if you wish. A more expedient method of selecting an option is to move the mouse pointer to the desired option and click.

To exit the Font dialog box without saving your changes,

16. Select **Cancel**

HANDS-ON ACTIVITY

In this exercise, you will use the *keyboard* to execute commands in a dialog box.

To open the Layout menu,

1. Hold down [Alt] and press **L** (for **L**ayout)

The Layout pull-down menu appears. To display the Line dialog box,

2. Press **L** (for **L**ine)

The Line Format menu appears as previously shown in Figure 2-11.

Notice that the first option, Tab Set, is followed by ellipses indicating that a sub-dialog box will appear when this option is selected. To select an option using the keyboard, you may either press the number preceding the option or type the underlined letter. To display the Tab Set sub-dialog box,

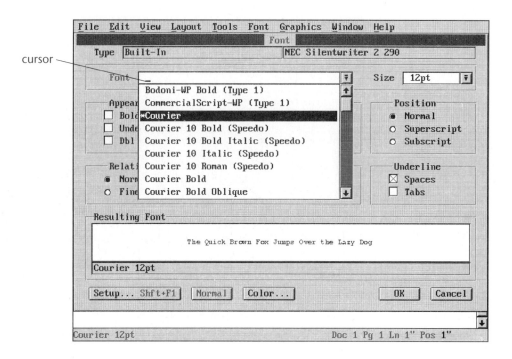

cursor

Figure 2-13

3. Press **1** or **T** (for _T_ab Set)

A sub-dialog box called Tab Set appears. To return to the previous dialog box, you can press [Esc].

4. Press [Esc]

The Line Format dialog box reappears. Now you are going to select the Paragraph Borders option by pressing the underlined letter.

5. Press **B** (for Paragraph _B_orders)

The Create Paragraph Border dialog box appears, as shown in Figure 2-14.

Notice that there are three command buttons at the bottom of the dialog box. The OK and Cancel command buttons do not have an underlined letter to execute the command from the keyboard. Pressing the function key [F7] will execute the OK command button, and pressing the [Esc] key will execute the Cancel command.

Notice that the OK command button is surrounded with a dotted box, indicating that it is the default and can, therefore, be executed by pressing [Enter]. However, the Cancel command button is not the default and also does not have an underlined letter by which to select the command. The default command button can be changed by pressing the [Tab] key. Each time [Tab] is pressed the next command button becomes the default option and is indicated with a dotted box. Pressing [Shift] + [Tab] makes the previous command button the default. To make the Off command button the default,

6. Hold down [Shift] and press [Tab]

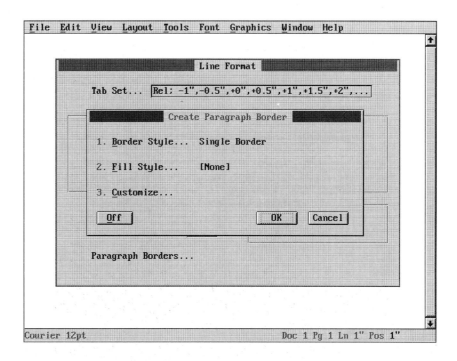

Figure 2-14

The Off command button now is surrounded by a dotted box. To make the Cancel command button the default option,

7. Press [Tab] twice

The Cancel command button is now the default. To exit the Create Paragraph Border dialog box,

8. Press [Enter]

The Line Format dialog box reappears. Notice the section of this dialog called Justification, which consists of radio buttons. Remember, only one radio button can be selected at a time. The selected option is indicated by a black dot in the radio button. To select the Justification option,

9. Press either **2** or **J** (for Justification)

In the Justification section, each radio button option is preceded by a number and also indicated with an underlined letter, thus allowing you to easily make a selection in the way you prefer. To select the Full option,

10. Press either **4** or **F** (for Full)

A black dot is placed in the radio button preceding the Full to indicate that it is the current selection.

Look at the third section called Line Spacing. A text box is present for this option so that you can type the desired line spacing. To select the Line Spacing option,

11. Press either **3** or **S** (for Line Spacing)

The text (1.0) in the text box is now highlighted, so whatever text you type replaces the highlighted text.

12. Type **2** (for double spacing)

13. Press (Enter)

    A check box is presented for the Hyphenation option. At present the Hyphenation option is turned off. To turn it on,

14. Press either **6** or **Y** (for Hyphenation)

    The check box now has an X in it to indicate that the option is turned on. Remember, a check box acts as a toggle—you turn it off the same way you turn it on. To turn it off,

15. Press either **6** or **Y** again

    There are two command buttons in the lower right-hand corner of the dialog box—OK and Cancel. Notice that the OK button has a dotted box around the button. This indicates that the option is the default and therefore can be executed by pressing (Enter) instead of using the mouse to select the button. To make the Cancel command button the default,

16. Press (Tab)

    The Cancel command button is now the default, so to exit without saving your settings,

17. Press (Enter)

    Now, you are going to access the Font menu by using the shortcut keys.

18. Press (Ctrl) + (F8)

    Now, you are going to experiment with drop-down list boxes.

    The Font dialog box appears, as shown in Figure 2-12. The Font and Size section of this dialog box are both drop-down list boxes. To select the Font option,

19. Press either **1** or **F** (for Font)

    A drop-down list box (shown in Figure 2-13) appears with a list of various options available for this feature. Notice that the cursor is blinking in an empty text box at the top of the list, indicating that you can type the desired option if you wish. To close the box without making a selection,

20. Press (Esc)

    To exit the Font dialog box without saving your changes,

21. Press (Esc) again

    NOTE: From this point forward in the book, the menu commands and dialog options will be indicated in the exercises by simply the command with the appropriate underlined letter. For example, to open the File menu, the exercise will read, "Select File." You may use either the keyboard or the mouse to select the command.

Using Scroll Bars

Some windows and dialog boxes have **scroll bars**. This component allows you to view the part of a document or information in a dialog box that cannot fit into the window. Only a mouse can be used to access or manipulate scroll bars. A window may have either a horizontal or a vertical scroll bar; sometimes a window has both. The horizontal scroll bar moves the display sideways, and the vertical scroll bar moves it up and down. A scroll bar has three parts, a **scroll button** and two **scroll arrows,** as shown in Figure 2-15.

The scroll arrow at the top of the vertical scroll bar is the up scroll arrow (as the arrow indicates). Similarly, the one at the bottom is the down scroll arrow. One selection of the scroll arrow (by clicking on it once) moves the cursor by one line in the specified direction. Positioning the mouse pointer on a scroll arrow and holding down the left mouse button causes the cursor to move continuously by line in the specified direction until the mouse button is released or the beginning or end of the information displays in the window.

Clicking on the scroll bar either above or below the scroll button moves the display one screen's worth in the specified direction. Dragging the scroll button up or down moves the display a distance proportional to the distance the box has moved. For example, if you position the scroll button halfway down the scroll bar, the middle of the information or file appears. Dragging the scroll button to the top of the scroll bar moves the display to the top of the information or file, and dragging the scroll button to the bottom of the scroll bar moves to the end of the file. With a little practice, you will soon be comfortable with this technique.

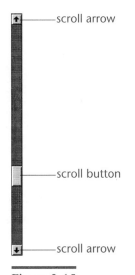

scroll arrow

scroll button

scroll arrow

Figure 2-15

Getting Help

WordPerfect's Help feature is accessed from the menu bar by choosing Help or by pressing F1.

The Contents options displays a help list for the following general information:

- Index   Features listed alphabetically
- How Do I...   Performing tasks
- Glossary   Meanings of terms
- Template   Function keys and their actions
- Keystrokes   Keystrokes and their actions
- Shortcut keys   Quickly accessing features
- Error Messages   Causes and solutions for common error messages

The How Do I... feature lists the most common tasks that you might want to do. For example, you might have questions such as "How do I print a document?" or "How do I change the top margin?" Topics can be selected from the following categories:

- Basics   • Writing Tools   • Macros
- Basic Layout   • Graphics/Equations   • Merge
- Advanced Layout

▌ **HANDS-ON ACTIVITY**

In this exercise, you are going to use the How Do I... option to learn how to save a document. Remember, if you prefer to execute a command using a keyboard shortcut, the keystrokes will be indicated with a √ symbol and will follow the menu commands.

1. Select **Help**

    √ Press F1

    The menu shown in Figure 2-16 appears.

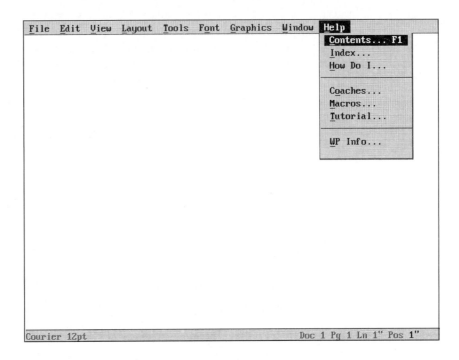

Figure 2-16

2. Select **How Do I...**

    The WordPerfect 6.0 How Do I... Help window appears, as shown in Figure 2-17.

3. Press the ↓ 3 times or click once and then double-click with the mouse on the subject called "Save a Document" under the Basics heading. Be sure "Save a Document" is highlighted

4. Select **Look**

    The Help window shown in Figure 2-18 appears, giving you step-by-step instructions on how to save a document. You may browse through the help information text either with the arrow keys or with the mouse. Compare your screen to the one in the figure.

    To move with the keyboard,

5. Press ↑ or ↓

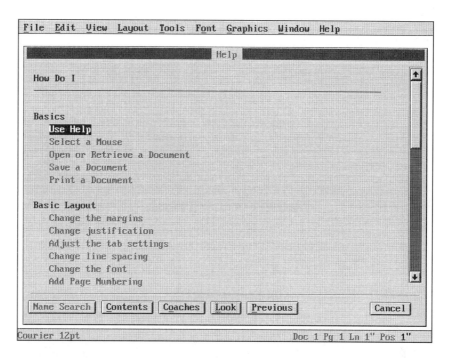

Figure 2-17

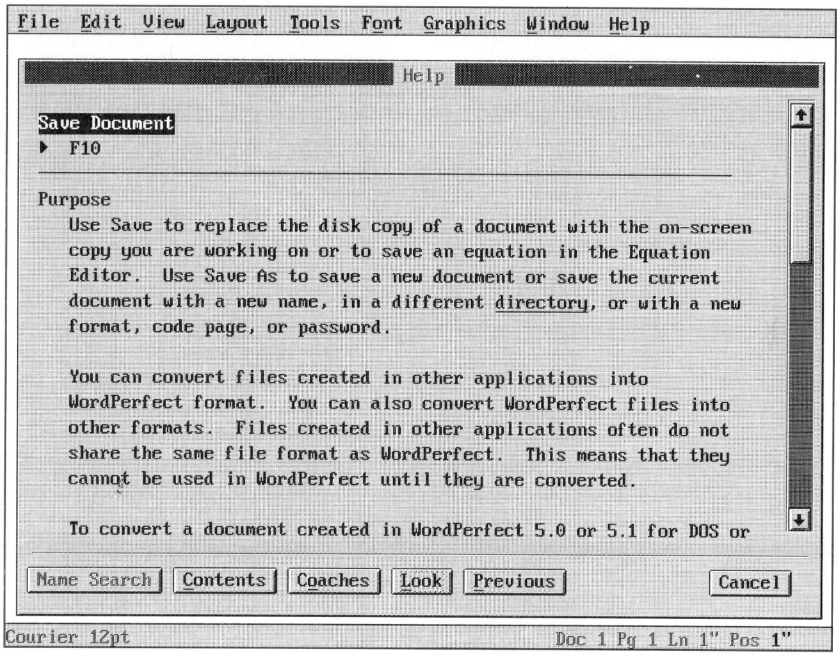

Figure 2-18

To move with the mouse, use the scroll bar along the right side of the help screen.

6. Select either the up or down arrow in the scroll bar, *or*

    Position the mouse pointer on the scroll button in the scroll bar (solid black in the text mode and resembling a "button" in the graphics mode), then hold down the left mouse button as you "drag" the button either up or down to scroll through the help text

To exit Help,

7. Select **Cancel**

√ Press Esc

NOTE: From this point forward, when you are to choose an option from the menu bar and an additional option from the pull-down menu then appears, the commands will be shown together in sequence. For instance, an instruction to select the File option from the menu bar and then choose Save from the pull-down menu would read "Select File ⇒ Save."

▌ HANDS-ON ACTIVITY

In the next exercise, you will use the Index Help feature, to search for help on the Print Preview feature.

1. Select **Help** ⇒ **Index**

The Help Index dialog box appears, as shown in Figure 2-19. An alphabetical listing of WordPerfect features appears. To search for a specific topic by name,

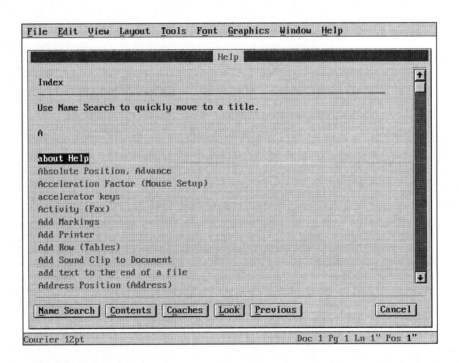

Figure 2-19

2. Select **N**ame Search

The cursor moves to the bottom of the screen and appears in the Name Search text box, thus allowing you to type in the topic.

3. Type **Preview**

4. Press Enter

5. Select <u>L</u>ook

The same Print Preview Help window appears as shown in Figure 2-20. To exit the Help menu,

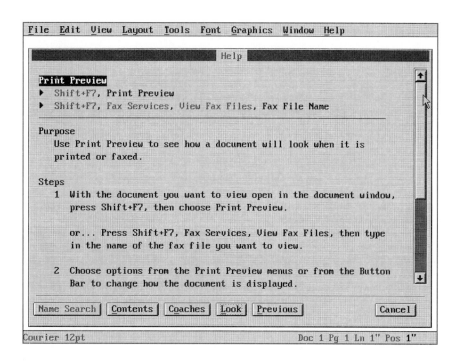

Figure 2-20

6. Select **Cancel**

√ Press Esc

Exiting WordPerfect

It is important that you exit WordPerfect in the proper manner for two reasons. First, WordPerfect creates temporary files during an editing session and they need to be properly closed and deleted (automatically by the program). Second, the WordPerfect system files are also open and need to be closed properly so that they do not become corrupted. Therefore, make it a rule to exit WordPerfect by selecting <u>F</u>ile ⇒ E<u>x</u>it WP (*Shortcut keys:* Home, F7).

If a file has not been saved, or if it has been changed by even one keystroke since the last time it was saved, the Exit WordPerfect dialog box presents you with a Save check box. Recall that check boxes allow you to switch a feature on or off. If there is an X inside the box, the feature is turned on; the absence of an X indicates that the feature is turned off. Notice that the Save feature in the dialog box is turned on, indicating that WordPerfect assumes you want to save the file and is expecting you to enter a file name if one has not previously been entered. To turn off the Save check box and instruct WordPerfect that you do not wish to have the file saved, either select the check box or press the letter preceding the box. Check boxes act as a toggle; to turn one on again, repeat the same process. To exit WordPerfect, press Enter.

▌ HANDS-ON ACTIVITY

You are finished with this editing session, so you are going to exit WordPerfect.

1. Select File ⇒ Exit WP

    √ Press Home, F7

    The Exit WordPerfect dialog box shown in Figure 2-21 appears.

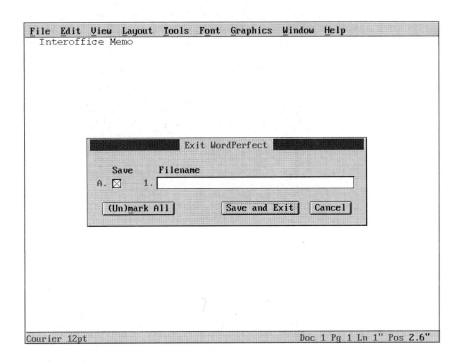

Figure 2-21

Since text was typed and then deleted, the Save check box has an X in it. WordPerfect assumes you want to save the text on your screen (in most cases you do) and is asking you to type in a file name. You do not wish to save since you deleted the text "Interoffice Memorandum"; therefore, to turn off the Save feature,

2. Select the **Save** check box

    √ Press **A**

    Notice that the X is removed and the dialog box now appears, as shown in Figure 2-22.

    To exit WordPerfect,

3. Select Exit

    √ Press Enter

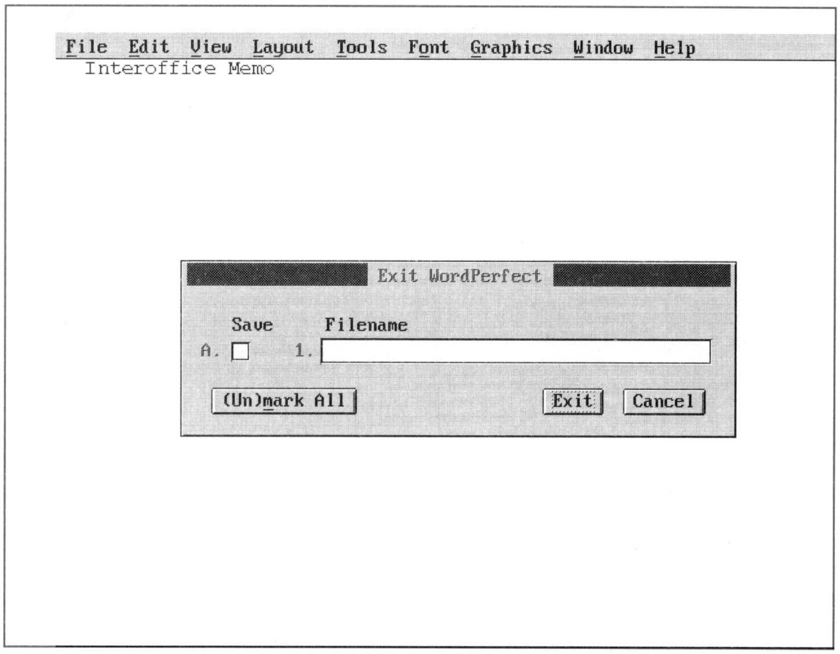

Figure 2-22

Review of Commands

Description	Menu Commands	Function Keys
Change the view mode	_____	_____
Use Help	_____	_____
Exit WordPerfect	_____	_____

Lesson Review

1. The information that displays in the left side of the Status Bar is:

2. The information that displays on the lower-right side of the document is:

3. The default settings for all margins are:

4. The default justification is set at:

5. List the three ways in which you can give WordPerfect a command.

6. What does a menu option followed by ellipses indicate?

7. What keystroke allows you to close a menu without making a selection?

8. Name the two views in which a WordPerfect window can be displayed.

9. What is the purpose of a dialog box?

10. Name two ways to invoke the Help feature.

▌ Assignments

2.1 Directions

1. Type your name and press Enter 6 times.

2. Note and record the vertical position of the cursor.

3. Using Backspace, delete all blank lines. (*HINT*: Your cursor should be positioned at the end of your name.) Note and record the horizontal position of the cursor.

2.2 Directions

1. Using either the keyboard or mouse, practice executing the following menu commands, using the right mouse button or Esc to cancel after each execution:

   Tools ⇒ Date ⇒ Format

   Font ⇒ Font

   Edit ⇒ Go to

2. Using the Help Index feature, display the shortcut key menu and note and record the shortcut keys for the Undo and Repeat features.

3. Using the Help Contents option, locate the Date feature. Note and record the steps to insert a date code in your document. (You will be using this feature in the next lesson.)

4. Exit WordPerfect without saving the text on your screen.

3

Creating a
One-Page Letter

Objectives

Upon completion of this lesson, you will be able to do the following:

- Use the Date feature
- Utilize the Enter key
- Bold and underline text as you type
- Move the cursor using the keyboard, mouse, and scroll bars
- Display the Reveal Codes screen
- Save a document with both Save As and Save
- Spell check a document
- Print a document

This lesson is designed to familiarize you with the WordPerfect document window and introduce you to the basic features of creating, saving, and printing a document.

Starting Point

Before beginning this lesson, load WordPerfect 6.0 and have a clear working screen.

Starting a New Document and Entering Text

Since WordPerfect automatically presents you with a blank document window when the WordPerfect program is started, nothing special needs to be done before you begin typing your document. If you make no formatting changes, the default settings will take effect: 1-inch top, bottom, left, and right margins; single spacing; and tabs set at every ½ inch.

There are many wonderful features that WordPerfect offers to make the generation of a document very easy, such as automatically inserting the date, word wrap (text is automatically moved to the next line when the end of the line is reached), and checking for spelling errors. The instructions that follow explain how to take advantage of these and other features while creating the letter shown in Figure 3-1.

51

(today's date)

Mr. James Jacobs
Technologies Unlimited
1075 Mountain Drive, Suite 200
Boulder, CO 80302

Dear Mr. Jacobs:

Thank you for your inqiry regarding the services provided by PencilPushers, Inc.
Our goals are to enhance the the pERformance of our clients by providing
administrative solutions without jeprodizing operating costs with added expense of
personnel and equipment.

Our company offers a **variety** of services ranging from general office staffing,
bookeping, word processing, client billing, as well as financial reporting, forcasting
and consulting. PencilPushers,Inc. incorporates the NASS Industry Production
Standard into its business practices and also subscribes tothe NASS Code of
Business Ethics.

For your review, enclosed is an information packette detailing each available service
including the costs, terms and conditions, as well as a list of client references.

We look forward to the **opportunity** to work with your company. I will be out of
town next week, but will contact you on August 16th to schedule an appointment
to discuss your specific needs.

Sincerely yours,

(your name)
President

Enclosure

Figure 3-1

Inserting the Date

WordPerfect will automatically insert the current date (according to the computer's clock) into your document. There are two options to consider when using the Date feature: Text and Code. The **Date Text** feature inserts the date the document is created, according to your computer's clock. But if the document is printed or edited at a later date, the inserted date remains unchanged. To insert the Date Text, from the menu bar, choose Tools ⇒ Date ⇒ Text (*Shortcut keys:* Shift + F5 , 1).

The **Date Code** feature also inserts the current date according to the computer's clock. However, if the document is later printed or edited, the date is updated to reflect the current date. To insert the Date Code from the menu bar, choose <u>T</u>ools ⇒ <u>D</u>ate ⇒ <u>C</u>ode (*Shortcut keys:* Shift + F5 , 2).

▌HANDS-ON ACTIVITY

You are the owner of an administrative support services company called PencilPushers, Inc., in Boulder, Colorado. You have staff that supports clients and manages the building services at three locations. You have received an inquiry from Mr. Jacobs regarding your services, and the letter you create and spell check in this lesson is in response to his letter.

In this exercise you will insert the current date using the Date Code feature. The cursor should be at the top of your document, and the status line should read "Ln 1" Pos 1"."

1. Select <u>T</u>ools ⇒ <u>D</u>ate

   ✓ Press Shift + F5

   The menu shown in Figure 3-2 appears.

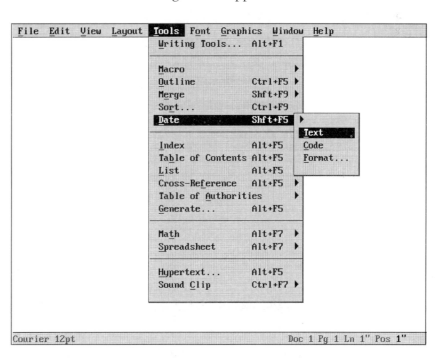

Figure 3-2

2. Select <u>C</u>ode

   The current date is inserted into your document.

▌Using the Enter Key

When you are entering text into a document, there are three occasions when you use the Enter key: to terminate a short line and position the cursor on the next line, such as with a date or inside address (name, address, city, state, and zip code); to create a blank line; and to end a paragraph. When you are typing a paragraph and the cursor approaches the right margin, do not press Enter —just keep typing. The words that cannot fit onto a line will be moved to the beginning of a new line. This feature is called **word wrap** and it will increase your typing speed by 20 percent!

▌ HANDS-ON ACTIVITY

The cursor is currently positioned at the end of the date. First, let's terminate that line and move the cursor one line down.

1. Press Enter

    Now, let's put some blank lines between the date and the inside address.

2. Press Enter 5 times

    Now type the inside address and press Enter at the end of each line. If you accidentally press the wrong key, to delete the last character typed, press Backspace .

3. Type the following text:

    ```
    Mr. James Jacobs
    Technologies Unlimited
    1075 Mountain Drive, Suite 200
    Boulder, CO 80302
    ```

4. Press Enter once

    You pressed Enter at the end of each line, and once more to create a blank line.

5. Type **Dear Mr. Jacobs:**

6. Press Enter twice

    As you type the following text to create the first paragraph, do not press Enter when the cursor approaches the right margin. WordPerfect will wrap the text that does not fit on one line to the next line.

    NOTE: Be sure to make the errors included in the exercise so that you can use the features of the spell check program, as shown a little later in this lesson.

7. Type the following text:

    ```
    Thank you for your inqiry regarding the services
    provided by PencilPushers, Inc. Our goals are
    to enhance the the pERformance of our clients
    by providing administrative solutions without
    jeprodizing operating costs with added expense
    of personnel and equipment.
    ```

    To end the first paragraph and begin typing the second paragraph,

8. Press Enter twice

9. Type `Our company offers a`

Before you continue typing the paragraph, there are two WordPerfect features we need to tell you about: Bold and Underline.

Bolding Text While Typing

As you are typing, any quantity of text may be boldfaced. Boldfaced text is darker both on-screen and when printed, for additional emphasis. To activate the **Bold** feature, from the Menu Bar choose Font ⇒ Bold (*Shortcut keys:* `F6`, or `Ctrl` + B). The font type and point size on the Status Bar are in bold to indicate that the Bold feature is active. Type the text to be in bold and then, to deactivate the feature, choose Font ⇒ Normal (*Shortcut keys:* `F6`, or `Ctrl` + B).

▌ HANDS-ON ACTIVITY

You are going to continue to type the second paragraph, including a word in boldface. You will use the shortcut key method to bold the word. To activate the Bold feature,

1. Press `Ctrl` + **B**

   Notice that the font and point size in the Status Line become bold to indicate that the feature is activated. (If you are using a color monitor, the Pos number in the status line changes color too.)

2. Type **variety**

   To deactivate the Bold feature,

3. Press `Ctrl` + **B**

4. Continue to type the remainder of the paragraph as shown below (include the errors):

   ```
   of services ranging from general office staffing,
   bookeping, word processing, client billing, as well
   as financial reporting, forcasting and consulting.
   PencilPushers, Inc. incorporates the
   ```

Now, you will learn to underline while typing.

Underlining Text While Typing

Any quantity of text may be underlined while typing. To activate the **Underline** feature, from the menu bar choose Font ⇒ Underline (*Shortcut keys:* `F8`, or `Ctrl` + U). The font type and point size on the Status Bar are underlined to indicate that the underline feature is active. Type the text to be underlined. To deactivate the underline feature, from the menu bar choose Font ⇒ Normal (*Shortcut keys:* `Ctrl` + U, or `F8`).

▌ HANDS-ON ACTIVITY

The specific titles "NASS Industry Production Standard" and "NASS Code of Business Ethics" will be underlined as you type the text.

To turn on the underline feature,

1. Select **Font**

    The Font pull-down menu appears, as shown in Figure 3-3.

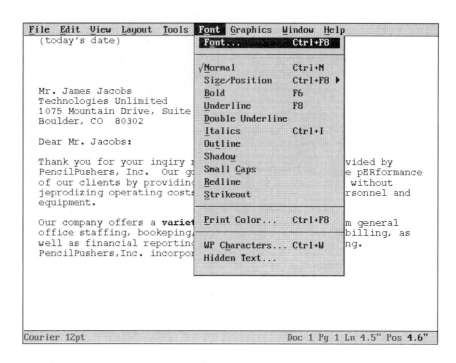

Figure 3-3

2. Select **Underline**

    ✓ Press Ctrl + U, or F8

    Notice that the Pos number on the Status Line is underlined, indicating that the underline function is on.

3. Type **NASS Industry Production Standard**

    Depending on the type of monitor that is attached to your computer, the underlined text is displayed either with a different shading, with a different color, or actually underlined.

    To turn off the Underline feature,

4. Select **Font** ⇒ **Normal**

    ✓ Press Ctrl + U, or F8

5. Type **into its business practices and also subscribes tothe**

    Now, let's turn on Underline.

6. Select **Font** ⇒ **Underline**

    ✓ Press Ctrl + U, or F8

7. Type `NASS Code of Business Ethics`

   Turn off the Underline feature:

8. Select F<u>o</u>nt ⇒ <u>N</u>ormal

   ✓ Press Ctrl + `U`, or F8

9. Type `.` (a period)

   To create a new paragraph,

10. Press Enter twice

11. Type the following text:

    ```
    For your review, enclosed is an information
    packette detailing each available service including
    the costs, terms and conditions, as well as a
    list of client references.
    ```

    To create another paragraph,

12. Press Enter twice

13. Type `We look forward to the`

14. On your own, bold and type the word `opportunity`

    CAUTION: Be sure to turn bold off.

15. Type `to work with your company. I will be out of town next week, but will contact you on`

▌ Hard Space (Keeping Two Words Together)

The **Hard Space** feature ensures that two words remain on the same line, such as the month and day in a date or initials in a person's name. The hard space feature inserts a hard space between the two words, instead of the regular space created using the Spacebar. To insert a hard space, type the first word; then press Home, Spacebar; then type the second word.

▌ HANDS-ON ACTIVITY

In this exercise, you will insert a hard space to keep the month name and day of the month on the same line.

1. Type `August`

   To insert a hard space,

2. Press Home, Spacebar

3. Type `16th`

   To complete the remainder of the paragraph,

4. Type `to schedule an appointment to discuss your spe-cific needs.`

5. Press ⌐Enter¬ twice

Moving Around in the Document

Your cursor is your point of action. When you want to insert or delete text, you must move the cursor to the place where the revision is to occur. Consequently, WordPerfect allows for various cursor movements that make it easy and fast for you to move the cursor throughout your document, using either the mouse or the keyboard. The cursor cannot be moved beyond the last keystroke of the document.

Moving with the Keyboard

You can move the cursor with the keyboard by using the four arrow keys located in the middle keypad (on an enhanced keyboard). Even though the arrow keys are repeating keys, when pressed once,

→	Moves one character to the right
←	Moves one character to the left
↑	Moves one line up
↓	Moves one line down

In addition, WordPerfect has provided the following keystroke sequences for more expedient movement:

Ctrl + →	Moves one word to the right
Ctrl + ←	Moves one word to the left
Home, ←	Moves to the beginning of a line
Home, →, or End	Moves to the end of a line
Ctrl + ↑	Moves up one paragraph
Ctrl + ↓	Moves down one paragraph
Home, Home, ↑	Moves to the beginning of a document
Home, Home, ↓	Moves to the end of a document

▌ HANDS-ON ACTIVITY

Let's experiment with the keystroke combinations to move the cursor. First let's move the cursor to the beginning of the document.

1. Press Home, Home, ↑

2. Press ↓ 6 times

   The cursor is at the beginning of the line that reads "Mr. James Jacobs."

   To move the cursor to the end of that line,

3. Press ⌷End⌷

    To move the cursor back to the beginning of the line,

4. Press ⌷Home⌷, ⌷←⌷

    To move the cursor to the end of your document,

5. Press ⌷Home⌷, ⌷Home⌷, ⌷↓⌷

    To move up by paragraph,

6. Press ⌷Ctrl⌷ + ⌷↑⌷ 4 times

    The cursor is positioned on the first character of the first paragraph, which reads, "Thank you for your inquiry regarding..."

    To practice moving to the next word or the previous word,

7. Press ⌷Ctrl⌷ + ⌷→⌷ 3 times

8. Press ⌷Ctrl⌷ + ⌷←⌷ 3 times

Using the Mouse to Position the Cursor

The cursor position can be moved using the mouse. Simply move the mouse pointer to the desired place and click the left mouse button once.

▌ HANDS-ON ACTIVITY

In this exercise, you will practice moving the cursor position using the mouse. If you do not have a mouse attached to your system, skip this exercise.

1. Move the mouse pointer to the beginning of the second sentence of the first paragraph, which reads, "Our goals are to..."

2. Click the left mouse button once

    Notice that the cursor is now positioned at the beginning of the word "Our."

3. Move the mouse pointer to the beginning of the second paragraph, which reads, "Our company offers a **variety**..."

4. Click the left mouse button once

Moving with Scroll Bars

Only a portion of your document can be seen in the WordPerfect windows —approximately 20 lines. The scroll bars can be used to view portions of your document not shown on the screen. If the scroll bars are not currently displayed in your document window, select View ⇒ Horizontal Scroll Bar or View ⇒ Vertical Scroll Bar. The component parts of a scroll bar were discussed in Lesson 2. Refer to Figure 2-8. Below is a recap of how to use the scroll bars to scroll through a document or list.

To Scroll	Action
One line up or down	Click on the up or down scroll arrow on the vertical scroll bar
One character to the left or right	Click on the left or right scroll arrow on the horizontal scroll bar
One screen up or down (if document is longer than 20 lines)	Click above or below the scroll box on the vertical scroll bar
One screen left or right (if document is wider than 8½" page)	Click to the left or right of the scroll box on the horizontal scroll bar
Continuously	Click and depress the left mouse button on one of the scroll arrows until the desired information is visible; release the mouse button
To any position	Drag the scroll box to the desired position; for example, positioning the scroll box halfway down the scroll bar displays the middle of the document

As you use the scroll bars to see additional text of your document, the cursor also moves.

▌ HANDS-ON ACTIVITY

If scroll bars are not displayed in your work area, follow the steps below.

1. Select <u>V</u>iew

   The <u>V</u>iew pull-down menu appears, as shown in Figure 3-4.

   If no check mark precedes <u>H</u>orizontal Scroll Bar and <u>V</u>ertical Scroll Bar, it indicates that the options are turned off. To turn on the horizontal scroll bar,

2. Select <u>H</u>orizontal Scroll Bar

   To turn on the Vertical scroll bar,

3. Select <u>V</u>iew ⇒ <u>V</u>ertical Scroll Bar

   The scroll bars will now be displayed on the right side and bottom of the screen. Compare your screen to the one shown in Figure 3-5.

▌ HANDS-ON ACTIVITY

Before experimenting with the mouse, let's use the keyboard to position the cursor at the top of the document.

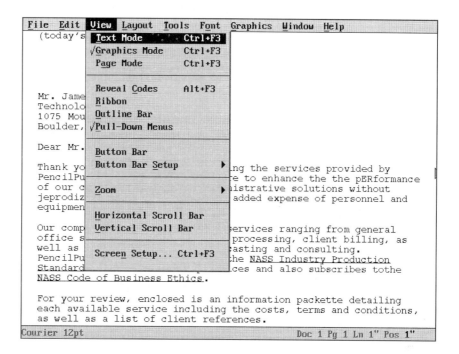

Figure 3-4

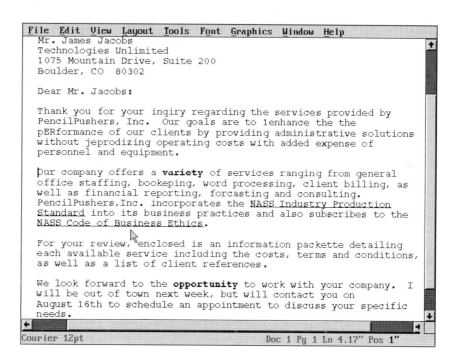

Figure 3-5

1. Press [Home], [Home], [↑]

    Now, let's use the mouse on the vertical scroll bar to move the cursor to the beginning of the first paragraph.

2. Click 13 times on the scroll bar down arrow

    The cursor is now located on the beginning of the first paragraph.

To move the cursor up two lines,

3. Click twice on the scroll bar up arrow

    The cursor is positioned at the beginning of the line that reads "Dear Mr. Jacobs."

    To move to the bottom of the document,

4. Position the mouse pointer on the scroll button, then drag the scroll button down to the bottom of the Scroll Bar. Release the mouse button.

    TIP: If your document is too wide to display on the current WordPerfect window, then you can use the horizontal scroll bars to pan from side to side.

Reveal Codes

Whenever you instruct WordPerfect to perform a special feature such as underlining or inserting a hard space, a specific code is embedded in the document for each feature. For example, when you instructed WordPerfect to turn on underlining, an [Und On] code was placed before the text with [Und Off] at the end. When the hard space was inserted, WordPerfect placed a [HSpace] code. However, in the normal document window, you are unable to view the codes until a special screen called **Reveal Codes** is activated.

NOTE: Appendix B has a list of all codes.

At first you may find the double screen a little confusing, but you will grow to depend upon Reveal Codes as one of the most useful WordPerfect editing features. You will learn to use the Reveal Codes screen to "debug" your documents by viewing, moving, copying, or removing codes.

To display the Reveal Codes screen, from the menu bar choose <u>V</u>iew ⇒ Reveal <u>C</u>odes (*Shortcut keys:* Alt + F3, or F11). The cursor displays in both screens. In the upper screen (normal workspace), it is a flashing vertical or horizontal line, and in the Reveal Codes screen, it shows as a block. The cursor moves simultaneously in both screens. To close the Reveal Codes screen, choose <u>V</u>iew ⇒ Reveal <u>C</u>odes from the menu bar (*Shortcut keys:* Alt + F3, or F11).

HANDS-ON ACTIVITY

Let's view some of the codes in your letter. First, make sure the cursor is located at the top of the document.

1. Press Home, Home, ↑

2. Select <u>V</u>iew ⇒ Reveal <u>C</u>odes

    ✓ Press Alt + F3, or F11

    The window splits into two screens, the lower one showing both the text and the codes inserted for each special function used. Compare your window to the one shown in Figure 3-6.

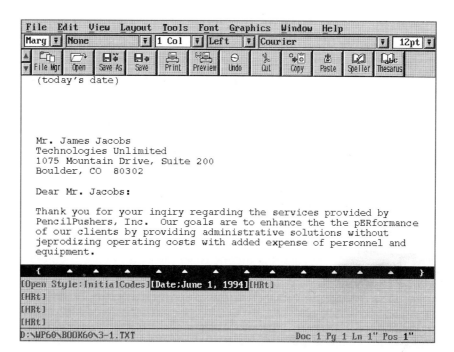

Figure 3-6

First you will see the code [Open Style:InitialCodes], which is automatically inserted into new documents to set the default formatting style for the entire document. Next, notice the [Date;*today's date*] code instructing WordPerfect to insert the current date. To the right of the [Date;*today's date*] is the [HRt] code, which stands for **hard return.** This is where you pressed [Enter].

When a cursor is positioned on a code, WordPerfect displays the full detail or information about the code. When the cursor is moved off the code, the code is shown in its compressed form, for example [Date].

▌ HANDS-ON ACTIVITY

Watch the Reveal Codes screen (lower window) to observe the changes in the [Date] code.

1. Press → once

   The cursor is now positioned on the [HRt] code. Notice that the [Date;*today's date*] code is compressed and is no longer expanded to display all the information, but only shows as [Date].

   To expand the [Date] code,

2. Press ←

   To observe wrapped paragraph coding, move down into the first line of the first paragraph of the letter.

3. Press ↓ 13 times

   At the end of the first line of the paragraph is a [SRt] code. This stands for **soft return,** which indicates that WordPerfect wrapped the text to the next line while you were typing the text.

If you move farther down into the second paragraph, you will notice the [Bold On] and [Bold Off] codes surrounding the word "variety" and the [Und On] and [Und Off] codes surrounding the two titles. These types of codes are called **paired codes.** One code instructs WordPerfect to turn on the feature and another turns it off. Do you see the [HSpace] code between August and 16th? Remember, the hard space code will always keep those two words on the same line.

Now let's exit the Reveal Codes screen.

4.   Select <u>V</u>iew ⇒ Reveal <u>C</u>odes

   ✓ Press (Alt) + (F3), or (F11)

Saving a Document

Your document is in the computer's memory and has not been saved. To save your document to disk, you can use either the menu selection, <u>F</u>ile ⇒ Save <u>A</u>s (*Shortcut key:* (F10)), or <u>F</u>ile ⇒ <u>S</u>ave (*Shortcut keys:* (Ctrl) + (F12)).

Using Save As

From the main menu option <u>F</u>ile there are two very similar selections for saving documents, **<u>S</u>ave** and **Save <u>A</u>s.**

When saving a document for the first time, you may select either the <u>S</u>ave or Save <u>A</u>s option. WordPerfect recognizes that your file has never been saved and will display a dialog box, allowing you to type a name for your new document.

But, if you had previously saved and named the currently displayed document, the <u>S</u>ave selection would assume that the file name will remain the same, not giving you the opportunity to type a different name. In the event that you want to save the file under a different name, you must use Save <u>A</u>s.

An example of a reason to use Save <u>A</u>s might be that you wrote a letter to Charlie, saving it as CHARLIE.LET, and now you would like to send the same letter with a few minor changes to Bob and save it as BOB.LET.

HANDS-ON ACTIVITY

Now save your letter on disk before you continue with other features in the lesson. The instructions below will save your document on a disk in drive A. If you wish to save your document on another disk, substitute the appropriate drive letters where drive A is indicated.

NOTE: When entering the document name, remember that it can be typed in uppercase or lowercase; it cannot exceed eight characters; and it cannot contain any spaces, or any of the following symbols: . " / \ [ ] : < > + = ; , | ^

Depending upon how your computer is configured, the assumed destination drive is usually drive C in the directory called \WPDOCS. When you are asked to input the document name, you may also type a different drive or directory, if you wish. Also, if you want to save your document on a floppy disk rather than the hard disk, type **A:** or **B:** with the file name, for example, **A:JOHN.LTR**.

1. Select <u>F</u>ile ⇒ **Save <u>A</u>s**

   ✓ Press `F10`

   The Save As dialog box appears, as shown in Figure 3-7.

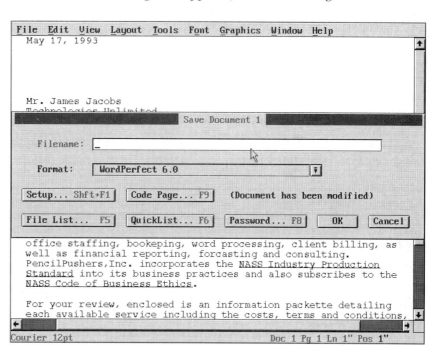

Figure 3-7

You are going to save your document as JACOBS.INQ. The cursor is positioned in the Filename text box, ready for you to type a name.

2. Type `A:JACOBS.INQ`

3. Select OK

   ✓ Press `Enter`

   To position the cursor at the end of the document, so that you can finish typing your letter,

4. Press `Home`, `Home`, `↓`

5. Type `Sincerely,`

6. Press `Enter` 4 times

7. Type your own name

8. Press `Enter`

9. Type `President`

10. Press `Enter` twice

11. Type `Enclosure`

12. Press Enter

Using Save

Earlier in the lesson, you used the File ⇒ Save As feature to save your file. To update the disk with changes you have made, from the menu bar choose File ⇒ Save (*Shortcut keys:* Ctrl + F12). WordPerfect *automatically replaces* the copy of the document on the disk. You are *not* prompted that the original file on the disk will be replaced with the version in memory (as you were in previous DOS versions of WordPerfect).

▌ HANDS-ON ACTIVITY

Now let's save your letter and update the old version of the file with the new one in memory.

1. Select File ⇒ Save

    ✓ Press Ctrl + F12

▌ Implementing the Speller

WordPerfect's **Speller** checks your documents for misspelled words, two occurrences of a word together, and irregular capitalization of text. To spell check a document, from the menu bar choose Tools ⇒ Writing Tools ⇒ Speller (*Shortcut keys:* Ctrl + F2). The Speller dialog box appears, as shown in Figure 3-8.

The options in the dialog box ask whether to check the current word, the current page, the entire document, or the remainder of the document

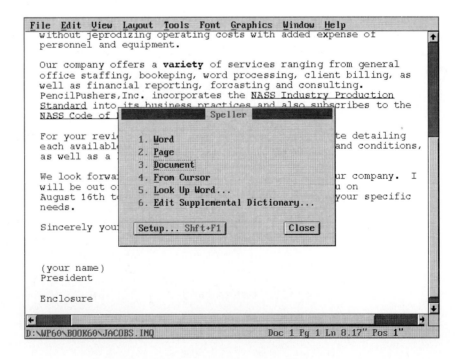

Figure 3-8

from the current cursor position to the end of the document. If you want to check a word or a page, your cursor must be somewhere on that word or page.

WordPerfect compares each word in a document against the words in its two dictionaries: the main dictionary (the file named WPUS.LEX, which contains approximately 125,000 words) and a supplemental dictionary (the file WP{WP}US.SUP). When Speller finds a word that is not in the main dictionary, for example a proper name or a term that is special to a particular industry (such as medical or legal), it flags it as misspelled. You have the option of adding the word to the supplemental dictionary to develop your own collection of special words (such as proper names or trade words that you use regularly).

During a spell check, the Speller is also automatically set to check for double words, numbers within a word, and irregular capitalization. If Speller finds two identical words next to each other, such as "that that," a "Duplicate Word Found" dialog box appears and you can either choose to delete the second occurrence of the word or leave the words and continue checking.

If Speller finds a word with irregular capitalization, such as "yOUR" or "YOur," it will flag the word. When irregular capitalization is found, the Irregular Case dialog box appears, and you have the option of choosing the correct capitalization, leaving the irregular capitalization as it is, or editing the word. You also have the option to Disable Case Checking during this Speller session.

CAUTION: Always save your document before and after a spell check. You may make a mistake unwittingly and need to return to the original form of the document.

HANDS-ON ACTIVITY

Before you begin this exercise, on your own, save the document. There are several misspelled words in your letter to Mr. Jacobs. Let's use WordPerfect's Speller to help you find them.

1. Select <u>T</u>ools ⇒ <u>W</u>riting Tools ⇒ <u>S</u>peller

    ✓ Press Ctrl + F2

    The Speller dialog box appears.

2. Select <u>D</u>ocument or press Enter

    NOTE: Remember, whenever an option in a dialog box is highlighted (text mode) or surrounded with a dotted box (graphics mode), it is the default option and can be selected by pressing Enter.

    "Jacobs" is the first word highlighted. Since it is a proper name, the Speller can only find "Jacob" in either the main or supplemental dictionaries. Since "Jacobs" is spelled correctly, you have three options. Skip <u>O</u>nce will bypass this occurrence of the word, but if "Jacobs" appears in your document again, the Speller will flag it again. Skip in this Document will bypass "Jacobs" every time Speller locates the word during this spell check. Add to the Dictionary will add it to the supplemental dictionary, so the word will never be flagged during any spell check. The word "Jacobs" appears again in the document, so to instruct Speller to bypass all occurrences,

3. Select **Skip in this Document**

The next word highlighted is "inqiry," which is spelled incorrectly; it should be "inquiry." The Word not Found dialog box contains a list of suggestions with letters to select them. The word "inquiry" is in the list, so it is easy for you to make the correction.

4. Select H for Inquiry

The incorrect word in the document (inqiry) is replaced by the correct word (inquiry). The speller continues.

The next word highlighted is "PencilPushers." This is an unusual proper name and the Speller has found no suggested possible replacement words. Since "PencilPushers" is the name of your company and will be used in all documents, add it to your supplemental dictionary so that the Speller will always know this name.

CAUTION: Make sure PencilPushers is spelled correctly before adding it to the supplemental dictionary.

5. Select **Add to Dictionary**

The second word "the" is highlighted, and the Duplicate Word Found dialog box appears. To delete the second occurrence of the word "the,"

6. Select **Delete Duplicate Word**

Next, "pERformance" is highlighted, and the Irregular Case dialog box appears. You want to replace "pERformance" with "performance," which is already highlighted.

7. Select **Replace Word**

The word "jeprodizing" is highlighted, but no suggested words are offered in the Word Not Found dialog box. Instead of looking up the correct spelling in a dictionary yourself, you can ask Speller to look it up for you. The Lookup feature will allow you to type the characters that you know are correct. When you are in doubt as to a character, type a question mark (?), and if there are several consecutive letters that you are unsure about, type an asterisk (*). The asterisk represents multiple characters and question mark represents one character. To instruct Speller to look up the word for you,

8. Select **Look Up**

The Look Up Word box appears with "jeprodizing" in the box titled "Word or Word Pattern:". "Jeprodizing" is highlighted, indicating that the word will be replaced when you begin to type your word pattern.

9. Type `je*d?zing`

   The Word or Word Pattern box appears as: "je*d?zing." Remember, the asterisk is telling WordPerfect that you are unsure of the multiple characters between the "e" and "d" and the question mark represents one unknown character between the "d" and "z."

10. Press [Enter]

    The correct spelling of "jeopardizing" now appears in the Suggestions word list. To replace the incorrect spelling with the suggested word,

11. Press [Enter]

    The word "bookeping" is now highlighted and the similar but wrong word "beekeeping" is offered in the suggested word list. This time, let's manually edit the misspelled word.

12. Select **Edit <u>W</u>ord**

    The cursor is placed in the document text so you may use normal editing keys to make the correction. The Speller dialog box appears with instructions.

13. Press [→] 4 times

    Edit "bookeping" to read "bookkeeping."

14. Type `ke`

    To exit the spell edit mode,

15. Press [F7] (Exit) or [Enter]

    Next, the word "forcasting" is highlighted and the correct spelling is shown in the suggested word list.

16. Select **<u>R</u>eplace Word** or press [Enter]

    Next, the speller highlights "NASS," which is correct in the document.

17. Select **<u>S</u>kip in this Document**

    Now the Speller highlights "tothe." These two words need to be separated with a space. To edit the phrase,

18. Select **Edit <u>W</u>ord**

19. Press [→] twice

20. Press [Spacebar]

21. Press [F7]

    The Speller stops on "packette." The correct spelling is "packet," listed in the suggested words.

22. Select C for "packet"

    Now the Speller questions the word "16th" since we combined numbers with alphabet letters.

23. Select **Ignore** **N**umbers

    Speller will probably stop at your name; if so, select the Skip in this Document option. Now, the spell check is complete.

24. Select OK

Printing a Document

To **print** the document displayed in the active window, choose <u>F</u>ile ⇒ <u>P</u>rint/Fax (*Shortcut keys:* [Shift] + [F7]). The Print dialog box appears, indicating the current printer. The Print dialog box allows you to print either the entire document or the current page. If you select the current page option, the cursor must be located in the page to be printed.

NOTE: If you have more than one printer available and the current printer selection is not the one you want, choose <u>S</u>elect... The Select Printer dialog box then appears. Move to the desired printer and choose <u>S</u>elect.

▌ HANDS-ON ACTIVITY

Before you print your letter, be sure your printer is on, the on-line light is illuminated, and the paper is properly aligned in the printer.

1. Select <u>F</u>ile ⇒ <u>P</u>rint/Fax

    ✓   Press [Shift] + [F7]

    The Print/Fax dialog box appears as shown in Figure 3-9. Notice that, in the Print section of the Print dialog box, <u>F</u>ull Document is selected, which indicates that the entire document will be printed.

2. Select **P**r**int**

Exiting WordPerfect

In Lesson 2, you exited WordPerfect without saving your file. When you execute the <u>F</u>ile ⇒ E<u>x</u>it WP option, you have the choice to save the file and exit, or exit without saving. Remember, it is important that you exit WordPerfect in the proper manner before turning off your computer.

▌ HANDS-ON ACTIVITY

You are finished with this editing session, so you are going to exit WordPerfect and during the exit procedure save your file.

1. Select <u>F</u>ile ⇒ E<u>x</u>it WP

    ✓ Press [Home], [F7]

    The dialog box shown in Figure 3-10 appears.

    Notice that the Save check box has an X in it to indicate that the file will be saved as you exit WordPerfect.

2. Select Save and Exit

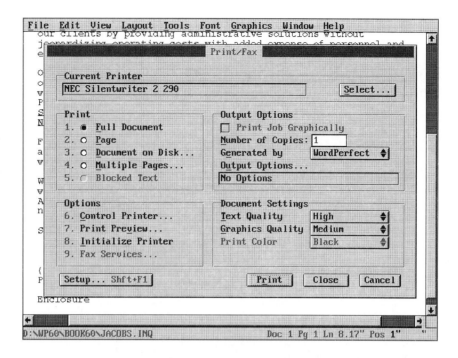

Figure 3-9

Figure 3-10

On Your Own

Review of Commands

Description	Menu Commands	Function Keys
Date Text	_____	_____
Date Code	_____	_____
Bold while typing	_____	_____
Underline while typing	_____	_____
Hard space	_____	_____
Display the scroll bars	_____	_____
Reveal Codes	_____	_____
Save a new document	_____	_____
Save already named document	_____	_____
Spell check a document	_____	_____
Print a document	_____	_____

Lesson Review

1. Name the two Date options and describe the difference between them.

   Code – Changes every time / Text will stay same

2. List two of the three times when you would use the [Enter] key.

3. If you were typing the following title of a book—*Using WordPerfect*—what commands would you use to underline it?

4. The keystrokes that would keep "June 27" from separating over two lines are

5. If you want to save and name a new document "Lesson 1," what command would you select?

6. What are the keystrokes to save the currently displayed, named document again after adding more material?

7. The keystrokes that move the cursor down to the next paragraph are

8. What do you select to see the codes that are inserted in your document?

9. The shortcut keys to bold words as you type are

10. Besides misspelled words, what other errors does Speller find?

11. The menu selections and the shortcut keys to print a document are

12. What is the proper procedure to save a document while exiting WordPerfect?

Assignments

3.1 Directions

1. Type the text shown below using the default formatting and the Date Code feature. Type the text as shown, including errors, plus any others you inadvertently make.

2. Bold "outstanding and unusual contributions."

3. Underline "April 3, 1995," and keep all parts of the dates together on a line.

4. Keep the words "Box" and "34" on the same line.

5. Save the document with the Save As feature as AWARDS.LS3.

6. Look at the Reveal Codes screen to see if your hard space commands are all in the right places (between the numbers in dates and between Campus Box and numbers).

7. Spell check and save the document again (this time with Save, using the same file name).

8. Print and exit the document.

(today's date)

The Distinguished Service Award Committee invites all employees to submit nominations for the Distinguished Service Award.

Distinguished Service Awads are given to college classified staff, contract administrators, and faculty who have worked at Boulder University for more than 10 years on a full time basis. Service is defined as continuous serice characterized by a high standard of quality, longevity, and significance. The emfasis should be on outstanding and unusual contributions which are clearly above and beyond the norm.

Please submit materials to the Faculty Senate Office, Campus Box 34 by April 3, 1995.

Basic Editing Features of WordPerfect 6.0

Objectives

Upon completion of this lesson, you will be able to do the following:

- Open a file
- Save a file using a new name
- Use the typeover mode
- Delete text
- Undelete text
- Undo a change
- Block text using the mouse or keyboard
- Delete a block of text
- Cut, copy, and paste text
- Insert new text
- Create a new paragraph
- Use the Thesaurus
- Underline and bold existing text
- Remove bold and underline
- Use case conversion
- Change the view of your text using the Zoom feature
- Display the document information

Starting Point

This lesson is designed to familiarize you with various features that enable you to insert and delete text, replace existing text, convert text from lower-case to uppercase, and vary your word choice. These tools can assist you in editing your documents swiftly and accurately.

Start WordPerfect 6.0 and insert your sample disk in drive A. A blank, unnamed document window should be displayed.

▌ Opening a Document

In previous lessons, you learned how to save a file to disk and clear the screen. When you want to edit or view an existing document, you must first open the file. Opening a file retrieves a copy of the file from disk and places it into a new document window. To **open a file**, choose File ⇒ Open (*Shortcut keys:* Shift + F10).

▌ HANDS-ON ACTIVITY

In this exercise, you will retrieve the inquiry letter to Mr. Jacobs you created in Lesson 3 named JACOBS.INQ.

1. Select File ⇒ Open

   ✓ Press Shift + F10

   The Open Document dialog box appears, shown in Figure 4-1.

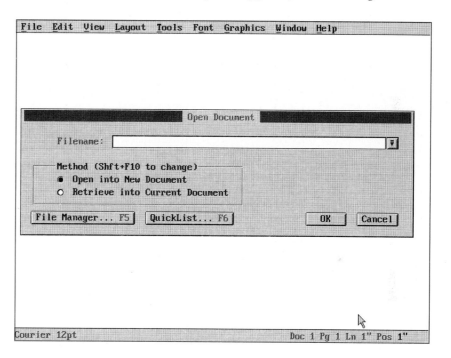

Figure 4-1

Notice that the option "Open into New Document" is selected. The file will open into a new document rather than "Retrieve into Current Document," which would combine the text in the newly opened document with any existing text in the current window.

Enter the name of the document in the "Filename" entry box to open the desired file. We are assuming that your file is located on a disk in drive A. If you are using a different drive, substitute the appropriate drive letter where A: is indicated.

2. Type **A:JACOBS.INQ**

3. Select **OK**

   ✓ Press Enter

   The Jacobs inquiry letter displays on the screen.

Now, let's close the file. Since no changes have been made, you do not need to save again.

4. Select <u>File</u> ⇒ Close

   ✓ Press F7, **N**, **N**

Now, try another method of selecting the same file to open.

5. Select <u>File</u> ⇒ <u>O</u>pen

   ✓ Press Shift + F10

This time, instead of typing the file name, you can display a list of the last four documents used by either pressing ⬇ or clicking on the browse arrow located at the right edge of the Filename entry box, as shown in Figure 4-2.

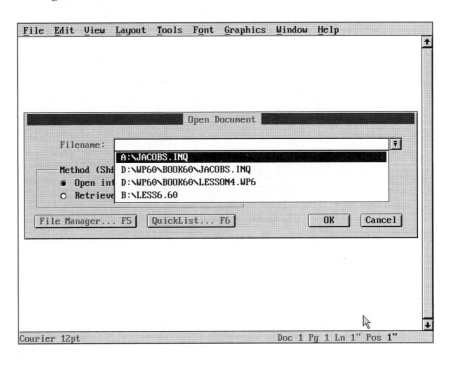

Figure 4-2

To display the last four documents you have used,

6. Press ⬇

7. Select **A:JACOBS.INQ**

8. Press Enter

   (Remember, a shortcut to opening a file using the mouse is to double-click on the file name.)

▌ Saving a File Using a New Name

The **Save <u>A</u>s** option in the <u>F</u>ile Menu allows you to save the document in the active window, using a new name. The original document remains un-changed on disk, which allows you to modify or edit the copy without alter-ing the original. You might want to use this feature when you have a standard contract on disk that you don't want to change, but you need a copy of it so that you can tailor the terms and conditions to a particular client.

To save a file with a new name, you choose <u>F</u>ile ⇒ Save <u>A</u>s (*Shortcut key:* F10). The Save As dialog box appears, and you type in the new file name. If you want the file to be saved in a different drive or directory, that information must precede the file name. For example, if you want the file named CONTRACT.TXT saved on drive A, in the Save <u>A</u>s text box you would type **A:CONTRACT.TXT**.

▌ HANDS-ON ACTIVITY

Mr. Jacobs's inquiry letter is currently displayed. You want to leave it as is, but need a similar letter for Ms. Alice Carter. To accomplish this task, you will use the Save <u>A</u>s feature to make a copy of Mr. Jacobs's letter.

1. Select <u>F</u>ile ⇒ **Save <u>A</u>s**

    ✓ Press F10

    The Save As dialog box appears. Now let's name the file CARTER.INQ on drive A. (If you are using a different drive, substitute the appropriate drive letter where we indicated drive A.)

2. Type **A:CARTER.INQ**

3. Select **OK**

    ✓ Press Enter

    Notice that the file name in the status line now reads "A:CARTER .INQ." You are no longer working with Mr. Jacobs's letter, but with Ms. Carter's.

    The CARTER.INQ letter is now in the active document window. In the next exercises you will use the editing keys to change the names, addresses, and wording in the body of the letter to convert this document from the Jacobs letter to the Carter letter. The completed Carter letter is shown in Figure 4-3 for your reference.

▌ Using Typeover

The **Typeover** feature allows you to type over existing text displayed in the active document. You press the Insert or Ins key to turn on Typeover. A "Typeover" prompt then appears at the lower left-hand corner of the status line to indicate that the feature is active. To turn off Typeover, simply press Insert again. The "Typeover" prompt in the status line disappears. (You ordinarily would work in the Insert mode.)

▌ HANDS-ON ACTIVITY

Let's use the typeover feature to change the name "Mr. James Jacobs" to "Ms. Alice Carter."

1. Position the cursor on the "r" in the word "Mr." at the beginning of the first line of the inside address block (in the graphics mode your cursor

(today's date)

Ms. Alice Carter
C & C Associates
22 Streamside Blvd.
Broomfield, CO 80038

Dear Ms. Carter:

Thank you for your inquiry regarding the on-site services provided by PencilPushers, Inc. Our goals are to enhance the performance of our clients by providing administrative solutions without jeopardizing operating budgets with added expenses for personnel and equipment.

Our company offers a **variety** of services ranging from general office staffing, bookkeeping, word processing, client billing, as well as financial reporting, forecasting and consulting. PencilPushers, Inc. incorporates the <u>NASS INDUSTRY PRODUCTION STANDARD</u> into its business practices and also subscribes to the <u>NASS CODE OF BUSINESS ETHICS</u>.

We will contact you next week to schedule an appointment to discuss your specific criteria. We look forward to the **opportunity** to work with your organization.

Sincerely,

(your name)
President

Enclosure

Figure 4-3

appears as a vertical line, so the line should be in front of the "r"; in the text mode your cursor appears as an underline and should be positioned under the "r")

2. Press Insert

   The lower left-hand corner of the Status line prompts "Typeover."

3. Type **s**

   Now, to continue to type over "James Jacobs" and replace with "Alice Carter,"

4. Position the cursor either in front of (if your cursor appears as a vertical line) or under (if your cursor appears as an underline) the "J" in the word James.

5. Type `Alice Carter`

6. Press [Insert] again to deactivate the Typeover feature

   Notice that the document name again displays at the left side of the status line (instead of the "Typeover" prompt).

Deleting Text

WordPerfect allows you to delete text by either blocking the text or using various keystroke combinations. In summary, to delete blocked text,

- Block the text to be deleted.

- Press either [Delete] or [Backspace].

Several keystroke combinations are available that allow you to delete various quantities of text without having to block:

Keystroke(s)	Deleted Text
[Backspace]	Character to the left of the cursor
[Delete]	Character to the right of the cursor
[Ctrl] + [Backspace]	Word at the cursor
or	
[Ctrl] + [Delete]	
[Ctrl] + [End]	From the cursor to the end of the line
[Ctrl] + [Page Down]	From the cursor to the end of the page
[Home], [Backspace]	From the cursor to the beginning of the current word
[Home], [Delete]	From the cursor to the end of the current word

HANDS-ON ACTIVITY

In this exercise you will use the Delete function to change the greeting on the letter from "Dear Mr. Jacobs" to read "Dear Ms. Carter."

1. Position the cursor either in front of (if your cursor appears as a vertical line) or under (if your cursor appears as an underline) the "r" in "Mr." in the greeting line

   NOTE: From this point forward in the book, if your cursor appears as a vertical line (graphics mode), position the cursor in front of the specified character. If your cursor appears as an underline (text mode), position the cursor under the specified character.

   To delete the current character,

2. Press [Delete]

   To type a new character (be sure you are *not* still in the typeover mode),

3. Type **s**

The new characters are always inserted to the left of the cursor.

Now let's delete the whole word "Jacobs:" and insert the new word "Carter."

4. Place the cursor someplace in the word "Jacobs" in the greeting line

5. Press Ctrl + Delete

6. Type `Carter:`

Now let's practice using the Backspace key to make some changes in the first paragraph of the letter.

7. Position the cursor at the end of the word "costs" in the last sentence of the first paragraph

8. Press Backspace 5 times

9. Now type the word `budgets` in its place

10. Position the cursor after the word "of" occurring later in the same sentence with either the mouse or the keyboard

11. On your own, perform the same steps to change the phrase "added expense **of** personnel" to "added expense **for** personnel"

Now, let's change the remaining lines of the inside address block to Ms. Carter's company name and address by deleting a whole line at a time.

12. Move the cursor to the "T" in Technologies Unlimited in the inside address block

To delete the entire line,

13. Press Ctrl + End

14. Now type `C & C Associates`

To move to the beginning of the street address line,

15. Press →

To delete this line of text,

16. Press Ctrl + End

17. Type `22 Streamside Blvd.`

18. On your own, delete the last address line, containing city, state, and zip

19. Type `Broomfield, CO 80038`

20. On your own, save the file

Undeleting Text

WordPerfect's **Undelete** feature stores your last three deletions in memory, so that you can either look at or restore them. In summary, to restore a deletion,

- Position the cursor where the deleted text is to be restored.

- Choose <u>E</u>dit ⇒ U<u>n</u>delete (*Shortcut key:* `Esc`)
- The last deletion is displayed; to restore it, select <u>R</u>estore.

  or

- To view the other two deletions, select <u>P</u>revious Deletion. Then to restore the displayed deletion, select <u>R</u>estore.

▌Undoing a Change

The **Undo** feature reverses the most recent change you made to your document. Most actions can be reversed by using Undo—for example, inserting and deleting text, and changing formatting such as margins and tabs. If you use Undo to restore your last deletion, the deleted text is restored at the original location. For example, if you delete a paragraph at the top of the document and then scroll to the end of the document, choosing Undo restores the text to its original location at the top of the document. In contrast, the Undelete command places the deleted text at the current cursor position.

If you delete a paragraph and then type some new text, choosing Undo does not restore the deleted paragraph (since it only works on your *last* action). Instead, Undo removes the new text because it is the most recent change. To restore the deleted text, you would need to use the Undelete command.

To use the Undo feature, choose <u>E</u>dit ⇒ <u>U</u>ndo (*Shortcut keys:* `Ctrl` + Z).

▌HANDS-ON ACTIVITY

Before beginning to experiment with Undo and Undelete, it would be a good idea to resave your letter.

1. Select <u>F</u>ile ⇒ <u>S</u>ave

   ✓ Press `Ctrl` + `F12`

   Now, let's see how Undo works.

2. Position the cursor somewhere in the first word of the first paragraph, which begins, "Thank"

3. Press `Ctrl` + `Delete`

   The word "Thank" is deleted.

   Now, let's move the cursor to the bottom of the document.

4. Press `Home`, `Home`, `↓`

   Now you are going to use the Undo feature to restore the deleted word to its original place.

5. Select <u>E</u>dit ⇒ <u>U</u>ndo

   ✓ Press `Ctrl` + z

   The word "Thank" is restored to its original position. Remember, Undo reverses the last change made to your document.

Now, let's experiment with the Undelete feature.

1. Position the cursor someplace in the word "you" in the phrase "Thank you for your inquiry" (the first sentence of the first paragraph)

2. Press Ctrl + Delete

The word "you" is deleted.

Now move the cursor to the bottom of the document.

3. Press Home, Home, ↓

Now you are going to use the Undelete feature to restore your deleted word; however, instead of being restored to its original position in the document, it will be restored at the position of the cursor, in this case at the end of the document.

4. Select **Edit** ⇒ U**n**delete

   ✓ Press Esc

The Undelete dialog box appears as shown in Figure 4-4.

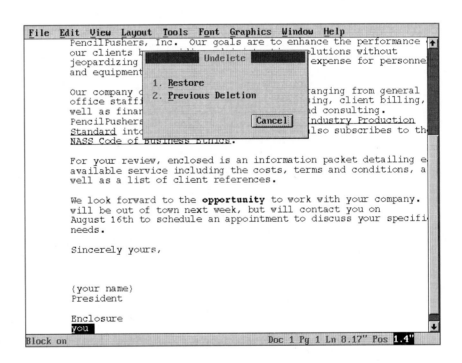

Figure 4-4

The deleted word is highlighted and shown at the bottom of the document. If you choose the Restore option, the word will be restored at the bottom of the document, which is not where it was originally deleted from. Since the deleted word will not be placed in its correct position, let's cancel Undelete.

5. Select **Cancel**

   ✓ Press Esc or Enter

Remember, the one main advantage of Undelete is that your last three deletions are saved, and you can restore any or all of the deletions. To view the previous deletions, select <u>P</u>revious.

To correct your mistake and restore the word "you" back to its proper place,

6. Position the cursor at the beginning of the word "for" in the phrase "for your inquiry regarding" (in the first sentence of the first paragraph)

7. Select <u>E</u>dit ⇒ U<u>n</u>delete

   ✓ Press Esc

8. Select <u>R</u>estore

The deleted word is positioned in its original place in the text.

Blocking Text

Before you can delete, move, copy, or enhance existing text, you must first learn how to block different quantities of text. **Block** means to select the text to be changed by highlighting. The two methods you can use to block text are the following:

- Dragging with the mouse
- Selecting <u>E</u>dit ⇒ <u>B</u>lock (*Shortcut keys:* Alt + F4, or F12) to turn on the Block mode, then using a directional arrow key to highlight the desired text

Using the Mouse to Block Text

You may block text by dragging the mouse. Position the mouse pointer at the beginning of the text to be blocked, then press and hold down the left mouse button and drag the mouse to the end of the text. Once the desired text is blocked, release the left mouse button. If you inadvertently block the wrong text, click the left mouse button once anywhere in the work area to turn Block off.

In addition to dragging the mouse, you can use the following shortcut mouse steps to select various quantities of text:

Selection Method	Text Selected
Double-click with the mouse pointer positioned on a word	One word
Triple-click with the mouse pointer positioned anywhere in the sentence	One sentence
Quadruple-click with the mouse pointer positioned anywhere in a paragraph	One paragraph

When using any of these methods, WordPerfect indicates when the Block mode is active with a "Block On" prompt in the lower-left corner of the status line.

Using the Keyboard to Block Text

With the keyboard you can also turn on Block mode by selecting Edit ⇒ Block (*Shortcut keys:* Alt + F4, or F12). The lower-left corner of the status line prompts "Block on" to indicate that the Block feature is active. Highlight the text to be affected by pressing the directional keys. Alternatively, after turning Block on, you can press a key to extend the selection to that character. For example, if your cursor is at the beginning of a sentence, you can turn on Block and type a period. The text from the cursor to the first period will be highlighted. The Block mode will not replace the blocked text with the character you type. To turn the Block feature off, press either Alt + F4, or F12 again, or press Esc.

▌ HANDS-ON ACTIVITY

It's time to get familiar with blocking and unblocking text using the mouse. *If you do not have a mouse attached to your PC, move to the next exercise.* The CARTER.INQ letter is on your screen.

1. Move the cursor to the beginning of the first paragraph that reads "Thank you for your inquiry..." (on the word "Thank") by moving the mouse pointer to the desired place and clicking the left mouse button once

2. Drag the mouse to highlight the words "Thank you"

3. Release the mouse button

   The block remains highlighted, waiting for the next WordPerfect function. Notice the "Block on" indicator in the status line. Compare your screen to the one shown in Figure 4-5.

Figure 4-5

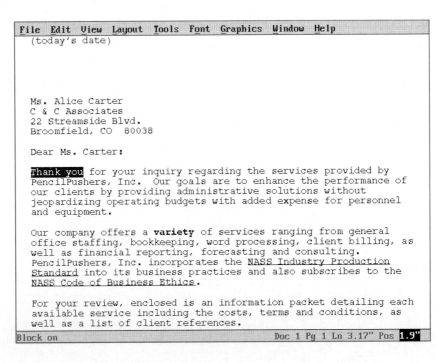

```
 File   Edit   View   Layout   Tools   Font   Graphics   Window   Help
 (today's date)




 Ms. Alice Carter
 C & C Associates
 22 Streamside Blvd.
 Broomfield, CO  80038

 Dear Ms. Carter:

 Thank you for your inquiry regarding the services provided by
 PencilPushers, Inc.  Our goals are to enhance the performance of
 our clients by providing administrative solutions without
 jeopardizing operating budgets with added expense for personnel
 and equipment.

 Our company offers a variety of services ranging from general
 office staffing, bookkeeping, word processing, client billing, as
 well as financial reporting, forecasting and consulting.
 PencilPushers, Inc. incorporates the NASS Industry Production
 Standard into its business practices and also subscribes to the
 NASS Code of Business Ethics.

 For your review, enclosed is an information packet detailing each
 available service including the costs, terms and conditions, as
 well as a list of client references.
 Block on                                    Doc 1 Pg 1 Ln 3.17" Pos 1.9"
```

To clear the block with the mouse,

4. Click the mouse anywhere in the document

Now let's use WordPerfect's Block mode (<u>E</u>dit ⇒ <u>B</u>lock) (*Shortcut keys:* Alt + F4 , or F12) to block text. <u>E</u>dit ⇒ <u>B</u>lock, Alt + F4 , or F12 are known as **toggle switches**, which means that you repeat the same menu options or press the same keystrokes to turn the feature off as you did to turn it on.

1. Position the cursor at the beginning of the word "Thank" in the first paragraph that reads, "Thank you for your inquiry..."

   To turn block on,

2. Select <u>E</u>dit ⇒ <u>B</u>lock

   ✓ Press Alt + F4 , or F12

   The "Block on" prompt is shown in the left corner of the status line.

3. Press → 6 times

   The word "Thank" and the space following are blocked.

4. Press Ctrl + →

   The first two words ("Thank you") of the paragraph are blocked.

5. Press End

   The first line of the first paragraph is blocked.

6. Press . (period)

   The first sentence is blocked.

7. Type (capital) W

   Text is selected up to the first capital "W," which is the word "We" located at the beginning of the fourth paragraph.

   To cancel the Block mode,

8. Select <u>E</u>dit ⇒ <u>B</u>lock

   ✓ Press either Esc , Alt + F4 , or F12

Deleting a Block

A portion of text can easily be deleted by first defining the text area with the Block function and then pressing either Backspace or Delete . The text is immediately removed from the document.

HANDS-ON ACTIVITY

Now, let's practice deleting an entire paragraph.

1. Move the cursor to the beginning of the third paragraph, which reads, "For your review, enclosed..."

2. Drag the mouse to highlight the entire paragraph, or use the keyboard to turn on Block mode and highlight with the arrow keys to the beginning of the next paragraph

   Compare your screen to the one shown in Figure 4-6.

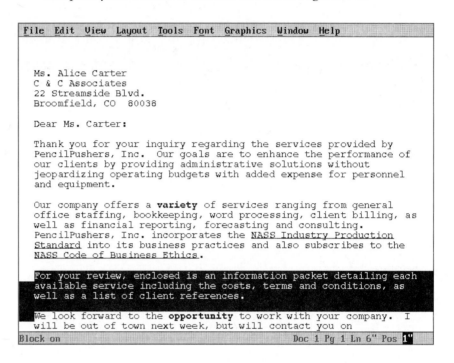

Figure 4-6

3. Press (Backspace) or (Delete)

   The resulting letter should now have three paragraphs.

   Remember, if you accidentally delete a block of text, it can be immediately restored by using the Undo or Undelete feature.

   NOTE: From now on, in this book you may use either the mouse or the keyboard to block text based on your own personal preference. However, only the keyboard steps will be given.

Cutting, Copying, and Pasting Text

Earlier in this lesson, you learned to block text, and then delete it. A similar concept applies when text is to be copied or moved (cut) from one part of a document and then pasted into a different location in the document.

WordPerfect provides a temporary storage area called a **buffer** that holds a piece of cut or copied text while you position the cursor in the new location for pasting. When you cut or copy text, it is placed in the buffer, where it remains until you cut or copy another quantity of text. Therefore, you can paste text from the buffer as many times as needed without having to block and cut or copy again.

Cut removes the information from the current location of the document and places the information in the buffer. By contrast, **Copy** leaves the information in its original location and places a copy of it in the buffer.

To cut or copy, first block the desired text, and then choose Edit ⇒ Cut and Paste, or Edit ⇒ Copy and Paste (*Shortcut keys:* Ctrl + F4). To insert the cut or copied text back into the document, position the cursor where the text is to be placed and press Enter .

▌ HANDS-ON ACTIVITY

You have decided to rearrange the final paragraph of your letter and make it into two separate sentences. Use the Cut and Paste feature to accomplish this task.

1. To move the first sentence of the last paragraph to the end of the paragraph, first block the sentence paragraph that reads, "We look forward to the **opportunity**..."

2. Select Edit ⇒ Block

   ✓ Alt + F4 , or F12

3. Press . (a period)

4. Press → twice

   Compare your document to the one shown in Figure 4-7.

Figure 4-7

```
 File  Edit  View  Layout  Tools  Font  Graphics  Window  Help

    Ms. Alice Carter
    C & C Associates
    22 Streamside Blvd.
    Broomfield, CO  80038

    Dear Ms. Carter:

    Thank you for your inquiry regarding the services provided by
    PencilPushers, Inc.  Our goals are to enhance the performance of
    our clients by providing administrative solutions without
    jeopardizing operating budgets with added expense for personnel
    and equipment.

    Our company offers a variety of services ranging from general
    office staffing, bookkeeping, word processing, client billing, as
    well as financial reporting, forecasting and consulting.
    PencilPushers, Inc. incorporates the NASS Industry Production
    Standard into its business practices and also subscribes to the
    NASS Code of Business Ethics.

    We look forward to the opportunity to work with your company.  I
    will be out of town next week, but will contact you on
    August 16th to schedule an appointment to discuss your specific
    needs.

    Sincerely yours,

 Block on                                    Doc 1 Pg 1 Ln 5.33" Pos 7.3"
```

5. Select Edit ⇒ Cut and Paste

   ✓ Press Ctrl + F4 , 1

6. Move the cursor to the space after the period at the end of the sentence as shown in Figure 4-8

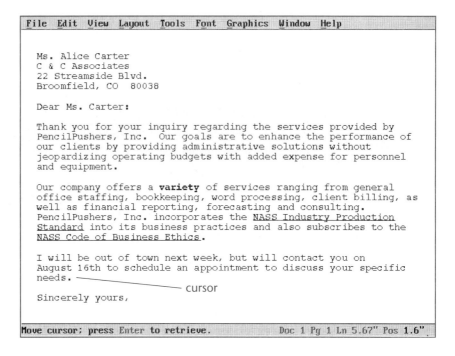

Figure 4-8

To paste the line at the beginning of the next sentence,

7.   Press [Spacebar] twice

8.   Press [Enter]

The cut sentence is pasted at the end of the paragraph. Compare your revised paragraph with Figure 4-9.

I will be out of town next week, but will contact you on August 16th to schedule an appointment to discuss your specific needs. We look forward to the **opportunity** to work with your company.

Figure 4-9

▌ Inserting Text

WordPerfect is automatically set to insert new text or characters. As you begin typing new text, all existing text from the cursor forward moves over to the right, making room for the new text. To insert new text, you position the cursor where the new text is to appear, and begin typing the text. As the text is typed, the original text is pushed along and automatically reformatted.

▌ HANDS-ON ACTIVITY

Ms. Carter specifically asked for information about your company's "on-site" services. In this exercise, you will insert the new word (on-site) in the middle of the first sentence.

1.   Position the cursor either in front of or under the "s" in the word "ser-vices" in the first line of the first paragraph

2. Type `on-site`

3. Press (Spacebar)

   To observe the reformatting of the paragraph,

4. Press (↓) several times

   The words "provided by" were pushed over to make room for your inserted word, and are now located at the beginning of the second line of the paragraph.

Creating a New Paragraph

A new paragraph can be created in two ways: splitting an existing paragraph into two, or creating a new paragraph between two existing paragraphs.

   To create a new paragraph, simply position the cursor where the new paragraph will begin and press (Enter) twice to terminate any existing paragraph and to insert a blank line between paragraphs.

HANDS-ON ACTIVITY

After reading the second paragraph of your letter, you have decided to split this paragraph in two. To create a new paragraph in the document,

1. Position the cursor either in front of or under the "P" in the word "PencilPushers" in the phrase that reads "PencilPushers, Inc. incorporates the NASS"

2. Press (Enter) twice

   After reading the letter again, you have decided that the two paragraphs should be one.

3. Position the cursor at the beginning of the third paragraph, which reads "PencilPushers, Inc. incorporates the NASS"

4. Press (Backspace) twice

Using the Thesaurus

WordPerfect includes a program called **Thesaurus**, which is similar to a book thesaurus. It displays **synonyms** (words with the same or similar meanings) and **antonyms** (words with opposite meanings) for words in your documents. This proves helpful if, for example, you've already used the same word several times and would like to find another to say the same thing, or even to select a word with a more precise "tone" that you wish to use. The Thesaurus displays a list of synonyms showing nouns, verbs, and adjectives.

   To use the Thesaurus, you first position the cursor in the pertinent word in your text and choose Tools ⇒ Writing Tools ⇒ Thesaurus (*Shortcut keys:* (Alt) + (F1)). The Thesaurus dialog box appears, with alternative words listed. If you do not like any of these alternatives, you can have the Thesaurus suggest additional choices by either double-clicking on a listed word that is preceded by a bullet, or selecting Look Up and typing a word in the Word box.

Once the desired replacement word is located, double-click on the word or move the highlighter to the desired word and choose R̲eplace.

■ HANDS-ON ACTIVITY

The first sentence of the fourth paragraph of your document ends with the word "needs." You will use the assistance of WordPerfect's Thesaurus to find an alternative word for "needs."

1. Position the cursor in the word "needs"

2. Select T̲ools ⇒ W̲riting Tools ⇒ T̲hesaurus

    ✓ Press Alt + F1 , **2**

    The Thesaurus dialog box appears, as shown in Figure 4-10.

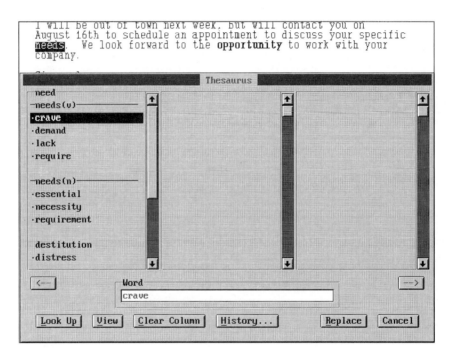

Figure 4-10

The word "needs" is listed as a verb (v) and as a noun (n). Also, the antonyms (ant) are shown if you scroll down toward the end of the list in the left column.

Notice that the Thesaurus window has a scroll bar so that you may use either the directional arrow keys or the mouse to browse up or down through the alternative words.

You like the word "requirement," but you would like to see if there are any better words. Notice that "requirement" is preceded by a bullet, indicating that there is another group of synonyms and antonyms available for that word. Let's look at those additional words:

3. Select by highlighting "requirement" and press Enter

    or

Double-click on "requirement" with the mouse

Your Thesaurus dialog box will now appear as shown in Figure 4-11.

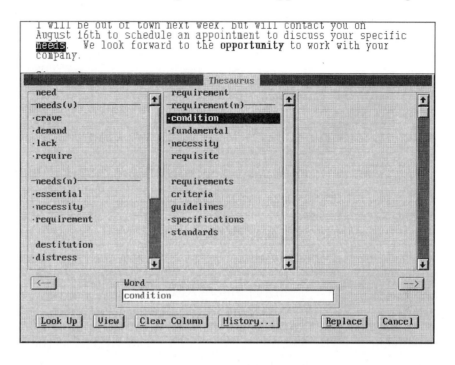

Figure 4-11

The second column now displays words developed from the word "requirement." You have decided on the word "criteria." To replace "needs" with "criteria,"

4. Highlight "criteria"

5. Select **Replace**

6. On your own, find a suitable synonym for the word "contact," also in the last paragraph and save the file

▌ Bolding and Underlining Existing Text

The way to boldface or underline text that has already been typed differs from the way you apply these features while you are typing. To bold existing text, you must "block" the text and then choose F<u>o</u>nt ⇒ <u>B</u>old (*Shortcut keys:* Ctrl + B, or F6). To underline existing text, you must "block" the text and then choose F<u>o</u>nt ⇒ <u>U</u>nderline (*Shortcut keys:* Ctrl + U, or F8). A pair of codes is placed around the text just as if you had applied the bold or underline while typing. To view the codes, activate the Reveal Codes screen by choosing <u>V</u>iew ⇒ Reveal <u>C</u>odes (*Shortcut keys:* Alt + F3 , or F11). Remember, the Underline codes are shown as [Und On] and [Und Off] and the bold codes are shown as [Bold On] and [Bold Off].

▌ HANDS-ON ACTIVITY

In this exercise, you will first apply underline and bold attributes to existing text in the Carter letter, then remove them, using Reveal Codes.

1. Place the cursor at the beginning of the word "PencilPushers" in the first paragraph

   The steps below use the keyboard to block the text "PencilPushers, Inc." Remember, if you prefer to use the mouse, the text can be blocked by dragging the mouse.

2. Select Edit ⇒ Block

   ✓ Press ⌐Alt⌐ + ⌐F4⌐, or ⌐F12⌐

3. Press ⌐Ctrl⌐ + ⌐→⌐ twice

4. Press ⌐←⌐ twice

   The phrase "PencilPushers, Inc." is now highlighted.

5. Select Font ⇒ Bold

   ✓ Press ⌐Ctrl⌐ + **B**, or ⌐F6⌐

▌ Removing Bold and Underline Attributes

There are two ways to remove bold and underline from text: use Font ⇒ Normal or Edit ⇒ Reveal Codes. When using the Font ⇒ Normal method, first block the text containing either the boldface or undelete attribute and then choose Font ⇒ Normal. When using the Reveal Codes method to remove the Bold, you must delete either the [Bold On] code placed before the boldface text or the [Bold Off] code placed after the text; the paired code will disappear as well. The same concept applies to removing the underline attribute; either delete the [Und On] code placed before the underline text or the [Und Off] code after the text.

▌ HANDS-ON ACTIVITY

You need to remove the bold codes from the phrase "PencilPushers, Inc." in the first paragraph of the letter. For practice, first remove the bold using Font ⇒ Normal, reinstate the bold with Edit ⇒ Undo, then remove the bold with Reveal Codes and attach underline.

1. Place the cursor at the beginning of the phrase "PencilPushers"

   Block the text either by dragging the mouse or using the following keystrokes:

2. Select Edit ⇒ Block

   ✓ Press ⌐Alt⌐ + ⌐F4⌐, or ⌐F12⌐

3. Press ⌐Ctrl⌐ + ⌐→⌐ twice

4. Press ⌐←⌐ twice

   Now, return to a normal font:

5. Select Font ⇒ Normal

   The bold is removed and the block of text returns to normal.

   To test the other method of removing bold with the Reveal Codes screen, first undo the removal of the underline.

6. Select <u>E</u>dit ⇒ <u>U</u>ndo

   ✓ Press Ctrl + **z**

   The bold is returned.

   To remove the bold using the Reveal Codes method,

7. Place the cursor at the beginning of the phrase "PencilPushers"

8. Select <u>V</u>iew ⇒ **Reveal <u>C</u>odes**

   ✓ Press Alt + F3 , or F11

9. Move with the directional arrow keys until you have highlighted the [Bold On] code in the Reveal Codes screen

10. Press Delete

    The bold is removed from the greeting.

11. Place the cursor again at the beginning of the phrase "PencilPushers"

12. On your own, block the text "PencilPushers, Inc." again

13. Select **F<u>o</u>nt** ⇒ <u>U</u>nderline

    ✓ Press F8 , or Ctrl + **u**

14. On your own, remove the underline using either method discussed above

    To close the Reveal Codes screen,

15. Select <u>V</u>iew ⇒ **Reveal <u>C</u>odes**

    ✓ Press Alt + F3 , or F11

Changing Text to Uppercase

WordPerfect has a wonderful feature called **Convert Case** that allows you to change existing text to all uppercase, all lowercase, or mixed case (initial caps). To do this, you first block the text to be converted and choose <u>E</u>dit ⇒ Con<u>v</u>ert Case and then choose either <u>U</u>ppercase, <u>L</u>owercase, or <u>I</u>nitial Case.

HANDS-ON ACTIVITY

You have decided that the phrase "<u>Industry Production Standard</u>" would be more prominent in all capital letters. Instead of retyping the text (and possibly introducing an error), you are going to use WordPerfect's Convert Case feature.

1. Place the cursor at the beginning of the phrase "<u>Industry Production Standard</u>" in the second paragraph of your letter

   To block the text,

2. Select <u>E</u>dit ⇒ <u>B</u>lock

   ✓ Press Alt + F4 , or F12

3. Press Ctrl + → 3 times

4. Select <u>E</u>dit ⇒ Con<u>v</u>ert Case

   ✓ Press Shift + F3

   The Convert Case menu appears, as shown in Figure 4-12.

Figure 4-12

5. Select <u>U</u>ppercase

6. On your own, also change the phrase "<u>Code of Business Ethics</u>" to uppercase

▌ Using Zoom

If you are in the <u>V</u>iew ⇒ <u>G</u>raphics mode, you have the ability to change the view of your document from 50% to 300% by using <u>V</u>iew ⇒ <u>Z</u>oom (*Shortcut keys:* Ctrl + F3 , 5). Zoom offers you the following options:

50% and 75%	The view decreases the size of the document so that you can see the general layout of the current page.
125%	The view displays the current page at approximately the size the text and graphics will appear when printed in a 12-point font.
150% to 300%	The view enlarges the text in the current page to the specified percent of magnification.
<u>M</u>argin Width	The view displays text horizontally from the left margin to the right.
Page <u>W</u>idth	The view displays a full horizontal view of the entire page from one edge of the screen to the other.
<u>F</u>ull Page	The view displays the entire page.

The default view is <u>M</u>argin Width and is set at that option each time WordPerfect 6.0 is started.

▌ HANDS-ON ACTIVITY

In this exercise, you are going to experiment with the various Zoom options to view the Carter file.

To position the cursor at the top of the document,

1. Press Home, Home, ↑

2. Select <u>V</u>iew ⇒ <u>Z</u>oom

   ✓ Press Ctrl + F3 , 7

   The Zoom menu appears, as shown in Figure 4-13.

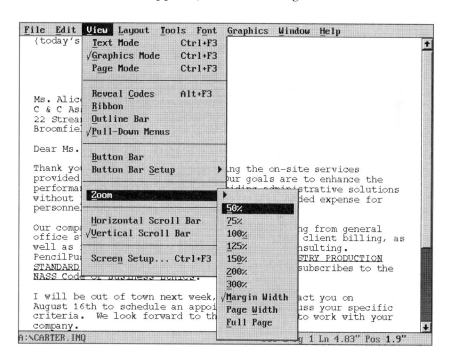

Figure 4-13

3. Select <u>F</u>ull Page

   Compare your view to the one shown in Figure 4-14.

   To view your document using 100%,

4. Select <u>V</u>iew ⇒ <u>Z</u>oom

   ✓ Press Ctrl + F3 , 7

5. Select 100<u>%</u>

   To return to the Margin Width option,

6. Select <u>V</u>iew ⇒ <u>Z</u>oom

   ✓ Press Ctrl + F3 , 7

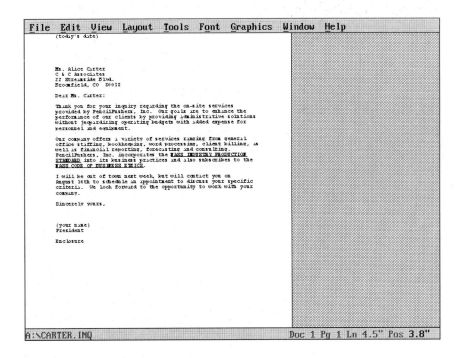

Figure 4-14

7.   Select **Margin Width**

Viewing Document Information

The **Document Information** feature shows you specific statistics about your document, such as how many characters, words, lines, sentences, paragraphs, and pages your document contains—a useful tool when you are writing an article or paper of a specified length. It also includes information on the average word length, average words per sentence, maximum words per sentence, and size of your document (in bytes). To view the Document Information screen, select Tools ⇒ Writing Tools ⇒ Document Information (*Shortcut keys:* Alt + F1 , 4).

HANDS-ON ACTIVITY

In this exercise, you will view the statistics of the Carter document.

1.   Select Tools ⇒ Writing Tools ⇒ Document Information

   ✓ Press Alt + F1 , **4**

   The Document Information window appears. Your screen should be similar to the one shown in Figure 4-15.

   To exit this feature,

2.   Select **OK**

   ✓ Press Enter

HANDS-ON ACTIVITY

The final steps in completing the letter are as follows:

1.   Spell check your document (Tools ⇒ Writing Tools ⇒ Speller or Ctrl + F2)

```
 File  Edit  View  Layout  Tools  Font  Graphics  Window  Help
   (today's date)                                                    ↑

   Ms. Alice Car┌────────── Document Information ──────────┐
   C & C Associa│                                          │
   22 Streamside│  Characters:                      816    │
   Broomfield, C│  Words:                           144    │
                │  Lines:                            40    │
   Dear Ms. Cart│  Sentences:                        15    │
                │  Paragraphs:                       13    │ices
   Thank you for│  Pages:                             1    │nce the
   provided by P│                                          │ solutions
   performance c│  Average Word Length:               5    │nse for
   without jeopa│  Average Words per Sentence:        9    │
   personnel and│  Maximum Words per Sentence:       26    │
                │  Document Size:                 2,050    │general
   Our company c│                                          │billing, as
   office staffi│                                          │.
   well as finan│              ┌────────┐                  │DUCTION
   PencilPushers │              │   OK   │                  │es to the
   STANDARD into │              └────────┘                  │
   NASS Code of └──────────────────────────────────────────┘

   I will be out of town next week, but will contact you on
   August 16th to schedule an appointment to discuss your specific
   criteria.  We look forward to the **opportunity** to work with your
   company.                                                           ↓
 A:\CARTER.INQ                              Doc 1 Pg 1 Ln 4.83" Pos 1.9"
```

Figure 4-15

2. Save the document (**File** ⇒ **Save** or `F10`)

3. Print the document (**File** ⇒ **Print/FAX** or `Shift` + `F7`)

4. Exit WordPerfect (**File** ⇒ **Exit WP** or `Shift` + `F7`)

On Your Own

Review of Commands

Description	Menu Commands	Function Keys
Open a file	_____	_____
Save a document, using a new name	_____	_____
Use typeover	_____	_____
Delete text:		
Block	_____	_____
Character left of cursor	_____	_____
Character right of cursor	_____	_____
Word at cursor	_____	_____
From the cursor to the end of a line	_____	_____
From the cursor to the end of a page	_____	_____
From the cursor to the beginning of a word	_____	_____

From the cursor to the
end of a word   _____   _____

Undelete text   _____   _____

Undo a change   _____   _____

Block text   _____   _____

Cut and paste text   _____   _____

Copy and paste text   _____   _____

Use the Thesaurus   _____   _____

Bold existing text   _____   _____

Underline existing text   _____   _____

Remove bold and
underline   _____   _____

Change text to uppercase   _____   _____

Change the zoom   _____   _____

Display document
information   _____   _____

▌ Lesson Review

1. What feature allows you to replace existing text on the screen? How is this feature activated?

2. List the two steps to delete a block of text.

3. What keystroke(s) deletes text from the cursor to the end of the page?

4. What keystroke(s) deletes the word at the cursor?

5. What steps would you take to underline text that has already been typed?

6. What are the two methods by which to remove bold from existing text?

7. Give one example of when you might use Undo, and one when you might use Undelete.

8. What is the difference between the Cut and Copy features?

9. List the two methods by which to activate the Block feature.

10. What does the Thesaurus feature do?

11. List the steps to change lowercase text to uppercase.

12. What information does the Document Information feature show?

▌ Assignments

4.1 **Directions**

1. Retrieve the AWARDS.LS3 file that you created in the end-of-chapter Assignments in Lesson 3.

2. Save it as AWARD.MEM.

3. Bold and underline the phrase "Distinguished Service Award Committee" and change it to uppercase.

4. Create a new paragraph after "on a full time basis."

5. Underline "high standard" in the second paragraph.

6. Using the Typeover mode, change the Campus Box to 58.

7. Using the Document Information feature, display the statistics for your document. Note the following information: document size, number of paragraphs, maximum words per sentence, and average words per sentence.

8. Spell check, save, print, and close the document.

9. Open AWARD.MEM and remove the underline that you added in step 3 above.

5

Formatting
Documents

Objectives

Upon completion of this lesson, you will be able to do the following:

- Use File Manager
- Align text for flush right and center
- Change the justification
- Change the margins
- Preview a document
- Vertically center a page
- Use tabs
- Change tab stops
- Create an envelope

This lesson incorporates formatting features such as centering a line and aligning text on the right margin. You will also learn how to change your document's margins, align columns of text using tabs, vertically center text on a page, and create an envelope using WordPerfect's automatic envelope creation tool.

Starting Point

Before beginning the lesson, start WordPerfect 6.0. A blank, unnamed document window should be displayed.

Using File Manager

WordPerfect provides a feature called **File Manager** that supplies a list of file names shown in alphabetical order along with a menu to perform file management functions such as open, look, delete, move, rename, print, and so on.

In Lesson 4, you learned how to open an existing document for editing by selecting File ⇒ Open, then typing the name of the desired document in the Filename text box. Occasionally, however, you may find yourself unsure of the spelling of a file name.

To use File Manager to open a document, you begin by selecting File ⇒ Open, but instead of typing the document name, you select File Manager (*Shortcut key:* F5). Then another dialog box titled "Specify File Manager List" will appear where you are to instruct WordPerfect which drive and directory to use. Then the File Manager window displays with the file names shown on the left and menu options shown on the right.

You may use either the mouse or the directional arrow keys to select the file of your choice, then select Open into New Document.

▌ HANDS-ON ACTIVITY

You want to edit the letter to Mark Johnson to add a section containing a tabulated list. In this exercise you first need to look at the text to make sure that you have selected the correct document name, then you will open the file for edits.

The completed Mark Johnson letter, along with the other sample files that coincide with the exercises in this book, is supplied for your convenience on a sample disk. Ask your instructor to provide you with a copy of this disk and insert it in the computer's drive.

NOTE: In this book we assume that you are using drive A for the sample disk and will give instructions to type **A:** *to access the disk. If you are using a different drive, substitute the appropriate drive letter where* **A:** *is shown.*

1. Select File ⇒ Open

    ✓ Press Shift + F10

    The Open Document dialog box appears, as shown in Figure 5-1.

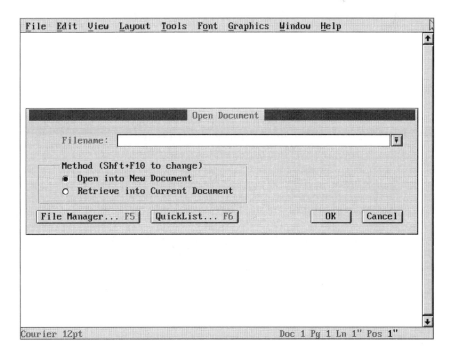

Figure 5-1

2. Select **File Manager**

    ✓ Press F5

    The Specify File Manager List dialog box appears, showing the directory where files are usually stored on your system, such as the screen shown in Figure 5-2.

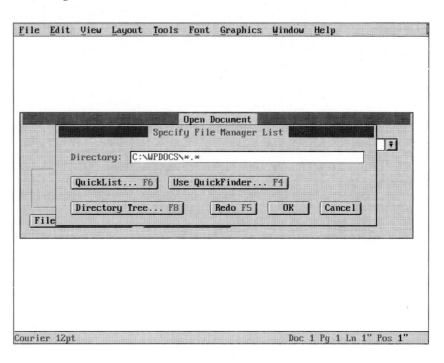

Figure 5-2

The defaults for the drive and directory are displayed in the Directory text box. To specify drive A for the location of your sample disk instead of the drive and directory shown,

3. Type **A:**

4. Select **OK**

    ✓ Press Enter

    The File Manager dialog box appears, displaying the contents of the student sample disk in drive A. Your list of file names will be similar to the list of files shown in Figure 5-3.

5. Select **JOHNSON.LTR**

    First, let's use the Look option to view the text before we open the document to make sure that we have selected the correct file name.

6. Select **Look**

    ✓ Press **3**

    The text from the JOHNSON.LTR file is displayed in the Look at Document window, shown in Figure 5.4. Notice that the file name and

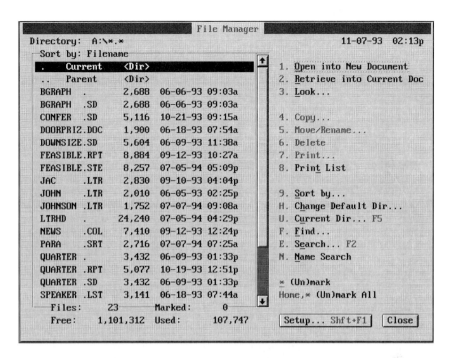

Figure 5-3

the revision date are shown at the top of the screen, there is a scroll bar on the right-hand side of the screen that allows you to browse through the text, and the Look menu is shown at the bottom of the screen.

NOTE: You have not actually opened the document for edits. You are not able to make any changes to the document in the "look" mode. You must "open" the file in order to work on the text.

Compare your screen with Figure 5-4.

When you are sure that this is the correct file, exit the Look at Document screen.

7. Select **Close**

   ✓ Press ⌗Enter⌗

   Now let's open the document.

8. Select **O**pen into New Document

   ✓ Press 1

   The letter appears on your screen and is ready for you to begin editing. Compare your letter to the one shown in Figure 5-5.

▌ **Aligning Text**

The feature **Layout** ⇒ **Alignment** allows you to align text in a number of different methods. This alignment can be done either before or after the text is typed and can be removed if not needed. In this lesson you will learn to apply the Center and Flush Right features while typing new text and then to add Center and Flush Right to existing text.

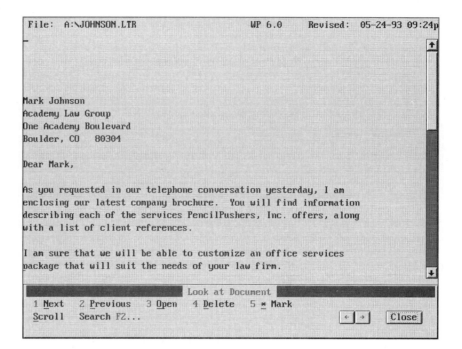

Figure 5-4

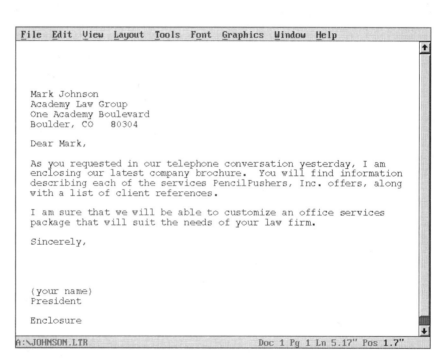

Figure 5-5

Using Flush Right

The **Flush Right** feature is used to align a single line of text at the right margin—for example, the date or a block of lines such as a company letterhead. To execute the Flush Right feature, choose Layout ⇒ Alignment ⇒ Flush Right (*Shortcut keys:* [Alt] + [F6]). If more than one line of text needs to be aligned on the right margin, block those lines of text first, and then choose Layout ⇒ Alignment ⇒ Flush Right. WordPerfect inserts a [Flsh Rgt] code when this feature is executed.

▍ HANDS-ON ACTIVITY

In this exercise you are going to use the automatic date feature that you learned in Lesson 3 to insert the current computer date. Then you will shift the date to the right margin, using the Flush Right feature.

1. Make sure the cursor is located at the top of the document

    Insert today's computer date:

2. Select Tools ⇒ Date ⇒ Text

    ✓ Press Shift + F5 , 1

    To flush-right the date,

3. Position the cursor in front of the first character of the date text

4. Select Layout ⇒ Alignment ⇒ Flush Right

    ✓ Press Alt + F6

    The date is now positioned on the right margin.

5. On your own, save the file

Centering a Line of Text

The **Center** feature in WordPerfect positions the cursor at the midpoint between the left and right margins. As you type the text, WordPerfect automatically centers it and inserts a [Cntr on Mar] code before it.

To center a line as you type it, position the cursor on the left margin and choose Layout ⇒ Alignment ⇒ Center (*Shortcut keys:* Shift + F6), type the text, and press Enter to terminate the line. If the text has already been typed, place the cursor in front of the text to be centered, and choose Layout ⇒ Alignment ⇒ Center. If more than one line of text needs to be centered, block the text and execute the Center command.

▍ HANDS-ON ACTIVITY

In this exercise you are going to insert a centered line after the first paragraph in the Johnson letter, which will serve as a heading to the tabulated section of text you will insert in the next exercise.

1. Position the cursor directly following the word "references" at the end of the first paragraph

2. Press Enter 3 times

    This will create three blank lines. Now move up into one of these blank lines to type the heading.

3. Press ↑ once

    The cursor is positioned on the second blank line. Now center a line.

4. Select <u>L</u>ayout ⇒ <u>A</u>lignment ⇒ <u>C</u>enter

   ✓ Press (Shift) + (F6)

   The cursor jumps to the middle of the screen.

5. Type `PencilPushers, Inc.`

6. Press (Enter)

7. On your own, save the file

   Compare your screen to Figure 5-6.

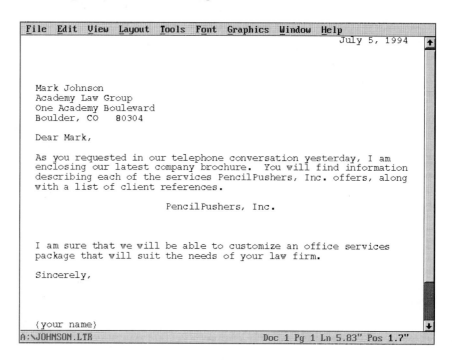

Figure 5-6

Changing the Justification

The **Justification** feature determines how the left and right margins will look. There are five settings available: Left, Right, Center, Full, and lastly the Full, All Lines option. The Left option aligns text evenly on the left margin, making the right margin uneven. The Right option aligns text evenly on the right margin, with an uneven left margin. The Center option centers the text on the page so that both margins are uneven, the Full option aligns both the left and right margins evenly, and the Full, All Lines option allows you to evenly space letters of a title or heading between the left and right margins. Full justification is traditionally used for books, newspapers, and newsletters. Right justification is good for aligning the date and return address at the right margin, and the center option would be appropriate for centering lines on a title page. Figure 5-7 indicates how each option looks.

The default setting is Left, because it is the alignment most used in correspondence and informal reports. To use the Justification feature—say, for a formal proposal—place the cursor within the paragraph that is to be

Left Justification:

Your prospectus, table of contents, transparency masters, and the introductory chapters on <u>A GUIDEBOOK TO WORDPERFECT 6.0</u> were received on September 20th. Thank you for the submittal.

Right Justification:

Your prospectus, table of contents, transparency masters, and the introductory chapters on <u>A GUIDEBOOK TO WORDPERFECT 6.0</u> were received on September 20th. Thank you for the submittal.

Center Justification:

Your prospectus, table of contents, transparency masters, and the introductory chapters on <u>A GUIDEBOOK TO WORDPERFECT 6.0</u> were received on September 20th. Thank you for the submittal.

Full Justification:

Your prospectus, table of contents, transparency masters, and the introductory chapters on <u>A GUIDEBOOK TO WORDPERFECT 6.0</u> were received on September 20th. Thank you for the submittal.

Full, All LInes

Your prospectus, table of contents, transparency masters, and the introductory chapters on <u>A GUIDEBOOK TO WORDPERFECT 6.0</u> were received on September   20th.   Thank   you   for   the   submittal.

Figure 5-7

changed. Choose <u>L</u>ayout ⇒ <u>L</u>ine ⇒ <u>J</u>ustification (*Shortcut keys:* Shift + F8, 1, 2) and specify the desired alignment.

WordPerfect has a new feature called **Auto Code Placement**. This feature tells WordPerfect to automatically place the justification code at the beginning of the paragraph in which the cursor is positioned. If the Auto Code Placement feature is turned off, the Justification option takes effect at the current position of the cursor. By default, this feature is automatically turned on. If the Auto Code Placement feature is on, a [Just] code is placed at the beginning of the paragraph. To make sure that Auto Code Placement feature is turned on, choose <u>F</u>ile ⇒ Se<u>t</u>up ⇒ <u>E</u>nvironment. If there is a check mark in the Au<u>t</u>o Code Placement check box, the feature is turned on.

When Justification for a paragraph is changed, the specified justification takes effect from the [Just] code forward in the document. In other words, all text from the [Just] code forward is formatted to the specified alignment, until another [Just] is encountered.

▌ HANDS-ON ACTIVITY

In this exercise you will turn Au<u>t</u>o Code Placement on and then format your document to Full justification.

1. Position the cursor at the beginning of the first paragraph, which reads, "As you requested..." (move with the arrow keys, or click with the mouse, to position the cursor)

   To check the status of Auto Code Placement,

2. Select File ⇒ Setup ⇒ Environment

   Make sure that there is a check mark on Auto Code Placement, indicating that this feature is on. If it is off, add a check mark to turn it on.

3. Select Auto Placement Code

4. Select OK

   ✓ Press [Enter]

   Now format the document to full justification.

5. Select Layout ⇒ Line ⇒ Justification

   ✓ Press [Shift] + [F8], 1, 2

   The menu shown in Figure 5-8 appears.

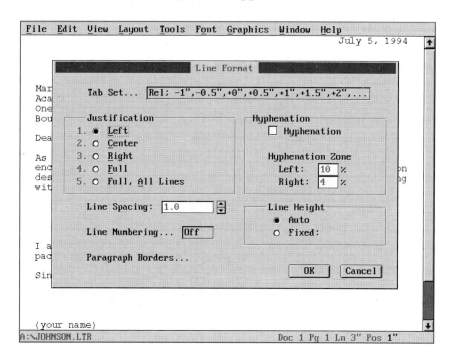

Figure 5-8

6. Select Full

7. Select OK

   ✓ Press [Enter]

   CAUTION: If you are using the keyboard steps, you will need to press [Enter] *again to close the Line Format dialog box.*

   All paragraphs of your document are now fully justified (both margins are even). Let's activate the Reveal Codes screen.

8. Select <u>V</u>iew ⇒ Reveal <u>C</u>odes

   ✓ Press `Alt` + `F3`, or `F11`

   NOTE: In the Reveal Codes screen you can see the detailed information about any code by positioning the cursor directly on the code so that it is highlighted. When you highlight [Just], it opens to display [Just: Full]—indicating that the type of justification is full.

   To exit the Reveal Codes screen,

9. Select <u>V</u>iew ⇒ Reveal <u>C</u>odes

   ✓ Press `Alt` + `F3`, or `F11`

10. On your own, save the file

▌ Changing Document Margins

Whenever you create a new document, the defaults for the margins (left, right, top, and bottom) are all set to 1-inch. These settings can be changed as many times as necessary within a document.

If the document top and bottom margins are changed, and the Auto Code Placement is on, WordPerfect places a [Top Mar:] or [Bot Mar:] code at the top of the current page. Thus, the new margins are in effect from the top of the current page forward.

If the Auto Code Placement feature is turned off, the margins take effect from the cursor position forward in the document. For example, if your cursor is positioned in the middle of a page and you change the top margin, the change will not take effect until the next page.

If the document left and right margins are changed and the Auto Code Placement is on, WordPerfect inserts a [Lft Mar:] or [Rgt Mar:] code at the beginning of the paragraph in which the cursor is positioned. The new left and right margins are in effect from the beginning of the paragraph forward in the document. If the Auto Code Placement is off, the margin changes take effect at the cursor position.

TIP: The Auto Code Placement feature is useful to ensure the correct placement of codes. To make sure the Auto Code Placement feature is turned on, choose <u>F</u>ile ⇒ Set<u>u</u>p ⇒ <u>E</u>nvironment. If there is a check mark in the Au<u>t</u>o Code Placement check box, the feature is turned on.

To change the current margin settings, choose <u>L</u>ayout ⇒ <u>M</u>argins (*Shortcut keys:* `Shift` + `F8`, 2). The Margin Format dialog box appears, allowing you to change the top, bottom, left, and right margins. To save the settings, choose OK.

▌ HANDS-ON ACTIVITY

In this exercise, you are going to change the left and right margins of your letter to ¾" and the top margin to 2".

1. Make sure that your cursor is positioned at the top of the document

2. Select <u>L</u>ayout ⇒ <u>M</u>argins

   ✓ Press `Shift` + `F8`, **2**

The Margin Format dialog box appears, as shown in Figure 5-9.

```
 File  Edit  View  Layout  Tools  Font  Graphics  Window  Help
                                              July 5, 1994        ▲
       ┌──────────────── Margin Format ────────────────┐
 Mark Johnson │ ┌─Document Margins────────────────────────┐ │
 Academy Law  │ │  1. Left Margin:            │1"        │ │
 One Academy  │ │  2. Right Margin:           │1"        │ │
 Boulder, CO  │ │                                         │ │
              │ │  3. Top Margin:             │1"        │ │
 Dear Mark,   │ │  4. Bottom Margin:          │1"        │ │
              │ └─────────────────────────────────────────┘ │
 As you requ  │ ┌─Paragraph Margins───────────────────────┐ │ day, I am
 enclosing ou │ │  5. Left Margin Adjustment: │0"        │ │ nformation
 describing e │ │  6. Right Margin Adjustment:│0"        │ │ rs, along
 with a list  │ │                                         │ │
              │ │  7. First Line Indent:      │0"        │ │
              │ │  8. Paragraph Spacing:      │1.0    │▲▼│ │
 I am sure t  │ └─────────────────────────────────────────┘ │ services
 package that │              ┌────────┐ ┌────────┐           │
              │              │   OK   │ │ Cancel │           │
 Sincerely,   │              └────────┘ └────────┘           │
              └──────────────────────────────────────────────┘
                                                              ▼
 {your name}                                                  ▼
 A:\JOHNSON.LTR                    Doc 1 Pg 1 Ln 1" Pos 1"
```

Figure 5-9

To enter the ¾" measurement for the left and right margins,

3. Select **L**eft Margin

   ✓ Press **1**

4. Type **.75** (for ¾")

5. Press (Enter)

6. Select **R**ight Margin

   ✓ Press **2**

7. Type **.75** (for ¾")

8. Press (Enter)

9. Select **OK**

   ✓ Press (Enter)

   NOTE: If you use the keyboard shortcut keys ((Shift) + (F8), 2) to open the dialog box, you will need to select Close to exit the Margin Format dialog box. When executing a command using the keyboard, in most instances exiting the dialog boxes will require closing an additional dialog box. Therefore, for the remainder of the book, use your own judgment when exiting a dialog box.

10. On your own, save the file

    If you display the Reveal Codes screen, you will see the codes [Lft Mar:] [Rgt Mar:]. If you position the cursor directly on one of the margin codes in the Reveal Codes screen, the code will expand to display the measurements [Lft Mar:0.75"] or [Rgt Mar:0.75"].

▐ **HANDS-ON ACTIVITY**

Now let's change the top margin to 2".

1. Be sure that your cursor is still located at the top of the letter

2. Select <u>L</u>ayout ⇒ <u>M</u>argins

    ✓ Press Shift + F8 , **2**

    The Margin Format dialog box appears.

    To enter the 2" measurement for the top margin,

3. Select <u>T</u>op Margin

    ✓ Press **3**

4. Type **2** (for 2")

5. Press Enter

6. Select **OK**

    ✓ Press Enter

7. On your own, save the file

    If you display the Reveal Codes screen, you will see the code [Top Mar:]. If you position the cursor directly on the margin code in the Reveal Codes screen, the code will expand to display the measurement [Top Mar:2"].

▐ **Previewing a Document**

Text displayed on the screen in the graphic view mode closely resembles the way it will appear when printed. However, features such as headers and footers, page numbers, footnotes, and so on are *not* displayed in the document screen. The **Print Preview** feature allows you to see the complete printed format of a document before you print it. While you are previewing it, the text is "Greeked"—made so small you cannot read it—and you are prevented from editing text. At least you can check that all elements are positioned correctly, possibly saving time and paper.

To activate this feature, choose <u>F</u>ile ⇒ Print Pre<u>v</u>iew (*Shortcut keys:* Shift + F7 , 7). Several commands are available in the Print Preview window. These commands may be issued either from the menu bar at the top of the screen or by clicking with the mouse on commands that are displayed as buttons just below the menu bar, called the Button Bar. The Button Bar can only be accessed by using the mouse.

When you first enter Print Preview, the current page is displayed at a certain percentage of its actual size, depending upon the document and previous view chosen. You can then change that view if you like (viewing options are discussed in a moment). When you are finished viewing the document, you may exit the view screen by selecting <u>F</u>ile ⇒ <u>C</u>lose, then clicking on the Close button (*Shortcut keys:* Esc , Esc).

Viewing Options

Various options for viewing the current page are available from either the Button Bar or the View menu.

100%	Shows the actual size of the print
200%	Shows the text twice its normal size
Zoom In	Increases the size of the text by 25 percent
Zoom Out	Decreases the size of the text by 25 percent
Zoom Area	To see a particular area, move the mouse pointer into the page, and vertical and horizontal lines forming crosshairs appear. Move the crosshairs to one corner of the area to be enlarged. Click and drag the mouse to the opposite corner. As you drag the mouse, a box is drawn on the screen, outlining the area. Click the mouse again and the selected area is displayed on the screen. Choose Reset from either the Button Bar or the View menu to return to the default scale.

Viewing Other Pages

If the document has more than one page, options for viewing the other pages are available from either the Button Bar or the Pages menu. These options allow you to view the Full Page or Facing Pages. When Facing Pages is selected, even-numbered pages are displayed on the left and odd-numbered pages on the right. To move forward one page, choose Next Page; to move backward, choose Previous Page. You can display a specific page by choosing the Pages ⇒ Go To Page option, typing the desired page number, and choosing OK.

▌ HANDS-ON ACTIVITY

In this exercise, you will view the one-page letter you currently have open on the screen.

1. Position the insertion point at the beginning of the letter

2. Select File ⇒ **Print Preview**

   ✓ Press Shift + F7 , 7

3. Select View ⇒ **Full Page** or click on the **Full Page** button

   The WordPerfect Print Preview window appears, with your document shown in a reduced view, giving you the format of the full page as shown in Figure 5-10.

4. Select View ⇒ **200% View** or click on the **Zoom 200%** button

   As you move down with the cursor, your text will appear in an enlarged state and you will only be able to see a portion of your document.

5. Select View ⇒ **Full Page** or click on the **Full Page** button

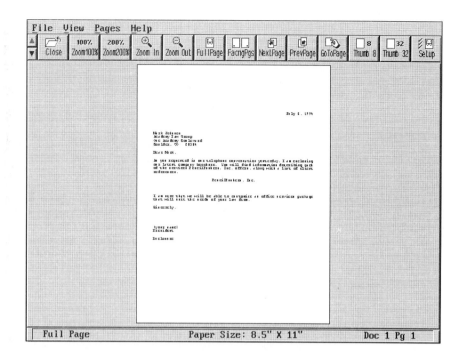

Figure 5-10

6.   Select **View** ⇒ **100%** **View** or click on the **Zoom 100%** button

Your text enlarges to actual size and displays the top half of the page on the screen.

To view the lower portion of the page,

7.   Press Home, ↓

To view the upper portion of the page,

8.   Press Home, ↑

To increase the size of the text by 25%,

9.   Select **View** ⇒ **Zoom In** or click on the **Zoom In** button

10. Select **View** ⇒ **Zoom In** again or click on the **Zoom In** button

The text is increased by another 25%.

To close the Print Preview window,

11. Select **File** ⇒ **Close** or click on the **Close** button

✓ Press F7 or Esc

We will now use Reveal Codes to remove the 2" top margin code and use Print Preview to check the results.

12. Move the cursor to the top of the document

13. Select **View** ⇒ **Reveal Codes**

✓ Press Alt + F3, or F11

To remove the 2" margin code,

14. Position the cursor on the [Top Mar:] code

Compare your screen to the one shown in Figure 5-11.

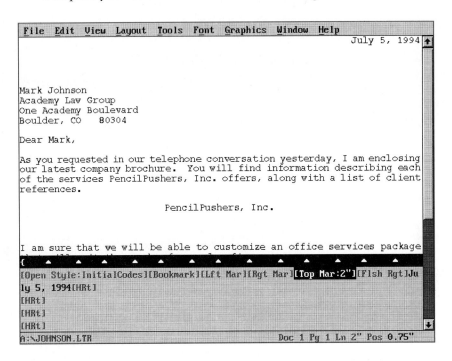

File Edit View Layout Tools Font Graphics Window Help
```
                                                       July 5, 1994

Mark Johnson
Academy Law Group
One Academy Boulevard
Boulder, CO   80304

Dear Mark,

As you requested in our telephone conversation yesterday, I am enclosing
our latest company brochure.  You will find information describing each
of the services PencilPushers, Inc. offers, along with a list of client
references.

                    PencilPushers, Inc.


I am sure that we will be able to customize an office services package
```
[Open Style:InitialCodes][Bookmark][Lft Mar][Rgt Mar][**Top Mar:2"**][Flsh Rgt]Ju
ly 5, 1994[HRt]
[HRt]
[HRt]
[HRt]
A:\JOHNSON.LTR   Doc 1 Pg 1 Ln 2" Pos 0.75"

Figure 5-11

15. Press Delete

The 2" margin change has been deleted and the document has returned to the default top margin of 1". To view the Print Preview screen,

16. Select File ⇒ Print Preview

✓ Press Shift + F7, **7**

17. Select View ⇒ Full Page or click on the **Full Page** button

To close the Print Preview window,

18. Select File ⇒ Close or click on the **Close** button

✓ Press F7 or Esc

▌ Vertically Centering a Page

The **Center Page** feature centers the text vertically on a page, between the top and bottom margins. To activate the Center Page feature, choose Layout ⇒ Page ⇒ Center Current Page (*Shortcut keys:* Shift + F8, 3, 2) to affect just the page where your cursor is placed, or select Layout ⇒ Page ⇒ Center Pages (*Shortcut keys:* Shift + F8, 3, 3) to center all pages in the document.

If the Auto Code Placement feature is on, WordPerfect inserts at the top of the page in which the cursor is positioned a [Cntr Cur Pg] code for the Center Current Page option and a [Cntr Pgs] code for the Center Pages. If the Auto Code Placement feature is off, you need to make sure that the cursor is positioned at the top of the page you want to be vertically centered.

REMEMBER: To view the Auto Code Placement settings, choose File ⇒ Setup ⇒ Environment. If a check mark precedes the Auto Code Placement option, it is turned on; if not, it is off.

▌ HANDS-ON ACTIVITY

Your letter to Mr. Johnson would look nicer if the text were centered vertically on the page. In this exercise, you use the Center Page feature to accomplish this task. (Be sure to move to the top of the page.)

1. Select Layout ⇒ Page ⇒ Center Current Page

    ✓ Press Shift + F8 , **3 , 2**

    An X marks the Center Current Page option in the Page Format dialog box as shown in Figure 5-12.

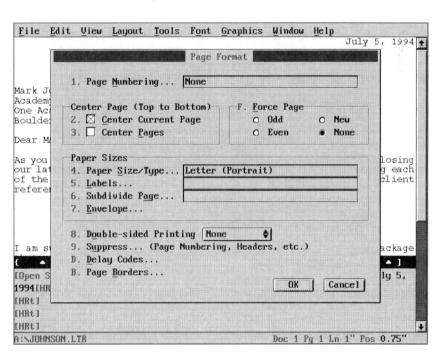

Figure 5-12

To exit this dialog box,

2. Select OK

    ✓ Press Enter

    Use Reveal Codes to view a [Cntr Cur Pg] code inserted at the beginning of the letter.

3. Select View ⇒ Reveal Codes

    Now, use the Print Preview feature to view your letter.

4. Select <u>F</u>ile ⇒ **Print Pre<u>v</u>iew**

✓ Press [Shift] + [F7], 7

(You may need to select Full Page.)

Compare your screen with Figure 5-13.

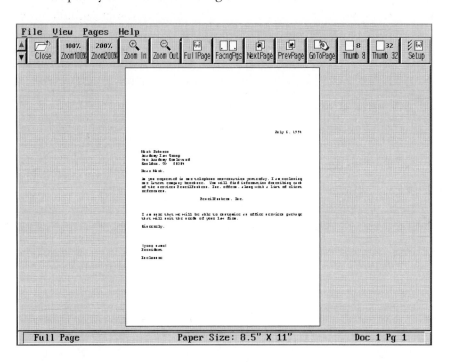

Figure 5-13

To exit the Print Preview window,

5. Select <u>F</u>ile ⇒ <u>C</u>lose

✓ Press [F7]

6. On your own, save the file

▌ Using Tabs

Tab stop positions are used to align columns, set up tables, and indent paragraphs. Tab stops are set much as they are on a typewriter: first you set the tab position and then you press [Tab] to move the cursor to the first tab stop. Each time you press [Tab] the cursor moves to the next defined tab stop. WordPerfect inserts a [Lft Tab] code each time the [Tab] key is pressed.

WordPerfect automatically sets up tab stops every half-inch. These tabs can either be placed in your documents as you type or can be inserted into existing text. Tabs can be removed with either the [Delete] or [Backspace] keys in the Reveal Codes mode.

▌ HANDS-ON ACTIVITY

In this exercise, you will insert a tab at the beginning of each paragraph and each line of the closing.

1. Position the cursor in front of the first character of the first paragraph

2. Press Tab

   The first line of the paragraph automatically tabs in ½ inch and the remaining lines of the paragraph reformat. As usual with all WordPerfect codes, to look at or to remove the [Lft Tab] code, use Reveal Codes.

3. Select **View** ⇒ **Reveal Codes**

   ✓ Press Alt + F3 , or F11

4. Using the Reveal Codes screen (lower window), position the cursor directly on the [Lft Tab] code

5. Press Delete

6. Close the Reveal Codes screen

7. On your own, insert a tab at the beginning of each paragraph

8. On your own, insert five tabs at the beginning of each line of the signature block

   Compare your letter to the one in Figure 5-14.

(today's date)

Mark Johnson
Academy Law Group
One Academy Boulevard
Boulder, CO   80304

Dear Mark,

   As you requested in our telephone conversation yesterday, I am enclosing our latest company brochure. You will find information describing each of the services PencilPushers, Inc. offers, along with a list of client references.

                              PencilPushers, Inc.

   I am sure that we will be able to customize an office services package that will suit the needs of your law firm.

                              Sincerely,

                              (your name)
                              President

Enclosure

Figure 5-14

9. On your own, save the file

Changing Tab Stops

WordPerfect automatically sets up tab stops every half-inch. The placement or type of tabs can be changed at any position in the document to accommodate the style desired in any text.

The two types of tab measurements available are Left Edge, or absolute, and Left Margin, or relative. **Left Margin tabs**, which are the default setting, are always measured relative to the left margin. For example, if you wish to set a tab stop ½ inch from the left margin, you would specify .5. All Left Margin tab stops "float" with the left margin. For example, if you have tab stops every ½ inch and decided to move your left margin ¼ inch to the right, all the tab stops will also move ¼ inch to the right. In other words, the tabs shift to new positions so that they remain the same distance from that margin. The code inserted for Left Margin or relative tab is [Tab Set:Rel;...].

Left Edge, or absolute, tab stops are measured from the left edge of the page, regardless of your current margin settings. For example, if you wanted a tab stop ½ inch in from the left edge of the text and the left margin is 1 inch, you would enter **1.5"** for the tab stop. If the left margin of a document is later changed, the tab stops do not float. For instance, if you have tab stops every ½ inch and you change the left margin from 1 inch to 1¼ inch, the first tab stop would be positioned ¼ inch from the left margin, instead of the original ½ inch. The code inserted for Left Edge tabs is [Tab Set:Abs...].

There are four tab alignments available. The following table describes the alignment of each tab setting:

Left Tab (L)	Aligns the text evenly on the left-hand side of the tab position
Center Tab (C)	Centers text over the center tab stop
Right Tab (R)	Aligns text evenly on the right-hand side of the tab position
Decimal Tab (D)	Aligns the decimal points of each number under the decimal tab position, thus aligning all the decimal points

An example of each alignment is shown in Figure 5-15.

Left	Center	Right	Decimal
Denver	Colorado	1,000	1,000.00
San Francisco	California	200	200.50
Columbia	South Carolina	10	10.75
Salt Lake City	Utah	1	1.

Figure 5-15

To change tab settings, you first position the cursor where the new tab settings are to take effect. If the cursor is placed in the middle of an existing paragraph, the new tab stops setting will start at the beginning of the paragraph unless the Auto Code Placement has been turned off. Select <u>L</u>ayout ⇒ Ta<u>b</u> Set (*Shortcut keys:* Ctrl + F11). The Tab Set dialog box will appear. To delete all tab stops, select the Clear <u>A</u>ll command button. To set a tab, move along the tab ruler with either the mouse or the left or right arrow keys to the desired location, then select the desired tab alignment by selecting the corresponding option button. You may also type the tab position in the <u>S</u>et Tab text box. When all the desired tabs are set, select the OK command button or press Enter.

▌ HANDS-ON ACTIVITY

In this exercise you are going to type the columnar table shown in Figure 5-16.

Service	Cost per Hour
Telephone Services	9.00
Clerical	14.00
Proofreading	18.00
Word Processing	20.00
Enhanced Word Processing	25.00
Desktop Publishing	35.00
Bookkeeping/Billing	25.00

Figure 5-16

The first step is to set two center tabs for the headings.

1. Make sure your cursor is positioned on a blank line two lines below the paragraph that reads "PencilPushers, Inc."

2. Select <u>L</u>ayout ⇒ Ta<u>b</u> Set

    ✓ Press Ctrl + F11

    The Tab Set dialog box appears, displaying "L" for left tabs set at every ½ inch, as shown in Figure 5-17. Notice that the Type of tab is relative, the alignment is set to Left, and the ruler displayed at the top of the screen has Left tabs set every ½ inch, which is the default setting.

    Your first task is to use the Clear <u>A</u>ll button (bottom of the dialog box) to clear existing tabs.

3. Select **Clear <u>A</u>ll**

    ✓ Press Ctrl + End

    Notice that the "L"s marking the default left tabs are removed.

    To set two Center tabs at 1.5" and 5.25",

4. Select <u>S</u>et Tab

5. Type `1.5`

    This will place the first tab 1½ inches from the left margin.

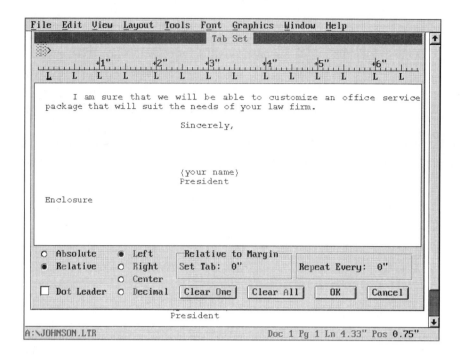

Figure 5-17

6. Press [Enter]

    The tab setting is placed in the ruler at the top of the dialog box, but it is marked as a Left-aligned tab. To change it to a Center tab,

7. Select **C**enter

    Create the next tab at 5.25 inches by using **S**et Tab in the box marked Relative to Margin.

8. Select **S**et Tab

9. Type **5.25**

    This will position the second centered tab at 5.25 inches from the left margin.

10. Press [Enter]

    Compare your Tab Set dialog box to the one shown in Figure 5-18.

    To exit the Tab Set dialog box and save your tab settings,

11. Select **OK**

    ✓ Press [F7]

12. Check your codes by activating the Reveal Codes screen (**V**iew ⇒ **Reveal C**odes or [Alt] + [F3], or [F11])

    If you highlight the [Tab Set] code, it will open to display the detailed code [Tab Set:Rel; +1.5"C, every +3.75"]). The code "Rel" means that the tabs are "relative" tabs, which are measured from the left margin. The first tab is at 1.5" centered (+ 1.5"C) and the next tab is positioned 3.75" away from the first tab.

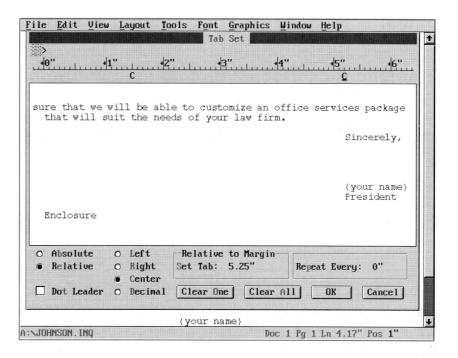

Figure 5-18

Now you are ready to type the headings.

CAUTION: Before you begin typing the headings, be sure your cursor is positioned to the right of the [Tab Set] code in the Reveal Codes screen so that WordPerfect types the text after the tab setting code, thus ensuring the new tab settings are in effect for the newly typed text.

13. Press → once

14. Press Tab

15. Type **Service**

16. Press Tab

17. Type **Cost per Hour**

18. Press Enter twice

▌ HANDS-ON ACTIVITY

The following steps will create the two-columnar list shown in Figure 5-16. For the list, you will need to create a left tab setting for the descriptions at .8"and a decimal tab setting for the costs at 5.25".

1. Make sure your cursor is positioned on a blank line two lines below the column headings that read "Service" and "Cost per Hour"

2. Select **Layout** ⇒ **Tab Set**

    ✓ Press Ctrl + F11

    Your first task is to clear all existing tabs.

3. Select **Clear All**

To set a left tab at .8",

4. Select Set Tab

To set the first tab at .8",

5. Type .8

6. Press Enter

NOTE: *Even though you cleared all existing tab locations, the type of tab defaulted to a centered since that was the type of tab used last.*

Change center to left type of tab.

7. Select Left

Create the next tab at 5.25".

8. Select Set Tab

9. Type 5.25

10. Press Enter

Now, the default tab setting is left, since that type was used last. Change it to a decimal aligned tab.

11. Select Decimal

To exit the Tab Set dialog box and save your tab settings,

12. Select OK

✓ Press F7

Now you are ready to type the items in the list.

13. Press Tab

14. Type Telephone Services

15. Press Tab

16. Type 9.00

17. Press Enter

18. On your own, continue to type the remaining items in the list shown in Figure 5-16

Your last task is to create another tab setting to set the tabs back to normal (every ½ inch) for the remainder of the document.

1. Make sure your cursor is positioned at the beginning of the last paragraph of the letter that reads "I am sure that we will be able to customize..."

2. Select Layout ⇒ Tab Set

✓ Press Ctrl + F11

Now, clear all tab settings.

3. Select **Clear** **A**ll

   ✓ Press Ctrl + End

   *NOTE: Make sure the **S**et Tab parameter displays a 0". If it does not, select **S**et Tab and type a 0.*

   Now, to set left tabs at every ½ inch beginning at 0, which indicates the left margin in the tab ruler,

4. Select **L**eft

5. Select **Repeat Every**

6. Type **.5**

7. Press Enter

   The tab set ruler will display a Left tab at every ½-inch mark, beginning at 0 in the tab ruler.

   To exit the Tab Set dialog box and save your tab settings,

8. Select **OK**

   ✓ Press F7

9. Check your codes by activating the Reveal Codes screen (**V**iew ⇒ **Reveal C**odes or Alt + F3 or F11)

   You will see a [Tab Set:Rel; O"L, every + 0.5"] code for tabs every ½ inch.

10. On your own, save the file

▌ Creating an Envelope

WordPerfect 6.0 has an envelope creation tool that will format an envelope for the current document displayed on your screen. This feature will automatically create a page break at the end of the document, create an envelope form, find the inside address lines in the displayed letter, and copy them to the envelope form.

A printer must be selected before you can use the Envelope feature. To see if a printer is selected, select **F**ile ⇒ **P**rint/Fax. If a printer is selected, the name of the printer will appear in the Current Printer option. If no printer is selected, choose the **S**elect option. The Select Printer dialog box appears in which you can select or add a printer definition.

▌ HANDS-ON ACTIVITY

In this exercise you will create and preview an envelope for the Johnson document.

1. Be sure that the JOHNSON.LTR file is displayed on your screen

2. Select **L**ayout ⇒ En**v**elope

   ✓ Press Alt + F12

The Envelope dialog box appears as shown in Figure 5-19.

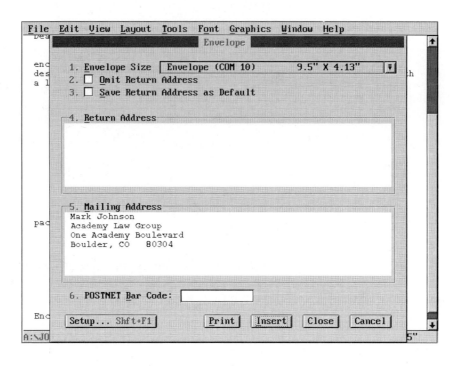

Figure 5-19

NOTE: *The inside address to Mark Johnson has already been located and copied to the addressee area of this dialog box. Accept these settings.*

3. Select **I**nsert

   ✓ Press Enter

   Automatically, a hard page break (indicated as a double horizontal line across the screen) is inserted at the end of the letter and an envelope is created with the correct address block copied from the displayed letter.

   To view the envelope using the Print Preview feature,

4. Select **F**ile ⇒ **Print Pre**view

   ✓ Press Shift + F7 , **7**

   Compare your screen to the one shown in Figure 5-20.

   To exit the Print Preview,

5. Select **F**ile ⇒ **C**lose or click on the **Close** button

   ✓ Press F7

6. Save the file and exit WordPerfect

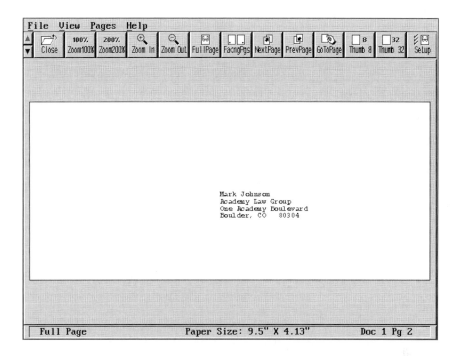

File   View   Pages   Help

Close Zoom100% Zoom200% Zoom In Zoom Out FullPage FacngPgs NextPage PrevPage GoToPage Thumb 8 Thumb 32 SetUp

Mark Johnson
Academy Law Group
One Academy Boulevard
Boulder, CO   80304

Full Page   Paper Size: 9.5" X 4.13"   Doc 1 Pg 2

Figure 5-20

Review of Commands

Description	Menu Commands	Function Keys
Open a file using File Manager		
Align text flush right		
Center text		
Apply Full justification		
Change document margins		
Preview a document		
Vertically center a page		
Change tab settings		
Create an envelope		

Lesson Review

1. What are the default settings for all margins?

2. What is the default justification?

3. What does the File Manager feature provide?

4. How is a hard page break indicated on your document screen?

5. What effect does the Auto Code Placement feature have on top and bottom margins?

6. List the five settings available in the Justification feature and describe the alignment of each.

7. The Print Preview option has a "zoom in" feature that will increase the size of the text by what percentage?

8. What menu options will show you whether the Auto Code Placement feature is turned on?

9. Name the four types of tab settings.

10. If you want your tab settings to "float" when a margin change occurs, what type of tab measurement should be selected?

11. What must be selected before an envelope can be created?

12. What menu command gives you right justification?

▌ Assignments

5.1 Directions

1. Begin with a blank screen to create the tabbed document shown in Figure 5-21.

2. Change the left and right margins to .75".

3. Center the first two lines for the title of the document.

4. Set the following tab stops (all Left tabs):

Dept	+0"
No.	+.8"
Title	+1.68"
Instructor	+4.33"
Room	+6.12"

   NOTE: If you need to estimate where the tab stops should be positioned in a new document, a good method to determine where to set them is to position the cursor at the left margin of a new line and press Tab. *Type the longest line in the first column; press* Tab *once; type the longest line in the second column; press* Tab; *and so on, until all the columns are represented. Position the cursor at the beginning of the line and display the Tab ruler. Clear all tabs and then set one tab for each column.*

5. Type the text shown in Figure 5-21 in the tabbed section.

6. Save the document as SCHEDULE.SPG.

7. Print and close the file.

```
                    Boulder Community College
                         Summer Schedule
    Dept    No.     Title                   Instructor    Room
    CMS     101     Information Systems      Palmer        WC 268
    CJC     340     Criminal Behavior        Copley        SO 108
    COM     241     Writing for Radio        Stoner        TE 116
    MGT     190     Strategic Management     Price         NC 1808
    MKT     301     Marketing Research       Downs         SO 313
```

Figure 5-21

5.2 Directions

1. Begin with a clear screen to create the document shown in Figure 5-22.

(today's date)

QUARTERLY REPORT

Eastern Region

Based upon the fiscal projections that each region prepared last year, this region has consistently met quota assignments in all product lines. In over half the product line, the Eastern Region has exceeded the projected quota by ten percent. Significant sales during the quarter were attributable to the efforts of the five top sales representatives:

M. J. Conover	Boston	100%
B. B. Hunt	New York	98%
R. A. Kane	Montreal	105%
K. V. Jordan	Ottawa	95%
G. O. Thomas	Washington	97%

Each of these sales representatives deserves particular recognition because they have been affiliated with their district offices for less than six months.

	Jan.	Feb.	Mar.	Apr.
Monthly Breakdown				
Boston	1,000.00	1,500.00	2,000.00	2,200.00
New York	2,300.00	2,100.00	2,200.00	1,800.00
Montreal	1,900.00	2,900.00	2,300.00	2,100.00
Ottawa	1,800.00	1,900.00	1,950.00	1,400.00
Washington	1,930.00	1,300.00	1,999.00	2,100.00

Figure 5-22

---

2. Change the justification to Full.

3. Use the Flush Right feature to place the date on the right margin and insert the date code.

4. Center and bold the heading "Quarterly Report."

5. When preparing to type the two tabbed sections, determine on your own the tab locations and appropriate tab alignment (left, right, center, decimal, and so on).

6. Vertically center the page.

7. Save it as REPORT.QTR.

8. Spell check, save, print, and exit.

6

Using the Button Bar and the Ribbon

Objectives

Upon completion of this lesson, you will be able to do the following:

- Describe the Button Bar
- Use features on the Button Bar such as the File Manager, print, envelope, and preview
- Create a custom Button Bar
- Edit a Button Bar
- Change the location and appearance of the Button Bar
- Display the Ribbon
- Execute features on the Ribbon such as Zoom and Justification

This lesson will show you how to display and use the Button Bar and the Ribbon. You will also learn to create, modify, and save a Button Bar.

Starting Point

Before beginning the lesson, start WordPerfect 6.0. The document window should be blank.

The Button Bar

In the previous chapters, you have been using the menu bar to give Word-Perfect a command. For the most frequently used options, WordPerfect provides a Button Bar to expedite the execution of a command. For example, to print a document, you choose File ⇒ Print/Fax. When the Button Bar is displayed, you would simply click on the Print button on the bar. The default Button Bar is shown in Figure 6-1.

As you can see, the Button Bar shows both pictures and words on the command buttons for the most commonly used features. To execute a command on the Button Bar, simply position the mouse pointer on the desired command button and click once. Commands on the Button Bar can only be accessed by using the mouse—there are no keystrokes available to choose command buttons.

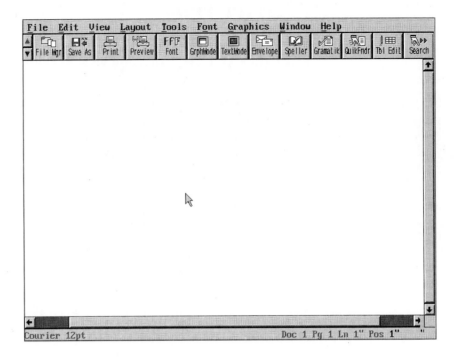

Figure 6-1

Before you can use the Button Bar, it must be displayed in the document window. To display it, choose <u>V</u>iew ⇒ <u>B</u>utton Bar. To remove the Button Bar, you use the same steps. Once the Button Bar is displayed, it will automatically display every time you load the WordPerfect program.

▌HANDS-ON ACTIVITY

In this exercise you are going to display the Button Bar.

1. Select <u>V</u>iew

    The <u>V</u>iew pull-down menu appears, as shown in Figure 6-2.

2. Select <u>B</u>utton Bar

    The default Button Bar appears.

Working with the Button Bar

As you can see, the Button Bar has command buttons that will allow you to access the File Manager, save a file as a new document, print, create an envelope, and so on. It also has other commands that you have not worked with yet, such as QuickFinder and Table Edit. To use the Button Bar, simply position the mouse pointer on the desired command button and click once. Remember, commands on the Button Bar can only be accessed by using the mouse.

▌HANDS-ON ACTIVITY

You will now use the Button Bar to open and print the letter to Mr. Jacobs called JACOBS.INQ. Since the Button Bar commands can only be executed

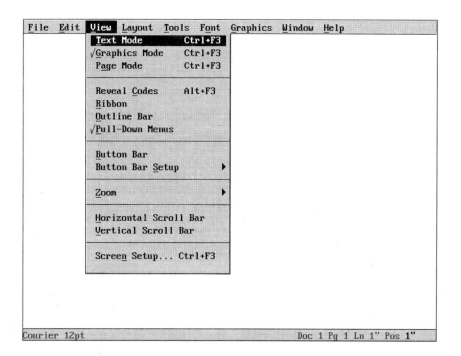

Figure 6-2

using the mouse, we are indicating the shortcut keystrokes, so that you can perform the exercise if you do not have a mouse connected to your system.

1. Click on **File Mgr** in the Button Bar

   ✓ Press F5

   The Specify File Manager List dialog box appears. To display the directory of drive A,

2. Type **A:** in the Directory text box

   If your data disk is in drive B, substitute B:

3. Press Enter

   The File Manager dialog box appears. Using the arrow keys,

4. Highlight **JACOBS.INQ**

5. Select <u>O</u>pen into New Document

   ✓ Press Enter

   (Remember, double-clicking on the file name is a fast method to open the file.)

   Your letter to Mr. Jacobs is in the document window.

   Now, print your document. Make sure your printer is on, the on-line light is illuminated, and the paper is properly aligned.

6. Click on **Print** in the Button Bar

   ✓ Press Shift + F7

7. Select P̲rint

▌ HANDS-ON ACTIVITY

As we stated, the default Button Bar has the most commonly used commands or features—one of those being the Envelope feature. Since you have not created an envelope for Mr. Jacobs's letter, you are going to use the Envelope command button on the Button Bar.

1. Click on **Envelope** in the Button Bar

   ✓ Press Alt + F12

   The Envelope dialog box appears, as shown in Figure 6-3.

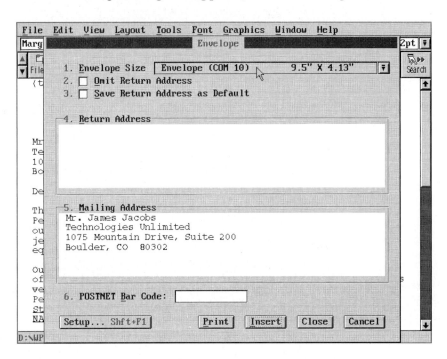

Figure 6-3

2. Select I̲nsert

   An envelope is created for your letter and placed at the bottom of the document.

   Use the Preview feature to view your envelope. First position your cursor at the bottom of your document.

3. Press Home, Home, ↓

4. Click on **Preview** in the Button Bar

   ✓ Press Shift + F7, **7**

   Compare your envelope to the one shown in Figure 6-4.

5. Click on **Close** in the Preview Button Bar

   ✓ Press F7

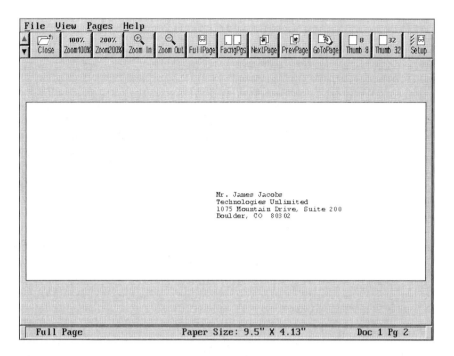

Figure 6-4

Creating Your Own Button Bar

WordPerfect allows you to create and customize your own Button Bar by inserting command buttons for the features you use the most. Once the Button Bar is created, you can easily change the Button Bar to your liking as you gain more experience working in WordPerfect. The Main Button Bar that WordPerfect activates when you choose View ⇒ Button Bar is called WPMAIN.WPB. You may edit this one or create one of your own. It is our recommendation, however, that you leave the Main Button Bar intact (particularly if you share your computer with someone else).

To create a new Button Bar, from the menu bar choose View ⇒ Button Bar Setup ⇒ Select ⇒ Create. The dialog box appears with the cursor blinking in the Button Bar Name text box. Type the name of the Button Bar and press Enter. To add a menu item, select the option Add Menu Item... and choose the menu feature the same way you do when working with it normally in WordPerfect. For example, to add the Print command, select File ⇒ Print/Fax. To add a feature such as bold or underline, select the Add Feature... option. A feature Button List dialog box appears with a list of WordPerfect features. Once you have added the desired features, select the OK command button. All Button Bar file names have a .WPB file extension and are saved in the \WP60\MACRO directory. The new Button Bar now displays at the top of your document window.

If you add more buttons than will fit on one row, WordPerfect must scroll one or more of them off the screen. When this occurs, left and right arrows appear to the left of the Button Bar. Click on these arrows to scroll the Button Bar in either direction.

▌ HANDS-ON ACTIVITY

You are going to create your own Button Bar and select several features that you have been using.

1. Select <u>V</u>iew ⇒ Button Bar <u>S</u>etup ⇒ <u>S</u>elect

    The Select Button Bar dialog box appears as shown in Figure 6-5.

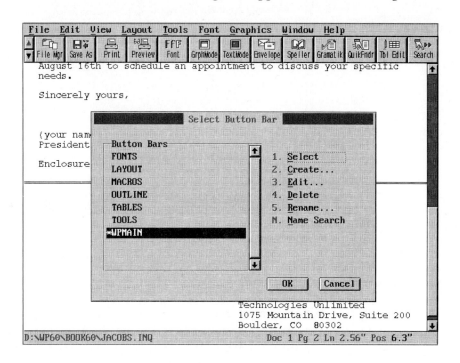

Figure 6-5

2. Select <u>C</u>reate

    The Button Bar Name dialog box appears as shown in Figure 6-6. WordPerfect is asking you to enter a name for your Button Bar.

3. Type **Train**

4. Select **OK**

✓ Press Enter or F7

    Notice that the Button Bar is now blank and the Edit Button Bar dialog box presents new menu options allowing you to add menu items and features to the bar. Compare your screen to the one shown in Figure 6-7.

    You are now going to add the following menu items to your Button Bar: Save As, Save, Print, Print Preview, Undo, Cut, Copy, Paste, File Manager, and Open. To add a menu item, simply choose the feature as if you were going to execute the command.

5. Select **Add M<u>e</u>nu Item**

    Notice that the menu bar is active and the <u>F</u>ile option is highlighted. To add the first item,

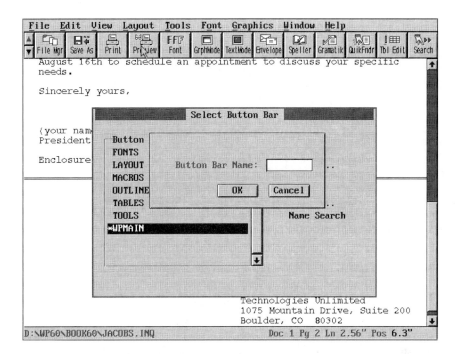

Figure 6-6

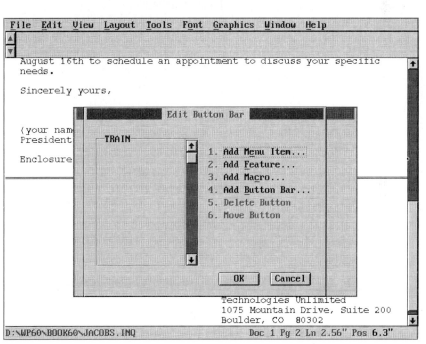

Figure 6-7

6. Select <u>F</u>ile ⇒ Save <u>A</u>s

   The "Save As" command button appears on your Button Bar.

7. Select <u>F</u>ile ⇒ <u>S</u>ave

8. Select <u>F</u>ile ⇒ <u>P</u>rint/Fax

9. Select <u>F</u>ile ⇒ Print Pre<u>v</u>iew

10. Select Edit ⇒ Undo

11. Select Edit ⇒ Cut

12. Select Edit ⇒ Copy

13. Select Edit ⇒ Paste

14. Select File ⇒ File Manager

15. Select File ⇒ Open

To exit the menu bar and return to the Edit Button Bar dialog box,

16. Press F7

Compare your screen to the one shown in Figure 6-8.

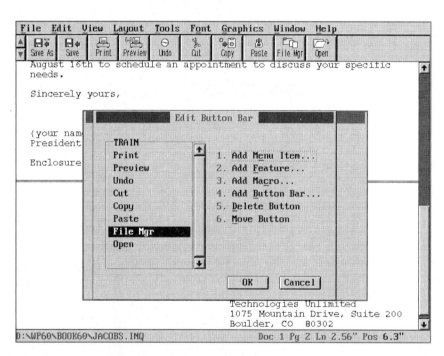

Figure 6-8

Now, you are going to add the following features to your Button Bar: JustFull (Justification Full), Speller, and Thesaurus.

17. Select **Add Feature**

The Feature Button List dialog box appears, as shown in Figure 6-9, with a long list of features in alphabetical order.

The first feature you are going to add is Justification Full. To locate this feature, you can press the ↓ until it is highlighted; a quick and easier method is to type part of the feature name.

18. Type `justfu`

The JustFull feature is now highlighted.

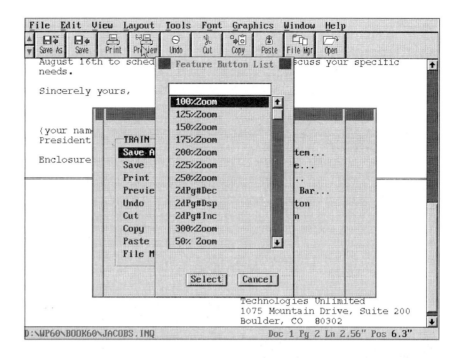

Figure 6-9

To add the JustFull feature to your Button Bar,

19. Press (Enter)

20. Repeat this process to add the following features: Speller and Thesaurus

    Compare your Button Bar to the one shown in Figure 6-10.

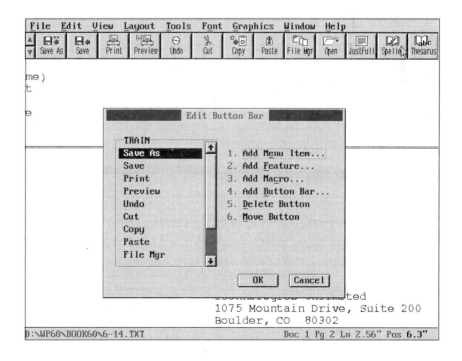

Figure 6-10

To save your Button Bar,

21. Select **OK**

    ✓ Press F7

    The Select Button Bar dialog box reappears. To select your Button Bar,

22. Make sure "Train" is highlighted

23. Press Enter

    You are returned to the document window, and your customized Button Bar appears at the top of your screen. To utilize your Button Bar,

24. On your own, use the Save button to update the JACOB.INQ letter

Selecting a Different Button Bar

You can create as many Button Bars as you need for various tasks. Besides the default Button Bar, WordPerfect also includes several other Button Bars (Fonts, Layout, Macros, Outline, Tables, and so on) that address specific tasks. To activate a specific Button Bar, choose <u>V</u>iew ⇒ Button Bar <u>S</u>etup ⇒ <u>S</u>elect. The Select Button Bar dialog box appears. Highlight the file name of the desired Button Bar and click on Select. The selected Button Bar is displayed on your screen.

▌ HANDS-ON ACTIVITY

You are going to activate the default Button Bar. Remember, it is called WPMAIN.

1. Select <u>V</u>iew ⇒ Button Bar <u>S</u>etup ⇒ <u>S</u>elect

   The Select Button Bar box appears.

2. Select **WPMAIN**

3. Select <u>S</u>elect

   ✓ Press 1

   The default Button Bar now appears at the top of your screen.

4. On your own, select your custom Button Bar, called **TRAIN**.

Editing a Button Bar

Editing a Button Bar is very simple. First, make sure the Button Bar you want to edit is displayed on the screen. From the menu bar, choose <u>V</u>iew ⇒ Button Bar <u>S</u>etup ⇒ <u>E</u>dit. The Edit Button Bar dialog appears. Use the menu to select the desired editing feature (Add Menu Item, Add Feature, Delete Button, Move Button, and the like). Once your modifications are complete, select OK or press F7.

CAUTION: Don't edit or modify the default Button Bar, WPMAIN. You might lose features that would have to be laboriously added again.

▌ HANDS-ON ACTIVITY

You have decided to delete the JustFull command button on your Train Button Bar and also to move the File Manager and Open buttons closer to the beginning of the bar, since you use them frequently. Make sure the Train Button Bar is displayed on your screen. Remember, the Button Bar displayed on your screen is the one that will be modified.

1. Select <u>V</u>iew ⇒ Button Bar <u>S</u>etup ⇒ <u>E</u>dit

    The Edit Button Bar dialog box appears. First, you are going to delete the JustFull command button.

2. Highlight **JustFull**

3. Select <u>D</u>elete Button

    A dialog box appears, asking if you wish to delete JustFull.

4. Select <u>Y</u>es

    The JustFull command button is deleted and the Button Bar is updated.

    Now, to move File Manager as the first button on the bar,

5. Highlight **File Mgr**

6. Select <u>M</u>ove Button

7. Press (Home), (Home), (↑)

    This will place the highlight at the beginning of the button list. To paste the button,

8. Select <u>P</u>aste Button

    ✓ Press (Enter)

9. Highlight **Open**

10. Select <u>M</u>ove Button

11. Press (Home), (Home), (↑)

12. Press (↓) once

    This will place the highlight on the Save As button. To paste the Open button,

13. Select <u>P</u>aste Button

    ✓ Press (Enter)

    To save the changes to your Button Bar,

14. Select **OK**

    ✓ Press (F7)

    Compare your Button Bar to the one shown in Figure 6-11.

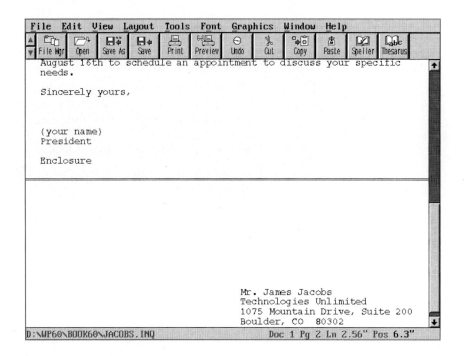

Figure 6-11

Changing the Position and Appearance of the Button Bar

The Button Bar does not have to be displayed at the top of your screen. It can be positioned horizontally at the bottom of the screen, or even vertically on the left or right of the screen. You can also change the appearance of the command buttons, by choosing to show only text or only pictures (icons). To change the position and appearance of the Button Bar, from the menu bar choose <u>V</u>iew ⇒ Button Bar <u>S</u>etup ⇒ <u>O</u>ptions.

▌ HANDS-ON ACTIVITY

In this exercise, you are going to change your Button Bar to be displayed on the left side of your document window and to show only text on the buttons.

1. Select <u>V</u>iew ⇒ Button Bar <u>S</u>etup ⇒ <u>O</u>ptions

    The Button Bar Options dialog box appears as shown in Figure 6-12.

2. Select <u>L</u>eft Side

3. Select Te<u>x</u>t Only

4. Select **OK**

    ✓ Press Enter

    Compare your Button Bar to the one shown in Figure 6-13.

5. On your own, display the Button Bar to your liking

    When you open a new file, the Train Button Bar will display in the position you last saved it.

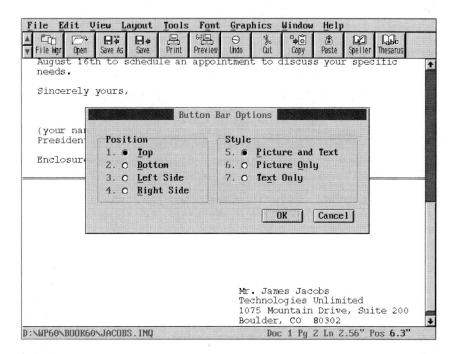

Figure 6-12

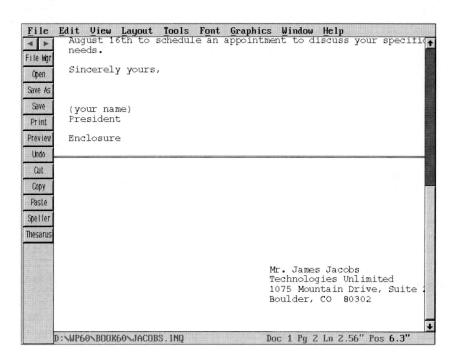

Figure 6-13

The Ribbon

In Lesson 5, you used the menu bar to change the justification of your document, while in Lesson 4 you used the View menu to change the display size of the text. The Ribbon allows you to quickly access features that change the size and appearance of text in a document, alter the view size of your document, select a font style and point size, change the justification setting, modify a paragraph level in an outline, and change the number of columns. (You will use the font, outline, and columns Ribbon features in later lessons in this book.)

The Ribbon can only be accessed with a mouse. Before you can use the Ribbon, it must be displayed in the document window. To display it, select <u>V</u>iew ⇒ <u>R</u>ibbon. Use the same steps to remove the Ribbon. Once the Ribbon is displayed, it will automatically display every time you load the WordPerfect program. The display of the Ribbon can be turned on or off (to save screen space) at any time. The settings made from the Ribbon are only in effect for the current document.

▌ HANDS-ON ACTIVITY

In this exercise, you are going to display the Ribbon.

1. Select <u>V</u>iew

    The <u>V</u>iew pull-down menu appears.

2. Select <u>R</u>ibbon

    Your screen should be similar to the one shown in Figure 6-14. Note that the browse buttons for each feature on the Ribbon have been indicated.

Using the Ribbon

Notice that each feature on the Ribbon has a browse button (down-pointing arrow) to the right of each option. When you click on the browse button, a drop-down list box displays the options for each feature. Click once to highlight the desired option, and double-click to execute the selection.

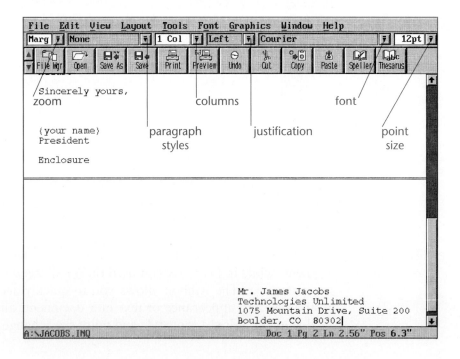

Figure 6-14

■ **HANDS-ON ACTIVITY**

In this exercise, you will use the Ribbon to change the display view of your document, using the Zoom drop-down list box. Be sure that your Ⴣiew is set to either Graphics or Page mode.

1. Position the cursor at the top of your document

2. Click on the **Zoom** browse button

   The Zoom drop-down list box appears as shown in Figure 6-15.

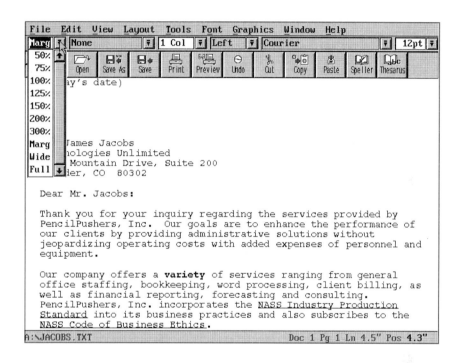

Figure 6-15

3. Double click on **200%**

   Your display view has been changed to 200%.

4. On your own, using the Zoom drop-down list box on the Ribbon, change the display view back to Marg (the Margin Width setting)

■ **HANDS-ON ACTIVITY**

In the next activity, you are going to use the Justification drop-down list box to change the text justification of your document. Make sure your cursor is at the top of the document.

1. Click on the **Justification** browse button

   The Justification drop-down list box appears.

2. Double-click on **Full**

   Your document is now Full justified.

3. On your own, using the Justification drop-down list box on the Ribbon, change the justification back to Left

4. Save the file and exit WordPerfect

On Your Own

Review of Commands

Description	Menu
Display the Button Bar	_____
Create a new Button Bar	_____
Select a Button Bar	_____
Edit a Button Bar	_____
Change location/appearance of Button Bar	_____
Display the Ribbon	_____

Lesson Review

1. Describe the physical appearance of the default Button Bar.

2. What is the major advantage of using functions from the Button Bar instead of the drop-down menus?

3. Must you select a command to display the Button Bar for every new document you begin?

4. If the answer to question 3 is no, which Button Bar is displayed when you open WordPerfect?

5. Is it possible to select the Button Bar command buttons via the keyboard?

6. How does WordPerfect accommodate a Button Bar that is longer than one row?

7. What are the general steps to create a new Button Bar?

8. What are the commands to select a different Button Bar?

9. What are the four possible locations for the Button Bar on your screen?

10. What are the three possible styles the Button Bar may have?

11. List any four of the six features that can be executed using the Ribbon.

12. What keystrokes are used to access the Ribbon?

13. What is the down-pointing arrow called that is located to the right of each feature on the Ribbon?

14. What does the down-pointing arrow indicate?

15. What menu commands turn off the Ribbon?

▌ Assignments

6.1 Directions

1. Create a Button Bar with the following commands on it: Save, Close, Print, Bold, Underline, Normal, Date Code, and Speller.

2. Save the new Button Bar as LETTER. (The .WPB file extension will automatically be added.)

3. Type the following letter, accessing all the relevant commands from your custom Button Bar (the slashes indicate new paragraphs):

(current date) / (leave six blank lines) / Dr. Louise Marold / 3456 Blair Place / Sunnyvale, CA 94067 / Dear Dr. Marold:/ Thank you very much for submitting your curriculum vita to us for consideration. However, at this time, all of our faculty positions are filled, and we are not hiring any new professors. / Your vita was very impressive, and we will keep it on file in case any openings arise. / Sincerely yours,/ Gerald Morrell, Chairman/ Information Systems Department

4. Using the Ribbon, select Full Justification.

5. Using the Ribbon, change the Zoom to 100%.

6. Spell check the letter.

7. Save the letter as MAROLD.LTR.

8. Print and close the file.

6.2 Directions

1. Add the following buttons to your LETTER.WPB Button Bar for use in future assignments: Cut, Copy, and Paste.

2. Move your Button Bar to the left side of the screen.

3. If you dislike the last placement of the Button Bar, move it to a desirable position.

7

Using File Manager

Objectives

Upon completion of this lesson, you will be able to do the following:

- Define the File Manager
- Describe the components of the File Manager dialog box
- Move around the File Manager dialog box
- View files on the hard disk
- Designate a default drive and directory
- Copy, rename, and delete a file
- Print files from the File Manager
- Mark and unmark file names for group functions
- Sort the file list
- Locate files with name search
- Use Find to locate files
- Search for specified text within files
- Set up QuickList and QuickFinder

This lesson is devoted to the File Manager and its many features. In Lesson 5 you used File Manager to look at a file and open it into a new document window for edits. Now let's explore some of the other File Manager options, such as how to delete or rename files, search for text in files, change drives or directories, sort the list of files, and mark files for group functions.

▌ Starting Point

Before beginning the lesson, start WordPerfect 6.0. The document window should be blank. Make sure the Train Button Bar and the Ribbon are displayed. Locate your sample disk and insert it into the appropriate drive. (Remember, the sample disk corresponding to these exercises is available from your instructor.)

*NOTE: Recall that in this book we assume you are using drive A for the sample disk and will give instructions to type **A:** to access the disk. If your sample disk is inserted in drive B, substitute **B:** wherever A is shown.*

What Is File Manager?

The File Manager function does exactly what the name implies—it manages files. Each time you create a new file, or open, delete, rename, or look at an existing file, the File Manager is working behind the scenes to help you achieve these tasks. The File Manager directs and manages the flow of data, keeping track of which files are stored on disk and which are open.

In addition to working with files, File Manager can help you manage the directories and subdirectories on the hard disk of your computer. In Lesson 1, you learned a few basics about hard disk directory tree structures. Now you can use File Manager to view a list of directories, move through existing directories, create new directories, and remove empty directories.

Some advantages to using File Manager for document organization are as follows:

- The File Manager does some of the same tasks as DOS, except that the screen is arranged in a dialog box format that is easier to use than DOS commands.

- The File Manager screen provides a clear listing of your files and directories in alphabetical order, making the items easy to locate.

- The File Manager screen shows information about each file, such as size and date or time the file was either created or last saved.

- With File Manager you can search through the contents of each file to locate specified text.

- File Manager can mark files so that you can copy, move, print, or delete specified marked files in groups rather than one at a time.

- Before you proceed with a menu choice, File Manager allows you to look at the contents of the file to make sure that you have selected the correct document name (an important benefit when you have dozens or hundreds of files).

Components of the File Manager Window

There are many ways to access the File Manager dialog box. Through the File menu you may select File Manager, Open, or Retrieve (*Shortcut keys:* Shift + F10, or F5).

HANDS-ON ACTIVITY

In this exercise, you will view the File Manager dialog box, using the File ⇒ File Manager menu method. Make sure your document window is blank.

1. Select **File** ⇒ **File Manager** or click on the **File Mgr** button on the Button Bar

   ✓ Press F5

The Specify File Manager List dialog box appears, verifying the current drive and directory as the location that you would like to view. In Figure 7-1, the current drive is C and the current directory is WPDOCS, shown as C:\WPDOCS\. Depending on your computer's individual configuration, your drive and directory may vary.

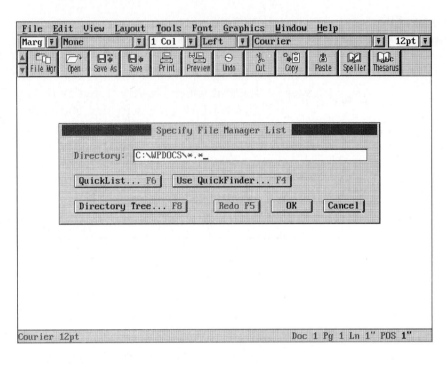

Figure 7-1

Check to see that your sample floppy disk is in the drive and specify drive A for the location of your sample files instead of the drive and directory shown.

2. Type **A:**

3. Select **OK**

    ✓ Press Enter

    The File Manager dialog box appears, displaying the contents of the student sample disk in drive A. Your list of file names will be similar to the list of files shown in Figure 7-2.

The components of the File Manager dialog box are listed as follows.

Left Side of the Dialog Box

*   The drive and directory that is currently displayed
*   The item on which the list of files is sorted (default is alphabetically by file name)
*   The list of files shown in five categories, from left to right:

    File name

    Extension

    Size of the file in bytes

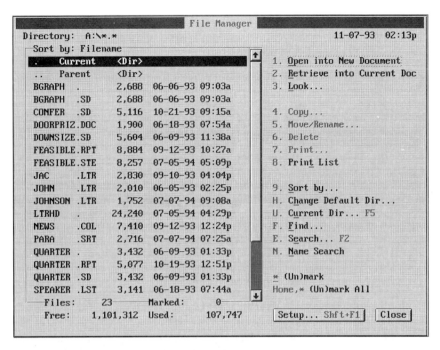

Figure 7-2

Date the file was created or last saved

Time the file was created or last saved

- The count of how many total files are in this current location and how many files are marked (tagged), shown at the bottom left

- Number of bytes that are free on the drive and the number of bytes that are used by the current list of files

Right Side of the Dialog Box

- The current date and time from the computer clock

- List of options (those in bold are available, those in nonbold are not available at this time depending on the placement of your cursor); the default option (indicated by a dotted border) is Open into New Document

- Setup... button (select if you would like to make WordPerfect setup changes)

- Close button (to exit this screen)

▌ Moving Around the File Manager Dialog Box

The highlighter is located at the top of the file list on the upper left-hand side of the dialog box. You may use either the mouse or the directional arrows to browse through the file names. For a convenient method of quickly moving through large lists of files using the mouse, use the scroll bar located between the file list and the option list.

▌ HANDS-ON ACTIVITY

In this exercise you will practice moving through various parts of the File Manager dialog box and closing the File Manager.

First, let's browse through the file name list. Either press the ⬇ on the keyboard or point and single-click with the mouse to select the file name JOHNSON.LTR.

CAUTION: Do not double-click with the mouse or you will inadvertently open the file.

1. Select **JOHNSON.LTR**

    NOTE: Now that you have moved the highlighter to a text file, all the file options on the right side of the screen have changed to bold. The displaying of the options in bold indicates that you may perform them on the highlighted file. Earlier, when the highlighter was located at the top of the file list on the directory marker (. Current), only part of the options were available since you had not yet selected a file.

2. Select **CONFER.SD**

3. If you have a mouse on your computer, try moving through the file list with the scroll bar

    Now close the File Manager dialog box and return to the document window.

4. Select **Close**

    ✓ Press Esc

Viewing Files on the Hard Disk

As well as using floppy disks for storage, you can store many more on the hard disk of the computer. Depending upon the configuration of your computer, the hard drive is usually C and the WordPerfect files are usually stored in a directory called C:\WPDOCS. If your configuration is different or if your computer is networked and it does not have drive C, skip the following exercise.

HANDS-ON ACTIVITY

In this exercise you will view a list of files in the WPDOCS subdirectory.

1. Select File ⇒ File Manager

    ✓ Press F5

    The Specify File Manager List dialog box appears, verifying the current drive and directory as the location that you would like to view.

    *NOTE: If your Directory text box already displays "C:\WPDOCS\ *.*", skip to step 3.*

    To view drive C and the WPDOCS directory,

2. Type `C:\WPDOCS`

3. Select **OK**

    ✓ Press Enter

The File Manager dialog box appears, displaying the contents of the directory WPDOCS on drive C.

Now exit this dialog box and return to the document window.

4. Select **Close**

    ✓ Press Esc

Designating a Default Drive/Directory

During a WordPerfect work session, you will save time if you "lock in" a particular drive or directory as **default**; for example, your working directory may be set to C:\WPDOCS. A default drive or directory means that every time you use the File menu to save, open, or retrieve documents, WordPerfect will automatically assume that you are using the default drive and directory. This default setting will remain in effect until you quit the current WordPerfect work session.

To designate a new drive/directory as the default from the File Manager dialog box, select Change Default Dir.

▌ HANDS-ON ACTIVITY

In this exercise, you will set the default drive to drive A. Again, if you are using a different drive to store your documents, substitute the appropriate drive letter.

1. On your own, start File Manager, listing the files on drive A

    The option Change Default Dir will make the current drive and directory the new default.

2. Select **Change Default Dir**

    The Change Default Directory dialog box appears, confirming the New Directory as drive A, as shown in Figure 7-3.

3. Select **OK**

    ✓ Press Enter

    Next, the Specify File Manager List dialog box appears, confirming that you would like to list all files on the default drive, indicated by the wild card reference (*.*). Confirm A:*.*.

4. Select **OK**

    ✓ Press Enter

    The screen rewrites (or refreshes) the view of the documents appearing on drive A.

    Drive A will be the automatic drive and directory location every time you access File Manager during the remainder of this WordPerfect session. Exit this dialog box.

5. Select **Close**

    ✓ Press Esc

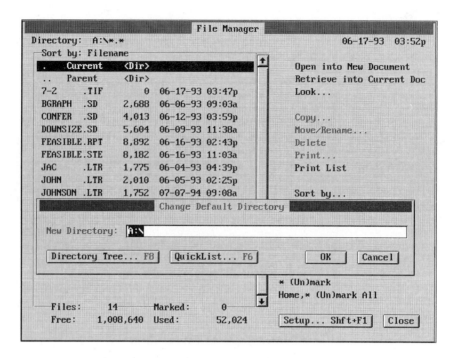

Figure 7-3

Let's test to make sure that drive A is the new default.

6. Select <u>F</u>ile ⇒ <u>F</u>ile Manager or click on the **File Mgr** button on the Button Bar

   ✓ Press F5

7. Close the File Manager dialog box

Copying a File

You can make a copy of an existing file on the same disk or in the same directory as long as you specify a new file name. When you copy a file and designate a new name, you then have two identical files on the same disk or directory but with different names.

You can also use the copy option to make a backup copy of a file, using the same name, onto a different disk. For example, you may have saved the original file on the hard disk (drive C) and want to make a backup copy of the file on drive A in case the original file is accidentally overwritten or deleted.

▌ HANDS-ON ACTIVITY

In this exercise, use the Copy option to copy JOHNSON.LTR to a new file NEW.LTR.

To begin this exercise, make sure you are starting from a blank document window, with your sample disk in drive A.

1. On your own, start File Manager listing files on drive A

2. Select **JOHNSON.LTR**

3. Select <u>C</u>opy

The Copy dialog box displays, asking where you wish to Copy High-lighted File to:. This box currently displays the drive, directory, and file name of the JOHNSON.LTR.

To copy to a new file called NEW.LTR on drive A,

4. Type **NEW.LTR**

    TIP: It is not necessary to include A:\ since drive A is assumed, because it is now your default for the remainder of the session.

    Complete this copy sequence.

5. Select **OK**

    ✓ Press [Enter]

    The file is copied. The File Manager screen rewrites (is refreshed) and the copied file NEW.LTR appears in the list of files on drive A.

    NOTE: The size, date, and time of NEW.LTR are exactly the same as for JOHNSON.LTR.

    To verify that the contents of the two letters are identical, look at the file NEW.LTR.

6. Select **Look**

    To exit the Look mode and return to the File Manager screen,

7. Select **Close**

    ✓ Press [Enter]

8. On your own, copy NEW.LTR to a second file called NEW2.LTR

9. On your own, close the File Manager dialog box

▌ Renaming a File

The Rename option in File Manager provides an easy way to change the name of a file without copying the file to a duplicate. During the rename procedure, you may also move the file by entering a different drive or directory location.

To rename a file, first select the file, making sure the file name is high-lighted, then select Move/Rename. You will then be asked to type the new name and/or location of the file.

▌ HANDS-ON ACTIVITY

To begin this exercise, make sure you are starting from a blank document window, with your sample disk in drive A.

1. On your own, start File Manager, listing files on drive A

2. Select **NEW.LTR**

3. Select **Move/Rename**

The Move/Rename dialog box is displayed, prompting for the New Name of the file, which can also include the new drive and/or directory names.

To rename the file from NEW.LTR to TEST.LTR,

4. Type **TEST.LTR**

    TIP: It is not necessary to include A:\ since drive A is assumed, because it is now your default for the remainder of the session. Your new file name replaces the existing file name and drive reference.

    Complete this rename sequence.

5. Select **OK**

    ✓ Press ⌈Enter⌉

    The file is renamed. The File Manager screen rewrites and the file NEW.LTR has been removed. The renamed version appears in the list of files under the name of TEST.LTR.

    NOTE: Remember, you do not have both versions of the file with Move/Rename.

6. On your own, close the File Manager dialog box

▌ Deleting a File

The Delete option on the File Manager menu enables you to delete (erase) unwanted files from disk.

CAUTION: Once a file has been deleted, you cannot recover the file without special recovery utility software. The file cannot be restored with Word-Perfect, so use extreme care when performing these steps.

▌ HANDS-ON ACTIVITY

In this exercise, you will delete the file TEST.LTR.

NOTE: The original file, JOHNSON.LTR, is still on disk and will not be affected.

Make sure you are starting from a blank document window, with your sample disk in drive A.

1. On your own, start File Manager, listing files on drive A

2. Select **TEST.LTR**

3. Select **D**elete

    The Delete dialog box displays, verifying the file name A:\TEST.LTR with the choice Yes or No.

    To delete the file TEST.LTR,

4. Select **Y**es

The file is deleted. The File Manager screen rewrites and the file NEW.LTR has been removed.

5. On your own, close the File Manager dialog box

Printing Files from File Manager

In previous lessons, you printed your document while it was displayed on the screen. WordPerfect also allows you to print a file from disk so that you can print without opening the file. You can print either the entire document or selected pages. You select Print from the File Manager menu to view a dialog box titled Print Multiple Pages, which gives you choices of pages to print (all is assumed). You would select "(all)" to print the entire document, or would type the numbers of specific pages you want to print. This could be, for example, individual random pages such as 1, 3, 4, and 6; or a continuous range of pages such as 3–7 (pages 3 through 7); or 5– (page 5 to the end of the document). Finally, you choose OK.

HANDS-ON ACTIVITY

You are going to print the JOHNSON.LTR from disk. Make sure that you are starting from a blank document window and your printer is ready.

1. On your own, start File Manager, listing files on drive A

2. Highlight the file **JOHNSON.LTR**

   CAUTION: Do not press [Enter] or double-click the mouse, which would open the file.

3. Select **P**rint

   The Print Multiple Pages dialog box appears as shown in Figure 7-4.

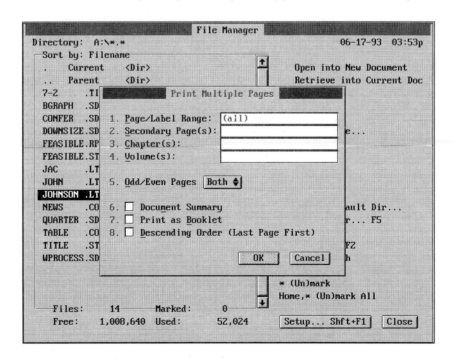

Figure 7-4

Since the JOHNSON.LTR file is a one-page document, we will accept this screen as is with "(all)" as the page range to print the entire document.

4. Select **OK**

5. Close the File Manager dialog box

Marking Files

So far you have performed file management functions with one file at a time. Many of the options on the File Manager menu, such as Copy, Move, Delete, Print, and Open, can also work with several files simultaneously. You first **mark** (tag) the desired files, then select the menu option.

To mark a file, select the file so that it is highlighted, then choose (Un)mark from the menu or press the asterisk (*). Repeat this process for each file that needs to be marked. File Manager places the asterisk (*) mark in front of each file name that you select. At the bottom of the file list, the number of currently marked files is shown, in addition to the number of bytes that these marked files use (helpful when you need to know whether a group of tagged files will all fit on a backup floppy disk).

Once a file has been marked, it can be unmarked by again highlighting the file name, selecting (Un)mark, or pressing the asterisk (*) a second time to remove the mark. To mark or unmark all files at once, select (Un)mark All or press [Home],*.

HANDS-ON ACTIVITY

In this exercise, you will practice marking and unmarking files with File Manager.

Make sure you are starting from a blank document window, with your sample disk in drive A.

1. On your own, start File Manager, listing files on drive A

2. Select **JOHNSON.LTR**

   Mark this file, using either the keyboard or the mouse.

3. Select (Un)mark

   ✓ Press *

   NOTE: *The selection highlighter automatically moves down to the next file.*

4. On your own, mark several more file names

   Notice the number of marked files and bytes used shown at the bottom of the file list.

5. On your own, close the File Manager dialog box and return to a blank document

   NOTE: *The marks disappear as soon as the File Manager dialog box is closed.*

▌Sorting the File Manager List

So far, File Manager has listed your documents in alphabetical order by file name. You can sort the list by any of the five columns on the left side of the File Manager dialog box: File name, Extension, Size, Date, or Time. Also, the sort can organize either in Ascending or Descending order.

▌HANDS-ON ACTIVITY

In this exercise, you practice sorting the files on drive A in several different ways: by extension, by size, and back to by name.

Make sure you are starting from a blank document window, with your sample disk in drive A.

1. On your own, start File Manager, listing files on drive A

    (It is not important to select a particular location on the file list, as the location of the highlighter does not affect the sort function.)

2. Select <u>S</u>ort by

    The File Manager Setup dialog box appears, displaying the default sort and display settings as shown in Figure 7-5.

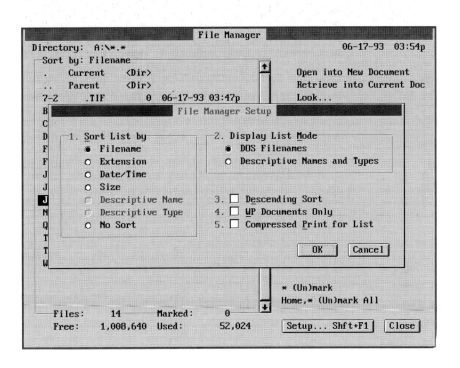

Figure 7-5

The "<u>S</u>ort List by" option on the Setup menu is used to change the way the files are sorted. Set the sort order to Extension.

TIP: You may first select <u>S</u>ort List by, to take the menu a step further so that numbers and underscores are placed on the choices: Filename, Extension, Date/Time, and so on. Or you may click directly on the options with the mouse to move the "radio button" to your choice.

3. Select <u>S</u>ort List by

4. Select <u>E</u>xtension

5. Select **OK**

   ✓ Press (Enter)

   The File Manager screen rewrites, displaying the files in alphabetical order by their extension.

   NOTE: If there are any files without an extension, they will be listed first, then all others with extensions. Files named with numbers precede those named with letters (123.LTR precedes TEST.LTR).

   Let's sort again by size in descending order (high to low).

6. Select <u>S</u>ort by

   At the File Manager Setup dialog box, set the sort order to Size.

7. Select <u>S</u>ort List by

8. Select <u>S</u>ize

   While the Setup dialog box is still displayed, activate the check box to sort in descending order.

9. Select D<u>e</u>scending Sort

   Make sure there is an X marking Descending Sort.

10. Select **OK**

    ✓ Press (Enter)

    The screen rewrites again, displaying the files in order of their size, in descending order from high to low.

11. On your own, sort in alphabetical order by file name in ascending order. Be sure to uncheck the X marking Descending order.

12. On your own, close the File Manager dialog box

▌ Locating Files with Name Search

The File Manager dialog box has an option called **Name Search**, used to move quickly to an alphabetical location in the file list on the current drive and directory. You can move to the exact specified file by typing the whole file name, or you can move to the general area by typing the first few letters of the file name. For instance, if you type **CARTER** as the name search phrase, the highlighter will move directly to the file CARTER.INQ. If you type **C** as the name search phrase, File Manager will move to the first file name beginning with C in the current list. **CAR** would be even more specific, and would probably hit the target unless you have a great many files.

▌ HANDS-ON ACTIVITY

In this exercise, you will locate the file JOHNSON.LTR with the Name Search option of File Manager.

Make sure you are starting from a blank document window, with your sample disk in drive A.

1. On your own, start File Manager, listing files on drive A

    CAUTION: Since you are going to search for the JOHNSON.LTR file by name, you must make sure that your file list is sorted alphabetically by Filename before beginning the search function. Perform a Sort by ⇒ Filename if necessary. Also, to sort the files A through Z, make sure that Descending Sort is not checked.

    TIP: Your cursor may be located at any position in the file list, since the location of the highlighter does not affect the Name Search function.

2. Select Name Search

    A small blank text box appears at the bottom of the file list screen where you are to type the beginning letter(s) of the desired file.

    Type the beginning letter of the JOHNSON.LTR file name.

    TIP: These searching functions are not case dependent, so you may use either uppercase or lowercase characters.

3. Type J

    The highlighter moved to the first name beginning with the letter J in the file list. You are still in the Name Search mode with the cursor still blinking in the Name Search text box. You may continue to type one or more of the remaining characters in the file name JOHNSON.LTR if you have more than one file beginning with the letter J, or you may move with the directional arrows to highlight the correct file name.

4. On your own, continue typing **JOHNSON** to highlight the file JOHN-SON.LTR

    To release the Name Search text box and return to the File Manager,

5. Point to the desired file name with the mouse pointer and click once, or press ⌞Esc⌟ to abandon the name search

    NOTE: After you have released the Name Search text box, the item numbers display again on the menu choices along the left side of the screen, meaning that these options are now available.

    Now that you have located the correct file, remember that you could select several options from the File Manager menu such as Open, Copy, Delete, and so on.

6. On your own, close the File Manager dialog box and return to a blank document screen

Using Search to Locate Files

Similar to the Name Search feature is the **Search** F2 option in the File Manager menu. Search also moves the highlighter to a file in the current drive and directory that matches a pattern you supply. The difference between Name Search and Search is that Search begins looking for the correct file name either forward or backward from the current position of your highlighter in the list of files, whereas the Name Search option automatically begins at the top of the list for each new search.

The Search option can be selected from the File Manager menu with the mouse, the keyboard, or the search function keys (forward search with F2, backward search with Shift + F2).

▌ HANDS-ON ACTIVITY

In this exercise, you will ask File Manager to search for the JOHNSON.LTR file, first from the top of the list and then from the bottom of the list.

Make sure you are starting from a blank document window, with your sample disk in drive A.

1. On your own, start File Manager, listing files on drive A

   CAUTION: Make sure that the cursor is located at the top of the file list and your files are sorted alphabetically by file name before beginning any search function. Perform a Sort by ⇒ Filename if necessary.

2. Press Home, Home, ↑

   To begin the search for JOHNSON.LTR,

3. Select Search

   ✓ Press F2

   The Search for Filename dialog box appears as shown in Figure 7-6, prompting you to type the name pattern for this search.

   Enter the file name for the search.

4. Type JOHNSON.LTR

5. Press Enter

   Begin the search.

6. Select Search

   ✓ Press F2

   Your highlighter is now placed on the JOHNSON.LTR file name in the file list.

   Now let's search for the same file, starting at the bottom of the list. First, move to the end of the file list.

7. Press Home, Home, ↓

   To begin the search for JOHNSON.LTR,

8. Select Search

```
┌──────────────────────────────────────────────────────────┐
│▓▓▓▓▓▓▓▓▓▓▓▓▓▓▓▓▓▓▓▓▓ File Manager ▓▓▓▓▓▓▓▓▓▓▓▓▓▓▓▓▓▓▓▓▓▓│
│ Directory: A:\*.*                              06-17-93  03:55p│
│ ┌Sort by: Filename─────────────────────┐▲                  │
│ │  .    Current     <Dir>               │  Open into New Document│
│ │  ..   Parent      <Dir>               │  Retrieve into Current Doc│
│ │  7-2     .TIF        0  06-17-93 03:47p│  Look...          │
│ │  BGRAPH  .SD     2,688  06-06-93 09:03a│                   │
│ │  CONFER  .SD     4,013  06-12-93 03:59p│  Copy...          │
│ │  DOWNSIZE.SD     5┌──Search for Filename──┐Rename...       │
│ │  FEASIBLE.RPT    8│                       │e              │
│ │  FEASIBLE.STE    8│ Text: [             ] │...            │
│ │  JAC     .LTR    1│                       │List           │
│ │  JOHN    .LTR    2│ □ Backward Search     │               │
│ │  JOHNSON .LTR    1│                       │by...          │
│ │  NEWS    .COL    7│ [Search F2]  [Cancel] │e Default Dir...│
│ │  QUARTER .SD     3└───────────────────────┘nt Dir... F5   │
│ │  TABLE   .COL  1,930  06-14-93 09:27a│  Find...           │
│ │  TITLE   .STE    911  06-17-93 11:16a│  Search... F2      │
│ │ ▓WPROCESS.SD   3,583  06-06-93 09:07a│  Name Search       │
│ │                                       │                    │
│ │                                       │▼ * (Un)mark        │
│ │                                       │  Home,* (Un)mark All│
│ └Files:    14───Marked:    0───────────┘                    │
│   Free: 1,008,640 Used:   52,024   [Setup... Shft+F1] [Close]│
└──────────────────────────────────────────────────────────┘
```

Figure 7-6

✓ Press F2

The Search for Filename dialog box appears, prompting you to type the name pattern for this search with the file name from the previous search still displayed. To accept JOHNSON.LTR,

9. Press Enter

Begin the search.

10. Select **Search**

✓ Press F2 or Enter

A dialog box appears, indicating that the file name was not found. To continue and clear this message,

11. Select **OK**

✓ Press Enter

Now try a backward search for the same file.

12. Select S**e**arch

✓ Press F2

The Search for Filename dialog box again appears. Accept the current file name.

13. Press Enter

To search from the bottom upward, make sure the Backward Search check box is marked.

14. Select <u>B</u>ackward Search

    Then begin the search.

15. Select **Search**

    ✓ Press F2 or Enter

    This time the file is found.

16. On your own, close the File Manager dialog box and return to a blank document

▌ Using Find to Search for Text Within Files

The <u>F</u>ind option in File Manager is used to search for all the files in the current directory containing a word or phrase that matches a pattern you provide.

The <u>F</u>ind menu gives you the choice of scanning only file names or only document summaries, or of scanning the actual text of the documents (which takes a bit more time). Find can read just the first page of the documents or the entire documents.

When the <u>F</u>ind option is complete, File Manager displays only the names of files containing the matching text. This provides you with a convenient method of grouping similar files together for functions such as copy, delete, open, and so on.

▌ HANDS-ON ACTIVITY

For example, in this exercise you will search for all the letters written to James Jacobs so that you can copy all his letters to a separate disk for storage. You will ask the <u>F</u>ind option to read the first page of all of your files, looking for "Jacobs" in the inside address. After the Find is complete, only the Jacobs letters will remain listed in File Manager. You will mark all the files so that they can be copied to a disk.

Make sure you are starting from a blank document window, with your sample disk in drive A.

1. On your own, start File Manager, listing files on drive A

2. Select <u>F</u>ind

   The <u>F</u>ind dialog box appears, displaying the Find options as shown in Figure 7-7.

   To search all the text of the files on drive A,

3. Select <u>E</u>ntire Document...

   The Find Word in Entire Document dialog box appears as shown in Figure 7-8. The Word Pattern text box is prompting for the phrase by which to find a word pattern.

   Enter the word pattern to find "Jacobs" in the inside address text of the letters.

4. Type `Jacobs`

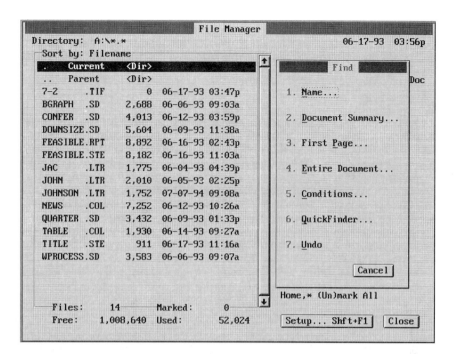

Figure 7-7

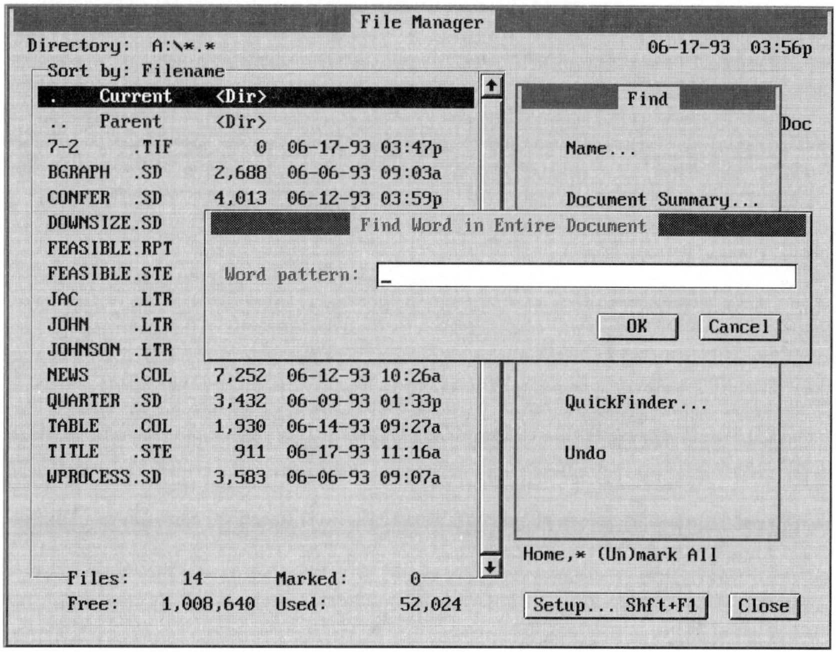

Figure 7-8

5. Select **OK**

    ✓ Press Enter

    The Finding Files message box appears while WordPerfect File Manager is reading the text of all the files in the current directory. You can see the total number of files processed as well as which file is currently being read.

When the find task is complete, only the files containing the word "Jacobs" will be displayed on the list of files. Even though the contents of your disk have not changed, the screen displays only the selected files for display.

6. On your own, use the <u>L</u>ook option to view the contents of the displayed files, verifying that they all contain the name "Jacobs"

Now, let's mark the Jacobs files to visualize grouping these similar files for copying, moving, or deleting.

7. Select **(Un)mark All**

✓ Press (Home), *

Now, unmark them all.

8. Select **(Un)mark All**

✓ Press (Home), *

Now, to bring back the list of all files from the current drive and directory, use the feature **.Current**, found at the upper left-hand corner of the list of files.

9. If you are using the keyboard, highlight **.Current** and press (Enter)

or

if you are using the mouse, double-click on **.Current**

The Specify File Manager List dialog box appears with the current drive and directory displayed, followed by the wild card symbols *.*, meaning all files.

To accept A:*.* as your current location,

10. Select **OK**

✓ Press (Enter)

All the files on the disk in drive A will now display.

11. On your own, close the File Manager dialog box and return to a blank document screen

▌ Using QuickList

QuickList is a fast approach WordPerfect offers in Version 6.0 to quickly list the files you use most often. You first define the QuickList setup with a name, such as RESUMES. Then you set the <u>F</u>ilename/Directory, which is the complete path name for the files to be located, including the drive, directory, and optional file name pattern. For example, if the resumes were all in the directory on drive C called JOBS, and were all named with an extension of .RES, the path name for the option <u>F</u>ilename/Directory would read: C:\JOBS *.RES. (The wildcard symbol * stands for any file name.)

▌ HANDS-ON ACTIVITY

In this exercise, you will set up a QuickList definition to list all inquiry letters (extension of .INQ) on drive A. Make sure you are starting from a blank document window, with your sample disk in drive A.

1. Select File ⇒ File Manager

    ✓ Press F5

    The Specify File Manager List dialog box appears and should be assuming A:*.* as the current default.

    If your Directory text box does not display A:*.* as the specified drive,

2. Type **A:**

    Do not press Enter . From the Specify File Manager List dialog box, access the QuickList option.

3. Select QuickList

    ✓ Press F6

    The QuickList dialog box appears as shown in Figure 7-9. Depending upon the way the WordPerfect 6.0 software was installed on your computer, you may see some QuickLists that are already set up for you. If the list is empty, then you know that no other QuickLists have been created. Either way, let's choose the create option to make a new QuickList.

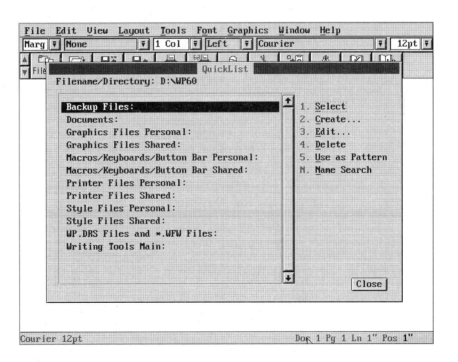

Figure 7-9

4. Select Create

The Create QuickList Entry dialog box appears as shown in Figure 7-10. It is prompting you for a description and a path name for the new index.

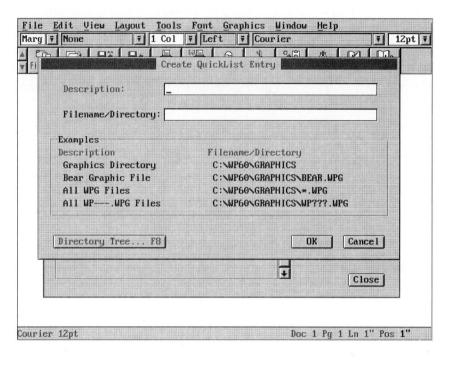

Figure 7-10

We will describe this index as INQUIRY LETTERS. Enter the Description text.

5. Type `INQUIRY LETTERS`

To move to the next blank text box in the dialog box,

6. Press (Enter), or (Tab), or (↓)

Enter the Filename/Directory location that will be indexed and the search pattern to be recalled. The examples shown on the lower portion of this dialog box are helpful to demonstrate some different hard disk variations to specify drives, directories, and file name patterns in the Filename/Directory text box.

We will search for inquiry letters on drive A, all files ending with .INQ (A:*.INQ).

7. Type `A:\*.INQ`

8. Press (Enter), or (Tab), or (↓)

To complete the Create QuickList Entry dialog box,

9. Select **OK**

✓ Press (Enter)

Your new QuickList descriptive name (INQUIRY LETTERS) appears in alphabetical order on the QuickList screen. To use the INQUIRY

LETTERS QuickList file as a search pattern, make sure the INQUIRY LETTERS QuickList is highlighted.

10. Select **U**se as Pattern

    The Specify File Manager List dialog box appears to verify the search syntax. It reads A:*.INQ.

11. Select **OK**

    ✓ Press [Enter]

    The QuickList has filtered the file names on drive A and the File Manager screen now only displays those ending with an .INQ extension.

12. Close the File Manager dialog box and return to a blank document

13. On your own, create another QuickList called LETTERS to search for files ending with .LTR on drive A

14. On your own, use your newly created QuickList called LETTERS to retrieve a file

▌ Using QuickFinder

WordPerfect's **QuickFinder** offers a faster way to search for words or phrases in documents than using the regular Search option from the File Manager menu. QuickFinder provides almost instantaneous results since it refers to an index rather than reading every word in each document while looking for a matching word pattern. Another advantage in using QuickList to search is that once you set up an index for searches, the setup is stored and can be used again at any time without rebuilding the search criteria.

To access QuickFinder, you begin by opening File Manager, either with the File option from the menu bar or by pressing [F5].

Creating a QuickFinder Index

To use QuickFinder, first you create an index, which is an alphabetical list of every word contained in all the files and directories you specify. An index file is named with an .IDX extension and is stored in a highly compressed format for QuickFinder access only. You cannot edit the index like a normal document, but you can use the Search Index menu to find files containing the words or phrases you need.

▌ HANDS-ON ACTIVITY

In this exercise, you will create an index file for all the inquiry files on your sample disk. Then the inquiry index file will be used to search for all inquiries containing the city name "Broomfield."

Make sure you are starting from a blank document screen, with your sample disk in drive A.

1. Select **F**ile ⇒ **F**ile Manager or click on the **File Mgr** button on the Button Bar

✓ Press F7

The Specify File Manager List dialog box appears and should be verifying A:*.* as the current default following your last exercise.

NOTE: If your Directory text box does not display A:*., type A: as the specified drive.*

2. Type **A:**

Do not press Enter. From the Specify File Manager List dialog box, access the Use QuickFinder option.

3. Select **Use QuickFinder**

✓ Press F4

The QuickFinder File Indexer dialog box appears as shown in Figure 7-11.

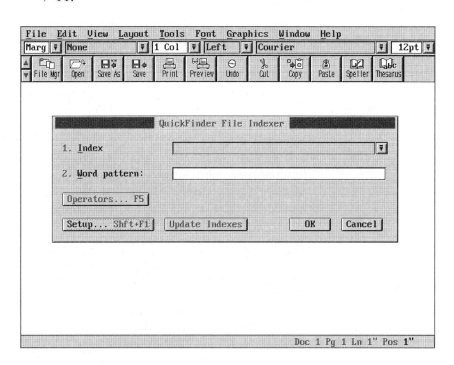

Figure 7-11

Before an index can be named, you must define the drive and directory location where the index files will be saved.

4. Select **Setup**

✓ Press Shift + F1

The QuickFinder File Indexes Setup dialog box appears, as shown in Figure 7-12. The option for Location of Files is the only option available (marked in bold and surrounded by a dotted box).

5. Select **Location of Files**

The QuickFinder Index Files dialog box appears, as shown in Figure 7-13.

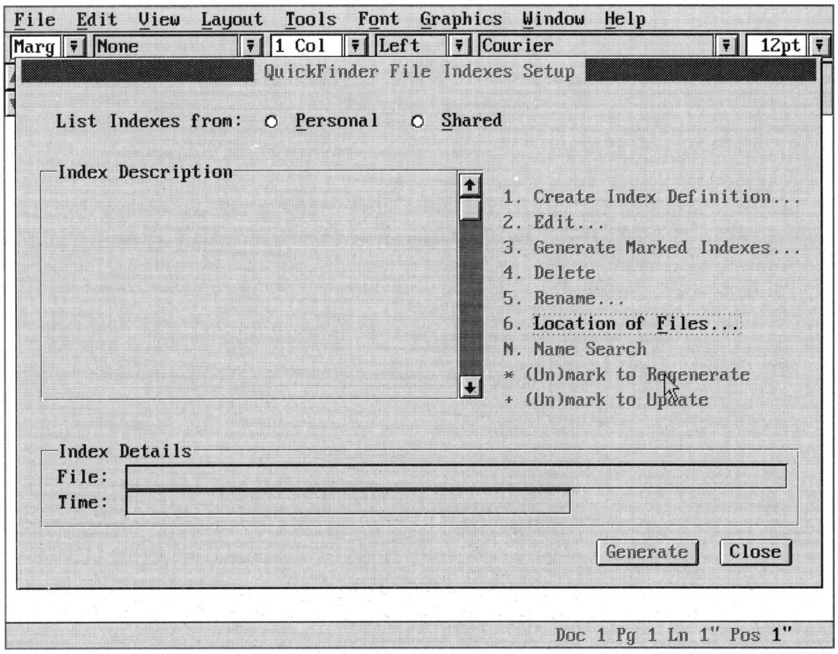

Figure 7-12

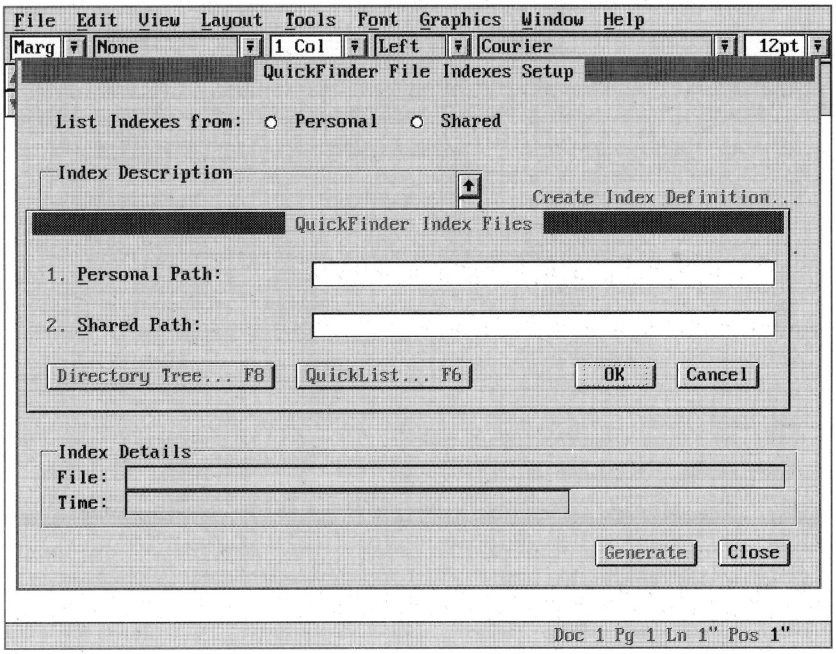

Figure 7-13

The options shown are to set either a personal path or a shared path for the location of the index file. Personal path would be used for a nonnetworked computer, whereas shared path would be used on a networked computer if you wanted to set up indexes that could be used by many different people using the network. You will be setting a personal path to drive A.

6.   Select **P**ersonal Path

7. Type **A:**

8. Select **OK**

   ✓ Press ⌷Enter⌷

The QuickFinder File Indexes Setup dialog box returns. Next you will create an index definition that includes the name and search path used to determine which files and directories are to be used for your word search.

9. Select <u>C</u>reate Index Definition...

The Create Index Definition dialog box appears, as shown in Figure 7-14.

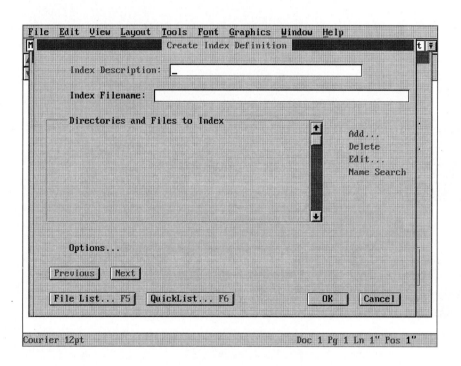

Figure 7-14

The cursor is positioned in the Index Description text box.

Since this index will be used to search all inquiry letters for specified cities, you will name the index Inquiry.

10. Type **Inquiry**

11. Press ⌷Enter⌷

The first eight characters of the descriptive name have been automatically inserted for the index file name. You may either accept this name with ⌷Enter⌷ or type a different name. We will accept "Inquiry."

12. Press ⌷Enter⌷

The Index Filename should read, "A:\INQUIRY.IDX."

13. Select <u>A</u>dd

The Add QuickFinder Index Directory Pattern dialog box now appears, as shown in Figure 7-15.

```
 File  Edit  View  Layout  Tools  Font  Graphics  Window  Help
M                          Create Index Definition                    t
       Index Description: inquiry

       Index Filename:  A:\INQUIRY.IDX
      ┌Directories and Files to Index──────────────────┐
      │       Add QuickFinder Index Directory Pattern   │
      │                                                 │
      │   Filename Pattern:                             │
      │                                                 │
      │   □ Include Subdirectories                      │
      │                                                 │
      │   [ File List... F5 ]  [ QuickList... F6 ]   [ OK ]  [ Cancel ]
      └─────────────────────────────────────────────────┘


       Options...

      [ Previous ]  [ Next ]

      [ File List... F5 ]  [ QuickList... F6 ]

Courier 12pt                              Doc 1 Pg 1 Ln 1" Pos 1"
```

Figure 7-15

You are being prompted for the Filename Pattern. Remember, a file name pattern specifies which files to read and can include drives, directories, and file name specifications with wild card characters, such as C:\WP60DOCS*.LTR.

NOTE: To set up a search index for all files on the hard disk starting at the root directory, you would enter C:*. as the file name pattern. Then mark the check box for including all subdirectories.*

In this example, you want to be able to use this index to search all inquiry files ending with the extension .INQ on drive A.

14. Type `A:\*.INQ`

15. Select **OK**

    ✓ Press [Enter] twice

The Create Index Definition dialog box returns displaying the name of your new index.

16. Select **OK**

The index file has been created. In review, the descriptive index name is Inquiry, the index file name is INQUIRY.IDX, and the file name search pattern is A:*.INQ (to read all inquiry files on drive A).

Up to this point, you have not instructed QuickFinder which words to search for, but only which drives, directories, and files to use for the search. At this time, a blank index structure has been set up but has not scanned the data files. To tell the index file to actually read the disk and alphabetize all the words in the specified file path, you must select Generate either from the QuickFinder File Indexes Setup menu or with the Generate button.

Make sure the Inquiry index is highlighted in the QuickFinder File Indexes Setup dialog box.

17. Select **Generate Marked Indexes...**

The generate screen displays with a status screen showing:

- The name of the index being used
- The elapsed time
- The number of files indexed
- The number of bytes processed
- The current completion status

After generation is complete, the QuickFinder File Indexes Setup dialog box returns. The generate item is no longer listed in bold on the menu, meaning that you have already used that option. Now we are ready to exit the QuickFinder File Indexes Setup dialog box.

18. Select **Close**

You have now returned to the QuickFinder File Indexer dialog box where you can specify the words or phrases to be selected by the index file for the search. You are searching for all the inquiry letters addressed to the city of Broomfield, CO.

19. Type **Broomfield**

20. Select **OK**

The File Manager list of files appears displaying only the file names containing the word "Broomfield."

21. On your own, one by one, move to each of the file names shown in the list, and select **Look** from the menu to view the text of the file. Check to see if the city of Broomfield is actually found in each of the files listed

22. Close the File Manager dialog box and return to a blank document

Using Existing Indexes for a Search

In this exercise, you will use the existing index INQUIRY to search for any inquiries containing the city name BOULDER.

Make sure you are starting from a blank document window, with your sample disk in drive A.

1. Select **File** ⇒ **File Manager** or click on the **File Mgr** button on the Button Bar

✓ Press F5

The Specify File Manager List dialog box appears and should be verifying A:*.* as the current default, following your last exercise.

NOTE: If your Directory text box does not display A:*., type* **A:** *as the specified drive.*

2. Type **A:**

   Do not press [Enter]. From the Specify File Manager List dialog box, access the QuickFinder option.

3. Select <u>U</u>se QuickFinder

   ✓ Press [Enter]

   The QuickFinder File Indexer dialog box appears.

4. Use either the mouse or the keyboard to open the drop-down list box in order to select your sample index, INQUIRY

5. Select **Inquiry** (double-click with the mouse)

   ✓ Press [Enter]

   The word pattern text box is prompting you for the search word or phrase.

6. Type **Boulder**

7. Select **OK**

   ✓ Press [Enter] twice

   The File Manager list of files displays the files containing the city of Boulder, CO. You may again want to use the Look option to verify that the correct files are listed.

8. On your own, close File Manager and return to a blank document window

Review of Commands

Description	Menu Commands	Function Keys
Copy a file		
Rename a file		
Delete a file		
Look at a file		
Sort files by name		
Mark all files		
Print a file from disk		
Use a QuickFinder index to search for a word		

▮ Lesson Review

1. List two advantages of using the File Manager.

2. What is the advantage of specifying a default drive?

3. What keystroke combination allows you to select and deselect all files in the File Manager?

4. What is a fast way to copy several files from one disk to another?

5. When you delete a file, can you Undo that deletion in WordPerfect?

6. What File Manager feature allows you to quickly locate a file name?

7. Do you need to open a document before you print it?

8. Why is QuickFinder faster than the File Manager Find feature for searching for words or phrases?

▮ Assignments

7.1 Directions

1. Access File Manager and display a list of the files on your sample disk in drive A.

2. Select the JOHNSON.LTR file.

3. Copy the file JOHNSON.LTR to a new file named PRACTICE .LTR.

4. Open the file PRACTICE.LTR and change the zip code from 80304 to 80203.

5. Save and Close the letter.

6. Access File Manager and display a list of the files on your sample disk in drive A.

7. Rename PRACTICE.LTR to SAMPLE.LTR.

8. Print a copy of SAMPLE.LTR from the File Manager menu.

9. Close File Manager.

7.2 Directions

1. Access File Manager and display a list of the files on your sample disk in drive A.

2. Sort the files by extension.

3. Mark all the files with an .INQ extension.

4. Now, unmark all files.

5. Sort the files alphabetically by file name in reverse (descending) order.

6. Use Find to locate all the documents containing the word "brochure."

8

Working with Multiple Documents

Objectives

Upon completion of this lesson, you will be able to do the following:

- Save a block of text to disk
- Open a clear document window
- Retrieve a file into an open document
- Switch to another document
- Frame a document window
- Cascade the open document windows
- Move and size a window
- Minimize and maximize a window
- Tile the open document windows
- Copy and paste information between document windows
- Close a document
- Exit all document windows and WordPerfect

This lesson will show you how to manage multiple documents, display more than one document on the screen, transfer information between two documents, and minimize and maximize windows.

Starting Point
Before beginning the lesson, start WordPerfect 6.0. The document window should be blank. Make sure the Train Button Bar and Ribbon are displayed. Locate the sample disk provided by your instructor used in Lesson 5. Open the document called JAC.LTR.

Saving a Block of Text
In the last few lessons, you have used the Block feature for many different purposes, such as cut and paste, case conversion, bolding and underlining text, and so on.

175

You can also use the Block feature to block a portion of a document, then save it as a new document. This feature is called **Block Save**. This allows you to retrieve the saved block of text into another document. This is called **boilerplating**—reusing the same text over and over again in a variety of documents. For example, if you write a variety of proposals, you might include a boilerplate passage describing your company. Rather than retyping this boilerplate text in each document, you can save the repeated information in its own file and then retrieve it into each new document that you create.

The steps for saving a block of text are as follows:

- Use the Block feature (<u>E</u>dit ⇒ <u>B</u>lock, Alt + F4, or F12) to highlight the boilerplate block of text you want to store in a separate file.
- Select <u>F</u>ile ⇒ Save <u>A</u>s or press F10
- The Save Block dialog box appears. Type the name and press Enter

▌ HANDS-ON ACTIVITY

You have received another inquiry about the services that your company, PencilPushers, Inc., provides and, instead of retyping the first paragraph in the JAC.LTR, you are going to use the Block Save feature. The JAC.LTR is located on the sample disk provided by your instructor, and it is the completed version of the letter you wrote to Mr. Jacobs in Lesson 3. For your reference, the first paragraph of the JAC.LTR is shown in Figure 8-1.

Thank you for your inquiry regarding the services provided by PencilPushers, Inc. Our goals are to enhance the performance of our clients by providing administrative solutions without jeopardizing operating costs with added expenses of personnel and equipment.

Figure 8-1

1. Position the cursor at the beginning of the paragraph

2. Select <u>E</u>dit ⇒ <u>B</u>lock

   ✓ Press Alt + F4, or F12

3. On your own, block the first paragraph, by either pressing the ↓ 5 times on the keyboard or quadruple-clicking with the mouse

4. Select <u>F</u>ile ⇒ Save <u>A</u>s

   ✓ Press F10

   The Save Block dialog box appears, as shown in Figure 8-2.

   To name the block of text,

5. Type `A:INTRO.PAR`

   The .PAR extension will identify the file as a boilerplate paragraph.

6. Select **OK**

   ✓ Press Enter

```
 File   Edit   View   Layout   Tools   Font   Graphics   Window   Help
Marg ▼ None                    ▼ 1 Col ▼ Left ▼ Courier                    ▼ 12pt ▼
▲ ┌┐   ┌→   ┌┐    ┌┐   ┌─┐   ┌─┐   ⊖    ✂    ┌─┐   ┌─┐   ┌─┐   ┌─┐
▼ File Mgr  Open  Save As  Save  Print  Preview  Undo  Cut  Copy  Paste  Speller  Thesarus
  (today's date)




   Mr┌──────────────────── Save Block ──────────────────────┐
   Te│                                                        │
   10│   Filename: ┌──────────────────────────────────────┐  │
   Bo│             └──────────────────────────────────────┘  │
     │                                                        │
   De│  ┌ File List... F5 ┐  ┌ QuickList... F6 ┐   ┌ OK ┐  ┌ Cancel ┐ │
   ▓▓└────────────────────────────────────────────────────────┘
   ▓▓PencilPushers, Inc.  Our goals are to enhance the performance of
   ▓▓our clients by providing administrative solutions without
   ▓▓jeopardizing operating costs with added expenses of personnel and
   ▓▓equipment.

     Our company offers a variety of services ranging from general
     office staffing, bookkeeping, word processing, client billing, as
     well as financial reporting, forecasting and consulting.
     PencilPushers, Inc. incorporates the NASS Industry Production
     Standard into its business practices and also subscribes to the
     NASS Code of Business Ethics.
 Block on                                    Doc 1 Pg 1 Ln 4.17" Pos 1"
```

Figure 8-2

Opening a Clear Document Window

WordPerfect allows you to have up to nine document windows open at one time. You can create new documents, open existing ones, or both. The File ⇒ New feature will give you a clear working document window in which you can create a new document. The status line will indicate the document number. For example, if you have one document open and you execute the File ⇒ New feature, the status line will read "Doc 2."

▌ HANDS-ON ACTIVITY

In this exercise, you are going to get a clear working document window in which you will create a letter to Dr. Mary Webster.

1. Select File ⇒ New

    You now have a clear working screen and the status line reads "Doc 2."

2. On your own, insert the Date Code and press ⟨Enter⟩ 6 times

3. Type:
    ```
    Dr. Mary Webster
    Flatirons Medical Center
    700 Grape Street
    Boulder, CO 80302

    Dear Dr. Webster:
    ```

Retrieving a File into an Open Document

When you execute the File ⇒ Open feature, WordPerfect automatically places the file into an empty document window. To retrieve a file into an existing file, you choose File ⇒ Retrieve. After you type the file name and press ⟨Enter⟩, the retrieve document is inserted at the position of the cursor.

▌ **HANDS-ON ACTIVITY**

In this exercise, you are going to retrieve into the current document the paragraph you blocked and saved from Mr. Jacobs's letter.

1. Position the cursor two lines below the salutation, "Dear Dr. Webster:"

2. Select <u>File</u> ⇒ <u>Retrieve</u>

   ✓ Press [Shift] + [F10]

   The Retrieve Document dialog box appears, as shown in Figure 8-3.

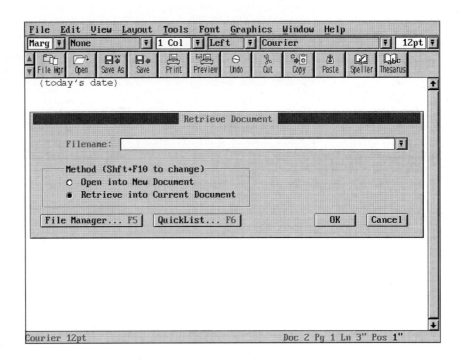

Figure 8-3

CAUTION: *Select the "Retrieve into Current Document" option but-ton if it is not already selected.*

The cursor is positioned in the Filename text box ready for you to type a file name.

3. Type **A:INTRO.PAR**

4. Select **OK**

   ✓ Press [Enter]

   Compare your document to the one shown in Figure 8-4.

   You are now going to open another file. The file is named JOHN.LTR and is located on the sample disk that is provided by your instructor. This is the letter to Mr. Johnson that you used in Lesson 5.

5. Select <u>File</u> ⇒ <u>Open</u>

   ✓ Press [Shift] + [F10]

> (today's date)
>
>
> Dr. Mary Webster
> Flatirons Medical Center
> 700 Grape Street
> Boulder, CO 80302
>
> Dear Dr. Webster:
>
> Thank you for your inquiry regarding the services provided by PencilPushers, Inc.
> Our goals are to enhance the performance of our clients by providing
> administrative solutions without jeopardizing operating costs with added expenses
> of personnel and equipment.

Figure 8-4

6. Type `A:JOHN.LTR`

7. Select **OK**

    ✓ Press Enter

    You now have three documents open. The JOHN.LTR is in the current document window; notice that the status bar reads "Doc 3."

Switching to Another Document

The **Switch** feature allows you to move between the current document window and the last document window accessed. If the Switch feature is executed when only one document window is open, a blank, working document window displays and the status line reads "Doc 2." To execute the Switch command, select <u>W</u>indow ⇒ <u>S</u>witch (*Shortcut keys:* Shift + F3).

By contrast, the **Switch To** feature displays a list of all open document windows, indicating the document file name alongside the corresponding document number shown in the status bar for each document. If a document has not been saved, the Switch To feature shows it as untitled and indicates the corresponding document number. To access the Switch To feature, select <u>W</u>indow ⇒ S<u>w</u>itch To (*Shortcut key:* F3). The Switch To Document dialog box appears, listing the open document windows. To switch to a specific window, type the number of the window or double-click on the file name with the mouse.

HANDS-ON ACTIVITY

In this exercise, you are going to experiment with both the <u>S</u>witch and the S<u>w</u>itch To features. The JOHN.LTR should be the active document window. To move to the last active document, which is the document to Dr. Webster,

1. Select <u>W</u>indow ⇒ <u>S</u>witch

✓ Press Shift + F3

The letter to Dr. Webster is now shown in Doc 2. Notice your status line.

Now you are going to use the S<u>w</u>itch To feature to move to Doc 1, which is the letter to Mr. Jacobs.

2. Select <u>**Window**</u> ⇒ S<u>**w**</u>**itch To**

    ✓ Press F3

    The Switch to Document dialog box appears, as shown in Figure 8-5.

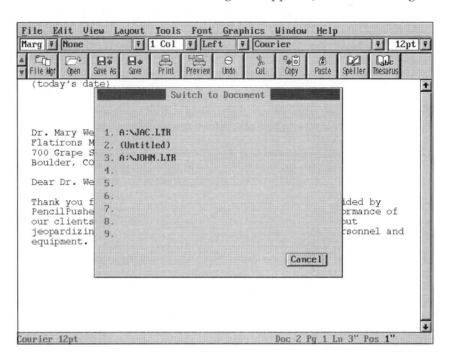

Figure 8-5

The Switch to Document dialog box indicates that document 2 is untitled, since you have not saved the letter to Dr. Webster. Now, you are going to display the JAC.LTR.

3. Press **1**

    A shortcut to move from one document window to another is available if you know the corresponding document number of the desired document. To display a specific window, press Home and then type the document number.

    Use the shortcut to move to Dr. Webster's letter in document 2.

4. Press Home

5. Type **2**

    Using the shortcut to move to the JOHN.LTR in document 3,

6. Press Home

7. Type **3**

▊ Framing a Document Window

Each time you start WordPerfect, a clear document window displays for you to begin typing text. The document window fills the entire screen. A document window can be displayed within a **frame**, thus providing **control tools** on the frame in which you can move, size, or exit a document window. The control tools can only be accessed by using a mouse. The document window you are currently working in is called the **active window**. The active window can be moved, sized, minimized, maximized, or closed.

To place a frame around a document window, select <u>W</u>indow ⇒ <u>F</u>rame (*Shortcut keys:* Ctrl + F3 , 1, 2). A frame is placed around the document window. Displaying a document window in a frame can be accomplished in any View mode—Text, Graphics, or Page. Figure 8-6 shows the control tools of a frame.

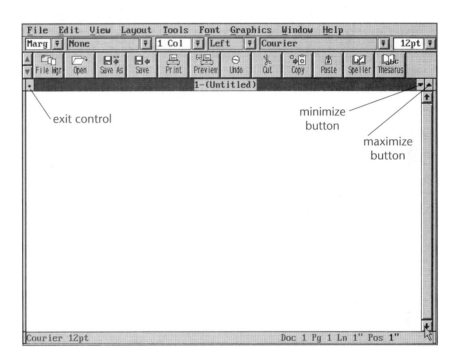

Figure 8-6

▊ HANDS-ON ACTIVITY

In this exercise, you are going to frame the active document window, which is the JOHN.LTR document.

1. Select <u>W</u>indow ⇒ <u>F</u>rame

    ✓ Press Ctrl + F3 , **1, 2**

    Compare your screen to the one shown in Figure 8-7.

▊ Cascading the Document Windows

Use the **Cascade** feature to automatically arrange all open windows so that they overlap with their title bars showing. When the Cascade feature is activated, all open document windows are automatically framed. To cascade all open document windows, select <u>W</u>indow ⇒ <u>C</u>ascade (*Shortcut keys:* Ctrl + F3 , 1, 5).

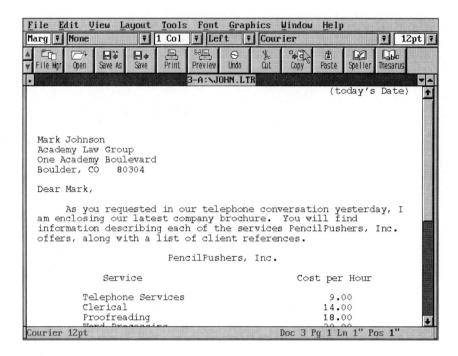

Figure 8-7

▌HANDS-ON ACTIVITY

With the three document windows you have open, in this exercise you will cascade them so that they overlap with their title bars showing. Then you will switch from one document to the next.

1. Select <u>W</u>indow ⇒ <u>C</u>ascade

    ✓ Press Ctrl + F3 , 1, 5

    You can now see the title bars for all three documents displayed at the top of the working window. Also, notice that in addition to the file name, a number indicates the order in which the files were opened. JOHN.LTR is the active file. It is the one on the top of the stack with a colored title bar (if you have a color monitor on your computer).

    Compare your screen to the one in Figure 8-8.

    Now switch the active file to JAC.LTR.

2. *Mouse Users:* Point to the title **JAC.LTR** and click

    Keyboard Users: Select <u>W</u>indow ⇒ <u>S</u>witch, then select **JAC.LTR**

    Now JAC.LTR is on the top with a colored title bar but the two other files are not neatly cascaded and need to be restacked.

3. Select <u>W</u>indow ⇒ <u>C</u>ascade

4. On your own, make JOHN.LTR the active window and use the Cascade feature to overlap the title bars of the 3 open windows

▌Moving a Window

To move a framed window with the mouse, position the mouse pointer in the title bar, drag the window to the desired position, and release the mouse button.

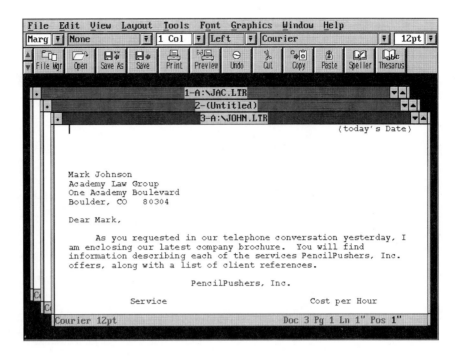

File Edit View Layout Tools Font Graphics Window Help

Marg ▼ None   ▼ 1 Col ▼ Left ▼ Courier   ▼ 12pt ▼

File Mgr | Open | Save As | Save | Print | Preview | Undo | Cut | Copy | Paste | Speller | Thesarus

1-A:\JAC.LTR
2-(Untitled)
3-A:\JOHN.LTR

(today's Date)

Mark Johnson
Academy Law Group
One Academy Boulevard
Boulder, CO   80304

Dear Mark,

    As you requested in our telephone conversation yesterday, I
am enclosing our latest company brochure. You will find
information describing each of the services PencilPushers, Inc.
offers, along with a list of client references.

                    PencilPushers, Inc.

            Service   Cost per Hour

Courier 12pt   Doc 3 Pg 1 Ln 1" Pos 1"

Figure 8-8

To move a framed window with the keyboard, press ⎡Ctrl⎤ + ⎡F3⎤, 1, 9, and use the directional arrow keys to move the window, then press ⎡Enter⎤ or ⎡F7⎤.

Remember, the document window must be framed before you can activate this feature.

▌HANDS-ON ACTIVITY

You are going to move the active window, JOHN.LTR, to the top of the screen. If you do not have a mouse attached to your computer, use the keyboard steps.

Mouse Steps

1. Position the mouse pointer in the title bar

    (The mouse pointer changes shape to a four-headed arrow.)

2. Hold down the left mouse button and drag the window to the top of the screen under the Button Bar

    A "ghost" outline appears, indicating the new position of the window.

3. Release the mouse button

    Compare your screen to the one shown in Figure 8-9.

4. On your own, use the Cascade feature to overlap the title bars of all open windows

Keyboard Steps

1. Press ⎡Ctrl⎤ + ⎡F3⎤

    The Screen dialog box appears, as shown in Figure 8-10.

2. Press **1** or **W** (for **W**indow)

    The Window dialog box appears, as shown in Figure 8-11.

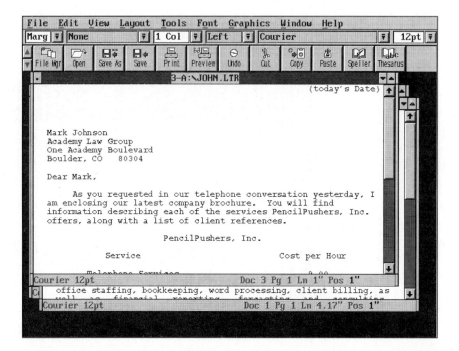

Figure 8-9

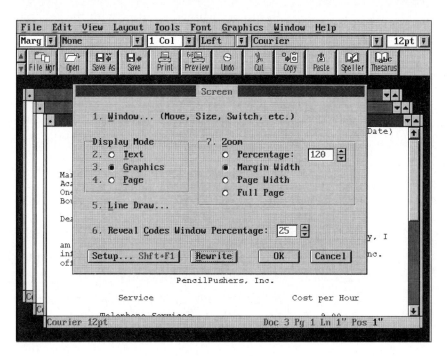

Figure 8-10

3. Press **9** or **M** (for Move)

4. Press ⬆ 3 times

5. Press ⬅ 5 times

6. Press either ⏎ Enter or F7

   Compare your screen to the one shown in Figure 8-9.

7. On your own, use the Cascade feature to overlap the title bars of all open windows

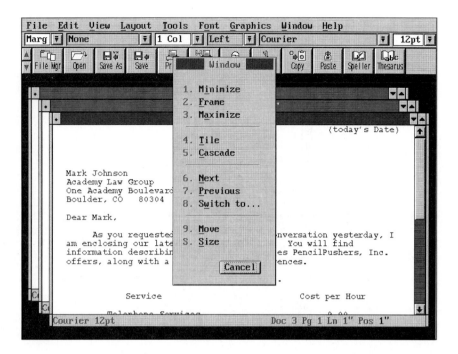

Figure 8-11

▌ Sizing a Window

You can change the size and shape of a framed document window. The minimum size for a document window is approximately 2 inches by 2 inches. The window you want to resize must be the active window and must be framed.

To change the size of a document window using the mouse, move the mouse pointer to a border or corner of the window. The mouse pointer changes to a two-headed arrow. Drag the mouse until the window becomes the desired size and shape, then release the mouse button.

To change the size of a framed document window using the keyboard, press Ctrl + F3, 1, S. Use the direction arrow keys to change the frame, then press either Enter or F7.

▌ HANDS-ON ACTIVITY

In this exercise, you are going to size the active document window, JOHN.LTR. If you do not have a mouse attached to your computer, use the keyboard steps.

Mouse Steps

1. Position the mouse pointer in the lower right-hand corner of the JOHN .LTR document window

    Compare your screen to the one shown in Figure 8-12.

2. Hold down the left mouse button and drag the window diagonally toward the upper-left corner of the window approximately 3 inches

3. Release the mouse button

    Compare your screen to the one shown in Figure 8-13.

4. On your own, use the Cascade feature to overlap the title bars of all open windows

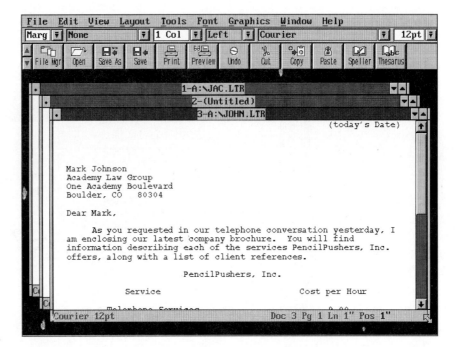

Figure 8-12

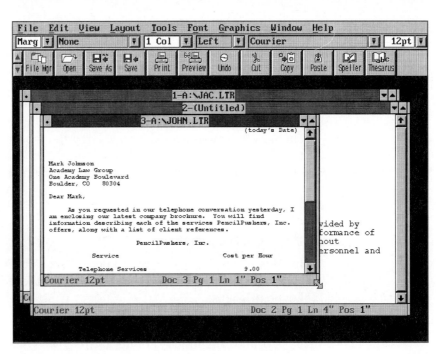

Figure 8-13

Keyboard Steps

1. Press Ctrl + F3

   The Screen dialog box appears.

2. Press 1 or W (for Window)

   The Window dialog box appears.

3. Press **S** (for <u>S</u>ize)

4. Press ⬅ 20 times

5. Press ⬆ 5 times

6. Press either [Enter] or [F7]

    Your screen should look similar to the one shown in Figure 8-13.

7. On your own, use the Cascade feature to overlap the title bars of all open windows

▌ Minimizing a Window

When a framed document window is **minimized,** the window is reduced to a small rectangle. This allows you to view several documents at one time. A document window cannot be minimized unless it is framed.

There are three ways in which to minimize a window:

- Click on the minimize arrow in the upper-right corner of the framed document window.

- Select <u>W</u>indow ⇒ M<u>i</u>nimize.

- Press [Ctrl] + [F3], **1, 1**

▌ HANDS-ON ACTIVITY

You are first going to minimize the active window, JOHN.LTR. If you do not have a mouse attached, move to "Keyboard Steps" section.

Mouse Steps

1. Click on the **minimize arrow**

    Compare your screen to the one shown in Figure 8-14.

Keyboard Steps

1. Press [Ctrl] + [F3]

    The Screen dialog box appears.

2. Press **1** or **W** (for <u>W</u>indow)

    The Window dialog box appears.

3. Press **1** (for M<u>i</u>nimize)

    Your screen should look similar to the one shown in Figure 8-14.

▌ HANDS-ON ACTIVITY

Now, you are going to use the menu method to minimize the next document window, which is the letter to Dr. Webster, currently untitled.

1. On your own, make the Dr. Webster letter the active document

2. Select <u>W</u>indow ⇒ M<u>i</u>nimize

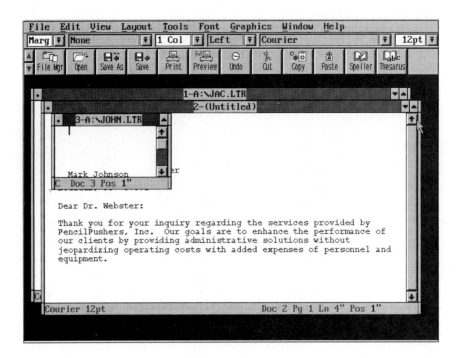

3. On your own, make active and minimize the last window, JAC.LTR, using the method of your choice

    Compare your screen to the one shown in Figure 8-15.

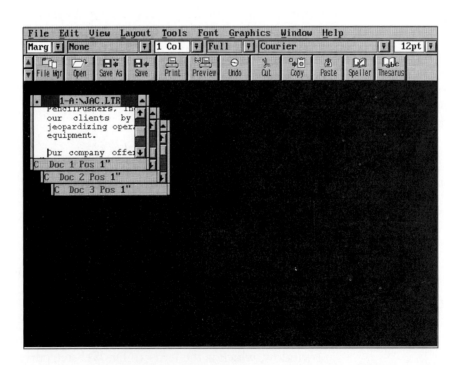

4. On your own, use the Cascade feature to overlap the title bars of all open windows

Notice that your windows have been rearranged. The letter to Mr. Jacobs is now the active window, since it was the last window minimized.

▌ Maximizing a Window

When a window is **maximized** it fills the entire screen, and if the document window was framed the frame no longer displays. As stated previously, whenever you start WordPerfect, you are automatically presented with a maximized document screen so that you can begin typing information. The full screen makes it easier to view and read your documents.

There are three ways in which to maximize a window:

- Click on the maximize arrow in the upper-right corner of the framed document window.
- Select <u>W</u>indow ⇒ <u>M</u>aximize.
- Press Ctrl + F3 , **1, 3**

▌ HANDS-ON ACTIVITY

You are going to maximize the active window, which is JAC.LTR. If you do not have a mouse attached to your computer, move to the "Keyboard Steps" section.

Mouse Steps

1. Click on the **maximize arrow**

   Your document is displayed full screen; notice that the frame has been removed.

Keyboard Steps

1. Select <u>W</u>indow ⇒ <u>M</u>aximize

   ✓ Press Ctrl + F3 , **1, 3**

   Your document is displayed full screen; notice that the frame has been removed.

▌ Tiling the Document Windows

The **Tile** option reduces all open documents into small windows that can all be viewed on the screen at once. To activate the tile feature, select <u>W</u>indow ⇒ <u>T</u>ile (*Shortcut keys:* Ctrl + F3 , 1, 4).

▌ HANDS-ON ACTIVITY

In this exercise, you are going to tile and then cascade the three open document windows.

1. Select <u>W</u>indow ⇒ <u>T</u>ile

   ✓ Press Ctrl + F3 , **1, 4**

   Compare your screen to the one shown in Figure 8-16.

2. On your own, cascade the open windows to see the difference between the two display options

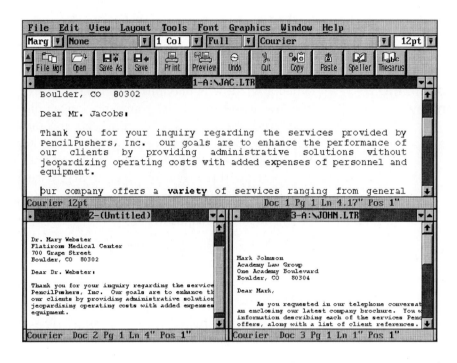

Figure 8-16

Copying and Pasting Between Document Windows

You can copy text, graphics, or codes from one WordPerfect document window to another. To copy, first use the Block feature to highlight what you want to copy, and then select <u>E</u>dit ⇒ <u>C</u>opy (*Shortcut keys:* Ctrl + C). The copied information is placed in a temporary storage area called a **buffer**. To paste the information, first make active the document window that you want to receive the information, and then position the cursor where the copied information is to be inserted. Finally, select <u>E</u>dit ⇒ <u>P</u>aste (*Shortcut keys:* Ctrl + V).

■ HANDS-ON ACTIVITY

You want to copy the first paragraph and the tabular information in Mr. Johnson's letter and paste them in the bottom of Dr. Webster's.

1. Make Mr. Johnson's letter (JOHN.LTR) the active window and maximize the window

2. Using the Block feature, highlight both the first paragraph and the table

    Compare your screen to the one shown in Figure 8-17.

3. Select <u>E</u>dit ⇒ <u>C</u>opy or click on the **Copy** button in the Button Bar

    ✓ Press Ctrl + C

    The copied text has been placed in the buffer. Now, we will use the document number method to switch to the letter to Dr. Webster, by pressing the Home key followed by the corresponding document number. Refer back to Figure 8-16 to see that the document number for the untitled (unsaved) Dr. Webster letter was 2. Now switch to it.

4. Press Home

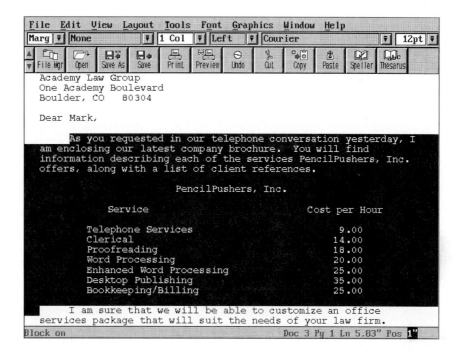

Figure 8-17

5. Type **2**

   To position the cursor at the end of the document,

6. Press [Home], [Home], [↓]

   To paste in the paragraph and tabular material,

7. Select **Edit** ⇒ **Paste** or click on the **Paste** button in the Button Bar

   ✓ Press [Ctrl] + **V**

8. On your own, copy the last paragraph and the signature block of the Mr. Jacobs letter (JAC.LTR) to Dr. Webster's letter

   Compare your document to the one shown in Figure 8-18.

   TIP: An easy way to save files when several documents are open is to tile the screen first and then move from one window to another, making each file active as you save.

   NOTE: If you do not have a mouse on your computer, you may use the menu commands **Window** ⇒ **Next**, **Window** ⇒ **Previous**, *or* **Window** ⇒ **Switch** *to move among tiled windows.*

9. On your own, tile the screen to display all open documents

10. Click in the JOHN.LTR window to make it active

11. Select **File** ⇒ **Save**

12. Click in the JAC.LTR window to make it active

13. Select **File** ⇒ **Save**

(today's date)

Dr. Mary Webster
Flatirons Medical Center
700 Grape Street
Boulder, CO 80302

Dear Dr. Webster:

Thank you for your inquiry regarding the services provided by PencilPushers, Inc. Our goals are to enhance the performance of our clients by providing administrative solutions without jeopardizing operating costs with added expenses of personnel and equipment.

As you requested in our telephone conversation yesterday, I am enclosing our latest company brochure. You will find information describing each of the services PencilPushers, Inc. offers, along with a list of client references.

PencilPushers, Inc.

Service	Cost per Hour
Telephone Services	9.00
Clerical	14.00
Proofreading	18.00
Word Processing	20.00
Enhanced Word Processing	25.00
Desktop Publishing	35.00
Bookkeeping/Billing	25.00

We look forward to the **opportunity** to work with your organization and will contact you next week to schedule an appointment to discuss your specific criteria.

Sincerely,

(your name)
President

Enclosure

Figure 8-18

▌ Closing a Document

You can close the active document window in any of the following ways:

- If the document window is framed, click on the Exit Control button.
  or
- Select File ⇒ Exit.

or

- Press F7 .

▌ HANDS-ON ACTIVITY

You are going to close the Mr. Johnson letter. If you do not have a mouse attached to your system, move to the "Keyboard Steps" section.

Mouse Steps

1. Press Home

2. Type **3**

   Make sure this document window is framed. If not, select <u>W</u>indow ⇒ <u>F</u>rame.

3. Click on the **Exit Control button**

   The document is closed.

Keyboard Steps

1. Press Home

2. Type **3**

   To close the document,

3. Select <u>F</u>ile ⇒ <u>C</u>lose

▌ Exiting All Document Windows

You can exit all document windows and be prompted to save each document before closing its window. To exit all document windows and WordPerfect, select <u>F</u>ile ⇒ E<u>x</u>it WP (*Shortcut keys:* Home + F7).

▌ HANDS-ON ACTIVITY

You are through for the day and wish to save your two document windows, then exit WordPerfect.

1. Select <u>F</u>ile ⇒ E<u>x</u>it WP

   ✓ Press Home , F7

   The Exit WordPerfect dialog box appears, as shown in Figure 8-19.

   Notice the Save check boxes. Document 1 (JAC.LTR) has no X in the check box, indicating that no changes have been made; therefore, the file does not need to be saved. Document 2 *does* have an X in the check box and the file name is blank. The Save and Exit command button is surrounded with a dotted box, indicating it is the default.

2. Press Enter

   Another dialog box appears, as shown in Figure 8-20.

   The cursor is blinking in the Filename text box.

3. Type `A:WEBSTER.INQ`

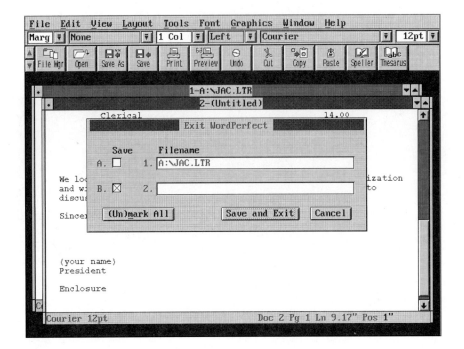

Figure 8-19

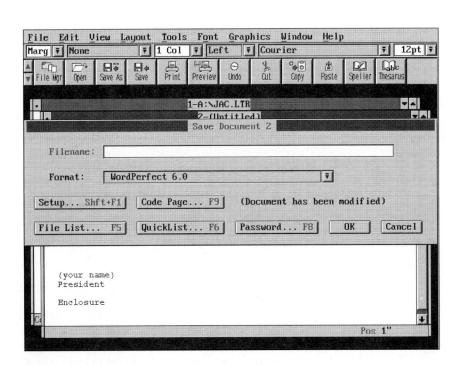

Figure 8-20

4. Select **OK**

    ✓ Press Enter

    The file is saved and you are exited from WordPerfect and returned to the DOS prompt.

Review of Commands

Description	Menu Commands	Function Keys
Block Save	_____	_____
Open a clear working screen	_____	_____
Retrieve a file	_____	_____
Switch	_____	_____
Switch To	_____	_____
Frame a window	_____	_____
Cascade document windows	_____	_____
Move a document window	_____	_____
Size a document window	_____	_____
Minimize a window	_____	_____
Maximize a window	_____	_____
Tile document windows	_____	_____
Copy	_____	_____
Paste	_____	_____
Close a document window	_____	_____
Exit all document windows	_____	_____

Lesson Review

1. Define the term boilerplating.

2. How many documents does WordPerfect allow you to have open at one time?

3. What is the difference between File Open and File Retrieve?

4. Explain the difference between the Switch feature and Switch To.

5. What must be accomplished before a document window can be sized or moved?

6. When documents are "cascaded," how do they appear on the screen?

7. When documents are "tiled," how do they appear on the screen?

8. What keystrokes allow you to access the control tools on a framed document window?

9. Explain how to size a document window using the mouse.

10. What control tool in a framed document window can be accessed to close the current window?

11. Describe a "minimized" document window.

12. Define the term maximized.

13. What does the down-pointing arrow indicate on a frame document window?

14. What menu commands allow you to close all document windows and exit the WordPerfect program?

15. Define the term buffer and tell when it is used.

16. Give two examples of when you might want to have more than one document open at once.

▌ Assignments

8.1   Directions

1. Open the document BGRAPH.SD. (It is on the sample disk provided by your instructor.)

2. Open the document WPROCESS.SD (located on the sample disk).

3. Use the Switch feature to move back to document 1 (BGRAPH.SD).

4. Position the cursor at the end of the document.

5. Cascade the two documents.

6. Tile the two documents.

7. Copy the first two paragraphs of WPROCESS.SD and paste them at the bottom of BGRAPH.SD.

8. Print, save, and close the two documents.

8.2   Directions

1. Open the MAROLD.LTR document.

2. Block save the body of the letter (two paragraphs) and name it VITA.

3. Access a clear document window.

4. Type the following information:

   (current date) / (six blank lines) / Dr. Kevin McMahon / 3000 Court Place / Denver, C0 80226 / Dear Dr. McMahon: / (two lines)

5. Retrieve the VITA document.

6. Type the following signature block:

   Sincerely yours, / (your name), Chairman / Information Systems Department

7. Print the document.

8. Use the Exit WP feature to exit all open document windows. Save the untitled document as MCMAHON.LTR.

9

Advanced Formatting Features

Objectives

Upon completion of this lesson, you will be able to do the following:

- Search for text and codes
- Replace text
- Number document pages
- Use advanced cursor movement
- View a document using the page mode
- Create headers or footers
- Edit a header or footer
- View soft page breaks
- Protect a block of text
- Create a hard page break
- Suppress a header or footer
- Specify a new page number
- Indent text
- Insert special characters
- Select a font

In this lesson you will use features that put the finishing touches on a document. You will learn how to use the indent, search, and replace features; how to place a footer in your document with page numbering; and how to center text vertically on a page.

Starting Point

Before beginning the lesson, start WordPerfect 6.0. The document window should be blank. Make sure the Train Button Bar and the Ribbon are displayed. Locate the sample disk provided by your instructor and open the document called FEASIBLE.RPT. Since this is a long document, we recommend that you print it for reference.

▌ Searching for Text and Codes

Instead of scrolling through a document when you want to modify text or delete a code, such as underlining, WordPerfect has a feature called **Search** that will assist you in locating either text or codes. You can search from the cursor forward or backward in a document.

You can search for text, codes, or a combination of both. When you are searching for text, WordPerfect will find text you are searching for (called the **search string**) even if it is part of another word. For example, if you search for the word "the," WordPerfect would also identify "their," "there," and "them." To search for whole words, the Search dialog box offers a check box to instruct WordPerfect to look only for whole words. This option is not automatically turned on, so be sure to put an X in the check box to activate the whole-words option.

If the search string is typed in lowercase, all occurrences of the text will be found. If you enter the search string in uppercase, only uppercase text is located. The table below illustrates case-sensitive searches:

Searching for	Finds
the	the, The, THE
The	The, THE
THE	THE

To activate the Search feature, choose <u>E</u>dit ⇒ Sear<u>c</u>h (*Shortcut key:* F2). The Search dialog box appears, and the cursor is in the Search For text box. The search string can consist of either text or codes. To search for text, type the text to be located. To search for codes, choose Codes (F5) to display the Codes dialog box. Highlight the desired code and choose Select. A shortcut to entering a code is to press the appropriate function key(s) that activate the specific feature.

Note that if you are using the keyboard to change options in the Search dialog box, there are no preceding numbers or underlined letters by which to select an option. After you have entered the search string, press ↓ to display the options with numbers and underlined letters.

When the Search feature is activated, WordPerfect will automatically search from the cursor to the end of the document. If you wish to search backward—in other words, from the cursor toward the top of the document—turn on <u>B</u>ackward Search in the Search dialog box by placing an X in the check box provided. To begin the search, choose S<u>e</u>arch or press F2 . When the first occurrence of the search string is found, the cursor is positioned at the end of the search string. To locate the next occurrence of the search string, select <u>E</u>dit ⇒ Sear<u>c</u>h (or press F2 twice). WordPerfect will display the last search string; therefore, to begin the search, select S<u>e</u>arch or press F2 .

▌ HANDS-ON ACTIVITY

Upon reflection you have decided that a 150MB disk drive would not be big enough to support tenants in a building of this size and need to change that text to 300MB. In this exercise, you are going to search for the word "150" and replace it with the "300."

1. Position the cursor at the beginning of the document (Home), Home), ↑)

2. Select on **E**dit ⇒ **Searc**h

   ✓ Press F2

   The Search dialog box displays, as shown in Figure 9-1.

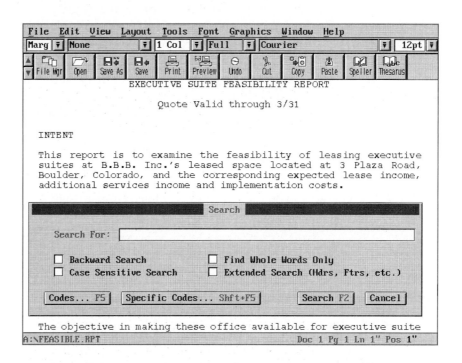

Figure 9-1

The cursor is positioned in the Search For text box.

3. Type **150**

4. Press Enter

5. Select S**e**arch

   ✓ Press F2

   WordPerfect locates the search strings and places the cursor one character to the right of it. To delete the word,

6. Press Ctrl + Delete

7. Type **300**

8. Press Spacebar once

   To see if there is another occurrence of the search string,

9. Select on <u>E</u>dit ⇒ Searc<u>h</u>

   ✓ Press [F2]

   The Search dialog box redisplays and your last search string is displayed in the Search For text box. To begin the search,

10. Select S<u>e</u>arch

    ✓ Press [F2]

    A message appears on the screen, "Not found." To clear the message,

11. Select **OK**

    ✓ Press [Enter]

▌ HANDS-ON ACTIVITY

In this exercise, you are going to implement a backward search to locate the word "revenues."

1. Position the cursor at the end of the document ([Home], [Home], [↓])

2. Select on <u>E</u>dit ⇒ Searc<u>h</u>

   ✓ Press [Shift] + [F2]

   The Search dialog box appears and the previous search string is located in the Search For text box.

   (Note that if you press [Shift] + [F2], the Backward Search check box is automatically turned on.)

3. Type **revenues**

   Be sure to type the word "revenues" in lowercase so that WordPerfect will find all occurrences.

4. Press [Enter]

   To search the document from bottom to top, mark the check box indicating reverse search.

5. Select <u>B</u>ackward Search

   Now, to begin the search,

6. Select S<u>e</u>arch

   ✓ Press [F2]

   To delete the word,

7. Press [Ctrl] + [Delete]

8. Type **income** and press the [Spacebar] once

   To find the next occurrence of the word "revenues," you are going to use the function key since it automatically defaults to a backward search.

9. Press [Shift] + [F2]

The last search string automatically displays in the Search For text box. To begin the search,

10. Press [Enter]

11. Select S**e**arch

✓ Press [F2]

12. On your own, continue the backward search and locate the remaining occurrences of the word "revenues," replacing each with the word "income."

▌ **HANDS-ON ACTIVITY**

In this exercise, you are going to use the Search feature to locate an underline code, so that you can delete it.

1. Position the cursor at the beginning of the document ([Home], [Home], [↑])

2. Select on **E**dit ⇒ Searc**h**

✓ Press [F2]

The Search dialog box displays.

3. Select **Codes**

✓ Press [F5]

The Search Codes dialog box appears, as shown in Figure 9-2.

4. Using the [↓] key, highlight the [Und On] code.

(Note that a quick way to get there is to press **U** and then press [↓] once.)

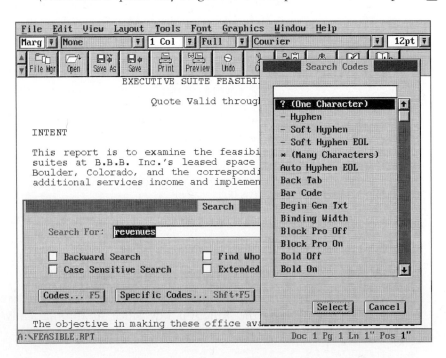

Figure 9-2

5. Select **Select**

   ✓ Press [Enter]

   NOTE: If the previous search string remains in the Search For box, it will be replaced with your new search string, or you may use [Del] or [Backspace] to remove it.

   An [Und On] code is now placed in the Search For text box. To begin the search,

6. Press [Enter]

7. Select S<u>e</u>arch

   ✓ Press [F2]

   When the underline code is located, the cursor is positioned one character to the right of the code. Display your Reveal Codes screen to see the position of the cursor and the underline code.

8. Select <u>V</u>iew ⇒ Reveal <u>C</u>odes

   ✓ Press [Alt] + [F3], or [F11]

   In the Reveal Codes screen, notice that the cursor is positioned on the "f" in the word "feasibility" and the [Und On] is to the left of the cursor.

   To delete the underline code,

9. Press [Backspace]

   Now, you are going to search for a bold code.

10. Select <u>E</u>dit ⇒ Sear<u>c</u>h

    ✓ Press [F2]

    The Search dialog box displays and the cursor is positioned in the Search For text box. Instead of using the Search Codes dialog box to insert a code, you are going to simply press the appropriate function key.

11. Press [F6]

    A [Bold On] code now displays in the Search For text box. To begin the search,

12. Press [Enter]

13. Select S<u>e</u>arch

    ✓ Press [F2]

    In the Reveal Codes screen, notice that the cursor is positioned on the "g" in the word "gross" and the [Bold On] code is to the left of the cursor. To delete the bold code,

14. Press [Backspace]

▊ Replacing Text

The **Replace** feature allows you *both* to locate *and* to replace text or codes in a single operation. You can do this in either the forward or backward direction, for a single occurrence or for all occurrences in the entire document. If you wish to implement this option for the entire document, make sure that the cursor is either at the very beginning or at the very end.

To activate the Replace feature, select Edit ⇒ Replace (*Shortcut keys:* [Alt] + [F2]). The Search and Replace dialog box appears. In the Search For text box, you enter the text and/or codes that are to be searched for, and in the Replace With text box, you type the replacement text and/or codes. WordPerfect will automatically replace all occurrences of the search string unless you choose one of two options—Confirm Replacement or Limit Number of Matches.

To replace one occurrence at a time, which allows you to confirm or reject the replacement, turn on the Confirm Replacement text box. When an occurrence of the text string is located, choose Yes to replace the occurrence, No to not replace the occurrence and skip to the next occurrence, or Replace All to automatically replace all remaining occurrences.

To replace a specified number of occurrences, turn on the Limit Number of Matches check box. WordPerfect will display a text box, allowing you to enter the number of times you want the search string replaced.

To close the dialog box and begin the Search and Replace feature, select Replace or press [F2].

▊ HANDS-ON ACTIVITY

In this exercise you want to replace the word "secretarial" with "administrative." You will initiate and use the Replace feature to accomplish this task.

1. Position the cursor at the top of the document ([Home], [Home], [↑])

2. Select Edit ⇒ Replace

    ✓ Press [Alt] + [F2]

    The Search and Replace dialog box appears, as shown in Figure 9-3.

    The [Bold On] code is positioned in the Search For text box from the previous exercise. To search for "secretarial,"

3. Type `secretarial`

4. Press [Enter]

    The cursor is now in the Replace With text box.

5. Type `administrative`

6. Press [Enter]

    To replace all occurrences without confirmation,

7. Select Replace

    ✓ Press [F2]

    The dialog box shown in Figure 9-4 appears.

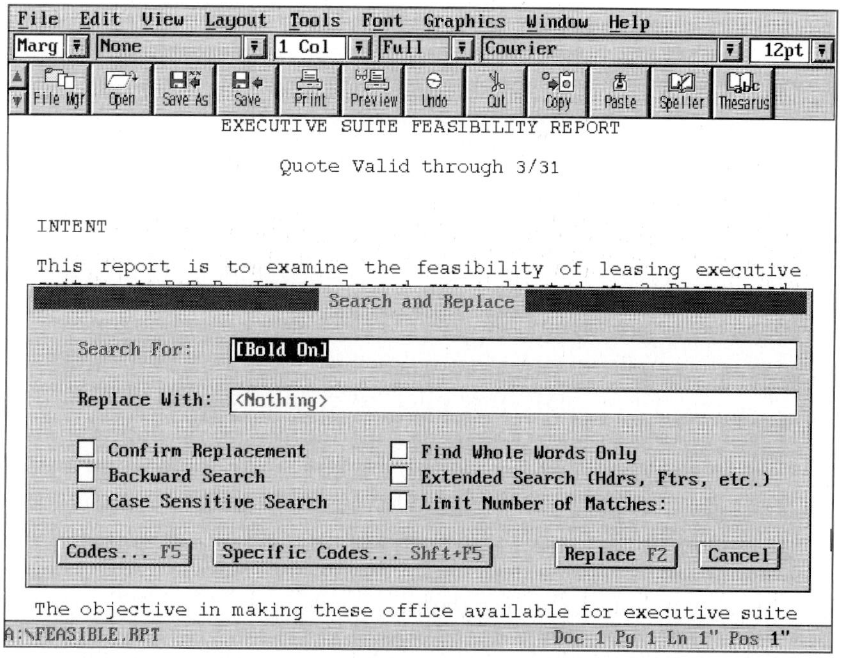

Figure 9-3

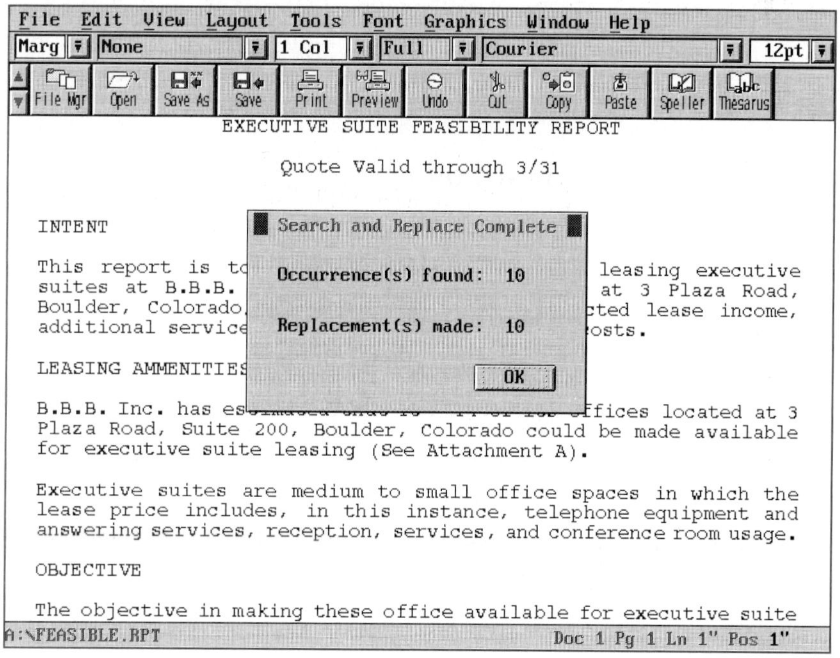

```
File   Edit   View   Layout   Tools   Font   Graphics   Window   Help
Marg ▼ None                    ▼ 1 Col ▼ Full ▼ Courier                    ▼ 12pt ▼
File Mgr  Open  Save As  Save  Print  Preview  Undo  Cut  Copy  Paste  Speller  Thesarus
                    EXECUTIVE SUITE FEASIBILITY REPORT

                        Quote Valid through 3/31


      INTENT

      This report is to examine the feasibility of leasing executive
┌──────────────────────────── Search and Replace ────────────────────────────┐
│                                                                              │
│  Search For:    │[Bold On]                                                │  │
│                                                                              │
│  Replace With:  │<Nothing>                                                │  │
│                                                                              │
│     ☐ Confirm Replacement        ☐ Find Whole Words Only                    │
│     ☐ Backward Search            ☐ Extended Search (Hdrs, Ftrs, etc.)       │
│     ☐ Case Sensitive Search      ☐ Limit Number of Matches:                 │
│                                                                              │
│   [ Codes... F5 ]   [ Specific Codes... Shft+F5 ]     [ Replace F2 ] [ Cancel ] │
└──────────────────────────────────────────────────────────────────────────────┘
      The objective in making these office available for executive suite
A:\FEASIBLE.RPT                                    Doc 1 Pg 1 Ln 1" Pos 1"
```

Figure 9-4

```
File   Edit   View   Layout   Tools   Font   Graphics   Window   Help
Marg ▼ None                    ▼ 1 Col ▼ Full ▼ Courier                    ▼ 12pt ▼
File Mgr  Open  Save As  Save  Print  Preview  Undo  Cut  Copy  Paste  Speller  Thesarus
                    EXECUTIVE SUITE FEASIBILITY REPORT

                        Quote Valid through 3/31


      INTENT
                    ┌──── Search and Replace Complete ────┐
      This report is t│                                   │leasing executive
      suites at B.B.B.│  Occurrence(s) found:   10        │at 3 Plaza Road,
      Boulder, Colorado│                                  │cted lease income,
      additional servic│  Replacement(s) made:   10       │osts.
                       │                                   │
      LEASING AMMENITIE│            [   OK   ]             │
                       └───────────────────────────────────┘
      B.B.B. Inc. has es────────────────────────────ffices located at 3
      Plaza Road, Suite 200, Boulder, Colorado could be made available
      for executive suite leasing (See Attachment A).

      Executive suites are medium to small office spaces in which the
      lease price includes, in this instance, telephone equipment and
      answering services, reception, services, and conference room usage.

      OBJECTIVE

      The objective in making these office available for executive suite
A:\FEASIBLE.RPT                                    Doc 1 Pg 1 Ln 1" Pos 1"
```

To clear the dialog box,

8. Select **OK**

   ✓ Press ⟨Enter⟩

Page Numbering

The **Page Numbering** feature will automatically number the pages of a document for you. The page numbering will begin on the page where the cursor is located. If the Auto Code Placement is active, a [Pg Num Pos] code is placed at the top of the current page to ensure that the code takes effect for the current and subsequent pages. If the Auto Code Placement is turned off, the code is placed at the cursor position and will not begin numbering until the following page. Remember, Auto Code Placement is set with the menu File ⇒ Setup ⇒ Environment ⇒ Autocode Placement.

The page number position can be specified on the top left, top center, top right, bottom left, bottom center, or bottom right. For the numbering methods, you can select Arabic numerals (1, 2, 3), lowercase Roman numbers (i, ii, iii), lowercase letters (a, b, c), uppercase Roman numerals (I, II, III), or uppercase letters (A, B, C).

If you are working with a large document, WordPerfect's page numbering feature offers a secondary page number to assist you in keeping track of a second set of page numbers. Chapter and volume page numbering is available for numbering larger subdivisions of a document.

Page numbers do not appear in a document window in either the Text or Graphics mode, although they will appear when you actually print the document or view with Print Preview. Also, page numbers can be seen in the View Page mode.

To insert a page number, position the cursor at the top of the page where the numbering is to begin (a safe choice for cursor position regardless of the status of Auto Code Placement) and select Layout ⇒ Page (*Shortcut keys:* Shift + F8, 3). The Page Format dialog appears. Select Page Numbering. The Page Numbering dialog box appears. Select Page Number Position to choose the position of the page number.

▌HANDS-ON ACTIVITY

In this exercise, you will use the Page Numbering feature to automatically place a page number in the bottom center of each page in your document.

1. Position the cursor at the top of the document (Home, Home, ↑)

2. Select Layout ⇒ Page

   ✓ Press Shift + F8, 3

   The Page Format dialog appears, as shown in Figure 9-5.

3. Select Page Numbering

   The Page Numbering dialog box appears, as shown in Figure 9-6.

   To specify the page number position as bottom center,

4. Select Page Number Position

   The Page Number Position dialog box appears, as shown in Figure 9-7. (Note the graphic representation of page number positions.)

5. Select Bottom Center

   To exit the Page Number Position dialog box,

6. Select OK

   ✓ Press Enter

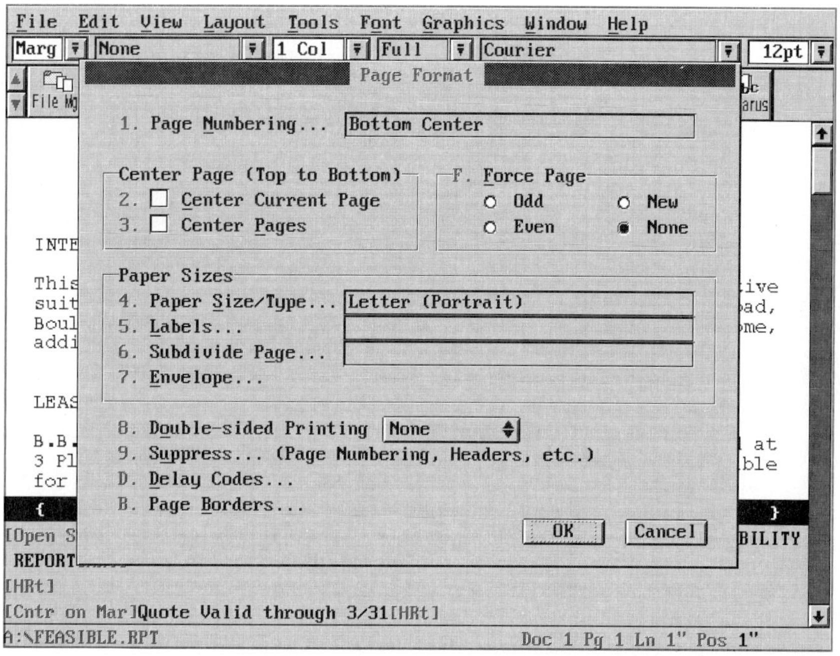

Figure 9-5

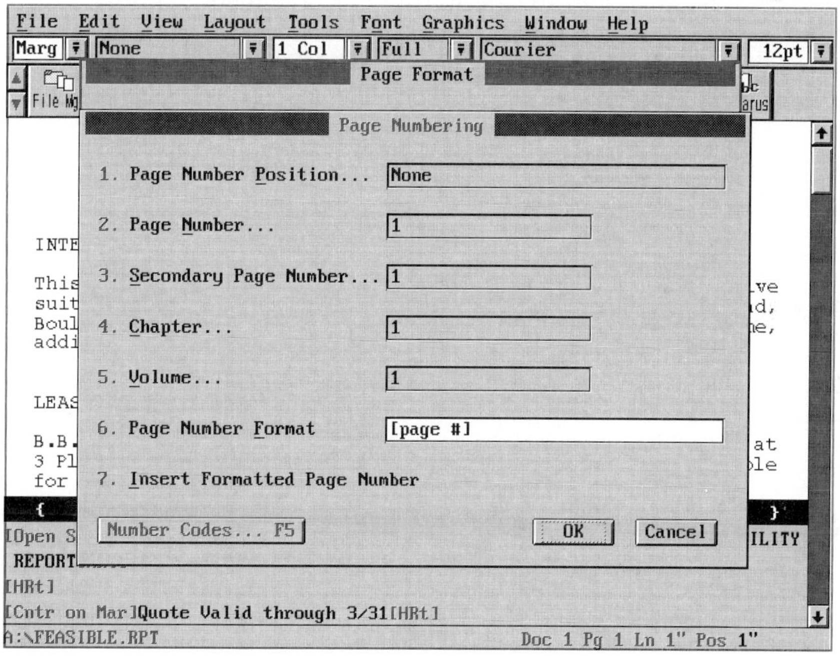

Figure 9-6

You are returned to the Page Numbering dialog box. Notice that the Page Number option is automatically set to 1, indicating that the first page of your document will be numbered as 1.

To exit and save your dialog settings,

7. Select **OK**

    ✓ Press Enter

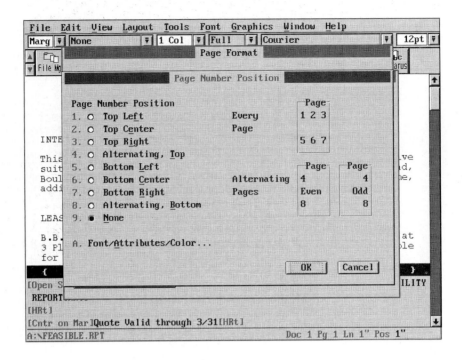

Figure 9-7

To return to your document window,

8. Select **OK** again

✓ Press [Enter]

9. Display the Reveal Codes screen and view the page number code ([Pg Num Pos])

10. On your own, use **File** ⇒ **Print Preview** to view your document as it will print; then use 100% zoom to get a closeup of your page numbers

▌ Advanced Cursor Movement

Since you are working with a multipage document, you will benefit from learning some shortcut keys that make it easier to move from page to page or to a specific page:

[Pg Up]   Moves the cursor to the first line of the previous page

[Pg Dn]   Moves the cursor to the first line of the next page

The Go to feature can be used in conjunction with other keys to move the cursor to a specified position. This feature is initiated by selecting **Edit** ⇒ **Go** to or by holding down [Ctrl] and pressing [Home]. A Go to dialog box appears.

[Go to], [↑]   Moves the cursor to the top of the current page

[Go to], [↓]   Moves the cursor to the bottom of the current page

| [Go to], *number,* Enter | Moves the cursor to the top of the specified page |
| [Go to], Ctrl + Home | Moves to your previous cursor position |

▌ HANDS-ON ACTIVITY

In this exercise, you are going to practice advanced cursor movement. Your cursor should be positioned at the top of your document.

1. Press Pg Dn twice

    Your cursor is at the top of page 3, and the status line is indicating page 3. To move up a page,

2. Press Pg Up

    The cursor is at the top of page 2. To go to the bottom of page 2,

3. Select **E**dit ⇒ **G**o to

    ✓ Press Ctrl + Home

    The Go to dialog box appears, as shown in Figure 9-8.

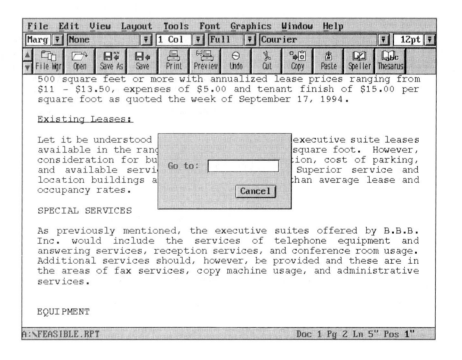

Figure 9-8

4. Press ↓

    The cursor is located at the bottom of page 2. Now, to go to the top of page 2,

5. Select **E**dit ⇒ **G**o to

    ✓ Press Ctrl + Home

    The Go to dialog box appears.

6. Press ⬆

The cursor is located at the top of page 2. Now, to position the cursor at the top of the document,

7. Press Home, Home, ⬆

Viewing a Document with the Graphics Page Mode

As we stated earlier, page numbers cannot be viewed in either the Text or Graphics modes. However, WordPerfect offers a view option called **Page mode** whereby you can view page numbers, headers and footers, footnotes, and labels. Page mode functions similarly to Graphics mode in that it is WYSIWYG (what you see is what you get).

To display Page mode, select <u>V</u>iew ⇒ <u>P</u>age (*Shortcut keys:* Ctrl + F3 , 4).

HANDS-ON ACTIVITY

In this exercise, you are going to turn on Page mode and then view your page numbers.

First, you will activate Page mode:

1. Select <u>V</u>iew ⇒ **<u>P</u>age**

   ✓ Press Ctrl + F3 , **4**

   Now, you will use the Go to feature to locate the cursor at the bottom of the page so that you can view your page numbers:

2. Press Ctrl + Home

   The Go to dialog box appears.

3. Press ⬇ twice

   Compare your page number to the one shown in Figure 9-9. (Look at the top portion of the Reveal Codes screen, *not* at the status line.)

4. On your own, view the remaining page numbers in your document

Creating Headers and Footers

At times you may want to print a date, name, title, page number, or phrase at the top or bottom of every page of a document. A **header** is text that is printed at the top of every page; a **footer** appears at the bottom of every page. You type your header or footer only once, in a special screen. Word-Perfect takes care of printing the header or footer on every page of the document, starting with the page where you activate the Header/Footer feature.

Headers and footers do not appear in a document window in either the Text or Graphics mode and can only be seen when the document is printed or Print Previewed. However, in the View Page mode, headers and footers can be seen in a document window and are displayed as they will appear when printed.

You can create two headers (labeled A, B) and/or two footers (labeled A, B) in a document. You might use two headers (or footers) when you want one header on odd-numbered pages and a different one on even-numbered

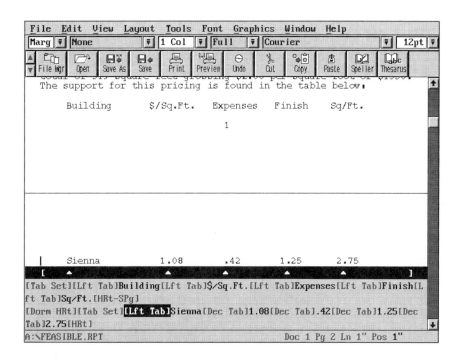

Figure 9-9

pages, as is done in this book. When the same header or footer is to be used on all pages, you simply specify Header A or Footer A.

When creating the header/footer text, you can use almost any WordPerfect feature, such as font changes, centering, flush right, date code, page number, and graphics (which will be covered in Lesson 13).

When WordPerfect enters header/footer text, it calculates the number of lines on the page at the same time. It prints headers at the top of the page just below the top margin, and adds a blank line between the header and the first line of text. Footers are printed just above the bottom margin, and one blank line is inserted between the last line of text and the footer.

To create a header or footer, position the cursor on the page where the header or footer is to first appear (normally at the beginning of the document). Select Layout ⇒ Header/Footer/Watermark (*Shortcut keys:* Shift + F8, 5). The Header/Footer/Watermark dialog box appears. Select either Headers or Footers. If you are creating one header or footer, select Header A (or Footer A). If you have already created one header or footer and are creating a second for alternating pages, select Header B (or Footer B), then choose OK. Another dialog box appears, in which you select the header/footer to be placed on All Pages, Even Pages, or Odd Pages, then choose Create. The WordPerfect Header (or Footer) window appears. Finally, type the text of the header or footer.

To include a page number, select Layout ⇒ Page ⇒ Page Numbering ⇒ Insert Formatted Page Number (*Shortcut keys:* Ctrl + P). To insert the current date, select Tools ⇒ Date ⇒ Code. To insert the file name, select Layout ⇒ Other ⇒ Insert Filename. When you are finished typing the text of the header/footer, press F7 to exit the dialog box and return to the document window. WordPerfect inserts a [Header A] code for Header A, a

[Header B] code for Header B, a [Footer A] code for Footer A, and a [Footer B] code for Footer B.

▌ HANDS-ON ACTIVITY

In this exercise, you are going to create a footer for your feasibility study that includes text and a page number.

1. Position your cursor at the top of the document (Home, Home, ↑)

2. Select Layout ⇒ Header/Footer/Watermark

   ✓ Press Shift + F8, 5

   The Header/Footer/Watermark dialog box appears, as shown in Figure 9-10.

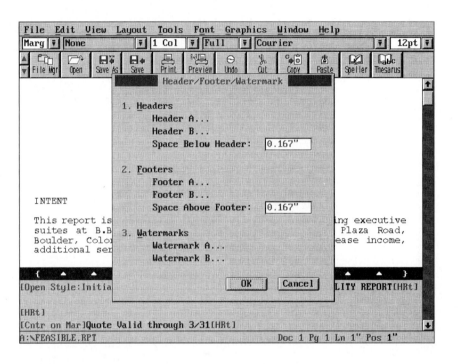

Figure 9-10

3. Select Footers

4. Select Footer A

   The Footer A dialog box appears, as shown in Figure 9-11.

5. Make sure the All Pages radio button is turned on

6. Select Create

   The Footer A window appears. To enter italicized text,

7. Press Ctrl + I

8. Type **Executive Suite Feasibility Report**

   To position the cursor on the right margin, using the Flush Right feature,

9. Press Alt + F6

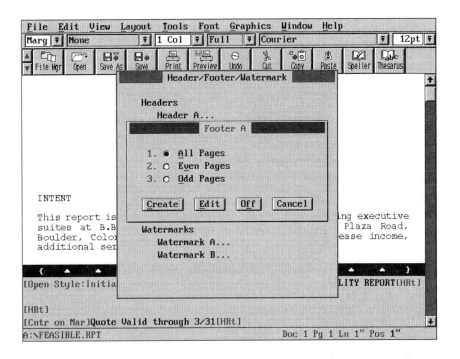

Figure 9-11

10. Type `Page`

11. Press (Spacebar)

    Now, to insert a page number,

12. Select <u>L</u>ayout ⇒ <u>P</u>age ⇒ Page <u>N</u>umbering ⇒ <u>I</u>nsert Formatted Page Number

    ✓ Press (Ctrl) + P

    A number 1 is placed in the Footer A screen, while in the Reveal Codes screen a [Formatted Pg Num] code is inserted. Compare your screen to the one shown in Figure 9-12.

    To exit and return to the document window,

13. Press (F7)

14. On your own, make sure you are in the Page mode; then view your footer

▌ **Editing a Header and Footer**

An existing header or footer may be edited at any time. If you have more than one header or footer, position the cursor on the page where the header or footer you want to edit is in effect. If you have only one header or footer, the cursor can be anyplace in the document. To edit a header or footer, select <u>L</u>ayout ⇒ <u>H</u>eader/Footer/Watermark (*Shortcut keys:* (Shift) + (F8), 5). Select either <u>H</u>eaders or <u>F</u>ooters and then choose either <u>A</u> or <u>B</u>, depending upon the header or footer you wish to edit. When another dialog box appears, choose the pages to be edited (<u>A</u>ll Pages, E<u>v</u>en Pages, or <u>O</u>dd Pages) and select <u>E</u>dit. Make the desired changes and press (F7).

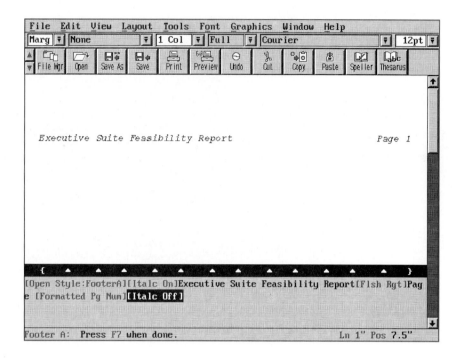

Figure 9-12

▍ **HANDS-ON ACTIVITY**

In this exercise, you are going to edit your footer by adding a graphic line and inserting both the file name and the date code. Since you only have one footer, it does not matter where your cursor is positioned.

1. Select <u>L</u>ayout ⇒ <u>H</u>eader/Footer/Watermark

   ✓ Press Shift + F8 , **5**

   The Header/Footer/Watermark dialog box appears.

2. Select <u>F</u>ooters

3. Select Footer <u>A</u>

   The Footer A dialog box appears. Make sure the <u>A</u>ll Pages radio button is turned on.

4. Select <u>E</u>dit

   The Footer A window displays. Now, you are going to insert a horizontal graphic line and a blank row above the existing footer text. (You will learn more about graphic lines in Lesson 13.)

5. Press Enter twice

6. Press ↑ twice

7. Select <u>G</u>raphics ⇒ Graphic <u>L</u>ines ⇒ <u>C</u>reate

   ✓ Press Alt + F9 , **2, 1**

   The Create Graphics Line dialog box appears, as shown in Figure 9-13.

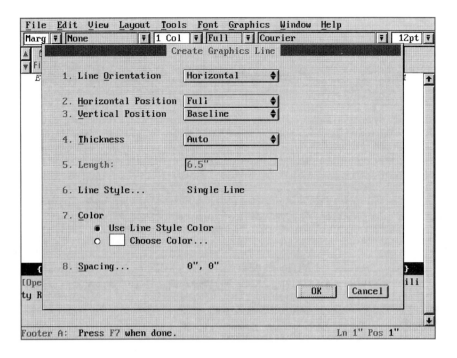

Figure 9-13

8. Select **Thickness**

9. Select **Set**

10. Type **.08**

11. Press ⌐Enter⌐

    To exit the Create Graphics Line dialog box,

12. Select **OK**

    ✓ Press ⌐Enter⌐

    To move to the end of the footer text,

13. Press ⌐Home⌐, ⌐Home⌐, ⌐↓⌐

    To position the cursor on the next line,

14. Press ⌐Enter⌐

    Now the next step is to insert the file name:

15. Select **Layout** ⇒ **Other**

    The Other Format dialog box appears, as shown in Figure 9-14.

16. Select **Insert Filename**

    The Insert Filename dialog box appears, as shown in Figure 9-15.

17. Select **Insert Filename**

    To return to the Footer A screen,

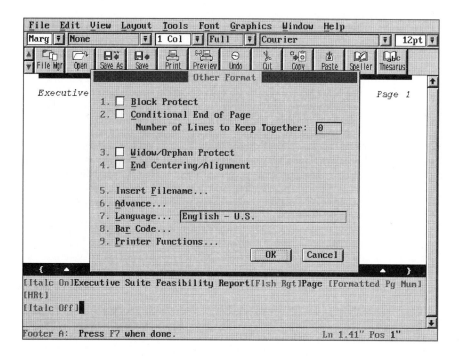

Figure 9-14

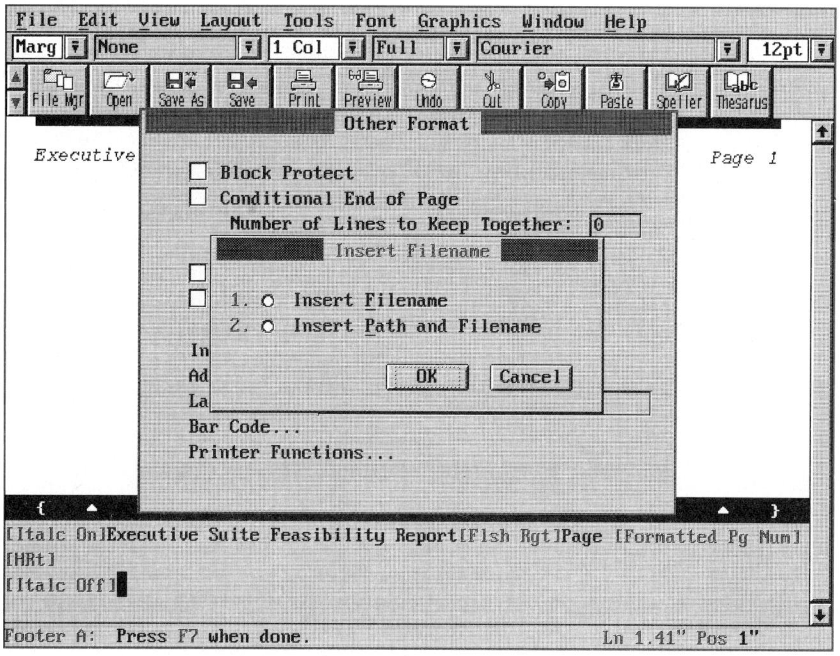

Figure 9-15

18. Select **OK** twice

✓ Press (Enter) twice

Notice that the file name displays in the Footer A screen, while in the Reveal Codes screen a [Filename] code is inserted. Now, you will insert the date code on the right margin. To position the cursor on the right margin, using the Flush Right feature,

19. Select <u>L</u>ayout ⇒ <u>A</u>lignment ⇒ <u>F</u>lush Right

  ✓ Press Alt + F6

20. Select <u>T</u>ools ⇒ <u>D</u>ate ⇒ <u>C</u>ode

  ✓ Press Shift + F5 , **2**

Compare your Footer A screen to the one shown in Figure 9-16.

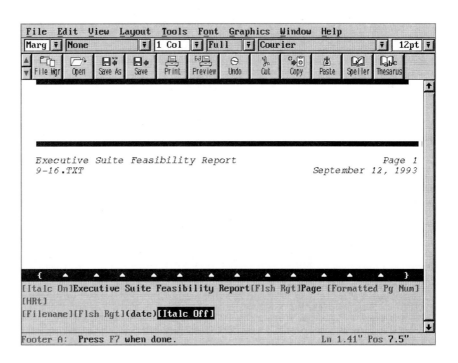

Figure 9-16

To exit and return to the document window,

21. Press F7

22. On your own, make sure you are in the Page mode; then view your footer

Viewing a Soft Page Break

WordPerfect automatically inserts a **soft page break** when the default number of inches (9.67) is reached on a page. A soft page break is shown in your document window as a single horizontal line. In the Reveal Codes screen it is shown as an [SPg] code. This type of page break may be altered by changing the top or bottom margins or by using various options such as the Block Protect feature, described shortly.

▌ HANDS-ON ACTIVITY

Let's look at one of the soft page breaks in your document. Your cursor should be positioned at the top of your document. Let's return to the Graphics mode:

1. Select <u>V</u>iew ⇒ <u>G</u>raphics Mode

2. Press [Pg Dn]

3. Press [↑] 4 times

Compare your document screen to the one shown in Figure 9-17.

```
 File   Edit   View   Layout   Tools   Font   Graphics   Window   Help
 Marg ▼  None            ▼  1 Col  ▼  Full    ▼  Courier            ▼  12pt ▼
 [File Mgr] [Open] [Save As] [Save] [Print] [Preview] [Undo] [Cut] [Copy] [Paste] [Speller] [Thesarus]
    Building          $/Sq.Ft.      Expenses      Finish        Sq/Ft.

    Sienna             1.08          .42          1.25          2.75

    Exeter              .92          .42          1.25          2.59
    Park               1.00          .42          1.25          2.67
    Meadow             1.13          .42          1.25          2.80

 These figures are based on straight lease space of approximately
 500 square feet or more with annualized lease prices ranging from
 $11 - $13.50, expenses of $5.00 and tenant finish of $15.00 per
 square foot as quoted the week of September 17, 1994.

 Existing Leases:

 Let it be understood that there are existing executive suite leases
 available in the range of $1.85 - $3.00 per square foot.  However,
 consideration for building and office location, cost of parking,
 and available services should be made.  Superior service and
 location buildings are maintaining higher than average lease and
 occupancy rates.

 SPECIAL SERVICES

 As previously mentioned, the executive suites offered by B.B.B.
 A:\FEASIBLE.RPT                              Doc 1 Pg 1 Ln 8.67" Pos 1"
```

Figure 9-17

Notice the solid horizontal line, indicating that the text below the line will be printed on another page. The next section illustrates how to use a Block Protect feature to prevent the default soft page break from splitting your table between two pages.

▌ Protecting a Block of Text

The **Block Protect** feature prevents a block of text, such as a tabular table or a chart, from being divided between two pages. To use this feature, select the block of text to be protected and choose <u>L</u>ayout ⇒ <u>O</u>ther ⇒ <u>B</u>lock Protect (*Shortcut keys:* [Shift] + [F8], 7, 1). A [Block Pro On] code is placed at the beginning of the blocked text and [Block Pro Off] is placed at the end. You can add or delete lines anyplace within the two codes and WordPerfect will keep the block of text on one page.

▌ HANDS-ON ACTIVITY

To ensure that the columnar table is not divided between the first and second pages, you will use the Block Protect feature.

1. Using the Block feature, highlight the entire columnar table

Compare your blocked text to that shown in Figure 9-18.

2. Select <u>L</u>ayout ⇒ <u>O</u>ther ⇒ <u>B</u>lock Protect

✓ Press [Shift] + [F8], **7, 1**

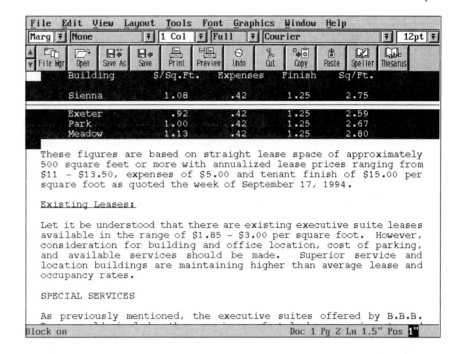

Figure 9-18

3. Select **OK**

   ✓ Press ⌐Enter⌐

   Notice the single horizontal line, indicating that the page break now precedes the columnar table. When the document is printed, the entire table will remain together on one page. Compare your document screen to the one shown in Figure 9-19.

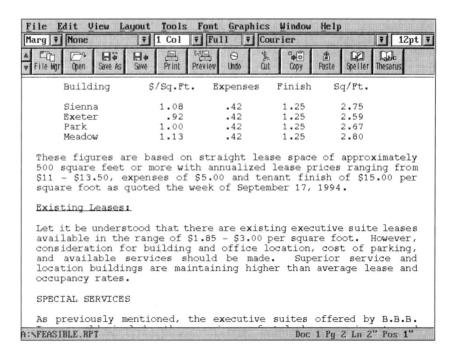

Figure 9-19

▌ Creating a Hard Page Break

The **Hard Page** feature inserts a mandatory page break at the position of the cursor; any text following the cursor will be printed on a new page. A page break is indicated in a document window as two solid horizontal lines. In the Reveal Codes screen it is indicated as an [HPg] code.

To insert a hard page break, move the cursor to the left of the character that is to be the first character of the new page, then choose Layout ⇒ Alignment ⇒ Hard Page (*Shortcut keys:* Ctrl + Enter). To delete a hard page code, in the Reveal Codes screen place the cursor on [HPg] code and press Delete.

▌ HANDS-ON ACTIVITY

You want to create a new blank page at the beginning of your document, so that you can create a title page for the feasibility report.

To position the cursor at the top of the document,

1. Press Home, Home, ↑

    Now, insert a hard page break:

2. Select Layout ⇒ Alignment ⇒ Hard Page

    ✓ Press Ctrl + Enter

    Your document window should appear as shown in Figure 9-20.

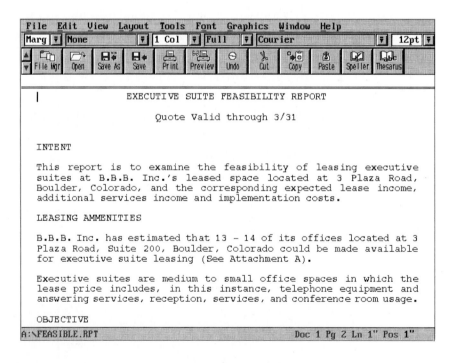

Figure 9-20

3. Press ↑

    Notice that the status line now reads "Pg 1." To create a title page,

4. Type the following text, centered and boldface, pressing Enter 6 times after each line (except after the last 2 lines press Enter twice):

```
EXECUTIVE SUITE FEASIBILITY REPORT
For
B.B.B. Inc.
(today's date)
Submitted by
PencilPushers, Inc.
(your name)
```

In Lesson 5, you learned to center a page top to bottom. You are now going to use that feature again to vertically center the text on your title page.

5. Select Layout ⇒ Page ⇒ Center Current Page

    ✓ Press Shift + F8 , 3, 2

6. Select OK

    ✓ Press Enter

7. Use the Print Preview (full page view) to view your title page

    Compare your title page to the one shown in Figure 9-21.

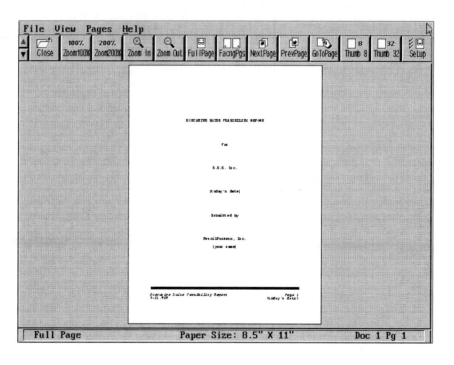

Figure 9-21

Notice that your footer appears at the bottom of the title page. The next section will tell you how to remove the footer from the title page but have it appear throughout the remainder of your document.

Suppressing a Header or Footer

The **Suppress** feature allows you to turn off any combination of page formats for the current page only—such as suppressing all page numbering, headers, and footers. To activate the Suppress feature, position the cursor on the page where the suppression is to occur and choose Layout ⇒ Page ⇒ Suppress (*Shortcut keys:* Shift + F8 , 3, 9). Select the item to be suppressed and choose OK. WordPerfect inserts a [Suppress] code when this feature is used.

HANDS-ON ACTIVITY

You are going to suppress Footer A on the title page of your report. Be sure that the cursor is positioned someplace on the first page.

1. Select Layout ⇒ Page ⇒ Suppress

    ✓ Press Shift + F8 , 3, 9

    The Suppress (This Page Only) dialog box appears, as shown in Figure 9-22.

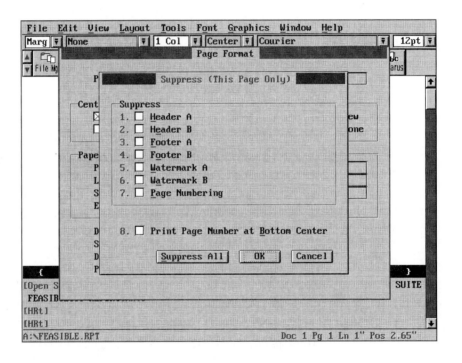

Figure 9-22

2. Select Footer A

    To exit and return to the document window,

3. Select OK twice

    ✓ Press Enter twice

4. On your own, use either the Print Preview feature or the Page mode to view your title page and the first page of your report

    Notice that Footer A is no longer displayed on the title page. Look at the first page of the report and notice that the page number is 2. In the next section, you will change the page number.

▦ Specifying a New Page Number

The Page Numbering feature you used earlier in this lesson allows you to specify a new page number. You might use this feature when you've created a title page and want the first page of the document to be numbered 1 instead of 2. Another instance might be when you instruct WordPerfect to generate a table of contents and you want the page number to begin with "i" (lowercase Roman numeral).

To specify a new page number, select <u>L</u>ayout ⇒ <u>P</u>age ⇒ Page <u>N</u>umbering (*Shortcut keys:* Shift + F8 , 3, 1). The Page Numbering dialog box appears. Select Page <u>N</u>umber to display the Set Page Number dialog box. Select New <u>N</u>umber, type the desired page number, and press Enter . Select OK three times to exit the dialog box and return to the document window.

▮ HANDS-ON ACTIVITY

When you last viewed your document, the first text page of the report was numbered as page 2. In this exercise, you are going to specify a new page number as 1.

1. Position the cursor on page 2 (the first text page of your report)

2. Select <u>L</u>ayout ⇒ <u>P</u>age ⇒ Page <u>N</u>umbering

    ✓ Press Shift + F8 , **3, 1**

    The Page Numbering dialog box appears.

3. Select Page <u>N</u>umber

    The Set Page Number dialog box appears as shown in Figure 9-23.

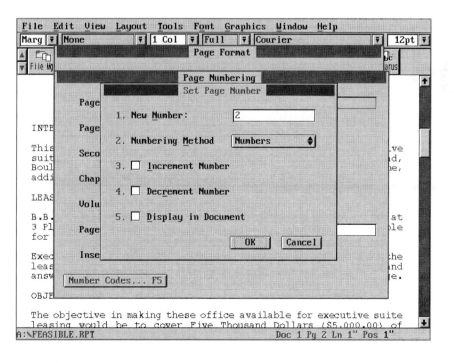

Figure 9-23

4. Select New <u>N</u>umber

5. Type **1**

6. Press Enter

To exit the dialog box and return to the document window,

7. Select **OK** 3 times

✓ Press Enter 3 times

8. On your own, change the bottom margin to .5 inches

NOTE: As always, your cursor position controls the location in the document where format changes begin. You should be positioned on the first text page so that the margin change begins there.

9. On your own, use either the Print Preview feature or the Page mode to view your title page and the first page of your report

▍ Indenting Text

The **Indent** feature indents an entire paragraph one tab stop from the left margin each time the feature is executed. This feature essentially sets a temporary left margin; the text automatically moves right, to the indent position, until Enter is pressed (at the end of the paragraph). The cursor then returns to the original left margin.

To utilize the Indent feature, tab stops must be set for each indent level desired. Choose Layout ⇒ Alignment ⇒ Indent (*Shortcut key:* F4). Each subsequent time Layout ⇒ Alignment ⇒ Indent is chosen, WordPerfect indents the text of the paragraph to the next tab position. Also, a [Lft Indent] code is inserted into the text each time the Indent feature is executed.

▍ HANDS-ON ACTIVITY

In your feasibility report to B.B.B. Inc., each main heading is indicated in all uppercase, and each subheading is shown in initial caps and underlined. For example, on the first text page the main headings are INTENT, LEASING AMENITIES, OBJECTIVE, and ESTIMATED COST PER SQUARE FOOT, and the subheading is <u>Monthly Gross Figures</u>. The subheadings would be distinguishable if they were indented one tab position or one-half inch. Therefore, you are going to implement the Indent feature to accomplish this task.

1. Position the cursor before or under the "M" in the phrase "Monthly Gross Figure"

2. Select <u>L</u>ayout ⇒ <u>A</u>lignment ⇒ <u>I</u>ndent

✓ Press F4

The title is moved .5" to the right. Now, indent the paragraph below:

3. Position the cursor before or under the "D" in the phrase "Due to current market..."

4. Select <u>L</u>ayout ⇒ <u>A</u>lignment ⇒ <u>I</u>ndent

✓ Press F4

Notice that all lines of the paragraph are aligned .5" in from the left margin. Compare your document window to the one shown in Figure 9-24.

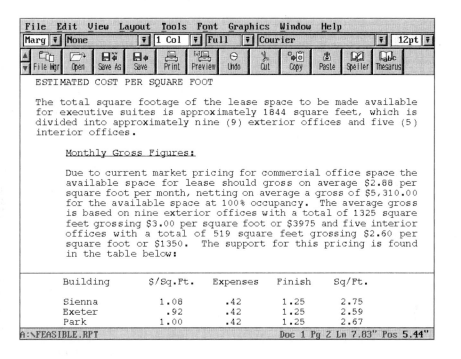

Figure 9-24

5. Position the cursor before or under the "T" in the phrase "These figures are based on straight..."

6. Select **L**ayout ⇒ **A**lignment ⇒ **I**ndent

   ✓ Press F4

7. On your own, indent all the remaining subheadings in the report, along with the subsequent paragraphs

Inserting Special Characters

WordPerfect offers a wide variety of special characters, such as bullets (• or ■); symbols for copyright (©), paragraph (¶), section (§); and characters such as ♥ just for fun.

Over 1600 characters (referred to as **WordPerfect Characters**) are divided into different groups or **character sets,** each containing the same type of characters. Some of the character sets available are Typographic Symbols, Math/Scientific, Greek, Hebrew, and Japanese.

To insert a WordPerfect character, position the insertion point where the character is to appear. Choose F**o**nt ⇒ **W**P Characters (*Shortcut keys:* Ctrl + W). The WordPerfect Characters dialog box appears. Choose **S**et to display a list of the WordPerfect character sets. Select the desired set and then choose **C**haracters. To select a specific character, either click on it or use the arrow keys to move the dotted selection box on to the character. To insert the character into your document, select **I**nsert.

▌ **HANDS-ON ACTIVITY**

In this exercise, you are going to add a bullet to the three items listed under the EQUIPMENT section on the second text page. The first item begins, "An IBM compatible..."

1.   Using the Search feature, locate "An IBM"

Compare your document window to the one shown in Figure 9-25.

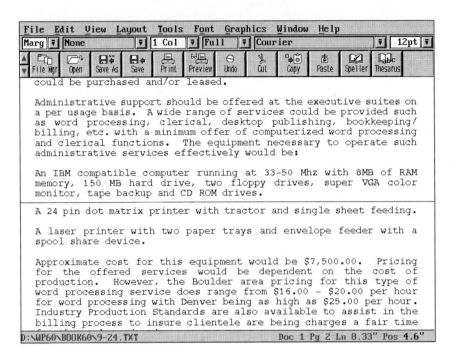

Figure 9-25

To position the cursor on the left margin,

2.   Press Home , ←

To indent the paragraph to the first tab stop,

3.   Select <u>L</u>ayout ⇒ <u>A</u>lignment ⇒ <u>I</u>ndent

✓ Press F4

Now insert the bullet,

4.   Select F<u>o</u>nt ⇒ <u>W</u>P Characters

✓ Press Ctrl + W

To move to the Set option,

5.   Press Tab

The WordPerfect Characters dialog box appears, as shown in Figure 9-26.

To display the list of WordPerfect character sets,

6.   Select <u>S</u>et

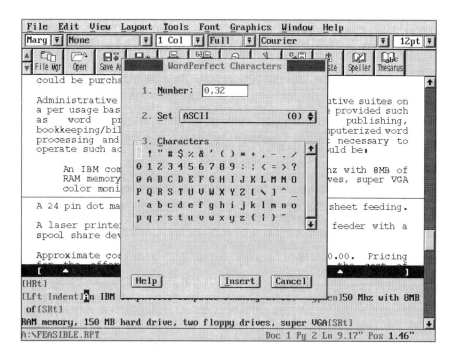

Figure 9-26

NOTE: *If you are using the keyboard, press* ⬇ *and press* Enter *to open the drop-down list box.*

7.   Select **T**ypographic Symbols

8.   Select **C**haracters

9.   Either use the arrow keys or click with the mouse to highlight the square bullet character (■) that is shown in Figure 9-27

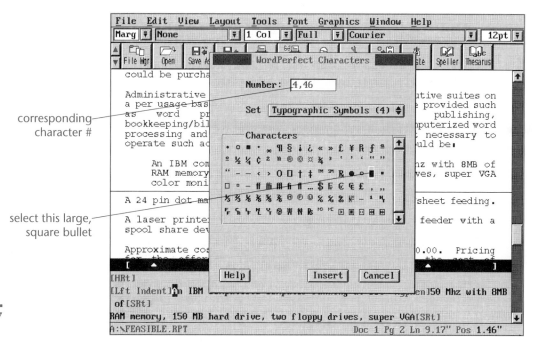

corresponding character #

select this large, square bullet

Figure 9-27

TIP: As you highlight the desired special character in the symbol chart, the character number displays at the top of this dialog box as shown in Figure 9-27. As an optional way to select the desired character, you may type the corresponding number of the character instead of highlighting the symbol. In this example, the bullet is character number 4,46 (no spaces).

To insert the character into your document,

10. Click on **Insert**

   ✓ Press Enter

To indent the paragraph to the next tab stop,

11. Select L̲ayout ⇒ A̲lignment ⇒ I̲ndent

   ✓ Press F4

12. Repeat this process for the two following paragraphs, which begin, "A 24 pin dot matrix..." and "A laser printer..."

Compare your paragraphs to Figure 9-28.

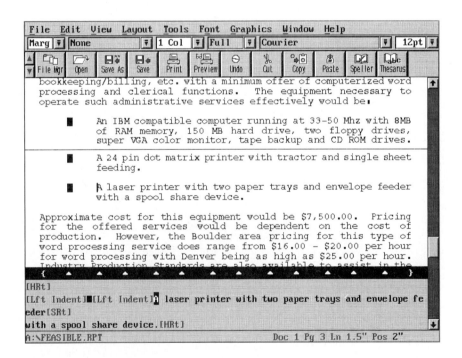

Figure 9-28

▓ Selecting a Font

A **font** is a complete set of characters in a specific typeface (such as Times Roman, Optima, Courier, and Helvetica), with a distinctive style or appearance (such as bold, italic, shadow, outline, and superscript) and a specific size such as 10-pt or 10-cpi. If the font you choose is **proportionally spaced**, the size is indicated in traditional typographic points (pt). Proportionally spaced means that different letters require different widths. For example, a capital "M" requires more space than a lowercase "i." There are 72 points per inch; therefore, if you select a point size of 72, the text will be approximately one inch in height. A 12-point font is the most common type size used, and is about the equivalent of 10-pitch type on a typewriter. If you choose a **monospaced** font (in which each letter requires the same amount of space), the size is indicated in characters per inch (cpi).

Two types of fonts can be used in WordPerfect—graphics fonts and printer fonts. If your printer supports graphics, then it has the capability of printing **graphics fonts**. WordPerfect 6.0 supports a number of graphics fonts, such as TrueType, CG Intellifont, Bitstream Speedo, and Type 1. Several Type 1 and Bitstream Speedo graphics fonts are included in the WordPerfect 6.0 program. Graphics fonts are generated graphically and are scalable, meaning that they can print in almost any size. Graphics fonts are also utilized as screen fonts; therefore, if you are in the Graphics or Page mode, the font appearance and exact size will be displayed as WYSIWYG (what you see is what you get). Graphics fonts take longer to print than printer fonts, however.

Each printer has its own built-in fonts that can be enhanced by cartridges, soft fonts, or print wheels. Both the built-in and supplemental fonts are called **printer fonts**. The printer fonts available to you depend upon the type of printer (whether laser, dot-matrix, or daisywheel), the amount of memory installed in the printer, and what (if any) supplemental products are being utilized.

Changing the Document's Initial Font

When WordPerfect was installed on your computer, an initial (default) font was selected by whoever did the installation. When new documents are created, WordPerfect automatically chooses that font for your document.

It is important to understand the difference between changing the Document Initial Font and making a regular font change within a document. If you select a font by choosing Font ⇒ Font, that selection affects the text from the cursor forward in the document until another font change is encountered. Selecting the Document Initial Font changes the font for the entire document, including page number, headers, footers, footnotes, endnotes, captions for graphics boxes, and so on. (You will learn about these features in future lessons.) When a document's initial font is changed, it doesn't matter where the cursor is located; *all* of the document's text is altered. So to change the font for the entire document, select Layout ⇒ Document ⇒ Initial Font ⇒ Font (*Shortcut keys:* Shift + F8, 4, 3, 1). Both the available graphics fonts and the printer fonts are listed. Highlight the desired font from the list box. If you selected a scalable font, select Size and enter the desired point size. Select OK to return to the document window.

Changing the Size and Appearance of a Font

You can change the size or appearance of a font either as you type the text or after it has been typed. In the latter case you must first block the text. Changes to the size of a font are based upon the current font selected. The options are Fine, Small, Large, Very Large, and Extra Large, and they work like this: if, for example, the current font is 12-point Times Roman and Large is selected, the text will change to the next size larger, or 14 points.

The examples below illustrate size changes for a Courier 12-point font with a Postscript printer selected.

Menu Selection	Result
Fine	Fine
Small	Small
Large	Large
Very Large	Very Large
Extra Large	Extra Large

You may also change the position of the text by applying either the Superscript or Subscript attribute as shown below:

Superscript ^{Text} Subscript $_{\text{Text}}$

To change the size of a font while typing the text, choose either Font ⇒ Size/Position, or Font ⇒ Font (*Shortcut keys:* Ctrl + F8) and turn on the check box of the desired size. Type the text. To turn off the feature, choose either Font ⇒ Normal (*Shortcut keys:* Ctrl + N) or Font ⇒ Font and turn off the check box of the current size.

If the text is already typed, block the text and either choose Font ⇒ Size/Position and select the desired size, or choose Font ⇒ Font (*Shortcut keys:* Ctrl + F8) and turn on the check box of the desired size.

The **Appearance** options control the style of the text. Available options are Bold, Underline, Double Underline, Outline, Shadow, Small Cap, Redline, and Strikeout. The following illustrates changes in appearance of a 10-point font rendered by a PostScript printer (the appearance of Outline, Shadow, and Redline will vary, depending on your printer):

Bold	**Bold**
Underline	<u>Underline</u>
Double Underline	<u>Double Underline</u>
Small Cap	Small Cap
Strikeout	~~Strikeout~~

To apply only one appearance as you enter text, choose Font, select the desired appearance, and type the text. To turn off the single appearance, select Font ⇒ Normal (*Shortcut keys:* Ctrl + N). If several appearances are to be applied while typing new text, select Font ⇒ Font (*Shortcut keys:* Ctrl + F8), turn on the check box of the desired appearances, and type the text. To turn off the feature, choose Font ⇒ Font and turn off the appropriate check boxes.

If the text is already typed, block the text and either choose Font and select the desired appearance, or choose Font ⇒ Font (*Shortcut keys:* Ctrl + F8) and turn on the check box of the desired appearances.

NOTE: If more than one attribute (size and/or appearance) is selected, choosing Font ⇒ Normal (Shortcut keys: Ctrl *+ N) will turn off all attributes. If the text is already typed, select the text and choose the appropriate command listed below:*

Appearance	Menu Commands	Shortcut Keystrokes
Bold	Font ⇒ Bold	F6 or Ctrl + B
Underline	Font ⇒ Underline	F8 or Ctrl + U
Italic	Font ⇒ Italics	Ctrl + I
Normal	Font ⇒ Normal	Ctrl + N
Double Underline	Font ⇒ Double Underline	
Outline	Font ⇒ Outline	
Shadow	Font ⇒ Shadow	
Small Caps	Font ⇒ Small Caps	
Redline	Font ⇒ Redline	
Strikeout	Font ⇒ Strikeout	

When either a Size or Appearance attribute is applied to text, WordPerfect enters a code to turn the attribute on and one to turn it off. The following table shows the feature and the codes that are used to indicate when the attribute is turned on and off.

Feature	On Code	Off Code
Fine	[Fine On]	[Fine Off]
Small	[Small On]	[Small Off]
Large	[Large On]	[Large Off]
Very Large	[Very Large On]	[Very Large Off]
Extra Large	[Ext Large On]	[Ext Large Off]
Subscript	[Subscpt On]	[Subscpt Off]
Superscript	[Suprscpt On]	[Suprscpt Off]
Bold	[Bold On]	[Bold Off]
Underline	[Und On]	[Und Off]
Double Underline	[Dbl Und On]	[Dbl Und Off]
Italics	[Italc On]	[Italc Off]
Outline	[Outln On]	[Outln Off]
Shadow	[Shadw On]	[Shadw Off]
Small Cap	[Sm Cap On]	[Sm Cap Off]
Redline	[Redln On]	[Redln Off]
Strikeout	[StkOut On]	[StkOut Off]

▌ HANDS-ON ACTIVITY

You are going to choose a different Document Initial Font for your feasibility report. Remember, the fonts that are available to you will depend upon your printer's capabilities or the graphics fonts that have been loaded. Also recall that when using the Document Initial font it does not matter where your cursor is positioned.

1. Click on **Layout** ⇒ **Document** ⇒ Initial **Font**

   The Document Initial Font dialog box appears, as shown in Figure 9-29.

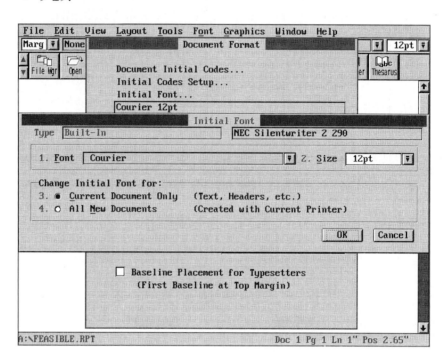

Figure 9-29

2. Select **Font**

   A list of fonts will appear according to the graphics fonts loaded and your printer's built-in fonts.

3. Choose a font to your liking and press ⌷Enter⌷

   Notice the **Size** option. If you choose a scalable font, make sure it is set to 12-pt.

4. Select **OK** twice

   ✓ Press ⌷Enter⌷ twice

   Now, you are going to apply the Large size to the title of your report.

   On the title page of your report,

5. Block **EXECUTIVE SUITE FEASIBILITY REPORT**

6. Select **Font** ⇒ **Siz/Position**

A pop-down menu appears, as shown in Figure 9-30.

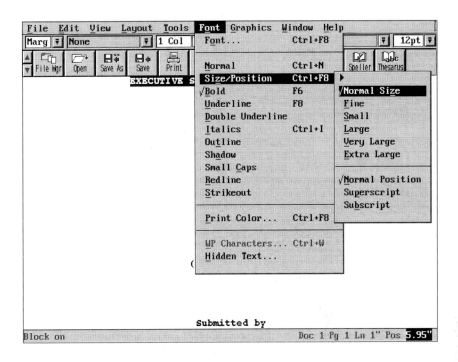

Figure 9-30

7. Select **Very Large**

To italicize the word "For" using the shortcut keys,

8. Block **For**

9. Press [Ctrl] + I

Now, you are going to change the size of the B.B.B. Inc. text by using the Font ⇒ Font menu.

10. Block **B.B.B. Inc.**

11. Select **Font ⇒ Font**

✓ Press [Ctrl] + [F8]

The font menu appears, as shown in Figure 9-31.

12. Select **Relative Size**

13. Select **Large**

14. Select **OK**

✓ Press [Enter]

15. On your own, apply the Large size to **PencilPushers, Inc.**

16. Save your document as **FEASIBLE.LS9**

17. Print the document and exit WordPerfect

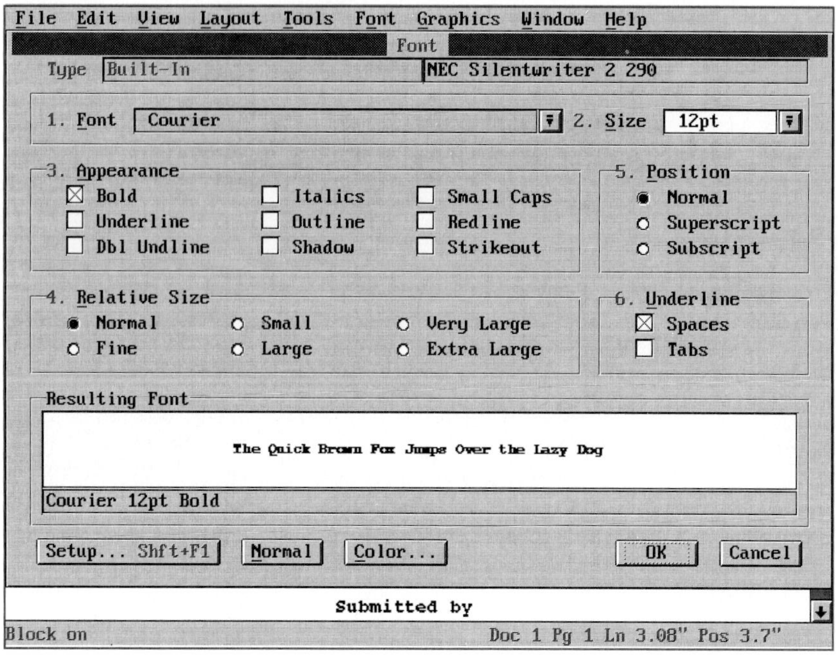

Figure 9-31

On Your Own

Review of Commands

Description	Menu Commands	Function Keys
Search		
Replace		
Apply page numbering		
Go to		
Page mode		
Create a header/footer		
Edit a header/footer		
Protect a block of text		
Create a hard page break		
Suppress a header/footer		
Specify a new page number		
Indent		
Insert WordPerfect characters		
Document Initial Font		
Change font		

Apply an appearance   _____   _____

Apply a size   _____   _____

▍ Lesson Review

1. Define a search string.

2. If the word "hello" is entered as a search string, which form of capitalization will be located?

3. What is the purpose of the Replace feature?

4. List the page numbering methods that can be used in a document.

5. Enter the keystroke combination to move the cursor to the bottom of the current page.

6. What is the purpose of the Page mode?

7. What are headers and footers?

8. When can you see a header or footer?

9. What is the command to include a page number in a header or footer?

10. What is the command to include the file name in a header or footer?

11. If only one footer is present in your document, where can the cursor be located to edit the footer?

12. Describe a soft page break.

13. What is the purpose of the Block Protect feature?

14. Describe the Suppress feature.

15. What happens when you use the Indent feature?

16. What is a font?

17. What is the difference between a proportionally spaced and a monospaced font?

18. Describe the difference between graphics fonts and printer fonts.

19. If the initial font is changed in a document, what text is affected?

20. You have just typed the text "WordPerfect 6.0." Describe the steps to apply the Large attribute.

Assignments

9.1 Directions

1. Open the document called DOWNSIZE.SD from the supplemental disk and save it as DOWNSIZE.LS9 to keep the original intact.

2. Create a title page with the following information centered, bold-faced, and attractively spaced. Also center the information vertically on the page.

> MOVING INFORMATION SYSTEMS APPLICATIONS FROM / LARGE SYSTEMS TO NETWORK MICROCOMPUTERS/ (DOWNSIZING)
>
>
> The Association of Information Systems/ London, England / 1994

3. Apply the Large attribute to the title and italicize the date.

4. Begin page numbering at the beginning of the document, specify bottom center, and be sure that the first page of text is numbered 1 (not 2).

5. Suppress the page numbering and headers or footers on the title page.

6. Change the document initial font to the font of your choice.

7. View the document with Print Preview.

8. Save and close the file.

9.2 Directions

1. Open the document called QUARTER.SD from the supplemental disk and save it as QUARTER.RPT to keep the original intact.

2. Replace all occurrences of "Eastern" with "Western."

3. Create a footer appearing on all pages that has the following information:

> Eastern Region Quarterly Report (left side) / Page # (right side) / file name (left side) / (current date)

4. Block protect the Monthly Breakdown table.

5. After the text "hot items", type the following paragraphs, using the indent feature before and after each number.

> 1. <u>Red Markers:</u> Red markers continue to lead all market sales. Face it, people love to highlight important information in red.
> 2. <u>Monogrammed</u> <u>coffee</u> <u>mugs:</u> It's a vanity item, but also a popular indirect selling tool.
> 3. <u>Personalized</u> <u>note</u> <u>pads:</u> They are becoming a "must" item for all companies.

6. Use Print Preview to view the document (print if desired).

7. Save and close the document.

10 Creating Tables

Objectives

Upon completion of this lesson, you will be able to do the following:

- Understand the basic structure of a table
- Create a table
- Move around in a table
- Insert rows and columns
- Delete rows and columns
- Undelete rows and columns
- Format text in cells
- Alter lines in a table
- Join cells
- Format columns in a table
- Shade cells
- Move and copy rows and columns
- Perform mathematical calculation in a table

WordPerfect's Table feature is one of the most innovative features that any word processing software company has ever developed. It offers the beginning user the simplicity of creating tabular columns without entering tabs or measuring and calculating tab settings. It also lets a user create complex forms and multicolumn documents, while incorporating a variety of font attributes and sizes.

Starting Point

Before beginning the lesson, start WordPerfect 6.0. The document window should be blank. Make sure the Train Button Bar and Ribbon are displayed. Graphics mode should be turned on.

Basic Structure of a Table

The basic structure of a table consists of **rows**, which run horizontally, and **columns**, which run vertically. Columns are labeled alphabetically from left to right, and rows are numbered sequentially from the top down, as shown in Figure 10-1. You can have up to 32 columns and 32,765 rows in one table.

	Column A	Column B	Column C
Row 1	Cell A1	Cell B1	Cell C1
Row 2			
Row 3		Cell B3	
Row 4			
Row 5			
Row 6			
Row 7			
Row 8	Cell A8	Cell B8	Cell C8

Figure 10-1

The rectangle where a row and column intersect is called a **cell**. Each cell has an **address**, consisting of its column letter plus row number, which indicates the cell's position in a table. The address of the cell where the cursor is located is indicated in the status line. For example, if the cursor is positioned in the first cell of the table, the status bar will indicate "Cell A1."

To create a table using the menu bar, choose Layout ⇒ Tables ⇒ Create (*Shortcut keys:* Alt + F7, 2, 1). The Create Table dialog box appears. Type the desired number of columns and rows and select OK. WordPerfect creates the table and automatically displays the Table Edit dialog box. Text cannot be entered into the table when this dialog box is present. Select Close (*Shortcut key:* F7) to close the dialog box and display the document window.

HANDS-ON ACTIVITY

As an owner of a small business, you know from experience that scheduling personnel for three buildings during the summer when most take vacations can be a task. The Table feature is going to help you easily organize your weekly scheduling and put it into a presentable format for your Pencil-Pushers employees. The table is shown in Figure 10-2 for your reference.

PencilPushers, Inc. Work Schedule			
Week of June 16th			
Day	**Spruce Bldg.**	**Walnut Bldg.**	**Pine Bldg.**
Monday	Karen Black	Susan Smith	Mike Nelson
Tuesday	Susan Smith	Joe Spence	Karen Black
Wednesday	Mike Nelson	Conley Blum	Susan Smith
Thursday	Rebecca Parker	Joe Spence	Mike Nelson
Friday	Rebecca Parker	Conley Blum	Susan Smith

Figure 10-2

1. On your own, center and bold the following headings, pressing [Enter] twice after each line:

   `PencilPushers, Inc. Work Schedule`
   `Week of June 16th`

   Don't forget to turn off the bold.

2. Select <u>L</u>ayout ⇒ <u>T</u>ables ⇒ <u>C</u>reate

   ✓ Press [Alt] + [F7], 2, 1

   The Create Table dialog box appears, as shown in Figure 10-3.

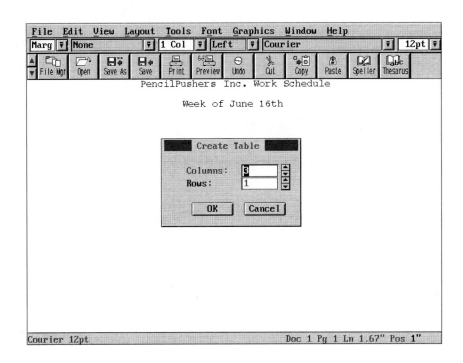

Figure 10-3

The cursor is positioned in the Columns text box and WordPerfect automatically displays 3 to create three columns. In your table you need four columns.

3. Type **4**

4. Press [Enter]

   The cursor is now positioned in the Rows option and the text box displays a 1. You need 5 rows.

5. Type **5**

6. Press [Enter]

7. Select **OK**

   ✓ Press [Enter]

The table is automatically created and the Table Edit dialog box is automatically opened, displaying the table menu at the bottom of the screen. Compare your screen to Figure 10-4.

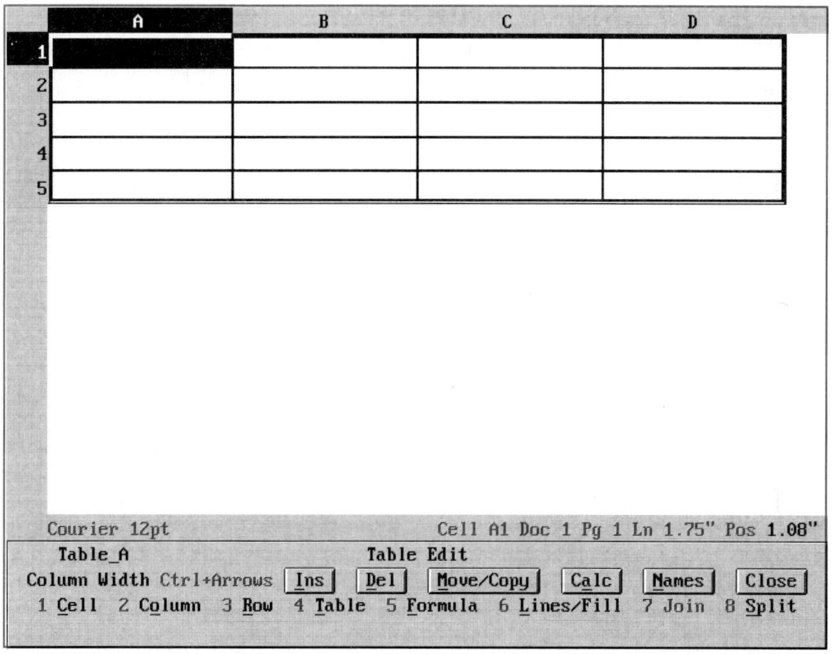

Figure 10-4

To exit the dialog box and return to the document window,

8. Select **Close**

   ✓ Press F7

You are now ready to begin typing your table. Notice that the status line now displays the cell address where the cursor is positioned. The cursor should be in the first cell (cell A1).

9. Type **Monday**

Do not press Enter. If you already have, press Backspace to delete the [HRt] code. To move to cell B1,

10. Press Tab

If you accidentally press Tab more than once, press Shift + Tab to back up one cell.

11. Type **Karen Black**

To move to cell C1,

12. Press Tab

13. Type **Susan Smith**

To move to cell D1,

14. Press Tab

15. Type **Mike Nelson**

To move to cell A2,

16. Press Tab

17. Type **Tuesday**

18. On your own, finish typing the remainder of the table shown in Figure 10-2 (column headings will be added later)

Moving Within a Table

As mentioned in the preceding section, Tab moves the cursor one cell forward; Shift + Tab moves it one cell back. You can also position the mouse pointer at any location within the table and click the mouse button to display the cursor. If there is no text in the cell where the cursor is located, the directional arrow keys move the cursor one cell in the direction of the arrow.

Listed below are additional keystrokes that can be used to move the cursor through a table. Remember, when using the Ctrl key in cursor movement, always hold down Ctrl while tapping the appropriate key for the desired cursor movement. When the Home key is required in a keystroke combination, tap Home (the Home key is never held down) and then tap the appropriate key for the desired cursor movement.

Press	Move To
Alt + ↓	Down one cell
Alt + ↑	Up one cell
Tab	Right one cell
Shift + Tab	Left one cell
[Go to], ↑	Beginning of text in a cell
[Go to], ↓	Last line of text in a cell
[Go to], Home, ↑ or Alt + Home, ↑	First cell in a column
[Go to], Home, ↓ or Alt + Home, ↓	Last cell in a column
[Go to], Home, ← or Alt + Home, ←	First cell in a row
[Go to], Home, → or Alt + Home, →	Last cell in a row
[Go to], Home, Home, ↑ or Alt + Home, Home, ↑	First cell in a table
[Go to], Home, Home, ↓ or Alt + Home, Home, ↓	Last cell in a table

▌ HANDS-ON ACTIVITY

In this exercise, you will practice moving the cursor with the keyboard.

NOTE: The [Go to] key combination is Ctrl *+* Home *.*

To move to the first cell in the table,

1. Press [Go to], Home , Home , ↑

    To move to the last cell in row 1,

2. Press [Go to], Home , →

    To move to the last cell in the table,

3. Press [Go to], Home , Home , ↓

    To move to the first cell in row 5,

4. Press [Go to], Home , ←

5. On your own, move to cell A1

▌ Inserting Rows and Columns

Rows and columns can be inserted at any time into a table. Therefore, even if you have not planned properly, rows and columns can easily be inserted. To insert a row or column, position the cursor where the new row or column should be inserted and access the Table Edit menu, selecting Layout ⇒ Tables ⇒ Edit (*Shortcut keys:* Alt + F11). Select Ins to display the Insert dialog box. Select either Columns or Rows, then specify the number of rows or columns to be inserted in the How Many option. You may instruct WordPerfect to insert rows or columns either before or after the cursor position. Select OK to exit the Table Edit dialog box and return to the document window.

One row can also be inserted in a document window by pressing Ctrl + Insert .

▌ HANDS-ON ACTIVITY

In this exercise, you are going to edit the table and insert two lines at the top of the table, so that you can enter a heading.

NOTE: The Table Edit dialog box is designed for changing the layout of the table, but does not allow you to type text in cells until you exit it.

1. Position the cursor someplace in the first row of the table

2. Select Layout ⇒ Tables ⇒ Edit

    ✓ Press Alt + F11

    To display the Insert dialog box,

3. Select Ins

    The Insert dialog displays as shown in Figure 10-5.

4. Select Rows

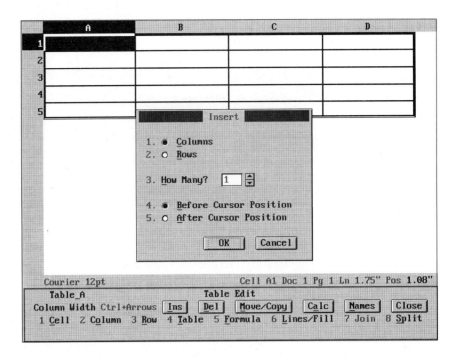

Figure 10-5

5. Select <u>H</u>ow Many?

The cursor moves to the <u>H</u>ow Many? text box.

6. Type **2**

7. Press [Enter]

Notice that the <u>B</u>efore Cursor Position radio button is selected, which will insert two rows above the current row 1.

8. Select **OK**

✓ Press [Enter]

The Table Edit dialog box redisplays and your table now has blank rows at the top of the table. Compare your screen to the one shown in Figure 10-6.

To exit the Table Edit dialog box and return to the document windows,

9. Select **Close**

✓ Press [F7]

10. Type the following text in the indicated cells:

cell A1:   Day
cell B1:   Spruce Bldg.
cell C1:   Walnut Bldg.
cell D1:   Pine Bldg.

11. Move to row 6 (Thursday, Rebecca Parker, Joe Spence, Mike Nelson)

As we mentioned earlier, you can easily insert one row in a document window by pressing Ctrl + Insert.

	A	B	C	D
1				
2				
3	Monday	Karen Black	Susan Smith	Mike Nelson
4	Tuesday	Susan Smith	Joe Spence	Karen Black
5	Wednesday	Mike Nelson	Conley Blum	Susan Smith
6	Thursday	Rebecca Parker	Joe Spence	Mike Nelson
7	Friday	Rebecca Parker	Conley Blum	Susan Smith

Courier 12pt   Cell A1 Doc 1 Pg 1 Ln 1.92" Pos 1.08"

Table_A   Table Edit
Column Width Ctrl+Arrows   [Ins]   [Del]   [Move/Copy]   [Calc]   [Names]   [Close]
1 Cell 2 Column 3 Row 4 Table 5 Formula 6 Lines/Fill 7 Join 8 Split

Figure 10-6

12. Press Ctrl + Insert

A blank row is inserted and the text in row 6 is now moved to row 7. Compare your table to the one shown in Figure 10-7.

File   Edit   View   Layout   Tools   Font   Graphics   Window   Help
[Marg ▼] [None   ▼] [1 Col ▼] [Left ▼] [Courier   ▼] [12pt ▼]
File Mgr Open Save As Save Print Preview Undo Cut Copy Paste Speller Thesarus

PencilPushers, Inc. Work Schedule

Week of June 16th

Day	Spruce Bldg.	Walnut Bldg.	Pine Bldg.
Monday	Karen Black	Susan Smith	Mike Nelson
Tuesday	Susan Smith	Joe Spence	Karen Black
Wednesday	Mike Nelson	Conley Blum	Susan Smith
Thursday	Rebecca Parker	Joe Spence	Mike Nelson
Friday	Rebecca Parker	Conley Blum	Susan Smith

Courier 12pt   Cell A6 Doc 1 Pg 1 Ln 3.2" Pos 1.08"

Figure 10-7

▌ Deleting Rows or Columns

To delete one row or column, position the cursor someplace in the row or column to be deleted. To delete more than one row or column, position the cursor in either the top-most row or the left-most column to be deleted. Select Layout ⇒ Tables ⇒ Edit (*Shortcut keys:* Alt + F11) to display the Table Edit dialog box. Select Del to display the Delete dialog box. Select either Columns or Rows, and specify the number of rows or columns to be deleted in the How Many? text box—the default is 1. Select OK to exit the Table Edit dialog box and return to the document window.

One row can also be deleted in a document window by pressing Ctrl + Del. The row in which the cursor is located will be deleted.

▌ HANDS-ON ACTIVITY

In this exercise, you are going to delete the two blank rows in your table using both methods—the Table Edit menu and Ctrl + Del in the document window.

1. Position the cursor someplace in row 2

2. Select Layout ⇒ Tables ⇒ Edit

    ✓ Press Alt + F11

    The Table Edit dialog box appears.

3. Select Del

    The Delete dialog box displays, as shown in Figure 10-8.

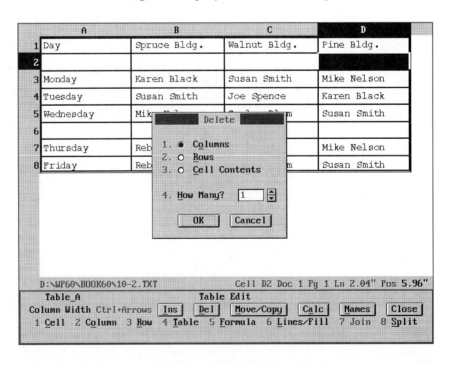

Figure 10-8

4. Select Rows

    Notice that the How Many? text box displays 1. To accept this response,

5. Select **OK**

    ✓ Press ⏎Enter

    The Table Edit menu redisplays. To close the dialog box and return to the document window,

6. Select **Close**

    ✓ Press ⎄F7

    Now, you are going to use the ⎄Ctrl + ⎄Del method to delete row 5 (the other blank row).

7. Position the cursor someplace in row 5.

8. Press ⎄Ctrl + ⎄Del

    A dialog box appears, asking if you want to delete the row. Compare your screen to the one shown in Figure 10-9.

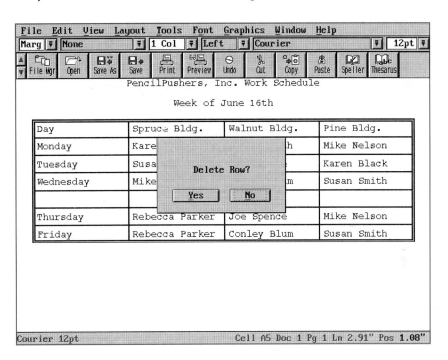

Figure 10-9

9. Select **Yes**

    ✓ Press ⏎Enter

▎Undeleting Rows and Columns

Deleted row(s) or column(s) may only be restored in the Table Edit dialog box. To restore a deleted row or column, position the cursor in the row or column that the restored row or column is to precede and select Layout ⇒ Tables ⇒ Edit (*Shortcut keys:* ⎄Alt + ⎄F11) to display the Table Edit dialog box. To activate the Undelete feature, press ⎄Esc. A dialog box appears, asking if you wish to undelete the row(s) or column(s); select Yes. The table is updated, restoring the last deletion. Exit the Table Edit dialog box to return to the document window.

▌ HANDS-ON ACTIVITY

In this exercise you are going to delete row 4, using the [Ctrl] + [Del] method, and then restore it, using the Undelete feature.

1. Position the cursor someplace in row 4

   To delete the row,

2. Press [Ctrl] + [Del]

   To respond to the dialog box and delete the row,

3. Select Yes

   ✓ Press [Enter]

   Now, to restore the deleted row,

4. Select Layout ⇒ Tables ⇒ Edit

   ✓ Press [Alt] + [F11]

   The Table Edit dialog box appears.

5. Press [Esc]

   A dialog box displays, asking if you wish to undelete the last row(s) deleted. Compare your screen to the one shown in Figure 10-10.

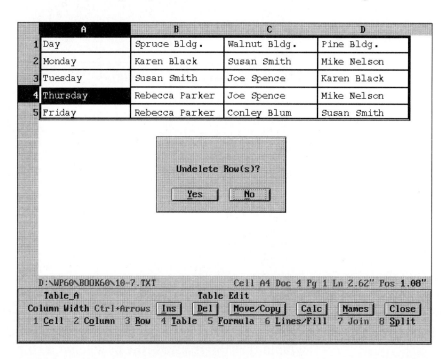

Figure 10-10

6. Select Yes

   ✓ Press [Enter]

The row is restored and the table is automatically updated.

To close the Table Edit dialog box and return to the document window,

7. Select **Close**

   ✓ Press F7

Formatting Text in Cells

WordPerfect offers many features for changing the appearance of text in a table, including appearance, size, and justification. Before any cells can be formatted, the Table Edit dialog box must first be opened.

To change the format for a cell, position the cursor in the cell to be affected. If more than one cell is to be formatted, use the Block feature to block or highlight those cells. Select **C**ell to display the Cell Format dialog box. The Appearance options allow you to change the way the text looks, and the Size options allow you to select the size of your text. When the Lock option is turned on, information in the cell cannot be changed. The Ignore When Calculating option instructs WordPerfect to ignore a cell during mathematical calculations. The Vertical Alignment determines where the text is to appear vertically in the cell. The Number Type option will be discussed in the "Performing Mathematical Calculations in Tables" section later in this lesson.

▌ HANDS-ON ACTIVITY

In this exercise, you are going to use the **C**ell option in the Table Edit dialog box to bold, italicize, and center the headings in your table.

1. Position your cursor in cell A1

2. Select **L**ayout ⇒ **T**ables ⇒ **E**dit

   ✓ Press Alt + F11

   The Table Edit dialog box appears. Now, you are going to block cells A1 through D1. The Block feature can be accessed in the Table Edit dialog box by pressing Alt + F4 , F12 , or by dragging with the mouse.

3. Press F12

   To block the entire row,

4. Press End

5. Select **C**ell

   The Cell Format dialog box appears, as shown in Figure 10-11.

   TIP: If you are using a mouse, you may prefer to quickly click on any of the items in the Cell Format dialog box to make the following selections, instead of using the menu steps.

6. Select **A**ppearance ⇒ **B**old

7. Select **A**ppearance ⇒ **I**talic

8. Select **J**ustification ⇒ **C**enter

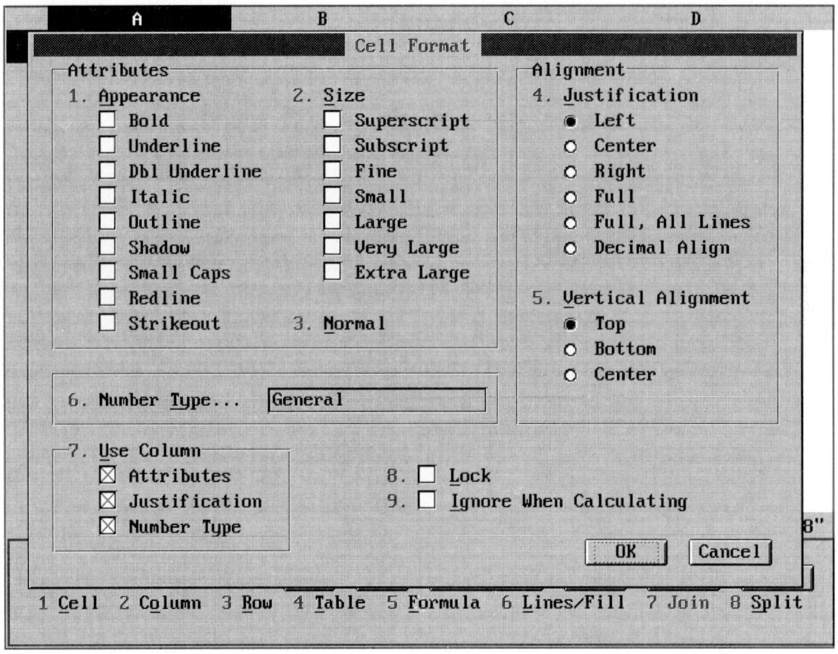

Figure 10-11

To exit the Cell Format dialog box,

9.   Select **OK**

✓ Press Enter

Compare your document to the one shown in Figure 10-12.

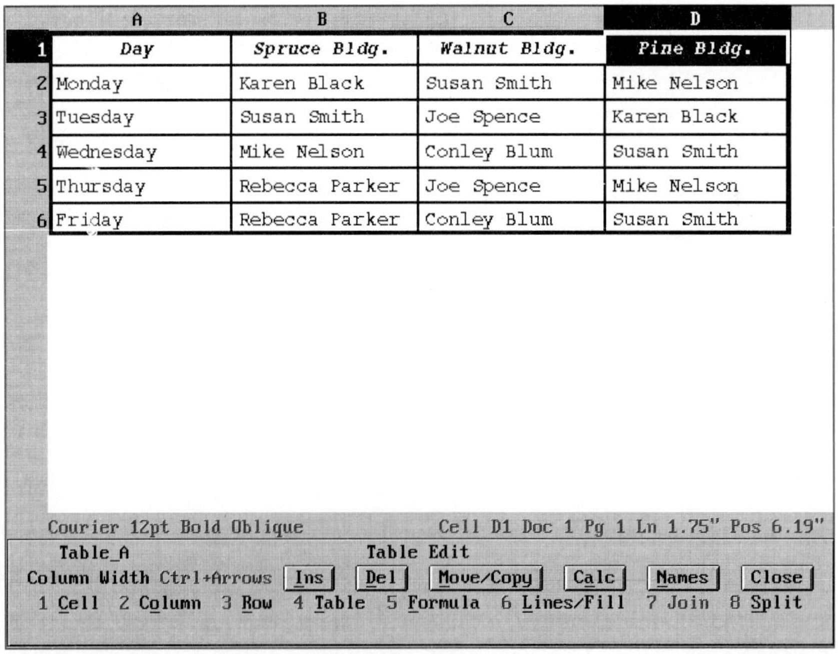

Figure 10-12

To exit the Table Edit dialog box and return to your document window,

10. Select Close

✓ Press F7

11. Save the document as SCHEDULE.16

12. Print the document

Altering the Lines in a Table

Lines can be changed or removed for the entire table, any single cell, or a group of blocked cells. To alter the lines for an entire table, position the cursor anywhere in the table and select Layout ⇒ Tables ⇒ Edit (*Shortcut keys:* Alt + F11) to display the Table Edit dialog box. Choose Lines/Fill to display the Table Lines dialog box and choose the desired line style. The Default Line option allows you to change the line style for the inside lines of the entire table. To alter all outside lines of the table, choose the Border/Fill option from the Table Lines dialog box.

To alter the lines for any part of a table, select Layout ⇒ Tables ⇒ Edit (*Shortcut keys:* Alt + F11) to display the Table Edit dialog box. To change a single cell, position the cursor in the cell or use the Block feature to highlight a group of cells and select the desired line element to be changed (Left, Right, Top, Bottom, Inside, or Outside). The Line Styles dialog box appears, offering you a variety of line styles or no lines.

HANDS-ON ACTIVITY

In this exercise, you are going to remove all the lines in your table.

1. Position the cursor anywhere in the table

   To display the Table Edit dialog box,

2. Select Layout ⇒ Tables ⇒ Edit

   ✓ Press Alt + F11

   To display the Table Lines dialog box,

3. Select Lines/Fill

   The Table Lines dialog box displays, as shown in Figure 10-13.

   The first step is to remove the inside lines for the entire table.

4. Select Default Line

   The Default Table Lines dialog box appears, as shown in Figure 10-14.

5. Select Line Style

   The Line Styles dialog box displays, as shown in Figure 10-15.

6. Select [None]

   To exit the Line Styles dialog box and return to the Table Edit dialog box,

7. Select Close twice

   ✓ Press Enter twice

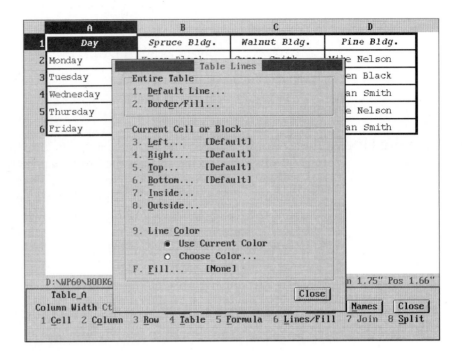

Figure 10-13

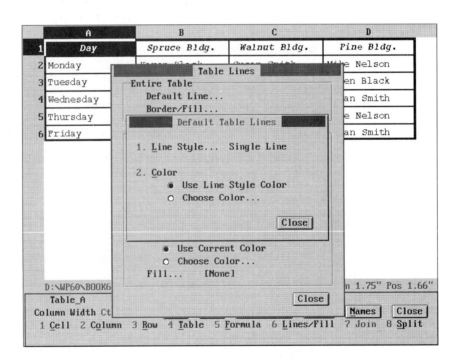

Figure 10-14

Now, remove the border or outside lines. Be sure the Table Edit dialog box is still open.

8. Select Lines/Fill

The Table Lines dialog box appears.

9. Select Border/Fill

The Table Border/Fill dialog box appears, as shown in Figure 10-16.

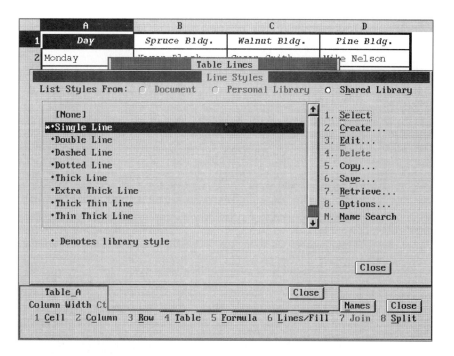

Figure 10-15

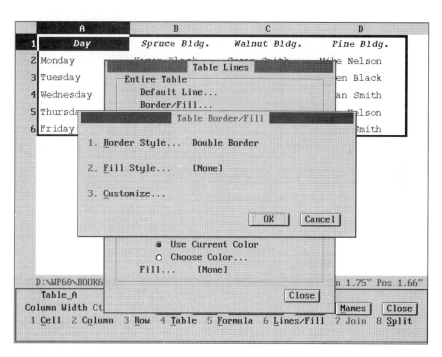

Figure 10-16

10. Select **B**order Style

    The Border Styles dialog box appears.

11. Select [None]

12. Select **OK**

    ✓ Press Enter

13. Select **Close**

    ✓ Press Enter

    The Table Edit dialog box reappears. To exit,

14. Select **Close**

    ✓ Press F7

    Compare your document to the one shown in Figure 10-17.

PencilPushers, Inc. Work Schedule			
Week of June 16th			
Day	*Spruce Bldg.*	*Walnut Bldg.*	*Pine Bldg.*
Monday	Karen Black	Susan Smith	Mike Nelson
Tuesday	Susan Smith	Joe Spence	Karen Black
Wednesday	Mike Nelson	Conley Blum	Susan Smith
Thursday	Rebecca Parker	Joe Spence	Mike Nelson
Friday	Rebecca Parker	Conley Blum	Susan Smith

Figure 10-17

Now, you are going to put a ruling line along the top and bottom of the table.

15. Position the cursor anywhere in the table.

16. Select **Layout** ⇒ **Tables** ⇒ **Edit**

    ✓ Press Alt + F11

17. Select **Lines/Fill**

18. Select **Border/Fill**

19. Select **Border Style**

20. In the Border Styles list box, on your own, move down with either the mouse or the ↓ to highlight **Thick Top and Bottom Border**

21. Choose **Select**

    To return to the Table Edit window,

22. Select **OK**

    ✓ Press Enter

23. Select **Close**

    ✓ Press F7

    To exit the Table Edit dialog box and return to the normal document window,

24. Select **Close**

    ✓ Press F7

Compare your document to the one shown in Figure 10-18.

PencilPushers, Inc. Work Schedule

Week of June 16th

Day	Spruce Bldg.	Walnut Bldg.	Pine Bldg.
Monday	Karen Black	Susan Smith	Mike Nelson
Tuesday	Susan Smith	Joe Spence	Karen Black
Wednesday	Mike Nelson	Conley Blum	Susan Smith
Thursday	Rebecca Parker	Joe Spence	Mike Nelson
Friday	Rebecca Parker	Conley Blum	Susan Smith

Figure 10-18

25. Save and exit the document

Joining Cells

The **Join** feature allows you to remove the boundaries (lines) between cells, combining the contents of the cells. Cells may be joined either before or after text is entered. You might, for example, want to join several cells to include a heading at the top of your table or to create preprinted forms. To join cells, you select Layout ⇒ Tables ⇒ Edit (*Shortcut keys:* Alt + F11) to display the Table Edit dialog box. Block the cells to be joined and select Join. The blocked cells are joined into a single cell.

NOTE: If you accidentally join cells that should not be joined, use the Split feature to put them back to their original state.

HANDS-ON ACTIVITY

In this exercise you are going to create the table shown in Figure 10-19. Notice that rows 1 and 2 of this document consist of only one column, therefore you can center the headings over the entire table. The first step is to create the table. Make sure you begin with a blank document screen.

1. Select **Layout** ⇒ **Tables** ⇒ **Create**

    ✓ Press Alt + F7 , 2, 1

    The Create Table dialog box appears. Specify 5 columns.

2. Type **5**

3. Press Enter

    The cursor is now positioned in the Rows option. Specify 9 rows.

4. Type **9**

5. Press Enter

6. Select **OK**

    ✓ Press Enter

PencilPushers, Inc.				
Revenue Summary				
Service	First Qtr	Second Qtr	Diff	% Diff
Clerical	18,725	17,640		
Word Processing	23,221	28,120		
Desktop Publishing	8,546	6,075		
Bookkeeping /Billing	21,498	19,681		
Misc.	2,501	3,968		
Total				

Figure 10-19

The table is automatically created and the Table Edit dialog box is opened. Now you are going to join cells A1 through E1.

7. Block cells A1 through E1

8. Select **J**oin

A dialog box appears, asking if you wish to join the cells.

9. Select **Y**es

✓ Press Enter

Cell A1 now spans the entire width of the table.

Compare your table to the one shown in Figure 10-20.

10. On your own, join cells A2 through E2

Now, you are going to format cell A1 by changing the Appearance to Bold, the Size to Very Large, and the Alignment to Center. The Table Edit dialog box should still be open.

TIP: Remember that cells may be formatted either before or after text is typed.

11. Position the cursor in cell A1

12. Select **C**ell

The Cell Format dialog box appears.

13. Select **A**ppearance

14. Select **B**old

15. Select **S**ize

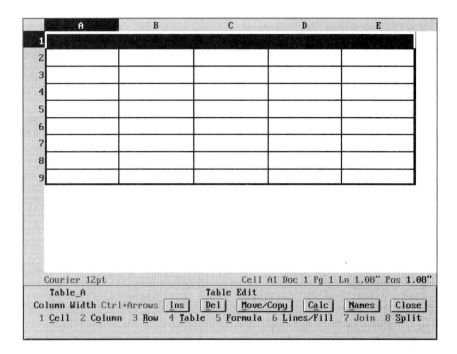

Figure 10-20

16. Select **V**ery Large

17. Select **J**ustification

18. Select **C**enter

    To exit the Cell Format dialog box,

19. Select **OK**

    ✓ Press Enter

20. On your own, move to cell A2 and change the Appearance to Bold and Italic, the Size to Large, and the Justification to Center

21. On your own, block cells A3 through E3 and change the Appearance to Bold and the Justification to Center

▋ **Formatting Columns in a Table**

To change the format for an entire column, display the Table Edit dialog box and position the cursor in the column to be affected. If more than one column is to be formatted, block *one cell* in each column; do not select all the cells in the columns. Select C**o**lumn to display the Column Format dialog box. The options in this dialog box are basically the same as in the Cell Format dialog box, with a couple of exceptions—Decimal Align Position and Column Margins. The Decimal Align Position option dictates the position of the decimal in a cell when the decimal align option is selected in the Alignment section of the dialog box. The Column Margins option allows you to change the left and right column margins.

One other parameter that has not been addressed, but that appears in both the Cell and Column Format dialog boxes, is the Number Type. This option allows you to change the way in which numbers display in your table. The default number type is General. The following options are available:

Format	Description	Example
General	Displays numbers without a thousands separator; negative number with a minus sign (-); no trailing zeros to the right of the decimal point.	2000 2000.05 2000.1 -2000
Integer	Displays numbers as counting numbers and negative numbers with a minus sign. Rounds numbers when necessary to eliminate decimals.	12 1 -1
Fixed	Allows you to display number to 15 decimal places. If a number has fewer decimal places than set, the empty decimal places are filled with zeros. Negative numbers are displayed with a minus and no thousands separator.	2000.00 2000.05 -2000 -2000.00
Percent	Displays numbers as percent values (multiplied by 100) with a trailing percent character (%). You may specify the number of decimal places.	7% 12.75%
Currency	Numbers display with dollar sign ($) and a thousands separator; the default is a comma (,). Negative numbers displayed either in parentheses, with a minus sign, or in CR/DR notation.	$10.75 $2,000 $2,000.00 ($2,000) -$2,000
Accounting	Similar to the Currency option, except the currency character is aligned at the left edge of the column.	$ 10.00 $ .50
Commas	Similar to the Fixed option, except commas are used for thousands separators and negative numbers are displayed in parentheses.	2,000.00 (2,000.00)
Scientific	Displays in scientific (exponential) notation. For example, if you specify 2 for the number of digits in a cell containing the number 450,000, the number is converted to 45e + 05.	1.2e + 02
Date	Converts dates into numeric values so that arithmetic functions can be performed. For example, date number 34,335 is displayed as January 1, 1994, or 1/1/94.	1/1/94 January 1, 1994
Text	Displays formulas as typed instead of with their computed values.	

▌HANDS-ON ACTIVITY

In the following exercise you are going to set columns B, C, and D to be right-aligned, so that your numbers will be properly aligned. You will also set the number type to commas.

1. Position the cursor in cell B4

2. Block cells B4 through D4

    Remember, when you are changing the format of more than one column, you need block only the first cell in each column in which the formatting is to take effect, as shown in Figure 10-21.

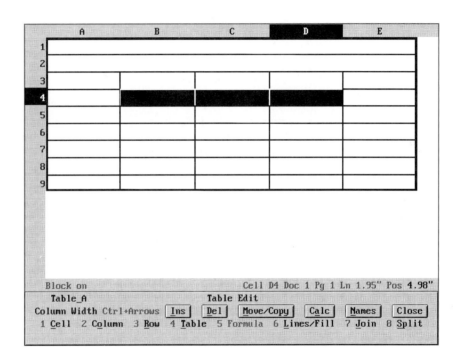

Figure 10-21

3. Select **C**olumn

    The Column Format dialog box appears.

    First, you will specify right alignment for the columns B, C, and D.

4. Select **J**ustification

5. Select **R**ight

    Now, to change the number type to commas,

6. Select Number **T**ype

    The Number Type Formats dialog box appears, as shown in Figure 10-22.

7. Select Co**m**mas

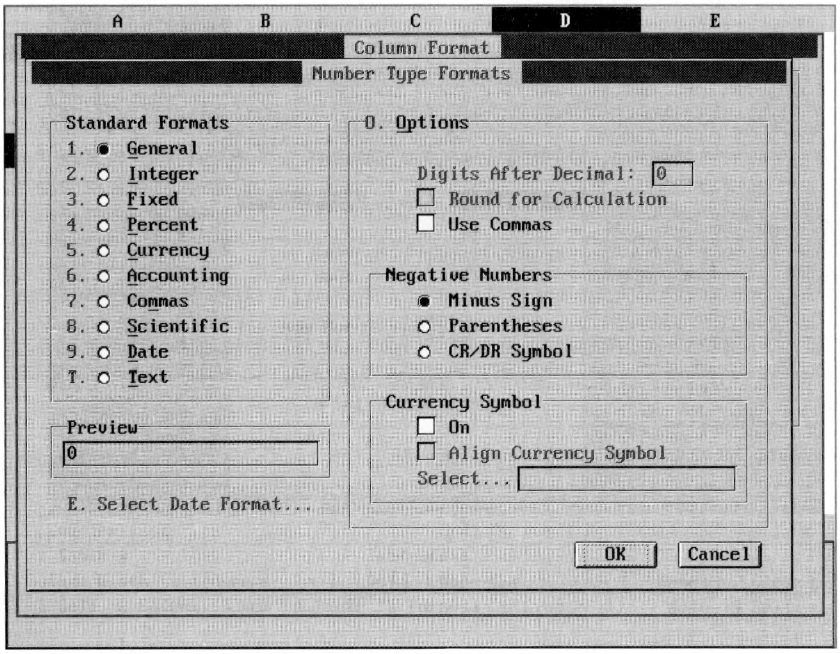

Figure 10-22

To specify the decimal places as 0,

8. Select <u>O</u>ptions

9. Select <u>D</u>igits After Decimal

10. Type **0**

11. Press (Enter)

To return to the Table Edit dialog box,

12. Select OK twice

✓ Press (Enter) twice

The next step is to format column E as right alignment and as percent with no decimal places. Make sure your cursor is in cell E4.

13. Select C<u>o</u>lumn

The Column Format dialog box appears. To specify right alignment,

14. Select <u>J</u>ustification

15. Select <u>R</u>ight

Now, to change the number type to percent,

16. Select Number <u>T</u>ype

17. Select <u>P</u>ercent

To specify the decimal places as 0,

18. Select <u>O</u>ptions

19. Select <u>D</u>igits After Decimal

20. Type 0

21. Press Enter

    To return to the Table Edit dialog box,

22. Select **OK** twice

    ✓ Press Enter twice

    To exit the Table Edit dialog box,

23. Press F7

24. Position the cursor in cell A1

25. Type `PencilPushers, Inc.`

    To move to cell A2,

26. Press Tab

27. Type `Revenue Summary`

    To move to cell A3,

28. Press Tab

29. Type `Service`

    Notice that WordPerfect followed your instructions to center, bold, and italicize the headings. To move to cell B3,

30. Press Tab

31. Type `First Qtr`

32. Press Tab

33. Type `Second Qtr`

34. Press Tab

35. Type `Diff`

36. Press Tab

37. Type `% Diff`

38. Press Tab

    The cursor is now positioned in cell A4.

39. Type `Clerical`

    To move to cell B4,

40. Press Tab

41. Type `18725`

CAUTION: Do not type the comma. Since you specified the number type as Commas, WordPerfect will automatically insert a comma whenever the number requires one.

42. Press Tab

43. Type **17640**

44. Press Tab 3 times

   The cursor is positioned in cell A5.

45. Type the remainder of the table as shown previously in Figure 10-19

   CAUTION: Remember, do not press Enter after typing the text in each cell. If the text is longer than the width of the cell, WordPerfect will automatically expand the cell to accommodate the text.

46. Save the document as **REVENUE.TBL**

Changing the Column Width

The easiest way to change the width of a table is to open the Table Edit dialog box, place the cursor in the column to be adjusted, and press Ctrl + → to increase the width or Ctrl + ← to decrease the width.

If you need a column to be a specific size, while in the Table Edit dialog box position the cursor in the column to be changed and select Column ⇒ Width. Type the desired width and press Enter.

HANDS-ON ACTIVITY

You are going to change the width of column A (using the Ctrl + → shortcut).

1. Position the cursor in cell A4

2. Display the Table Edit dialog box

3. Press Ctrl + → 8 times

4. Position the cursor in cell B4

5. Press Ctrl + → once

6. Position the cursor in cell C4

7. Press Ctrl + → once

   Compare your document to the one shown in Figure 10-23.

Shading Cells

Cells can be shaded to add interest to a table. You can use shading in titles or to emphasize a particular cell or column. To do this, display the Table Edit dialog box and block the cells to be shaded. Select Line/Fill to display the Table Lines dialog box. Select Fill to display the Fill Style and Color dialog box. Select Fill Style to display the Fill Styles dialog box. Choose the desired shading (10% to 100% or None). If you wish the entire table to be shaded, at the Table/Lines dialog box select the Border/Fill option.

PencilPushers, Inc.				
Revenue Summary				
Service	**First Qtr**	**Second Qtr**	**Diff**	**% Diff**
Clerical	18,725	17,640		
Word Processing	23,221	28,120		
Desktop Publishing	8,546	6,075		
Bookkeeping/Billing	21,498	19,681		
Misc.	2,501	3,968		
Total				

Figure 10-23

TIP: Although you cannot have different levels of shading in a single table, you can create two (or more) tables next to each other and specify varying percentages of shading for each table. For example, if you want the title of a table to have a different shading from the rest of the table, create a table with one row and column for the title, and then create another table for the remainder of the text.

Figure 10-24 shows the way different types of shading appear.

▌ HANDS-ON ACTIVITY

In this exercise, you are going to shade the title of your table.

1. Position the cursor in cell A1

2. Display the Table Edit dialog box

3. Select **L**ines/**Fill**

   The Table Line dialog box appears.

4. Select **F**ill

   The Fill Style and Color dialog box appears, as shown in Figure 10-25.

5. Select **Fill St**y**le**

   The Fill Styles dialog box appears, as shown in Figure 10-26.

6. Select **10% Shaded Fill**

7. Press Enter

8. Select **OK**

   ✓ Press Enter

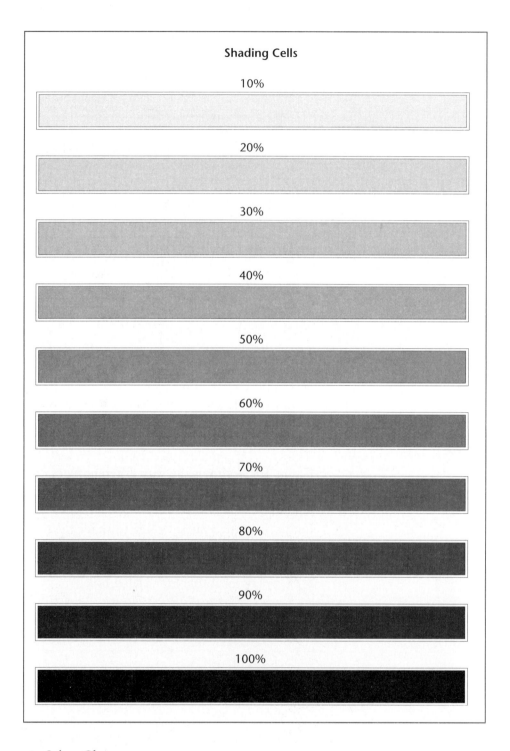

Figure 10-24

9. Select **Close**

   ✓ Press ⌨️Enter⌨️

10. On your own, block E3 through E9 and shade these cells as 10%

    Compare your document to the one shown in Figure 10-27 (page 266).

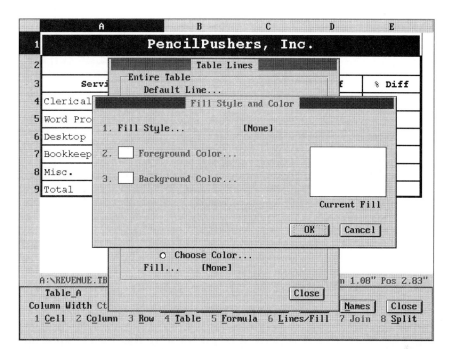

Figure 10-25

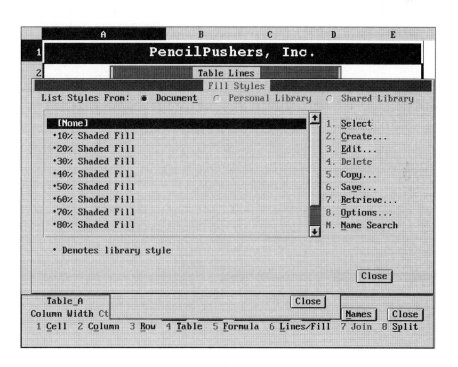

Figure 10-26

To exit the Table Edit dialog box,

11. Press F7

12. Save your document

PencilPushers, Inc.				
Revenue Summary				
Service	First Qtr	Second Qtr	Diff	% Diff
Clerical	18,725	17,640		
Word Processing	23,221	28,120		
Desktop Publishing	8,546	6,075		
Bookkeeping/Billing	21,498	19,681		
Misc.	2,501	3,968		
Total				

Figure 10-27

Moving or Copying Rows and Columns

The Move/Copy feature in the Table Edit dialog box allows you to move a block of text, cell(s), row(s), or column(s). To move or copy one row or column, position the cursor in the appropriate row or column. If several cells, rows, or columns are to be moved or copied, use the Block feature to highlight the appropriate quantity. Select the Move/Copy option. The Move dialog box appears, in which you select the area of text to either Move or Copy. Position the cursor where the cut or copied text is to be placed and press Enter.

▌ HANDS-ON ACTIVITY

In this exercise, you are going to move the row that reads "Clerical" to follow "Bookkeeping."

1. Position the cursor someplace in the row that reads "Clerical" (row 4)

2. Display the Table Edit dialog box

3. Select Move/Copy

   ✓ Press Ctrl + F4

   The Move dialog box appears, as shown in Figure 10-28.

4. Select Row

5. Select Move

   The "Clerical" row has been removed from the table and placed in the cut and paste buffer (a temporary area to hold text while it is being moved). The screen prompts, "Move cursor; Press Enter to retrieve."

6. Move the cursor into the row that reads "Misc."

7. Press Enter

   To exit the Table Edit dialog box,

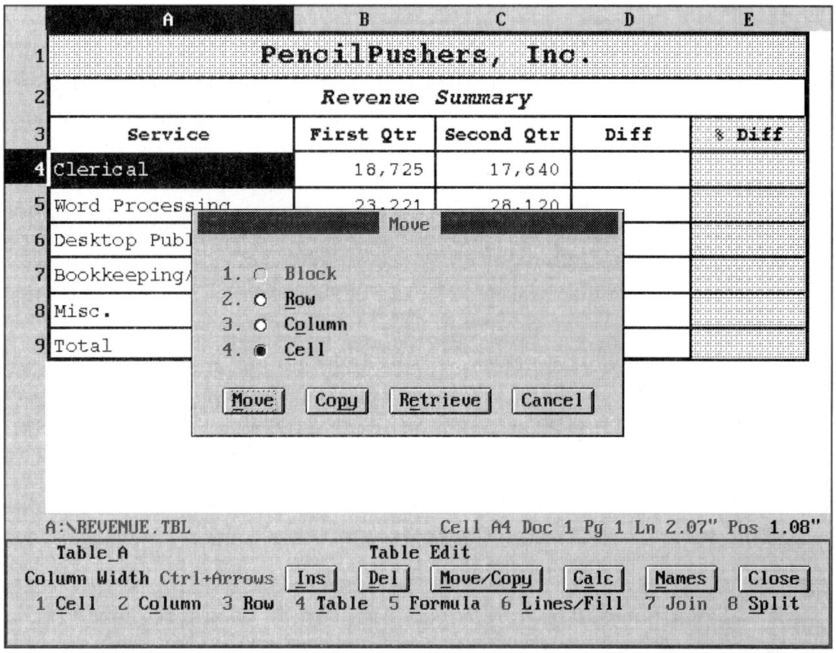

Figure10-28

8. Select **Close**

    ✓ Press `F7`

Performing Mathematical Calculations in Tables

WordPerfect has the capability of performing mathematical calculations within a table. Formulas can include addition, subtraction, multiplication, and division. Any combination of the following arithmetic operators can be used in a formula:

+   Addition

–   Subtraction

*   Multiplication

/   Division

These operators will work with numbers, cell addresses, or both. Formulas can contain numbers, cell addresses, or both. If a formula contains two or more operators, they are calculated from left to right. By enclosing any part of a formula in parentheses, you order that portion of the formula to be calculated first. If parentheses are nested (one set enclosed within another), the numbers within the deepest level are calculated first. Listed below are some sample formulas:

Formula	Result
A1 + B1	Adds the contents of cells A1 and B1
D2*100/B2	The contents of cell D2 are multiplied by 100 and then divided by the contents of cell B2
5/(G1 + 50)	Adds the contents in cell G1 to 50, and then divides 5 by that number

WordPerfect 6.0 has over 100 spreadsheet **functions**, which are built-in formulas to perform various calculations. These functions are prerecorded formulas that have already been verified for accuracy. The Functions option is located in the Table Formula dialog box, and the Functions are listed in alphabetical order. Functions can be used in cells, formulas, or even other functions.

Most functions have a similar format, which consists of two parts: the function name followed by parentheses. If information, called an **argument**, is required, WordPerfect displays the keywords inside the parentheses. For example, in the Function list, the POWER function appears as POWER (number1, number2). Two arguments (number1, number2) are presented in this function, and each describes the type of information needed. Notice, also, that the arguments are separated by a comma. If a function is followed by an empty parenthesis, no arguments are needed. For example, the DATE function appears as DATE().

Using Ranges

A **range** is a group of one or more cells that form a rectangle that is contiguous (one whose sides all touch). A range can be a single cell, a row, a column, several rows or columns, or even the entire table. All cells in a range must be adjacent to one another. It is advantageous to define a range, since commands and formulas can be performed on more than one cell at a given time, giving you unpredictable results if the range is not defined correctly. Figure 10-29 indicates legal and illegal ranges.

A **range address** consists of cell addresses that specify the first and last cell in the range, separated by a colon. In Figure 10-30, Range 1 consists of one row (beginning at cell A4 and ending at cell G4); therefore, the range is defined as A4:G4. Range 2 is one column (beginning at cell C1 and ending at cell C8); so the range is defined as C1:C8. Range 3 in the figure is one cell, so the range address is F2:F2. Range 4 consists of a block of cells with several row and columns; when defining this range, specify from the upper-left corner to the lower right—for instance, this range is E6:G8.

A range is defined by highlighting it, by using either the cursor or the mouse pointer. To define a range, move the cell pointer to a beginning or corner cell and select point mode, or press F4 to anchor the cell. Once a cell is anchored, you can use the cursor or mouse to highlight the remainder of the range.

Creating a Formula

To enter a formula, position the insertion point in the cell where the formula is to be entered. Display the Table Edit dialog box and select Formula. The Table Formula dialog box displays, allowing you to enter a formula using arithmetic operators or functions. To display an alphabetical list of functions select Functions or press F5.

▌ HANDS-ON ACTIVITY

In this exercise, you are going to create a formula that will calculate the difference between the two three-month time periods.

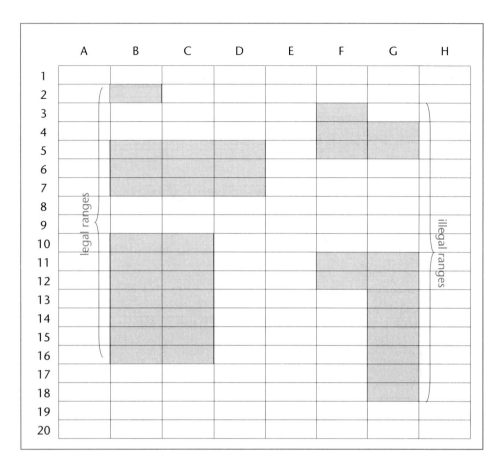

Figure 10-29

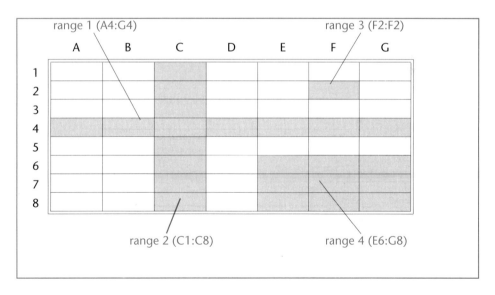

Figure 10-30

1. Position the cursor in cell D4

2. Display the Table Edit dialog box

3. Select **F**ormula

   The Table Formula dialog box appears, as shown in Figure 10-31.

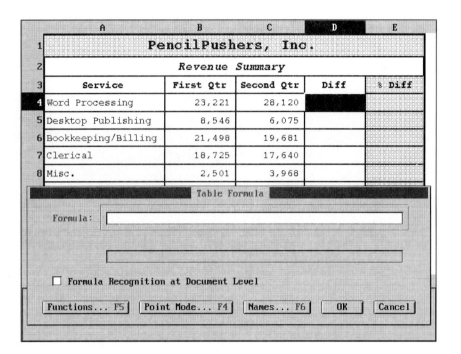

Figure 10-31

Enter the following formula to subtract the contents of cell B4 from the contents of cell C4 (be sure to type a minus sign (–) and not a dash when entering the formula):

4. Type **C4-B4**

5. Press ⟨Enter⟩

    To exit the Table Formula dialog box,

6. Select **OK**

    ✓ Press ⟨Enter⟩

    Notice that the result instantly appears in the cell and the formula appears in the lower-left corner of the dialog box. The resulting difference should be an increase of 4,899.

    To return to the document window,

7. Select **Close**

    ✓ Press ⟨F7⟩

▋ **Copying a Formula** A formula can easily be copied from one cell to another cell or to adjoining rows or columns. WordPerfect will automatically adjust the copied formula to reflect the correct cell address. For example, if the original formula is A1 + A2 and the formula is copied to column B, the formula will be adjusted to read B1 + B2.

To copy a formula, position the insertion point in the cell that contains the formula to be copied, display the Table Edit dialog box, and select the Move/Copy option. Select the Cell option and choose Copy. To copy to a specific cell, choose To Cell and enter the cell address. To copy the formula to the right, choose <u>R</u>ight and enter the number of times it is to be copied, or to copy the formula down, choose <u>D</u>own and enter the number of times the formula is to be copied.

▌ HANDS-ON ACTIVITY

In this exercise you are going to copy the formula down five times (from cell D5 through D9). The cursor should still be positioned in cell D4.

1. Display the Table Edit dialog box

2. Position the cursor in cell D4

3. Select <u>M</u>ove/Copy

   The Move dialog box appears.

4. Select <u>C</u>ell

5. Select Cop<u>y</u>

   The Copy Cell dialog box appears, as shown in Figure 10-32.

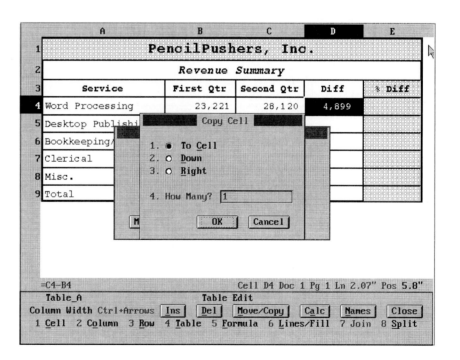

Figure 10-32

6. Select <u>D</u>own

   The cursor instantly moves to the How Many? text box.

7. Type **5**

8. Press Enter

9. Select OK

   The result in cell D9 displays a zero. After you total the B and C columns in cells B9 and C9, you will recalculate the formula in D9.

NOTE: Negative numbers in column D are displayed with a minus sign.

▊ HANDS-ON ACTIVITY

Now, you are going to create a formula that will calculate the percentage difference between the two quarters. The Table Edit dialog box should still be open.

1. Move the cell pointer to E4

2. Select <u>F</u>ormula

   The Table Formula dialog box appears.

3. Type **D4/B4**

4. Press (Enter)

   To exit the Table Formula dialog box,

5. Select **OK**

   ✓ Press (Enter)

6. On your own, copy the formula from cell E4 down 5 rows

   Compare your table to the one shown in Figure 10-33.

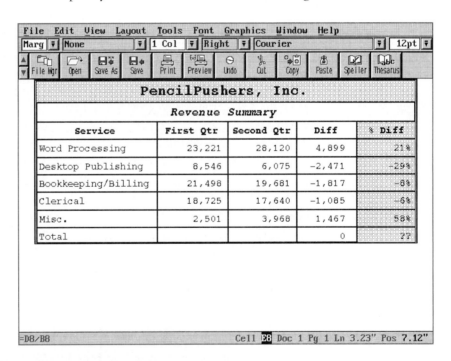

Figure 10-33

▊ HANDS-ON ACTIVITY

In this exercise, you are going to use the SUM function to total the First Quarter column.

1. Move the cursor to cell B9

2. Display the Table Edit dialog box

3. Select <u>F</u>ormula

The Table Formula dialog box appears. To display the Table Functions dialog box,

4. Select **Functions** or press F5

Compare your screen to the one shown in Figure 10-34.

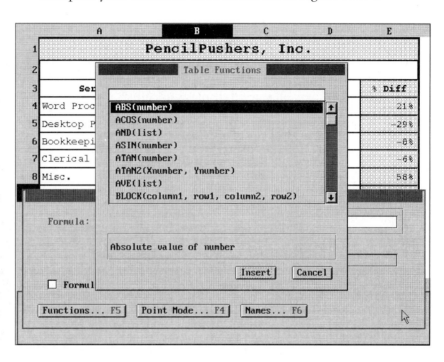

Figure 10-34

Use either the scroll bar or the arrow keys to

5. Highlight **SUM(list)**

TIP: A quick way to get there is to type SUM.

6. Select **Insert**

The Formula text box appears as SUM(). You are now going to block the range of cells that you want WordPerfect to total.

7. Select **Point Mode**

✓ Press F4

Remember, to specify a range you define the beginning and ending cells.

8. Move to cell B8

Now, you need to anchor that cell so that you can block the remainder of the range to be totaled. To anchor the cell,

9. Select **<u>S</u>tart Block**

✓ Press F4

10. Press ↑ 4 times

Cells B8 through B4 are blocked to define the range.

11. Select **OK**

    ✓ Press [Enter]

    The Table Formula dialog box reappears and the Formula text box reads SUM(B4:B8). To accept the formula,

12. Press [Enter]

13. Select **OK**

    ✓ Press [Enter]

    The total displays in cell B9.

14. On your own, copy the formula to the right one column

    The formulas in cells D9 and E9 need to be updated.

15. Select **C**alc

    Compare your document to the one shown in Figure 10-35.

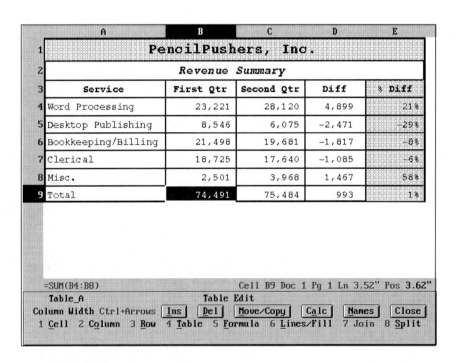

Figure 10-35

16. Exit the Table Edit dialog box

17. Save and print the document

18. Exit WordPerfect

On Your Own

Review of Commands

Description	Menu Commands	Function Keys
List the commands to:		
Create a table	_____	_____
Insert a row	_____	_____
Delete a row	_____	_____
Undelete a row	_____	_____
Format cells	_____	_____
Alter lines in a table	_____	_____
Join cells	_____	_____
Format columns	_____	_____
Change column width	_____	_____
Shade cells	_____	_____
Move a row	_____	_____
Create a formula	_____	_____
List the operators or functions to:		
Add	_____	_____
Subtract	_____	_____
Multiply	_____	_____
Divide	_____	_____
Sum	_____	_____
List the keystrokes to move the cursor in a table:		
Up one cell in the current column	_____	_____
Down one cell in the current column	_____	_____
One character to the left	_____	_____
One character to the right	_____	_____
To the next cell	_____	_____
To the previous cell	_____	_____
To the beginning of the text in a cell	_____	_____
To the last line of text in a cell	_____	_____

To the first cell in a column	_____	_____
To the last cell in a column	_____	_____
To the first cell in a row	_____	_____
To the last cell in a row	_____	_____
To the first cell in a table	_____	_____
To the last cell in a table	_____	_____

▌ Lesson Review

1. What is the intersection of a row and column called?

2. What is an example of a cell address?

3. What keystrokes move to the first cell in a row?

4. What is the maximum number of columns allowable in one table?

5. What keystrokes will insert a row in a document window?

6. Where should the cursor be positioned if you want to delete three rows?

7. List the steps to undelete a row or column.

8. How can text be entered in the Table Edit dialog box?

9. What happens when you join four cells, such as A1, B1, C1, and D1?

10. What are some of the size attributes available?

11. What must be done to format more than one cell?

12. What happens when the Lock option is turned on?

13. List some of the Line Style options available in the Line Styles dialog box.

14. In the Table Edit dialog box, which option allows you to change the shading of a cell?

15. What formula would total cells A1, A2, A3?

16. What is the most efficient way to expand and contract column widths?

17. What is a function?

18. How does 100% shading appear?

19. What is a range?

20. List the steps to define a range.

▍ Assignments

10.1 Directions

1. Create a table consisting of the following:

   Title (Row 1): CMS CLASS SCHEDULE—shaded 30%, bold, centered, and large font

   Subtitle (Row 2): Fall Semester—large font, centered, and italic

   Column headings (Row 3): Course No., Name, Instructor, Room, Time—centered

   Data (Rows 4–9):

CMS201	Intro Computers	Landry	CN217	8:00
CMS305	File Design	Morrell	WC265	9:00
CMS306	Database	Garman	WC268	10:00
CMS311	COBOL	DiBrell	CN217	11:00
CMS223	Word Processing	Larsen	WC267	12:00
CMS323	LAN/WAN	Morris	CN215	1:00

2. Save the file as **SCHEDULE.CMS.**

3. Print and exit.

10.2 Directions

1. Design a table containing the following information:

   Title (Row 1): CMS Expenses

   Subtitle (Row 2): First Quarter

   Column Heads (Row 3): Faculty Travel / Jan. / Feb. / March / Total

   Data (Rows 4–11):
   (first row)Landry / 1230 / 600 / (empty)
   (second row)Monroe / 989 / 1079 / (empty)
   (third row)Pence / 1160 / (empty) / 939
   (four row)Morrell / 680 / 400/ /329
   (fifth row)Shaw / 760 / (empty) / (empty
   (sixth row)Morris / (empty / 739 / (empty)
   (seventh row)Prins / (empty) / (empty / 1123
   (eighth row)Freeman / empty / 1261 / (empty)
   (ninth row)Total / (empty) / (empty) / (empty)

2. Save the table as EXPENSES.CMS.

3. Calculate totals horizontally (row 12) and vertically (column E).

4. Save again, print, and exit.

11

Setting Up
Text Columns

Objectives

Upon completion of this lesson, you will be able to do the following:

- Create parallel columns
- Create newspaper columns
- Change column width
- Move and copy columns
- Convert parallel columns to a table
- Retrieve a file

This lesson introduces you to setting up text columns. WordPerfect 6.0 allows for the creation of up to 24 side-by-side text columns. Two different types of text columns can be created—newspaper and parallel.

Starting Point

Before beginning the lesson, start WordPerfect 6.0. The document window should be blank. Make sure the Train Button Bar and Ribbon are displayed.

Types of Text Columns

Two different styles of text columns are available: newspaper and parallel. **Newspaper columns** are designed for text that flows continuously from one column to the next. When the first column is filled with text, the cursor automatically moves to the top of the next column, and so on, through all the columns. If you want to end a column before its bottom is reached, choose <u>L</u>ayout ⇒ <u>A</u>lignment ⇒ Hard <u>P</u>age (*Shortcut keys:* Ctrl + Enter) to insert a hard page break. The **Balanced Newspaper columns** style is a new feature with WordPerfect 6.0; however, it functions the same as newspaper columns, except that each column on a page is adjusted to be equal in length.

Parallel columns are designed for documents in which information in the first column relates to information in the second (and subsequent) columns, as it does in a table. Examples of this type of document include employment resumés. In a resumé, the first column might consist of a job title, employer, and dates of employment; the second column would hold the job description. The first and second columns for each job would likely be of different length, but for each job both columns would need to begin on the same line. In other words, the first line of each column in the group is kept on the same line. **Parallel Block Protect** columns prevent a column block or group from being split by a soft page break.

Examples of both columns are shown in Figure 11-1.

Newspaper-Style Columns

Newspaper-style columns are designed for documents such as newsletters or magazine articles, in which the text continuously flows from the top to the bottom of each column on a page and from column to column. Text flows smoothly from one column to the next, even if text is added or deleted. An entire document can be designed with newspaper columns or you may want to divide only a portion of the document into columns. This feature has great versatility.

Parallel Columns

Block 1

Block 2

Parallel columns are designed to align the first line of each unit. Each column can have a varying number of lines, but WordPerfect will always keep the first line of the unit uniform.

When typing text in the Parallel column style, you first type the text of the first column, and then press [CTRL]+[ENTER] to position the cursor in the next column. Then you type its text.

Figure 11-1

Creating Columns

To create columns, there are three basic steps:

- Define the columns.
- Type the text.
- Turn off the Column feature.

Defining the Columns

To begin a document that will have columns, move the cursor where the Columns feature is to start and choose Layout ⇒ Columns (*Shortcut keys:* Alt + F7, 1). The Text Columns dialog box appears. If you choose the default settings presented in this dialog box, WordPerfect will automatically create two newspaper columns with evenly divided columns according to the existing margins in the document separated by a ½-inch gutter. A **gutter** is the space between columns.

The Column Type parameter offers four choices: Newspaper, Balanced Newspaper, Parallel, and Parallel with Block Protect. Enter the desired number of columns in the Number of Columns option; up to 24 columns can be specified. WordPerfect will automatically and equally divide the specified number of columns between the left and right document margins, inserting between columns the gutter measurement specified in the Distance Between Columns option. The Line Spacing Between Rows option only applies to Parallel columns or Parallel with Block Protect columns, and it specifies the line spacing between each group or unit.

To specify uneven columns, choose Custom Width and designate the desired margins for each column.

Newspaper style columns can be turned on with the Ribbon. When this method is used, WordPerfect automatically defines newspaper style columns and equally divides the specified number of columns between the left and right document margins, inserting a ½-inch gutter between columns. To use the Ribbon method, position the cursor where the columns are to begin, move the mouse pointer to the Columns browse button, and click to display the list, as shown in Figure 11-2. Double-click on the desired number of columns.

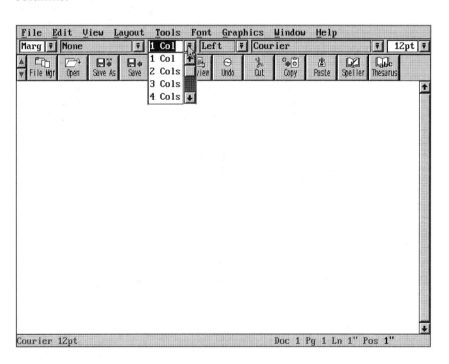

Figure 11-2

Typing the Text

When typing parallel columns, type the text and choose Layout ⇒ Alignment ⇒ Hard Page (*Shortcut keys:* Ctrl + Enter) to position the cursor in the next column. Choosing Layout ⇒ Alignment ⇒ Hard Page (*Shortcut keys:* Ctrl + Enter) after typing the last column moves the cursor to the beginning of the first column. Remember, the Line Spacing Between Rows option in the Text Column dialog box dictates the line spacing between each group or unit.

When you type the text in newspaper columns, a new column is automatically started when the cursor reaches the bottom of a column. To force text to the next column, position the cursor before the text that you want on the next column and choose Layout ⇒ Alignment ⇒ Hard Page (*Shortcut keys:* Ctrl + Enter).

Turning Columns Off

Turning columns off is necessary only if you are combining regular text or columns with different types or widths of columns in one document. To turn columns off, choose Layout ⇒ Columns ⇒ Off (*Shortcut keys:* Alt + F7, 1, F).

Creating Newspaper Columns

Remember, there are two ways to define newspaper columns: using the Ribbon and using the Text Column dialog box. The Ribbon is the easiest method with which to create newspaper columns. However, one drawback is that uneven column widths and specific gutter widths cannot be selected when using this method.

When columns have been defined, a [Col Def] code is inserted at the cursor position. If you expand the code, it appears as [Col Def:Newspaper;*n*]. The *n* represents the specified number of columns. If the Balanced Newspaper columns option is selected, the expanded code appears as [Col Def: Newspaper with Balance;*n*]. After the first column is typed, WordPerfect automatically inserts an [SCol] code (soft column) at the bottom of the column and the cursor automatically moves to the top of the next column. If you want to end a column before the bottom of the page, select Layout ⇒ Alignment ⇒ Hard Page (*Shortcut keys:* Ctrl + Enter), at which time WordPerfect inserts an [HCol] code (hard column) and moves the cursor to the top of the next column. When you turn columns off, a [Col Def] code is placed at the cursor position. If the code is expanded, it appears as [Col Def:Off].

▌HANDS-ON ACTIVITY

In this exercise, you will create a two-column newsletter, using the Ribbon method. *Remember, you must have a mouse attached to your system to access the Ribbon.* If you do not have a mouse, follow the keyboard method shown with a ✓. The newsletter is shown in Figure 11-3 for your reference. Do not be concerned if your lines and columns break differently.

1. Change the left and right margins to .5"

2. Select **Courier 10 cpi** or **Courier 12 pt** as the Document Initial Font

   Now you are ready to begin typing your document.

3. Select **Center, Bold**, and **Very Large**

4. Type `Newsletter`

   (Don't forget to turn off the Bold and Very Large attributes.)

5. Press Enter 4 times

Newsletter

Third Quarter   Volume VI, Number 1

A Word About Our Company

In order to provide more information on how we can assist you with administrative and support services, PencilPushers, Inc. prepares this "newsletter" quarterly. The intent of this newsletter is to update you on community affairs, the local business environment, and the computer industry. Our focus as a company is to provide the office support services you would want your own secretarial staff to provide.

Team Work

In business today, there is a growing trend toward team performance and discovering how employees can work more effectively together through communication and successful interdependent relationships. The Team Building Corporation specializes in developing relationships within their clients' organizations.

Team Building Corporation is offering a one-day free seminar to introduce a series of dynamic and interactive activities to address critical interpersonal topics such as team building, managing change, communication skills, and interpersonal development for self-directed work teams.

Environmentally Aware

The Boulder Chamber is forming an Environmental Committee to focus on a broad range of interrelated environmental issues. A summer retreat has been scheduled to determine the committee's scope of work. To register for the Environmental Committee or to attend the planning retreat, call the Chamber at 444-2000.

Conducting New Business

A monthly networking and educational program for owners of businesses less than two years old. It features networking opportunities and a monthly topic of concern to newer businesses. New owners will gain support, have educational programs, networking opportunities, and help in growing their businesses. Next session is September 20. Call Catherine Pyle at 422-3000 to make a reservation.

Fall Conference

Take Note! Here is a quick way to update yourself on the latest trends and developments in the computer and communications industry. The 10th Annual Computer Conference will be held October 9 - 13th at the Mile-Hi Convention Center, Denver, Colorado. Presenters are highly skilled and knowledgeable in today's fastest changing industry. For your convenience, sessions are broken down into half day and all day sessions. To register, call the Conference Registration Office at 444-1212.

Targeting New Products

WordPerfect Corporation announces

Figure 11-3 (page 1)

Now you need to choose the Font size of Small.

6. Select F*ont* $\Rightarrow$ F*ont* $\Rightarrow$ <u>R</u>elative <u>S</u>ize $\Rightarrow$ <u>S</u>mall

7. Select **OK**

WordPerfect 6.0 for DOS to be released this month. Among the new and enhanced features are additional spreadsheet functionality, the ability to fax directly within WordPerfect, WYSIWYG editing, scalable fonts, selectable merge, and a DOS version of the QuickFinder. This version is touted to be the best yet and beta test sites agree.

The Corporate Network

Probably no one needs to be convinced that computers empower individuals to do their jobs better and more efficiently. But what about individuals working together that need to share information and files? Individuals working on standalone computers need to share information and work together. However, sharing information in this type of network is called "Sneaker Net"-- put your sneakers on and walk the information down the hall. A local area network (LAN) is made up of computers and shared devices that are physically connected by cables. LANs allow entire buildings and campuses to share expensive resources, such as laser printers, scanners, CD-ROM players, large capacity disk drives, software programs, etc. The cost of providing and maintaining a network is large, but the cost of not providing it is even larger.

The Darker Side of Computing

If someone mentions they have a virus, it may not be a physical illness. Computers seem to also occasionally have an illness called a virus. A virus is no more than a small program written so as to "hide itself" on diskettes and transfer to any PCs/disks it comes in contact with, directly or via a computer network. The program code is "triggered" by some event (such as a particular date) and then activates some pre-programmed code to, for example, display a message on your screen, corrupt data or erase files. The danger is that viruses can replicate themselves on many disks without being noticed, so they can spread widely before being triggered.

Our suggestion is be a "Wise Owl" and follow the four tips below for "safer computing":

1. If your software allows, apply write-protect tabs on all program disks before installing the software.

2. Do not install software if you do not know where it's been.

3. Keep backups of your important files, especially corporate financial statements.

4. Bring your disks to the computer lab and use the virus detection software on the machines to check for viruses.

Awards

Ms. Priscilla Singer of Basin Enterprises was awarded the prestigious honor of "Business Person of the Year." Ms. Singer founded Basin Enterprises ten years ago and has successfully built a reputable company. Ms. Singer's business is located in the Spruce Building.

Figure 11-3 (page 2)

✓ Press ⌊Enter⌋

8. Type **Third Quarter**

To move the cursor to the right margin, choose the Flush Right feature:

9. Select <u>L</u>ayout ⇒ <u>A</u>lignment ⇒ <u>F</u>lush Right

   ✓ Press `Alt` + `F6`

10. Type `Volume VI, Number 1`

    (Be sure to turn Small off.)

11. Press `Enter` 3 times

    You are now ready to define your newspaper columns.

12. Position the mouse pointer on the Columns browse button in the Ribbon and click

    Compare your document window to the one shown in Figure 11-4.

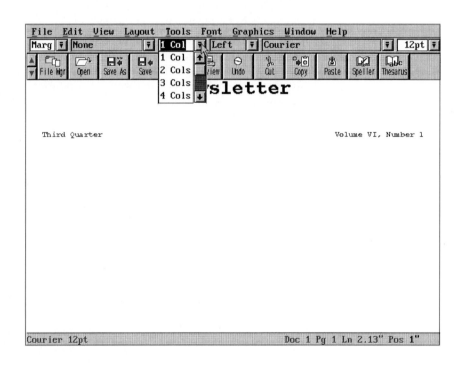

Figure 11-4

13. Move the mouse pointer to the 2 Cols option and double-click

    ✓ Press `Alt` + `F7` , `1`

    ✓ Press `Enter`

14. Display the Reveal Codes screen and notice that the [Col Def] code and the status line both display the Col number

▌ Retrieving a File into an Open Document

In Lesson 8 you learned to retrieve a text file into an already open document. If you recall, the <u>F</u>ile ⇒ <u>R</u>etrieve feature inserts the specified document at the cursor position. This feature proves extremely handy when you want to combine portions of two existing documents and customize a new one.

▌ **HANDS-ON ACTIVITY**

Instead of your typing a long document, the newsletter document is supplied on your sample disk. Insert the data disk into a floppy drive. In this exercise, we will refer to the drive as A; however, if you are using a different drive, substitute the appropriate drive letter.

1. Select <u>F</u>ile ⇒ <u>R</u>etrieve

   The Retrieve Document dialog box appears. The cursor is blinking in the Filename text box.

2. Type `A:NEWS.COL`

3. Select **OK**

   ✓ Press Enter

   Notice that the text automatically wraps into two columns. Compare your document to the one shown in Figure 11-3.

   Also, notice that the Column indicator on the Ribbon now displays 2 to indicate that two columns have been defined.

4. Save the document as **NEWSLTR.COL**

5. Use the Print Preview feature to view the document

   Notice that the columns on the second page are uneven.

   Now, you are going to change the column definition to the Balanced Newspaper style, so that the columns will be automatically balanced.

▌ Changing the Column Type

To change the column definition from newspaper style to balanced newspaper or vice versa, the cursor can be positioned anywhere within the columns if the Auto Code Placement feature is turned on. However, if the Auto Code Placement feature is turned off, make sure the cursor is at the beginning of columns; otherwise your columns will not align correctly. You must use the Text Column dialog box to accomplish this task.

▌ **HANDS-ON ACTIVITY**

In this exercise, you are going to change the column definition from newspaper to balanced newspaper. We are assuming that the Auto Code Placement is turned on. If not, position the cursor at the beginning of column 1.

1. Select <u>L</u>ayout ⇒ <u>C</u>olumns

   ✓ Press Alt + F7 , 1

   The Text Column dialog box appears, as shown in Figure 11-5.

2. Select **Column <u>T</u>ype**

3. Select **Balanced N<u>e</u>wspaper**

   To exit the dialog box,

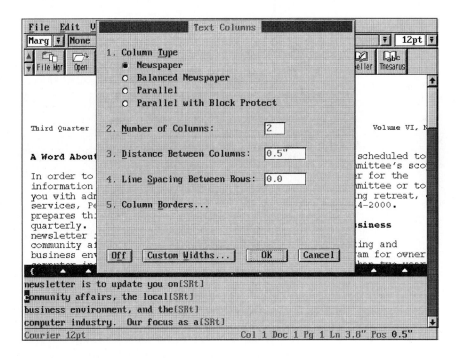

Figure 11-5

4. Select **OK**

   ✓ Press [Enter]

5. Use the Print Preview feature to view the document

   Notice that the columns in the second page are almost equal in length.

   To turn columns off,

6. Position the cursor at the bottom of the document

7. Select **L**ayout ⇒ **C**olumns ⇒ O**f**f

   ✓ Press [Alt] + [F7], **1, F**

8. Save and close the file

▪ Creating Parallel Columns

Basically, you follow the same steps to create parallel columns as you did newspaper, with one exception. The Line **S**pacing Between Rows option in the Text Column dialog box dictates the space between each group or unit.

At the point where the columns are defined, a [Col Def] code is inserted. If you expand the code, it appears as [Col Def:Parallel;*n*]. The *n* represents the specified number of columns. If the Parallel with Block Protect option is selected, the expanded code appears as [Col Def:Parallel with Protect;*n*].

After the text for the first column is typed and you choose **L**ayout ⇒ **A**lignment ⇒ Hard **P**age (*Shortcut keys:* [Ctrl] + [Enter]), to move the cursor to the next column insert an [HCol] code (hard column). Do this in each column. When you turn columns off, a [Col Def] code is placed at the cursor position. If you expand the code, it appears as [Col Def:Off]. Figure 11-6 illustrates the expanded codes for parallel columns.

```
[Col Def:Parallel;n]
xxxxxxxxxxxxxxxxx    xxxxxxxxxxxxxxxx    xxxxxxxxxxxxxxxx
xxxxxxxxxxxxxxxxx    xxxxxxxxxxxxxxxx    xxxxxxxxxxxxxxxx
xxxxxx[HCol]         xxxxxxxxxxxxxxxx    xxxxxxxxxxxxxxxx
                     xxxxxxxxxxxxxxxx    xxxxxxxxx[HCol]
                     xxxxxx[HCol]


xxxxxxxxxxxxxxxx     xxxxxxxxxxxxxxxx    xxxxxxxxxxxxxxxx
xxxxxxxxxxxxxxxxx    xxxxxxxxxx[HCol]    xxxxxxxxxxxxxxxx
xxxxxxxxxxxxxxxx                         xxxxxxxxxxxxxxxx
xxxxxxxxxxxxxxxx                         xxxxxxxxxx[THCol]
xxxxxxxxx[HCol]                          [Col Def:off]
```

Figure 11-6

▌ HANDS-ON ACTIVITY

You are now ready to begin the exercise to create parallel columns. When defining the columns, you will specify three columns, and you will define a different width for each one.

In the last several weeks at the headquarters of PencilPushers, several people have dropped by the reception desk in both the Spruce and Pine buildings, requesting information on services and pricing. You are going to use the parallel columns feature to create a small flyer that you can hand out to inquiring individuals. The flyer is shown in Figure 11-7 for your reference.

1. On your own, change the left and right margins to .5"

2. On your own, set the Document Initial Font to **Courier 10** cpi or **Courier 12 pt**

    Now you are ready to begin typing your document.

3. First, on your own, turn on **Center, Bold,** and **Extra Large**

4. Type `PencilPushers, Inc.`

    (Don't forget to turn off the Bold and Extra Large features.)

5. Press Enter twice

6. Now, on your own, turn on **Center, Bold, Italics,** and **Very Large**

7. Type `Scope of Services`

8. Press Enter 3 times

    Now you are ready to define the parallel columns.

9. Select **Layout** ⇒ **Columns**

    ✓ Press Alt + F7, **1**

10. Select **Column Type**

11. Select **Parallel**

PencilPushers, Inc.

Scope of Services

CLERICAL	Mailings, small or bulk (sorting & physical mailing only); typing miscellaneous labels, envelopes; filing; copying; miscellaneous small tasks.	$14.00
PROOFREADING	Available for all general text, excluding highly technical text.	$18.00
WORD PROCESSING	Manuscript text, business letters, personalized letters, contracts, proposals, mailing lists (typing and maintenance), bulk mailings, statistical typing, reports, special projects, etc.	$20.00
RESUME SERVICE	Complete services from initial interview to defining the scope of the resume to the finished product.	$20.00
ENHANCED WORD PROCESSING	Data conversion of other word processing files; text which incorporates some desktop publishing features (i.e. columns, tables) without using a desktop publishing program.	$25.00
DESKTOP PUBLISHING	Newsletters, Promotions, Layouts, Flyers, Corporate Reports, etc.	$35.00
BOOKKEEPING AND BILLING	Checkbook reconciliations, full-charge bookkeeping, payroll, financial reporting, financial statements, client billing, etc. Areas of billing expertise - service companies, real estate and therapy services.	$25.00
CONSULTING	Available in the areas of office procedures, office efficiencies, staffing, bookkeeping procedures and executive suites.	$40.00

(All Services are quoted on a per hour basis)

Figure 11-7

To specify the number of columns,

12. Select **N**umber of Columns

The cursor jumps to the Number of Columns text box.

13. Type **3**

14. Press Enter

Notice the Line **S**pacing Between Rows parameter. The current setting is 1, which specifies one blank row between each group or unit in the columns. To specify the custom column widths,

15. Select **Custom Widths**

    The Text Columns dialog box displays, adding a Custom Widths window, and column 1 is highlighted, as shown in Figure 11-8.

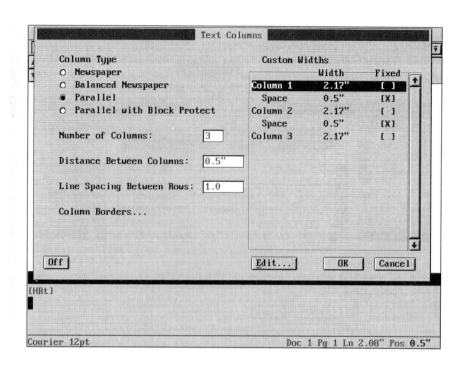

Figure 11-8

To change the width for column 1,

16. Select **Edit**

    ✓ Press ⌗Enter⌗

    Another dialog box appears at the bottom of the screen, as shown in Figure 11-9. Column 1 appears in the title of the dialog box, indicating that the changes made will affect column 1.

17. Select **Width**

    The cursor moves to the **W**idth text box.

18. Type **1.5**

19. Press ⌗Enter⌗

    There are several reasons why WordPerfect might adjust column widths, so if you want the width of the current column to remain unchanged, turn on the **F**ixed option.

20. Select **Fixed**

    To specify column 2,

21. Select **Next** twice

```
┌─────────────────────────────── Text Columns ──────────────────────────────┐
│                                                                          │▼│
│  Column Type                      Custom Widths                            │
│  ○  Newspaper                                   Width      Fixed           │
│  ○  Balanced Newspaper           │Column 1      2.17"      [ ]│▲           │
│  ●  Parallel                     │ Space        0.5"       [X]│            │
│  ○  Parallel with Block Protect  │Column 2      2.17"      [ ]│            │
│                                  │ Space        0.5"       [X]│            │
│  Number of Columns:     [3  ]    │Column 3      2.17"      [ ]│            │
│                                  │                           │            │
│  Distance Between Columns:  [0.5"]│                          │            │
│                                  │                           │            │
│  Line Spacing Between Rows: [1.0]│                           │            │
│                                  │                          │▼│           │
│  Column Borders...               └─────────────────────────────┘          │
│                                                                           │
│   ┌─────┐                    ┌──────────── Column 1 ──────────────┐       │
│   │ Off │                    │                                    │       │
│   └─────┘                    │  1. Width:      [2.17"    ]         │       │
│ [HRt]                        │  2. ☐ Fixed                         │       │
│                              │                                    │       │
│                              │  [Next] [Previous] [ OK ] [Cancel] │       │
│ Courier 12pt                 └────────────────────────────────────┘       │
```

Figure 11-9

Notice that the title in the dialog box now reads "Column 2." To adjust the width for column 2,

22. Select **W**idth

   The cursor moves to the **W**idth text box.

23. Type **3.75**

24. Press (Enter)

25. Select **F**ixed

   To specify column 3,

26. Select **N**ext twice

   The dialog box now reads, "Column 3."

27. Select **W**idth

28. Type **.75**

29. Press (Enter)

30. Select **F**ixed

31. Select **OK**

   Compare the Custom Widths window to the one shown in Figure 11-10.

   To exit the Text Columns dialog box and return to the document window,

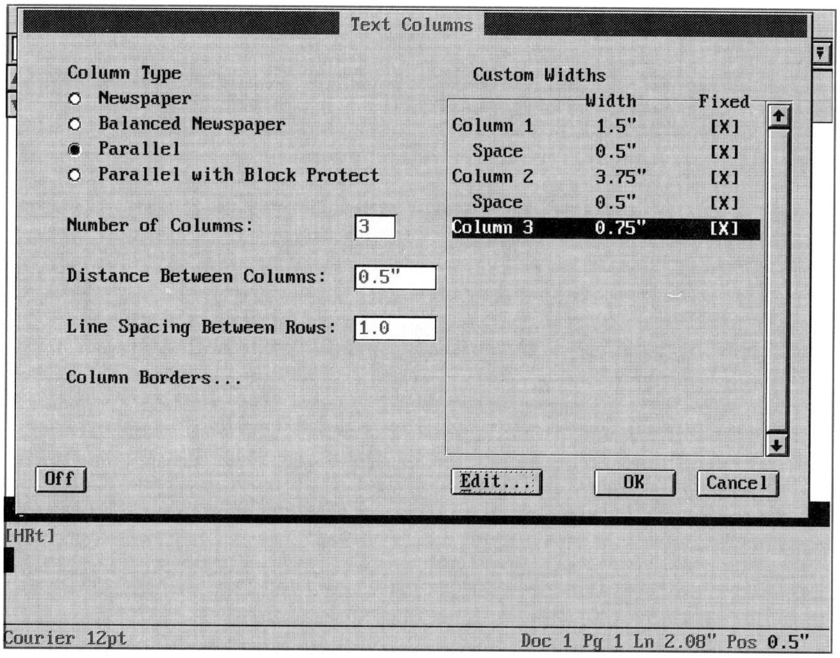

Figure 11-10

32. Select **OK**

    Notice that the Column indicator on the Ribbon now displays 3 to indicate that three columns have been defined. Now, you are ready to begin typing the first column.

33. Type `CLERICAL`

    CAUTION: Do not press Enter.

    To move the cursor to column 2,

34. Select <u>L</u>ayout ⇒ <u>A</u>lignment ⇒ Hard <u>P</u>age

    ✓ Press Ctrl + Enter

    Notice that the status bar reads "Col 2." Now type the second column:

35. Type `Mailings, small or bulk (sorting & physical mailing only); typing miscellaneous labels, envelopes; filing; copying; miscellaneous small tasks.`

    CAUTION: Do not press Enter.

    To move the cursor to column 3,

36. Select <u>L</u>ayout ⇒ <u>A</u>lignment ⇒ Hard <u>P</u>age

    ✓ Press Ctrl + Enter

    Once again, notice that the status bar reads "Col 3." Now type the text for the third column:

37. Type `$14.00`

Do not press ⌅Enter⌆. Now move the cursor to the beginning of the first column:

38. Select <u>L</u>ayout ⟹ <u>A</u>lignment ⟹ Hard <u>P</u>age

    ✓ Press ⌊Ctrl⌋ + ⌊Enter⌋

    The cursor is positioned in the first column. Type the text of the second block in the first column.

39. Type `PROOFREADING`

    Position the cursor in the second column.

40. Select <u>L</u>ayout ⟹ <u>A</u>lignment ⟹ Hard <u>P</u>age

    ✓ Press ⌊Ctrl⌋ + ⌊Enter⌋

41. Type `Available for all general text, excluding highly technical text.`

    Now let's move to the third column.

42. Select <u>L</u>ayout ⟹ <u>A</u>lignment ⟹ Hard <u>P</u>age

    ✓ Press ⌊Ctrl⌋ + ⌊Enter⌋

43. Type `$18.00`

44. Select <u>L</u>ayout ⟹ <u>A</u>lignment ⟹ Hard <u>P</u>age

    ✓ Press ⌊Ctrl⌋ + ⌊Enter⌋

45. On your own, type the remainder of the columns as shown in Figure 11-11

    Now, you need to turn columns off.

46. Select <u>L</u>ayout ⟹ <u>C</u>olumns ⟹ O<u>f</u>f

    ✓ Press ⌊Alt⌋ + ⌊F7⌋, `1`, `F`

    To type the last line in your document,

47. On your own, turn on **Center**, **Italics** and **Fine**

48. Type `(All Services are quoted on a per hour basis)`

    (Don't forget to turn off the Italics and Fine attributes.)

49. Press ⌊Enter⌋

50. Save the document and name it `SERVICES.COL`

▌ Moving the Cursor in Columns

The ⌊←⌋ and ⌊→⌋ keys move the cursor horizontally within a column, while ⌊↑⌋ and ⌊↓⌋ move the cursor vertically by line within a column. The following table indicates the keystrokes to move from column to column.

WORD PROCESSING	Manuscript text, business letters, personalized letters, contracts, proposals, mailing lists (typing and maintenance), bulk mailings, statistical typing, reports, special projects, etc.	$20.00
RESUME SERVICE	Complete services from initial interview to defining the scope of the resume to the finished product.	$20.00
ENHANCED WORD PROCESSING	Data conversion of other word processing files; text which incorporates some desktop publishing features (i.e. columns, tables) without using a desktop publishing program.	$25.00
DESKTOP PUBLISHING	Newsletters, Promotions, Layouts, Flyers, Corporate Reports, etc.	$35.00
BOOKKEEPING AND BILLING	Checkbook reconciliations, full-charge bookkeeping, payroll, financial reporting, financial statements, client billing, etc. Areas of billing expertise - service companies, real estate and therapy services.	$25.00
CONSULTING	Available in the areas of office procedures, office efficiencies, staffing, bookkeeping procedures and executive suites.	$40.00

Figure 11-11

Press	To Move
Ctrl + Home, →	One column to the right
Ctrl + Home, ←	One column to the left
Ctrl + Home, End	To the last column
Ctrl + Home, Home, ←	To the first column
Ctrl + Home, ↑	To the top of the current row
Ctrl + Home, ↓	To the bottom of the current row

▌ HANDS-ON ACTIVITY

On your own, experiment with moving the cursor from column to column.

▌ Changing Column Widths

To change the width of a column, position the cursor someplace within the group or unit where the change is to take effect. If the Auto Code Placement feature is turned off, make sure the cursor is at the beginning of the unit to be changed; otherwise your columns will not align correctly.

Select <u>L</u>ayout ⇒ <u>C</u>olumns ⇒ Custom <u>W</u>idths. Select the column or gutter to be changed and select <u>E</u>dit. Type the desired dimension and press (Enter).

▌ HANDS-ON ACTIVITY

You are going to change the width of the first column to 1.75" and the second column to 3.5".

1. Position the cursor someplace in the first line, which reads "CLERI-CAL"

2. Select <u>L</u>ayout ⇒ <u>C</u>olumns

   ✓ Press (Alt) + (F7), 1

3. Select Custom <u>W</u>idths

   Column 1 is highlighted in the Custom Widths window. To change the width for column 1,

4. Select <u>E</u>dit

   ✓ Press (Enter)

5. Select <u>W</u>idth

   The cursor moves to the Width text box.

6. Type 1.75

7. Press (Enter)

   Leave the <u>F</u>ixed option turned on. Now, to specify column 2,

8. Select <u>N</u>ext twice

   The title in the dialog box now reads "Column 2."

9. Select <u>W</u>idth

   The cursor moves to the <u>W</u>idth text box.

10. Type 3.5

11. Press (Enter)

12. Select OK

    To exit the Text Columns dialog box and return to the document window,

13. Select OK

    The text automatically readjusts to the altered column widths.

▌ Moving or Copying Columns

The first step in moving or copying a column is to block the text you want to move or copy, using the Block feature. You may block any amount of text from one corner to the opposite corner either by dragging the mouse diagonally, or by moving the cursor before the first character, turning Block on, and using the directional arrow keys to highlight through the last character of the unit or group. After the text has been blocked, choose Cut or Copy in the Button Bar or Edit ⇒ Cut or Copy. To paste the text, position the cursor where the text is to be inserted and choose the Paste button in the Button Bar or Edit ⇒ Paste.

▌HANDS-ON ACTIVITY

In this exercise, you are going to move the "BOOKKEEPING AND BILL-ING" section between the "PROOFREADING" and "WORD PROCESS-ING" sections.

CAUTION: Before you begin this exercise, save your document in case you are unsuccessful in the cut/paste procedure. In that event you could close the file without saving the changes and then open it again.

1. Position the cursor in front of the first "B" in the phrase "BOOKKEEP-ING AND BILLING"

    To turn the Block feature on,

2. Select Edit ⇒ Block

    ✓ Press F12

3. Press ↓ twice

    The BOOKKEEPING AND BILLING unit is completely blocked. Compare your screen to the one shown in Figure 11-12.

4. Select Edit ⇒ Cut or click on the Cut button in the Button Bar

    ✓ Press Ctrl + X

Figure 11-12

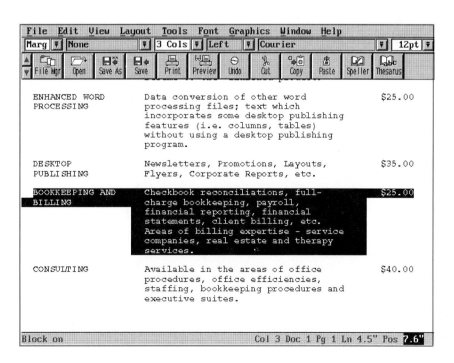

5. Position the cursor on the "W" in the phrase "WORD PROCESSING"

6. Select **Edit** ⇒ **Paste** or click on the **Paste** button in the Button Bar

   ✓ Press Ctrl + **V**

   Compare your document to Figure 11-13.

File Edit View Layout Tools Font Graphics Window Help

| Marg ▼ | None | 3 Cols ▼ | Left ▼ | Courier | 12pt ▼ |

File Mgr Open Save As Save Print Preview Undo Cut Copy Paste Speller Thesarus

CLERICAL	Mailings, small or bulk (sorting & physical mailing only); typing miscellaneous labels, envelopes; filing; copying; miscellaneous small tasks.	$14.00
PROOFREADING	Available for all general text, excluding highly technical text.	$18.00
BOOKKEEPING AND BILLING	Checkbook reconciliations, full-charge bookkeeping, payroll, financial reporting, financial statements, client billing, etc. Areas of billing expertise - service companies, real estate and therapy services.	$25.00
WORD PROCESSING	Manuscript text, business letters, personalized letters, contracts, proposals, mailing lists (typing and maintenance), bulk mailings, statistical typing, reports, special projects, etc.	$20.00
RESUME SERVICE	Complete services from initial interview to defining the scope of	$20.00

A:\SERVICES.COL   Col 1 Doc 1 Pg 1 Ln 2.08" Pos 0.75"

Figure 11-13

7. Save your document

Converting Parallel Columns to a Table

Should you decide that you would like to have your parallel columns converted into a table, the task is quite easy. Simply select the text to be converted to a table, and select Layout ⇒ Tables ⇒ Create (*Shortcut keys:* Alt + F7, 2, 1). The Create Table from Block dialog box appears. Choose the Parallel Columns option and OK.

HANDS-ON ACTIVITY

In this exercise, you are going to convert your parallel columns into a table with lines to separate the categories of services, descriptions, and fees.

CAUTION: Before you begin this exercise, save your document in case you are unsuccessful in converting your columns to a table. In that event you could close the file without saving the changes and then open it again.

1. Position the cursor at the beginning of the table (on or before the "C" in "CLERICAL")

To turn the Block feature on,

2. Select <u>E</u>dit ⇒ <u>B</u>lock

   ✓ Press F12

3. Press Home, Home, ↓

4. Press ↑ twice

   All units in the parallel columns are blocked.

5. Select <u>L</u>ayout ⇒ <u>T</u>ables ⇒ <u>C</u>reate

   ✓ Press Alt + F7, 2, 1

   The Create Table from Block dialog box appears, as shown in Figure 11-14.

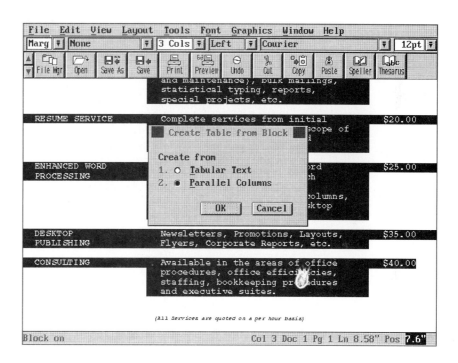

Figure 11-14

6. Select <u>P</u>arallel Columns

7. Select **OK**

   You are placed in the Table Edit dialog box. You may need to adjust some of your column widths. If so, use the Ctrl + arrow keys method.

8. Close the Table Edit dialog box

   Compare your document to the one shown in Figure 11-15.

9. Select <u>F</u>ile ⇒ Save <u>A</u>s

   ✓ Press F10

PencilPushers, Inc.

Scope of Services

CLERICAL	Mailings, small or bulk (sorting & physical mailing only); typing miscellaneous labels, envelopes; filing; copying; miscellaneous small tasks.	$14.00
PROOFREADING	Available for all general text, excluding highly technical text.	$18.00
BOOKKEEPING AND BILLING	Checkbook reconciliations, full-charge book-keeping, payroll, financial reporting, financial statements, client billing, etc. Areas of billing expertise - service companies, real estate and therapy services.	$25.00
WORD PROCESSING	Manuscript text, business letters, personalized letters, contracts, proposals, mailing lists (typing and maintenance), bulk mailings, statistical typing, reports, special projects, etc.	$20.00
RESUME SERVICE	Complete services from initial interview to defining the scope of the resume to the finished product.	$20.00
ENHANCED WORD PROCESSING	Data conversion of other word processing files; text which incorporates some desktop publishing features (i.e. columns, tables) without using a desktop publishing program.	$25.00
DESKTOP PUBLISHING	Newsletters, Promotions, Layouts, Flyers, Corporate Reports, etc.	$35.00
CONSULTING	Available in the areas of office procedures, office efficiencies, staffing, bookkeeping procedures and executive suites.	$40.00

(All Services are quoted on a per hour basis)

Figure 11-15

10. Name the document **SERVICES.TBL**

11. Print the document and exit WordPerfect

On Your Own

Review of Commands

Description	Menu Commands	Function Keys
Define columns	_____	_____
Turn columns off	_____	_____
Retrieve a file	_____	_____
Convert parallel columns into a table	_____	_____

List the keystrokes to move the cursor in columns:

Description		Function Keys
One column to the right		_____
One column to the left		_____
Last column		_____
First column		_____
To the top of the current row		_____
To the bottom of the current row		_____

Lesson Review

1. What is the difference between newspaper style and parallel columns?

2. What is the purpose of balanced newspaper columns?

3. What is the purpose of the Parallel Block Protect feature?

4. What is the maximum number of columns that can be defined?

5. What keystrokes move the cursor from the bottom of one parallel column to the beginning of the next?

6. When is it necessary to enter a column-off code?

7. What keystroke combination moves the cursor to the next column?

8. What keystroke combination moves the cursor to the previous column?

9. Define a gutter.

10. What is an alternate method to creating newspaper columns with default settings?

11. What are the steps to copy a column?

12. When changing a column definition, where should the cursor be positioned, if the Auto Code Placement is turned off?

13. List the steps to convert parallel columns into a table.

14. What is the amount of gutter space (space between columns) automatically set in WordPerfect?

15. What option in the Text Columns dialog box allows you to change the size of a column?

▌ Assignments

11.1 Directions

1. Create three parallel columns, using the default settings.

2. Type in the following information, bolding and capping the title and column headings.

CMS 201 CLASS		
LANGUAGE	PRIMARY USES	COMMENTS
Assembler	Systems	Highly efficient; system dependent; difficult to read and understand
BASIC	Education	Simple to learn; limited simple program functions
C	Systems	Developed by Bell Laboratories as part of the UNIX operating system
COBOL	Business	Old language; wordy; extensive file-handling capability; durable
FORTRAN	Scientific	Old language; has limitations, but very popular in science
Pascal	Education Systems Scientific	Excellent structured language; limited I/0

3. Change the gutter space to .20".

4. Save the document as CLASS.COL.

5. Print and exit.

11.2 Directions

1. Open CLASS.COL.

2. Save as CLASS.TBL.

3. Convert the parallel columns into a table.

4. Save again, print, and exit.

11.3 Directions

1. Center and type a title "Call for Papers" in a large, scalable, bold italic font.

2. Set up two newspaper style columns using the default settings and turn columns on.

3. Retrieve the document CONFER.SD from your data disk.

4. Check to see that the columns are equal length and that they stop in grammatically acceptable places.

5. Save the document as CONFER.COL.

6. Print and exit.

12 Creating and Editing Macros

Objectives

Upon completion of this lesson, you will be able to do the following:

- Create (record) a macro
- Use (play) a macro
- Edit a macro
- Assign an Alt key name to a macro
- Create pauses in a macro

In this lesson you will learn a most valuable and timesaving feature called macros. Macros record commands that perform a task, and they will replay automatically whenever you call upon them. You will learn to record, play, and edit simple macros.

Starting Point

Before beginning the lesson, start WordPerfect 6.0. The document window should be blank. Make sure the Train Button Bar and Ribbon are displayed. Locate your sample disk and insert it into the appropriate drive.

What Is a Macro?

The Macro feature allows you to save or **record** frequently used keystrokes such as text characters and menu selections. The recorded keystrokes are saved in a file in the \WP60\MACROS directory, which is automatically created during the WordPerfect installation process. All macro files have a .WPM file extension. After the macro has been recorded and saved in a file, you can use (or **play**) the macro anytime, and WordPerfect will automatically execute the saved keystrokes for you, conserving time and preventing errors.

Macros are time-savers that are most useful when you use the same text or series of keystrokes on a regular basis. Examples include the name of your company, the closing of a letter, or form letters, such as an interoffice memorandum.

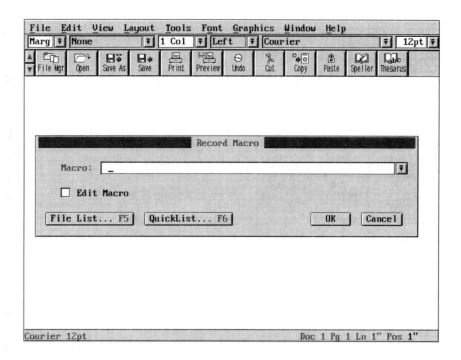

Figure 12-2

6. Press [Enter] 4 times

7. Type your name

8. Press [Enter]

9. Type **Chief Executive Officer**

   Now, to stop the recording of this macro and save the macro file,

10. Select <u>T</u>ools ⇒ <u>M</u>acro ⇒ <u>S</u>top

    ✓ Press [Ctrl] + [F10]

11. Since the macro had already been saved at the point when you stopped the recorder, close the file without saving

▍ Playing a Macro

When you play a macro, WordPerfect executes all the saved keystrokes, starting at the current position of the cursor. To play a macro, from the Menu Bar choose <u>T</u>ools ⇒ <u>M</u>acro ⇒ <u>P</u>lay (*Shortcut keys:* [Alt] + [F10]). The Play Macro dialog box appears, where you may type the name of the desired macro or select from a list of macro file names displayed in a drop-down box. Highlight the macro file name to be played and select it either by pressing [Enter] or by double-clicking with the mouse.

▍ HANDS-ON ACTIVITY

Since you wrote the letter to Mr. Johnson back in Lesson 5, your title has been changed to Chief Executive Officer. The letter has not yet been mailed, so play your newly created macro to update the closing.

1. Open the file **JOHNSON.LTR**

2. Block the closing section of the letter, as shown in Figure 12-3

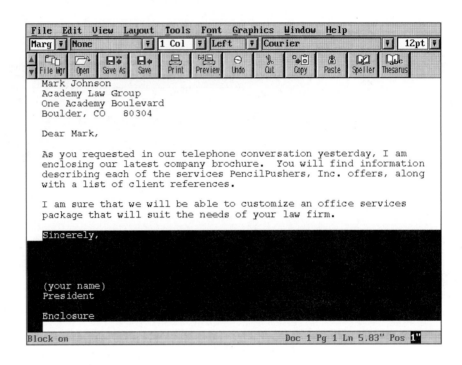

Figure 12-3

To delete the old signature block,

3. Press [Delete]

Now, play your SIG macro to insert the new signature block.

4. Select **T**ools ⇒ **M**acro ⇒ **P**lay

✓ Press [Alt] + [F10]

The Play Macro dialog box appears, as shown in Figure 12-4.

You may either type the name of the desired macro or choose from a list of macro names by selecting the browse button on the drop-down list box.

5. Select the **browse button** on the Macro list box

✓ Press [↓]

6. Select **SIG.WPM**

7. To play the macro, double-click with the mouse

✓ Press [Enter]

The new signature block is automatically inserted for you. Leave your letter to Mr. Johnson on the screen, and go on to the next section.

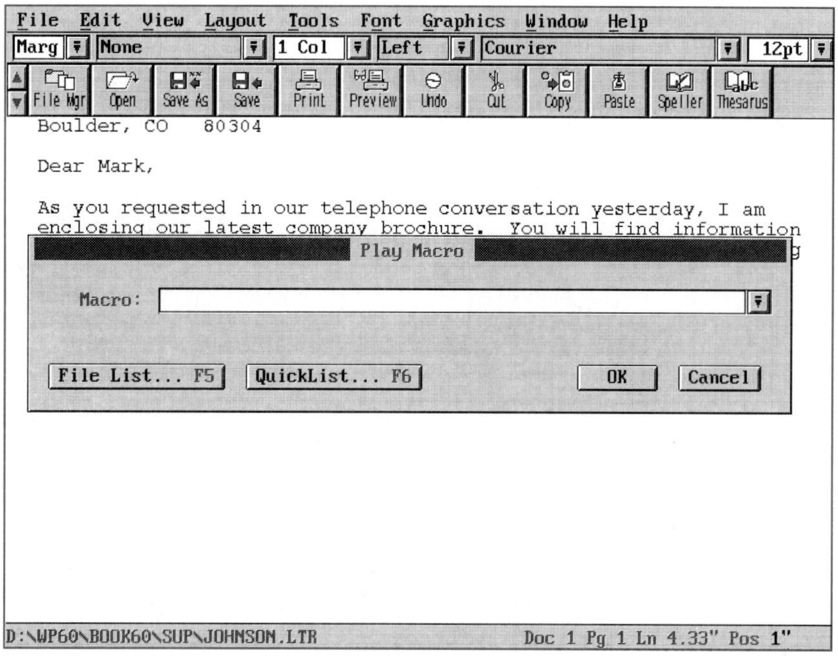

```
┌──────────────────────────────────────────────────────────────────┐
│ File  Edit  View  Layout  Tools  Font  Graphics  Window  Help      │
│ ┌Marg▼┐┌None         ▼┐┌1 Col▼┐┌Left  ▼┐┌Courier          ▼┐┌12pt▼┐│
│ ▲ ┌─┐  ┌─┐  ┌─┐  ┌─┐  ┌─┐  ┌─┐  ┌─┐  ┌─┐  ┌─┐  ┌─┐  ┌─┐  ┌─┐        │
│ ▼ File Mgr Open Save As Save Print Preview Undo Cut Copy Paste Speller Thesaurus│
│       Boulder, CO   80304                                          │
│                                                                    │
│       Dear Mark,                                                   │
│                                                                    │
│       As you requested in our telephone conversation yesterday, I am│
│       enclosing our latest company brochure.  You will find information│
│   ┌──────────────────────────Play Macro──────────────────────────┐ g│
│   │                                                               │  │
│   │   Macro: ┌──────────────────────────────────────────────┐▼┐  │  │
│   │          └──────────────────────────────────────────────┘   │  │
│   │                                                               │  │
│   │   ┌─File List... F5─┐ ┌─QuickList... F6─┐      ┌─OK─┐ ┌Cancel┐│  │
│   │   └─────────────────┘ └─────────────────┘      └────┘ └──────┘│  │
│   └───────────────────────────────────────────────────────────────┘  │
│                                                                    │
│                                                                    │
│                                                                    │
│                                                                    │
│ ┌─────────────────────────────────────────────────────────────────┐│
│ │D:\WP60\BOOK60\SUP\JOHNSON.LTR          Doc 1 Pg 1 Ln 4.33" Pos 1"││
│ └─────────────────────────────────────────────────────────────────┘│
└──────────────────────────────────────────────────────────────────┘
```

Figure 12-4

Editing a Macro

In case you create a macro and then find a misspelling or other minor error, WordPerfect allows you to edit the macro. Macros are stored as regular documents—you can open, edit, and resave them, using the same commands you use with other documents.

When editing a macro, it is extremely important that you enter the commands in the exact syntax—the proper format—they require, so that your macro will execute properly. Use extreme caution when editing a macro to be sure that each command you enter is typed correctly.

There are two ways to access the macro file for editing. First, you could open the file in the conventional method from either the Button Bar or File ⇒ Open ⇒ File Manager (*Shortcut key:* F5). But, since macros are stored in the \WP60\MACROS subdirectory instead of your normal document directory, you will have to go through many extra steps to locate the macro file. A more efficient method of opening a macro file for edits is to select Tools ⇒ Macro ⇒ Record ⇒ Edit Macro. Then, when you open the drop-down list box or select File List, the macro directory is automatically suggested and a file list of only macro files is displayed. You then select the correct macro file and it automatically opens for edits.

After you make the desired changes to the macro, choose File ⇒ Close (*Shortcut key:* F7). Choose Yes to save your changes.

▌ HANDS-ON ACTIVITY

You are going to edit your SIG macro, using the Tools menu to add a blank line at the end of the macro and the company name, PencilPushers, Inc.

1. Select <u>T</u>ools ⇒ <u>M</u>acro ⇒ <u>R</u>ecord

   ✓ Press Home, Ctrl + F10

   The cursor is blinking in the Macro text box of the Record Macro dialog box. Since the Record Macro dialog box is used for both record and edit, in order to edit, you must mark the Edit Macro check box.

2. Press Tab

3. Select <u>E</u>dit Macro

   Instead of typing the entire drive and directory to locate the SIG macro, let's use the drop-down list box for available names of macro files.

4. Select the **browse button** on the Macro list box

   ✓ Press ↓

5. Select **SIG.WPM**

6. To open the macro, double-click with the mouse

   ✓ Press Enter

   Compare what appears on your screen with the macro shown in Figure 12-5. If you made any mistakes during the recording of your macro, it will not look exactly like the figure.

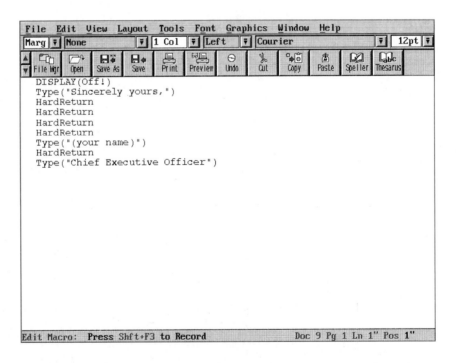

Figure 12-5

Each command in the macro instructs WordPerfect to execute a particular command or feature just as you would do from the keyboard. For example, **Type** is a command that tells WordPerfect to type everything within the quotation marks and parentheses following Type. Therefore, line 2 of your macro instructs WordPerfect to type the phrase "Sincerely yours," at the cursor position in the document. Then lines 3 through 6 (the HardReturn commands) insert new blank lines into the document.

Now, move to the bottom of the macro file.

7. Press (Home), (Home), (↓)

This positions the cursor at the end of the macro file on a blank line.

Now tell WordPerfect to insert a new line.

8. Type **HardReturn** (with no space)

9. Press (Enter)

Now add the name of your company.

10. Type **Type("PencilPushers, Inc.")**

11. Press (Enter)

12. Type **HardReturn**

13. Press (Enter)

Compare your macro file to the one shown in Figure 12-6.

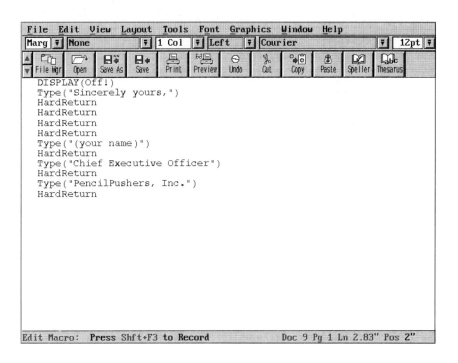

Figure 12-6

Now close and save your macro file.

14. Select <u>F</u>ile ⇒ <u>C</u>lose

   ✓ Press (F7)

15. Choose <u>Y</u>es to save your changes

▌ **HANDS-ON ACTIVITY**

Your letter to Mr. Johnson is still on the screen. Let's play your edited macro.

1. Block and delete the signature block

2. Select <u>T</u>ools ⇒ <u>M</u>acro ⇒ <u>P</u>lay

    ✓ Press [Alt] + [F10]

    The Macro Play dialog box appears.

3. Select the **browse button** on the Macro list box

    ✓ Press [↓]

4. Select **SIG.WPM**

5. Double-click with the mouse

    ✓ Press [Enter]

    The edited signature block is automatically inserted for you.

6. Close the letter to Mr. Johnson and choose <u>Y</u>es to save your changes

▌ **Editing Macros with the File Menu**

So far we have used the Tools menu to edit a macro file. As discussed earlier, a macro file can be accessed just like any other document, not only with the special macro menus. Now let's use <u>F</u>ile ⇒ <u>O</u>pen to view the macro text.

▌ **HANDS-ON ACTIVITY**

In this exercise, you will open the macro file SIG.WPM, then print the macro text. Make sure you begin with a blank document screen.

1. Select <u>F</u>ile ⇒ <u>O</u>pen

    ✓ Press [Shift] + [F10]

2. Type `C:\WP60\MACROS\SIG.WPM`

3. Select **OK**

    ✓ Press [Enter]

    TIP You may also use File Manager to locate the file.

    As you can see, the macro text appears on the screen ready for edits. Therefore, you can use either the <u>F</u>ile ⇒ <u>O</u>pen menu or the <u>T</u>ools ⇒ <u>M</u>acro ⇒ <u>R</u>ecord ⇒ <u>E</u>dit Macro menu with exactly the same results.

    Now, print the macro. Make sure your printer is ready.

4. Select <u>F</u>ile ⇒ <u>P</u>rint/Fax ⇒ <u>P</u>rint

    ✓ Press [Shift] + [F7], then [Enter]

5. Close the file without saving

Creating a Macro Using an ALT Key Combination

In the previous exercise you created a macro called SIG for your signature block. The advantage to naming macros with long names is that the name is descriptive (SIG for signature), but the disadvantage is that there are several menu steps involved to play the macro.

Now you will create an ALT key combination macro that uses the [Alt] key plus one alphabet letter. The advantage to ALT macros is that even though the record steps are the same, to play an ALT macro, simply press [Alt] and the alphabet letter.

HANDS-ON ACTIVITY

In this exercise, you will create a macro that implements the flush right and date functions, to enter today's date on the right margin of your document. The macro will be named ALTD (for Date).

1. Select <u>T</u>ools ⇒ <u>M</u>acro ⇒ <u>R</u>ecord

   ✓ Press [Ctrl] + [F10]

   The Record Macro dialog box appears with the cursor blinking in the Macro text box, waiting for you to type the name of the new macro.

2. Type or press [Alt] + **D**

3. Select **OK**

   ✓ Press [Enter]

   First, invoke the flush right command.

4. Select <u>L</u>ayout ⇒ <u>A</u>lignment ⇒ <u>F</u>lush Right

   ✓ Press [Alt] + [F6]

   Now, insert the computer date.

5. Select <u>T</u>ools ⇒ <u>D</u>ate ⇒ <u>T</u>ext

   ✓ Press [Shift] + [F5], **1**

6. Press [Enter]

   Stop the macro recorder.

7. Select <u>T</u>ools ⇒ <u>M</u>acro ⇒ <u>S</u>top

   ✓ Press [Ctrl] + [F10]

8. Close the file without saving

   There are two ways to play an ALT key macro: select <u>T</u>ools ⇒ <u>M</u>acro ⇒ <u>P</u>lay from the menu, or press [Alt] plus the alphabet letter used to name the macro.

9. Position the cursor in a blank document window

   Play the macro.

10. Press [Alt] + **D**

    ✓ Select <u>T</u>ools ⇒ <u>M</u>acro ⇒ <u>P</u>lay

Creating a Macro That Pauses

In creating some types of documents, it may be useful to have a macro create the standard parts of the letter or form and then pause for you to insert the variable text from the keyboard. An interoffice memorandum provides a good example of this. The beginning of the document is always the same; the headings "To," "From," and "Subject" are always used. The rest, however, varies, so you need to have the macro temporarily stop to allow you to insert the names of the individuals to whom the memo is directed, whom it is from, the subject, and so on.

When creating a macro that pauses, you can embed a pause command with <u>T</u>ools ⇒ <u>M</u>acro ⇒ <u>C</u>ontrol ⇒ Macro Record <u>P</u>aused (*Shortcut keys:* Ctrl + Pg Up, [Macro Record Paused]). When the Pause command is encountered in a macro, it temporarily stops the macro until the user presses Enter, at which time the macro continues playing.

▌ HANDS-ON ACTIVITY

One of the most widely used forms for correspondence in the business environment today is the interoffice memorandum. In this exercise you create a macro named MEM1 that produces an interoffice memorandum, pausing in the appropriate places for user input. The memo form you will create is shown in Figure 12-7 for your reference.

In this exercise, you will record the macro up to the first pause location, then switch back and forth between the edit mode and the record mode to complete the macro while inserting the Pause command where needed. Make sure you begin from a clear document window.

1. Select <u>T</u>ools ⇒ <u>M</u>acro ⇒ <u>R</u>ecord

   ✓ Press Ctrl + F10

   The Record Macro dialog box appears and the cursor is in the Filename text box.

2. Type **MEM1**

3. Select **OK** or press Enter

   (If a dialog box stating "C:\WP60\MACROS\MEM1.WPM already exists" displays, either select "Replace" or change the name from MEM1 to MEM2.)

   The lower-left corner of the Status Bar will prompt "Recording Macro."

   To center the heading, INTEROFFICE MEMORANDUM,

4. Select <u>L</u>ayout ⇒ <u>A</u>lignment ⇒ <u>C</u>enter

   ✓ Press Shift + F6

   Now, turn on the Bold feature.

5. Select <u>F</u>ont ⇒ <u>B</u>old

   ✓ Press F6 or Ctrl + **B**

6. Type **INTEROFFICE MEMORANDUM**

```
┌─────────────────────────────────────────────────────────┐
│                                                           │
│                 INTEROFFICE MEMORANDUM                    │
│                                                           │
│                                        (today's date)     │
│                                                           │
│                                                           │
│   TO:                                                     │
│                                                           │
│   FROM:                                                   │
│                                                           │
│   SUBJECT:                                                │
│                                                           │
│   ━━━━━━━━━━━━━━━━━━━━━━━━━━━━━━━━━━━━━━━━━━━━━━━━━━━━      │
│                                                           │
│                                                           │
│                                                           │
│                                                           │
│                                                           │
│                                                           │
│                                                           │
│                                                           │
│                                                           │
│                                                           │
│                                                           │
│                                                           │
│                                                           │
│                                                           │
│                                                           │
│                                                           │
│                                                           │
│                                                           │
└─────────────────────────────────────────────────────────┘
```

Figure 12-7

Turn Bold off.

7. Select **Font** ⇒ **Normal**

    ✓ Press Ctrl + **N**, or F6

8. Press Enter 4 times

    Now use the Flush Right Date macro (made in an earlier exercise) to position the date code on the right margin.

9. Press [Alt] + D

10. Press [Enter] 3 times

11. Bold and type **TO:**

    (Don't forget to turn off bold or to return to Normal.)

12. Press [Tab] twice

    The status line should read "POS 2"."

    You are now located at the position where the first PAUSE command should be inserted. Thus, the macro will type all the headings and then wait for the user to type the name of the memo's recipient. The pause will suspend the macro until the user presses [Enter] and then the macro will continue.

    The pause command can be inserted either from the record mode or the macro editor. First, let's stop the macro recorder and switch to the edit mode.

13. Select <u>T</u>ools ⇒ <u>M</u>acro ⇒ <u>S</u>top

    ✓ Press [Ctrl] + [F10]

    Now switch to the Macro Edit mode to embed the pause.

14. Select <u>T</u>ools ⇒ <u>M</u>acro ⇒ <u>R</u>ecord

    ✓ Press [Ctrl] + [F10]

15. Type **MEM1**

16. Select **OK**

    ✓ Press [Enter]

17. Select <u>E</u>dit

    Compare your macro text with the macro shown in Figure 12-8. Remember, if you made a mistake during the recording of your macro, it will not appear exactly like the one in the figure.

    Move to the bottom of the macro.

18. Press [Home], [Home], [↓]

    NOTE: If you are not on a blank line at the bottom of the macro, press [Enter] *to create a blank line and move the cursor to the blank line.*

19. Type **Pause**

20. Press [Enter] to move the cursor to the next line.

    Now switch back to the Macro Record mode to continue the next memo heading. Keep watching the left-hand side of the status line, which tells you which mode WordPerfect is in.

21. Press [Shift] + [F3]

```
DISPLAY(Off!)
Center
AttributeAppearanceOn(Bold!)
Type("INTEROFFICE MEMORANDUM")
AttributeAppearanceOff(Bold!)
HardReturn
HardReturn
HardReturn
HardReturn
NEST("ALTD")
HardReturn
HardReturn
HardReturn
AttributeAppearanceOn(Bold!)
Type("TO:")
AttributeAppearanceOff(Bold!)
Tab
Tab
```

Figure 12-8

22. Press Enter twice

    Turn on bold for the next heading.

23. Select F**o**nt ⇒ **B**old

    ✓ Press F6, or Ctrl + **B**

24. Type **FROM:**

    Turn off bold.

25. Select F**o**nt ⇒ **N**ormal

    ✓ Press Ctrl + **N**, or F6

26. Press Tab once (the status line should read "POS 2″")

    Now insert a pause using the Macro Control option.

27. Select **T**ools ⇒ **M**acro ⇒ **C**ontrol

    ✓ Press Ctrl + Pg Up

    From the Macro Control dialog box,

28. Select the **Macro C**ommands button

    To move to the Pause command, use the ↓ on the keyboard, the scroll bar with the mouse, or type the first letter(s) of the command.

29. Type **P**

30. Select **I**nsert

    ✓ Press Enter

31. Press (Enter) twice

32. On your own, enter bold text for "SUBJECT," followed by a tab and a pause, and press (Enter) 3 times

To spruce up the appearance of your memo, you are going to insert a horizontal graphic line. The next lesson, Lesson 13, will give you an in-depth look at graphic elements, including lines.

NOTE: Make sure you are still in the Record mode.

33. Select <u>G</u>raphics ⇒ Graphic <u>L</u>ines ⇒ <u>C</u>reate

✓ Press (Alt) + (F9), 2, 1

The Create Graphics Line dialog box appears as shown in Figure 12-9.

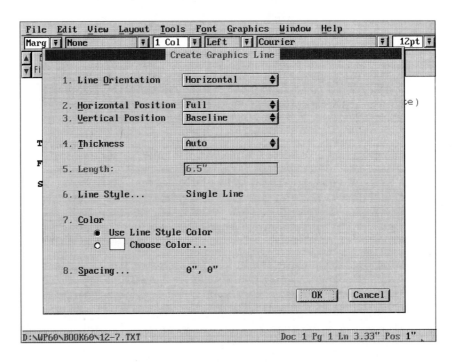

Figure 12-9

The default thickness of the line is .013" and the dialog box is currently showing "Auto" for its setting. To make the line thicker,

34. Select <u>T</u>hickness ⇒ <u>S</u>et

35. Type **.05** (for .05 inches)

36. Press (Enter)

37. Select **OK**

✓ Press (Enter)

38. Press (Enter) 3 more times

Return to the Edit mode once again to check your work before you end and save the macro.

39. Press [Shift] + [F3]

Compare your macro line by line with the one shown in Figure 12-10. Make any corrections necessary.

```
DISPLAY(Off!)
Center
AttributeAppearanceOn(Bold!)
Type("INTEROFFICE MEMORANDUM")
AttributeAppearanceOff(Bold!)
HardReturn
HardReturn
HardReturn
HardReturn
NEST("ALTD")
HardReturn
HardReturn
HardReturn
AttributeAppearanceOn(Bold!)
Type("TO:")
AttributeAppearanceOff(Bold!)
Tab
Tab
Pause
HardReturn
HardReturn
AttributeAppearanceOn(Bold!)
Type("FROM:")
AttributeAppearanceOff(Bold!)
Tab
Pause
HardReturn
HardReturn
AttributeAppearanceOn(Bold!)
Type("SUBJECT:")
AttributeAppearanceOff(Bold!)
Tab
HardReturn
HardReturn
HardReturn
GraphicsLineCreate
GraphicsLineThickness(0.05")
GraphicsLineHorizontalPosition(FullAlign!)
GraphicsLineVerticalPosition(Baseline!)
GraphicsLineLength(6.5")
GraphicsLineEnd(Save!)
HardReturn
HardReturn
HardReturn
```

Figure 12-10

Now, go back to the Record Macro screen.

40. Press ⌈Shift⌉ + ⌈F3⌉

    To end the recording of your macro,

41. Select **Tools** ⇒ **Macro** ⇒ **Stop**

    ✓ Press ⌈Ctrl⌉ + ⌈F10⌉

42. Close your document without saving it

▌HANDS-ON ACTIVITY

You should now have an empty document window on your screen. Use your MEMO macro to inform the staff at PencilPushers, Inc. that you will be on vacation for a week beginning on July 1.

1. Select **Tools** ⇒ **Macro** ⇒ **Play**

    ✓ Press ⌈Alt⌉ + ⌈F10⌉

    The Play Macro dialog box appears.

2. Select the **browse button** on the Macro list box

    ✓ Press ⌈↓⌉

3. Highlight **MEM1.WPM**

4. Select by double-clicking with the mouse

    ✓ Press ⌈Enter⌉

    The macro types the headings and the date, then stops at "TO:" so that you can enter the addressee.

5. Type `All Staff`

6. Press ⌈Enter⌉

    The macro resumes execution. The "FROM:" line appears and the cursor is positioned so that you can enter your name.

7. Type your name

8. Press ⌈Enter⌉

    Again, the macro resumes playing; the "SUBJECT:" line appears and the macro pauses.

9. Type `Vacation`

10. Press ⌈Enter⌉

11. Type `This is to advise you that I will be on vacation for one week starting on July 1st. Ms. Joan Browning will administer the duties of my office during my absence.`

Compare your memo to the one shown in Figure 12-11.

INTEROFFICE MEMORANDUM

(today's date)

TO: All Staff

FROM: (your name)

SUBJECT: Vacation

This is to advise you that I will be on vacation for one week starting on July 1st. Ms. Joan Browning will administer the duties of my office during my absence.

Figure 12-11

12. Save your memo and name it `VACATION.MEM`

13. On your own, print your document

14. Close the document

Review of Commands

Description	Menu Commands	Function Keys
Create (record) a macro	_____	_____
Stop recording a macro	_____	_____
Edit a macro	_____	_____
Switch from record to edit	_____	_____

Lesson Review

1. Define a macro.

2. What are three examples of when you might use a macro?

3. What steps are performed to edit a macro using the Tools menu?

4. What steps are performed to edit a macro using the File menu?

5. What are the two different macro-naming methods you can use?

6. Name the default directory in which WordPerfect stores macros.

7. How can you create a document that will pause to let you insert information?

8. List the steps to play a macro called DOCUMENT.WPM and a macro called ALTS.WPM.

Assignments

12.1 Directions

1. Create the following macro for the form of a standard letter; name it STANDLET.

   (Begin recording) 2 inches from the top of the page, enter the date code. Leave several lines for the inside address and type **Dear** at the left margin. Leave several blank lines and type **Sincerely yours,** leave 4 blank lines and type your name and **Accounting Systems Department.** (End recording)

2. Play the macro to test it. (Clear the screen without saving.)

3. Edit the macro and change Sincerely yours, to Very truly yours,.

4. Play the macro again to test your changes and print the contents on the screen.

5. Close your file without saving it.

12 2 Directions:

1. Play the STANDLET macro.

2. Insert the following text into your letter shell:

Sharon Lucas / 879 Arapahoe Street / Boulder, CO 80302 / Ms. Lucas: / You have been randomly selected from members of the Boulder Business Council to participate in a survey to determine the extent to which businesses in the Boulder area utilize outside accounting or bookkeeping services. These services can range from full charge bookkeeping, occasional temporary help, or end-of-year tax preparation. / I would appreciate your taking a few minutes of your time to fill out the enclosed inquiry, fold and tape it, and mail it in the enclosed envelope. The results will be tabulated and presented at one of your future BBC meetings.

3. Save the letter as **LUCAS.SVY.**

4. Spell check, save again, print, and exit.

13

Enhancing Your Documents with Graphics

Objectives

Upon completion of this lesson, you will be able to do the following:

- Define WordPerfect's graphics boxes
- Create a graphics box
- Resize a graphics box
- Create a text box
- Create a table box
- Create a user box
- Move a graphics box
- Add a caption to a box
- Edit a graphics image
- Enlarge and reduce a graphics image
- Move, rotate, and flip a graphics image
- Change the fill attributes of a graphics image
- Create a shadow border
- Create, edit, and move graphics lines
- Use watermark images

This lesson introduces you to the graphics boxes and lines that are available for your use. You will learn how to add graphics, tables, and text to these boxes, as well as how to enhance your documents with graphics lines. You will manipulate these boxes by moving them, resizing them, adding shadow borders, adding captions, and so on.

Starting Point

Before beginning the lesson, start WordPerfect 6.0. Open the sample file NEWSLTR.COL and change the column definition to Newspaper instead of Balanced Newspaper. Make sure that the Train Button Bar and the Ribbon are displayed.

What Is a Graphics Box?

WordPerfect's **graphics boxes** allow you to add pictures (graphics) to enhance the appearance of your documents. WordPerfect has a number of graphics files built in, or you can use a graphics image from one of the many software packages supported by WordPerfect. When working with graphics, there are three basic steps:

- Type your text.
- Create an empty box in which to place the graphics.
- Fill the box with text, a graphics image, a table, a chart, a drawing, or an equation.

After the box has been filled, the graphics can be expanded or contracted, moved horizontally or vertically, and rotated any number of degrees. WordPerfect automatically flows the text around the inserted graphics box. If either the View ⇒ Graphics or View ⇒ Page modes are turned on, the graphics is visible on the screen. If not, only the outline of the specific box is displayed.

Types of Graphics Boxes

There are eight types of graphics boxes available for your use: Figure, Table, Text, User, Equation, Button, Watermark Image, or Inline Equation. Each graphics box has a different style or appearance (such as border, fill type, corner style). Even though each box is different in appearance, there is no constraint as to what contents can be placed into a particular box. Therefore, you can put an image, text, table, or equation in any type of box. For example, you could put an equation in a figure box or text in a table box. The appearance of each box is described below, along with the suggested usage of each.

Figure box	This box appears with a frame around the perimeter and is typically used for clip art images, charts, logos, or drawings.
Table box	This box appears with a ruling line above and below the box and is typically used for a table, spreadsheet table, statistical data, or text.
Text box	This box appears like the Table box, except that it is shaded and is typically used for quotes, sidebars, and textual information that you want set off from the main document.
User box	This box has no frame or shading—in fact, it is invisible, and therefore is suitable for any contents.
Button box	This box appears as a 3-D push button and is typically used to graphically illustrate a keystroke, push button, or icon, as well as text, clip art images, or drawing.
Watermark Image	A watermark image is printed behind the text of a document, like the faint image on fine writing paper.

Remember that any of the graphics boxes can contain a graphics, a chart, a drawing, a table, text or an equation.

NOTE: From this point forward, the less often used equation boxes will not be addressed, because of the limited length of this book.

Each box type is automatically numbered consecutively. That is, if you have both table and figure boxes, the table boxes are numbered separately from the figure boxes. If a box is deleted or added, the remaining boxes *of that type* are automatically renumbered. Box numbers are not displayed, unless a caption is added to the box. Figure 13-1 will give you an idea of the default format and numbering style of each box except for the equation boxes.

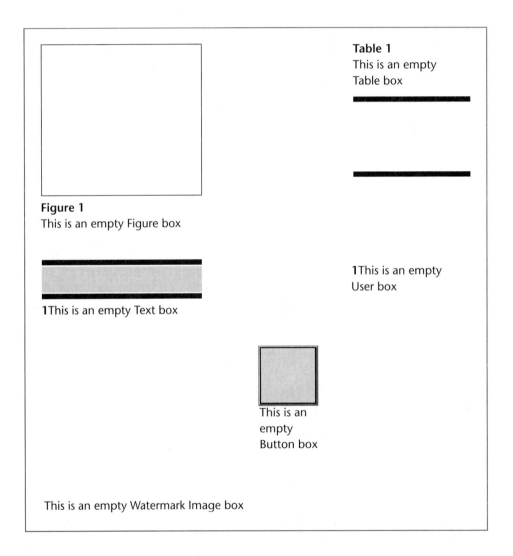

Figure 13-1

Inside the figure:

Figure 1
This is an empty Figure box

Table 1
This is an empty Table box

1This is an empty User box

1This is an empty Text box

This is an empty Button box

This is an empty Watermark Image box

Creating a Graphics Box

If you fill graphics boxes with a graphics image, the image is initially a separate file. Once the graphics is placed into the box, however, it becomes a part of the current document. WordPerfect has provided a number of graphics images for your use. These files reside in the WP60\GRAPHICS directory and have a .WPG file extension. Graphics images can be imported from other software programs into your WordPerfect document. Figure 13-2 shows a list of formats currently supported by WordPerfect.

Graphics Formats Supported by WordPerfect 6.0

Format	Description
CGM	Computer Graphics Metafile
DHP	Dr. Halo PIC Format
DXF	AutoCAD Format
EPS	Encapsulated PostScript
GEM	GEM Draw Format
HPGL	Hewlett-Packard Graphics Language Plotter File
IMG	GEM Paint Format
MSP	Microsoft Windows (2.x) Paint Format
PCX	PC Paintbrush Format
PIC	Lotus 1-2-3 PIC Format
PNTG	Macintosh Paint Format
PPIC	PC Paint Plus Format
TIFF	Tagged Image File Format
WPG	WordPerfect Graphics Format

Figure 13-2

There are two methods by which to add a graphics to a document. The first method (Graphics ⇒ Graphics Boxes ⇒ Create) allows you to select the graphics box of your choice and place text, a compatible image file, a drawing, a table, or an equation inside the box. The second method (Graphics ⇒ Retrieve Image) is used to retrieve and convert from other software a clip art image, a chart, or a drawing into a document; WordPerfect automatically uses a figure box for this method. When this method is used, you are simply prompted for a file name, and after you specify it the graphics image is automatically placed in a figure box. This is the most expedient method; however, you are *not* presented with a dialog box in which to add a caption or make any changes.

Specifying a Box Type

When choosing the Graphics ⇒ Graphics Boxes ⇒ Create (*Shortcut keys:* Alt + F9, 1, 1) option, the Create Graphics Box dialog box appears. Select Filename to enter the name of the file and choose OK. The default box style is Figure, so if you wish to select a different box style, choose the Based on Box Style option. The Graphics Box Styles dialog box appears and you are presented with a list of the eight styles.

Anchoring a Graphics Box

The Create Graphics Box dialog box also has an Attach To option, which allows you to specify to what quantity of text (a single character, a paragraph, or a page) you want the graphics attached. If that quantity of text is moved, the graphics box moves with it. There are four options available: Fixed Page, Page, Paragraph, and Character.

The Fixed Page option attaches a graphics box to a fixed position on the page and can only be positioned relative to the top and left edges of the page.

The Paragraph option ties the graphics to the paragraph in which the cursor is positioned. If the paragraph moves to another page, the graphics will move with it. The graphics box is positioned vertically relative to the top of the paragraph and horizontally relative to the paragraph margins.

When a graphics box is attached to a page with the Page option, you can specify that the box either stay on that page or move from page to page with the surrounding text.

If the Character option is selected, the box is treated as a single character, regardless of the size.

Default Placement and Sizing

When a graphics box is created, it is placed at the right margin at the same vertical position as the cursor. The default width for a figure, table, text, and user box is 3.25", and a button box is 1". The height of the graphics box is proportionate to the item placed in the box. A watermark image default size is full page (6.5" x 9").

When a graphics box is created, WordPerfect automatically inserts a [Box (Anchor):Edit Num *n*;Type Box;*filename*;*caption*] code. The (Anchor) specifies whether the graphics is attached to a Fixed Page, Paragraph, Page, or Character. The Edit Num *n* is a document box number automatically assigned to the box. Each graphics box created is numbered sequentially. If you want to add a caption or edit the box, the document box number will need to be specified if you are using the keyboard method to select a graphics box.

▌ HANDS-ON ACTIVITY

You are going to place a figure graphics box in the first paragraph of your newsletter. You will use the quicker method of creating a graphics box. Be sure you have the NEWSLTR.COL document open and View Graphics or Page mode turned on.

1. Position the cursor at the beginning of the first line of the first paragraph, which reads, "In order to provide more information..."

2. Select <u>G</u>raphics ⇒ <u>R</u>etrieve Image

   The Retrieve Image File dialog box appears, as shown in Figure 13-3.

   To get a listing of the graphics files that come with the WordPerfect program,

3. Select **File List**

   ✓ Press F5

   The Select List dialog box appears, indicating the default drive and directory of the graphics files. If your path is not correct, type in a new one.

4. Select **OK**

   ✓ Press Enter

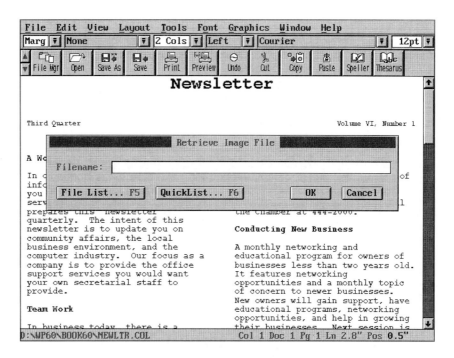

Figure 13-3

The File List dialog box appears, as shown in Figure 13-4.

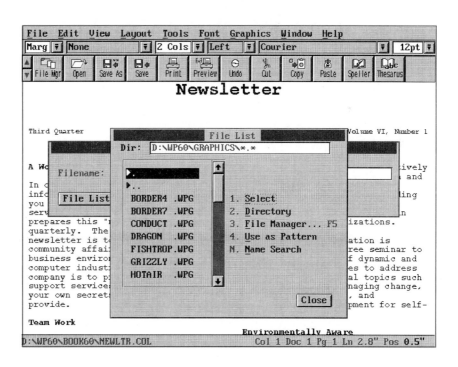

Figure 13-4

You are now going to select the graphics file called PENPUSH.WPG.

5.   Highlight **PENPUSH.WPG**

6. Select **S**elect

✓ Press [Enter]

Compare your document window to the one shown in Figure 13-5.

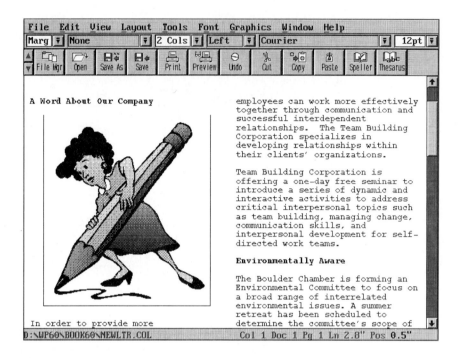

Figure 13-5

WordPerfect automatically applied a figure box to the image, and placed the graphics box on the right margin of the first column. The default width of a graphics box is 3.25" and the height is proportionate to the item in the box.

7. Display the Reveal Codes screen and notice the [Box (Para):Edit Num 1; Figure Box;PENPUSH.WPG;] code that WordPerfect inserted

The Box (Para) means that the box is anchored to the first paragraph of your newsletter. The Edit Num 1 is a document box number automatically assigned to the box. If you want to add a caption or edit the box, the document box number will need to be specified.

▌ Resizing a Graphics Box

Before you can change the size of a graphics box, you must first specify which graphics box is to be altered. A graphics box can either be specified or selected, using the mouse or the keyboard.

To select a graphics box using the *mouse*, the Graphics or Page mode must be active. Position the mouse pointer anywhere inside the box and double-click the left mouse button. The Edit Graphics Box dialog box displays. (Remember, to use the method, the Graphics or Page mode must be activated.)

To select a graphics box using the *keyboard*, select <u>G</u>raphics ⇒ Graphics <u>B</u>oxes ⇒ <u>E</u>dit (*Shortcut keys:* [Alt] + [F9], 1, 2). The Select Box to Edit dialog box appears. Select the Document Box <u>N</u>umber option, type the number of the box to be edited and press [Enter], then select Edit Box. (Remember, WordPerfect automatically assigns a sequential number to all graphics boxes and it is displayed in the Edit Num *n* portion of the [Box (Anchor):Edit Num *n*;Type Box:filename;caption] code.) The Edit Graphics Box dialog box appears, which offers you the capability to change the size of the box.

▌ HANDS-ON ACTIVITY

Before you can make any adjustments to your graphics, you will first need to select it and then change the size. This exercise will take you through the *keyboard* steps.

1. Select <u>G</u>raphics ⇒ Graphics <u>B</u>oxes ⇒ <u>E</u>dit

    ✓ Press [Alt] + [F9], 1, 2

    The Select Box to Edit dialog box appears, as shown in Figure 13-6.

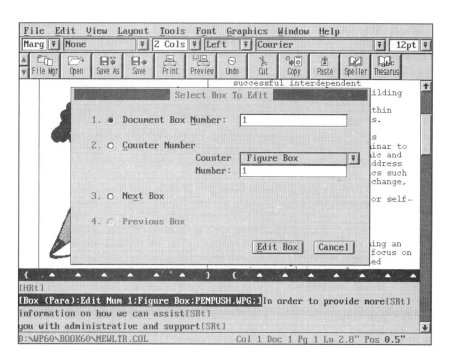

Figure 13-6

Notice that the Document Box <u>N</u>umber parameter is indicating graphics box 1. To edit this box,

2. Select <u>E</u>dit Box

    The Edit Graphics Box dialog box appears, as shown in Figure 13-7.

    You are going to alter your size by entering a specific dimension.

3. Select Edit <u>S</u>ize

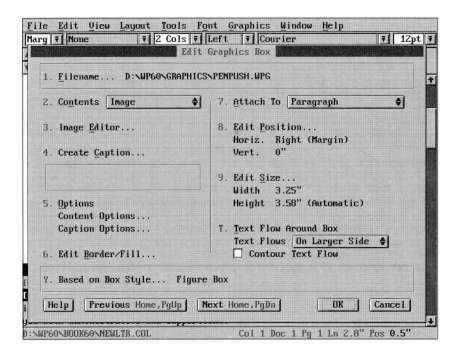

Figure 13-7

The Graphics Box Size dialog box appears, as shown in Figure 13-8.

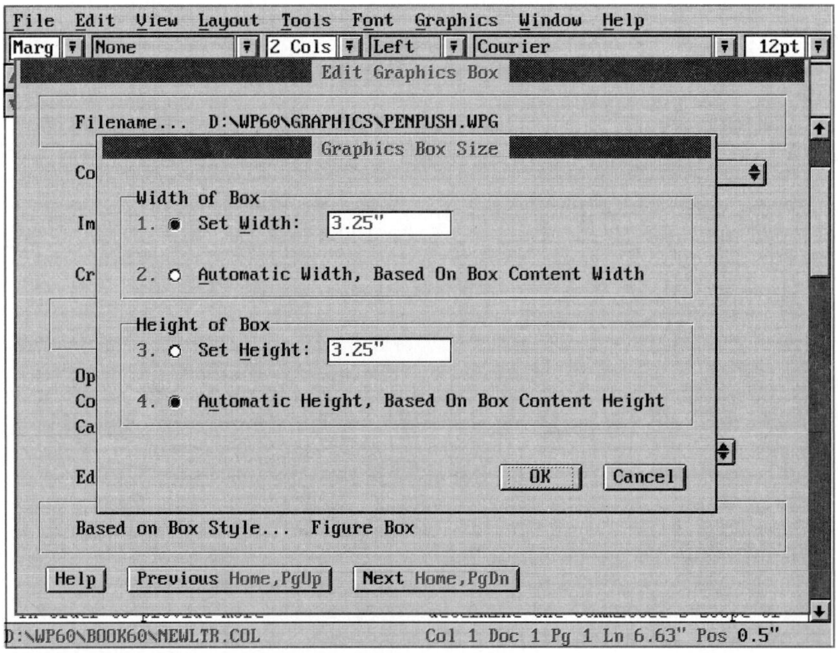

Figure 13-8

4. Select Set **W**idth

5. Type **1.25**

6. Press ⌨Enter⌨

7. Select Set <u>H</u>eight

8. Type **1.25**

9. Press [Enter]

To save your settings and return to the document window,

10. Select **OK** twice

   ✓ Press [Enter] twice

Compare your graphics box to the one shown in Figure 13-9.

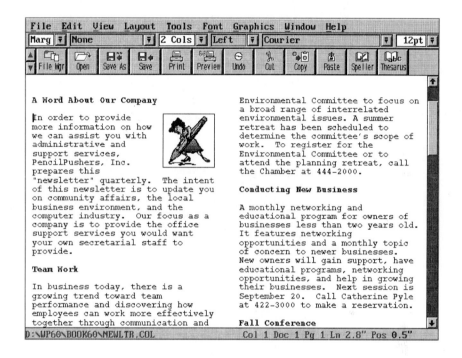

Figure 13-9

NOTE: If you have a mouse, complete this exercise and then move to the next section, "Resizing a Graphics Box Using the Mouse." If you do not have a mouse, just read the next section.

11. Select <u>E</u>dit ⇒ <u>U</u>ndo

   Notice that your graphics box is now back to its original size. You are now going to use the mouse to select and size your graphics. If you do not have a mouse attached to your system, skip to the "Creating a Text Box" section.

Resizing a Graphics Box Using the Mouse

The easiest way to resize a graphics box is with the mouse. However, before it can be resized, it must first be selected. To select a graphics box, position the mouse pointer inside the box and click the left mouse button once. WordPerfect indicates that the graphics box is selected, by outlining the graphics with a dashed line and surrounding the perimeter with eight small black boxes. To deselect a graphics box, position the mouse pointer outside the box, and click the mouse once.

The eight black boxes that surround the box are called **sizing handles.** To resize a box, position the mouse pointer on one of the sizing handles (the mouse pointer changes to a double-headed arrow), hold down the left mouse button, and drag the sizing handle until the box is the desired size.

To change two sides of the box, use one of the sizing handles at the four corners of the box. To change only one side of the box, use a sizing handle on the side you wish to alter.

▌ HANDS-ON ACTIVITY

In this exercise, you are going to resize the "PenPush" graphics box.

The first step is to select the graphics box.

1. Position the mouse pointer inside the graphics box and click the left mouse button once

Compare your graphics box to the one shown in Figure 13-10.

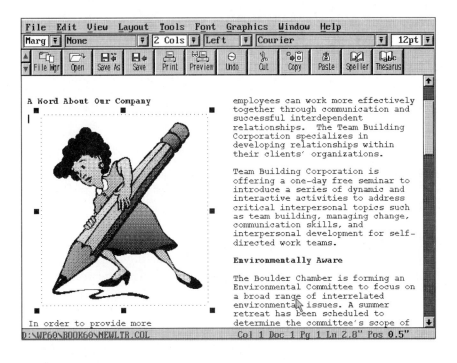

Figure 13-10

2. Position the mouse on the lower-left sizing handle, as shown in Figure 13-11

    Notice that the mouse pointer turns into a double-headed arrow. To make the graphics box smaller,

3. Drag the mouse diagonally toward the upper-right corner of the graphics box as shown in Figure 13-12

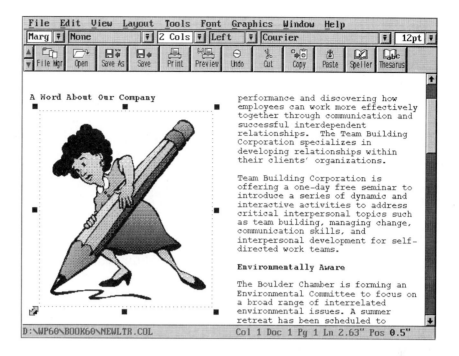

Figure 13-11

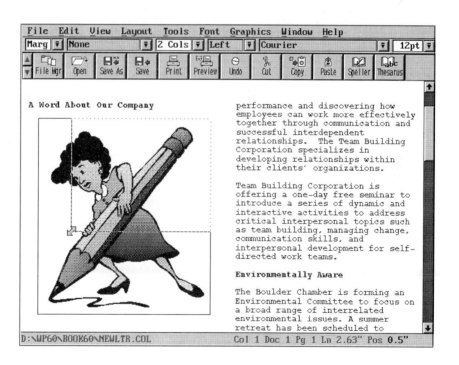

Figure 13-12

Notice that, as you drag the mouse, an outline of the resized box is shown. Make the box approximately 1.25" x 1.25".

4. Release the mouse

    To deselect the box,

5. Point the mouse pointer outside the box and click once

6. For consistency in future exercises in this lesson, on your own, go back through the menu steps (<u>G</u>raphics ⇒ Graphics <u>B</u>oxes ⇒ <u>E</u>dit) and manually set both the width and height of the PENPUSH graphics to 1.25"

▌ Creating a Text Box

A text box is created in the same way as a figure box. When the Create Graphics Box dialog box appears, select the Based on Box Style option and change the selection to Text Box. If you wish to create or edit the text or a table that is to be placed in the box, WordPerfect provides a Text Editor for that purpose. It is advisable, however, that you first edit the box size in the Create Graphics Box dialog box, *before* you create or edit text or tables in the Text Editor.

To display the Text Editor, select the <u>E</u>dit Text option in the Create Graphics Box dialog box. The Text Editor functions just like a document window and allows you to type text, define columns, create tables, change font style and size, cut and paste text, rotate text, retrieve an existing document, and add graphics boxes with images or text.

▌ HANDS-ON ACTIVITY

In this exercise, you are going to create a text box in which you will type the table of contents for your newsletter. This text table will be anchored to the page so that it will always remain at the same position, no matter how much text is added, deleted, or moved.

1. Position the cursor at the top of the document

    To create the text box,

2. Select <u>G</u>raphics ⇒ Graphics <u>B</u>oxes ⇒ <u>C</u>reate

    ✓ Press Alt + F9 , 1, 1

    The Create Graphics Box dialog box appears. First, you will need to specify the type of box.

3. Select **Based on Box St<u>y</u>le**

4. Highlight **Text Box**

5. Select <u>S</u>elect

    ✓ Press Enter

    The next step is to tell WordPerfect that you want the table of contents anchored to the Fixed Page.

6. Select <u>A</u>ttach To

7. Select <u>F</u>ixed Page Position

    The next step is to change the width of the box. This is an important step—remember, you always want to specify the correct width of the box before creating or editing text in the Text Editor.

8. Select **Edit** **S**ize

The Graphics Box Size dialog box appears, as shown in Figure 13-13.

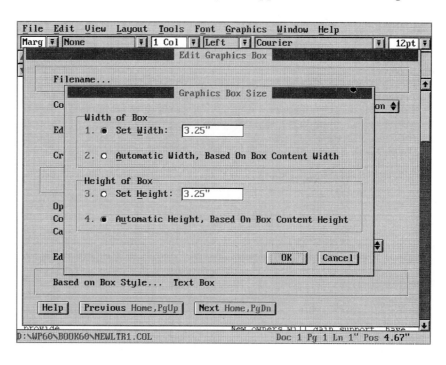

File   Edit   View   Layout   Tools   Font   Graphics   Window   Help
Marg ▼ None   ▼ 1 Col ▼ Left ▼ Courier   ▼ 12pt ▼
                         Edit Graphics Box
  Filename...
                         Graphics Box Size
Co   on ⬍
      ┌Width of Box────────────────────────────────
Ed   │ 1. ● Set **W**idth: 3.25"
      │
Cr   │ 2. ○ **A**utomatic Width, Based On Box Content Width
      └
      ┌Height of Box───────────────────────────────
      │ 3. ○ Set **H**eight: 3.25"
Op   │
Co   │ 4. ● **A**utomatic Height, Based On Box Content Height
Ca   └
      ⬍
Ed   OK   Cancel

  Based on Box Style... Text Box

  Help   Previous Home,PgUp   Next Home,PgDn
  provide   New owners will gain support have
D:\WP60\BOOK60\NEWLTR1.COL   Doc 1 Pg 1 Ln 1" Pos 4.67"

Figure 13-13

The width of your columns is 3.5", so you will want to specify that dimension for your box width.

9. Select **Set W**idth

10. Type **3.5**

11. Press (Enter)

Be sure the Height of Box parameter is set to A**u**tomatic Height, Based on Box Content Height. This is the default setting and will adjust the box according to the amount of text you enter in the Text Editor.

12. Select **OK**
Now you are ready to display the Text Editor and type the table of contents.

13. Select **Cr**eate Text

The Text Editor appears, as shown in Figure 13-14.

14. Select **Large, Bold,** and **Italics**

15. Type **Inside This Issue:**

16. Press (Enter) twice

17. Turn off the Large attribute

18. Type **A Word About Our Company**

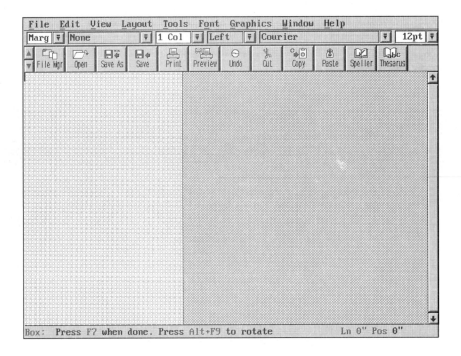

Figure 13-14

Now you will use the Flush Right feature to move the cursor to the right margin; however, you also need dot leaders. You can move the cursor to the right margin and create dot leaders in one simple operation:

19. Press [Alt] + [F6] twice

20. Type **1**

21. Press [Enter]

22. Continue typing the remainder of the table, as shown below. Be sure to press [Alt] + [F6] twice to move the cursor to the right margin and create the dot leaders. Press [Enter] twice after each line, except the last one. After the last line, press [Enter] once

Team Work 1

Environmentally Aware 1

Conducting New Business 1

Fall Conference 2

Targeting New Products 2

The Corporate Network 2

The Darker Side of Computing 2

Awards 3

To exit the Text Editor,

23. Press F7

You are returned to the Create Graphics Box dialog box. There is one final step that needs to be performed. Notice the Edit Position parameter. The horizontal and vertical positions are relative to the upper-left corner of the page. In other words, with these current settings your graphics box will be placed one inch from the top left edge of the page. To calculate where your table of contents should be placed, subtract the height of the box shown in the Edit Size parameter from 10 inches. WordPerfect is measuring from the top edge of the page, plus you want a one-inch bottom margin.

24. Select **Edit Position**

The Fixed Page Position dialog box appears, as shown in Figure 13-15.

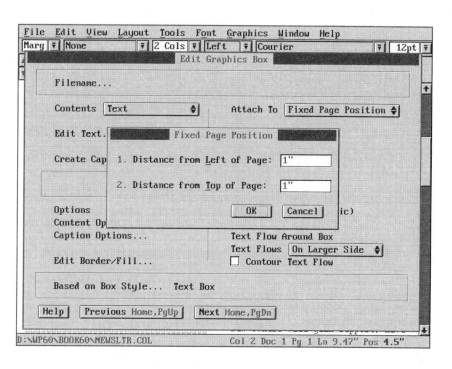

Figure 13-15

First, you will specify where the box is to be placed relative to the left edge of the page. Your left margin is .5", so that is where the box should be positioned.

25. Select **Distance from Left of Page**

26. Type **.5**

27. Press Enter

28. Select **Distance from Top of Page**

Since you want the bottom of the text box to be placed along the bottom margin, you will subtract the box height (3.5") from 10" (the page size less the bottom margin).

NOTE: The measurements of your graphics box may differ due to font differences between computer setups. Calculate the automatic height from the page size, less the bottom margin.

29. Type **6.5**

30. Press (Enter)

To exit the Create Graphics Box dialog box,

31. Select **OK**

✓ Press (Enter)

32. Use the Print Preview feature to view your newsletter

Compare your screen to the one shown in Figure 13-16. Notice that the title "Team Work" is in the first column and the text regarding this subject has been placed at the top of the second column.

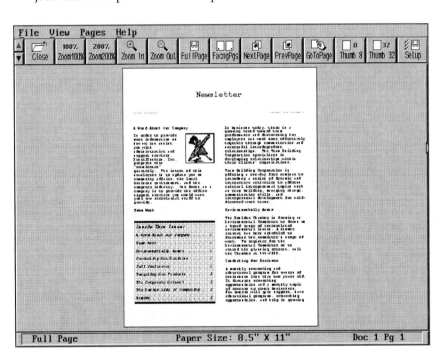

Figure 13-16

To correct this problem,

33. Exit the Print Preview screen

34. Position the cursor before or under the "T" in "Team Work"

35. Press (Ctrl) + (Enter)

▌ Creating a Table Box

You create a table box the same way a figure or text box is created. Remember, you can place either text, a graphics image, or an equation in a table box. A table box appears with a ruling line above and below the graphics box.

▌**HANDS-ON ACTIVITY**

In this exercise, you are going to create a table box and place a table inside the box. The table is located on your sample disk.

1. At the top of page 2, column 1, locate the text "Next session is September 20"; and delete this sentence

    In its place,

2. Type **The fall schedule is shown in the table below.**

3. Position the cursor in front of or under the "F" in the next subheading, "Fall Conference"

4. Press [Enter] twice

5. Press [↑] twice

6. Select <u>G</u>raphics ⇒ Graphics <u>B</u>oxes ⇒ <u>C</u>reate

    ✓ Press [Alt] + [F9], **1, 1**

    The Create Graphics Box dialog box appears. First, you will need to specify the type of box.

7. Select **Based on Box St<u>y</u>le**

8. Highlight **Table Box**

9. Select <u>S</u>elect

    ✓ Press [Enter]

    The next step is to change the width of the box. Since the column width is 3.5", that is the dimension you will specify.

10. Select **Edit <u>S</u>ize**

    The Graphics Box Size dialog box appears.

11. Select **Set <u>W</u>idth**

12. Type **3.5**

13. Press [Enter]

    Be sure the Height of the Box parameter is set to A<u>u</u>tomatic Height, Based on Box Content Height. This is the default setting and will adjust the box according to the amount of text you enter in the Text Editor.

14. Select **OK**
    Now you are ready to display the Text Editor and retrieve the table.

15. Select **Cr<u>e</u>ate Text**

    The Text Editor appears.

16. Select <u>F</u>ile ⇒ <u>R</u>etrieve

The Retrieve Document dialog box appears. In the instructions below, we specify drive A. If your sample disk is located in a different drive, substitute the correct drive letter where we indicate A.

17. Type `A:TABLE.COL`

18. Press Enter

The table is retrieved into the Text Editor. To exit the Text Editor,

19. Press F7

You are returned to the Create Graphics Box dialog box.

To exit the Create Graphics Box dialog box,

20. Select **OK**

✓ Press Enter

21. Use the Print Preview feature to view your newsletter

▓ Creating a User Box

You create a user box the same way a figure or text box is created. Remember, you can place either text, a graphics image, or an equation in a user box. A user box has no borders or shading.

▌ HANDS-ON ACTIVITY

In this exercise, you are going to create a user box and place a graphics image inside the box.

1. Position the cursor in front of the "I" in the phrase "If someone mentions they have a virus," (page 2, column 2, just beneath the heading "The Darker Side...")

2. Select **Graphics** ⇒ **Graphics Boxes** ⇒ **Create**

✓ Press Alt + F9 , 1, 1

The Create Graphics Box dialog box appears. First, you will need to specify the type of box.

3. Select **Based on Box Style**

4. Highlight **User Box**

5. Select **Select**

✓ Press Enter

The next step is to change the width of the box. Since WordPerfect automatically makes the width of a user box 3.25",

6. Select **Edit Size**

The Graphics Box Size dialog box appears.

7. Select **Set Width**

8. Type `1.5`

9. Press [Enter]

Be sure the Height of the Box parameter is set to A̲utomatic Height, Based on Box Content Height. This is the default setting and will adjust the box according to the graphics image retrieved.

10. Select **OK**

Now, you are going to specify the file name.

11. Select F̲ilename

The Retrieve File dialog box appears.

12. Type `DRAGON.WPG`

13. Select **OK**

✓ Press [Enter]

To return to the document window,

14. Select **OK**

✓ Press [Enter]

15. Use the Print Preview feature to view your newsletter; compare the second page to the one shown in Figure 13-17

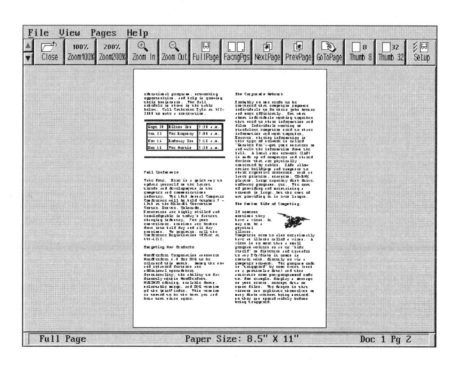

Figure 13-17

▌ Moving a Graphics Box

A graphics box can be moved either by using the mouse or through the Create Graphics Box dialog box. To move a graphics box using the *mouse*, select the graphics box, position the mouse inside the box (the mouse pointer changes to a four-headed arrow), press the mouse button, and drag the graphics to the new location. Release the mouse.

To change the location of a graphics box using the *keyboard*, choose Graphics ⇒ Graphics Boxes ⇒ Edit and specify the number of the graphics box. The Edit Graphics Box dialog box appears. Select the Edit Position option, and choose the desired vertical and horizontal position of the box.

▌ HANDS-ON ACTIVITY

In this exercise, you are going to use the menu to move the location of the dragon graphics.

1. Select Graphics ⇒ Graphics Boxes ⇒ Edit

    ✓ Press Alt + F9 , **1 , 2**

    The Select Box to Edit dialog box appears. Make sure the Document Box Number parameter is indicating 4. If not, select the Document Box Number option and type **4**.

2. Select Edit Box

    The Edit Graphics Box dialog box appears. To change the location of the graphics,

3. Select Edit Position

    The Graphics Box Size dialog box appears.

4. Select Horizontal Position

5. Select Left

    To exit the Paragraph Box Position dialog box,

6. Select OK

    ✓ Press Enter

    To return to the document window,

7. Select OK

    ✓ Press Enter

    NOTE: If you have a mouse, continue with the following steps in this exercise.

8. Select Edit ⇒ Undo

    Notice that your graphics box is now back to its original location. You are now going to use the mouse to select and move your graphics. If you do not have a mouse attached to your system, skip to the next section, "Adding a Caption to a Box."

    First, you must select the graphics.

9. Position the mouse pointer inside the graphics box, then click the left mouse button once

    WordPerfect indicates that the box is selected by outlining it with a dashed box and placing eight small black boxes (sizing/moving handles) around the box.

10. Move the mouse pointer into the graphics box

   The mouse pointer changes to the shape of a cross of double-headed arrows. Compare your graphics box to the one shown in Figure 13-18.

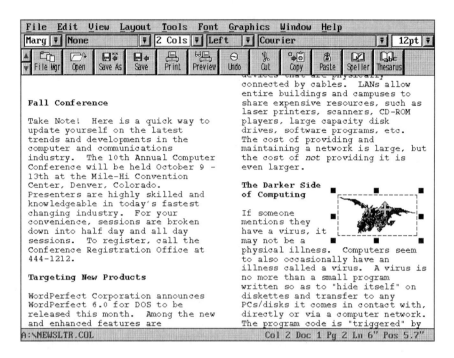

Figure 13-18

11. Hold down the left mouse button and drag the graphics box to the left edge of the column; then release the mouse button

   Compare your graphics to the one shown in Figure 13-19.

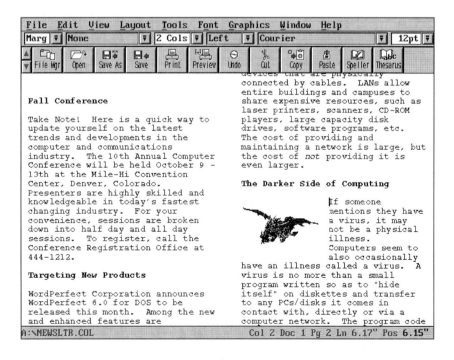

Figure 13-19

Adding a Caption to a Box

A caption may be created that includes the number of the graphics box along with a description of the contents; the caption moves with the box. If you do not want the caption to be numbered, simply press [Backspace] to delete the number. When the Edit Graphics Box appears, select the Create Caption option. Type the caption and press [F7].

▌ HANDS-ON ACTIVITY

In this exercise, you are going to add a caption to the user box that contains dragon. Your caption will contain only descriptive text.

1. Select the graphics using either the mouse method (double-click in the graphics with the Graphics or Page mode active) or the keyboard method (<u>G</u>raphics ⇒ Graphics <u>B</u>oxes ⇒ <u>E</u>dit) and type **4** (to specify graphics box 4)

    The Edit Graphics Box appears.

2. Select **Create Caption**

    The Caption Editor appears, with a 1 in the upper-left corner of the window, as shown in Figure 13-20. First, you will need to delete the number.

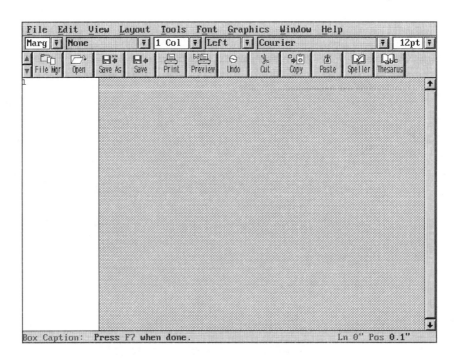

Figure 13-20

3. Press [Backspace]

4. From the F<u>o</u>nt menu, select Italics and Fine

5. Type **Beware of Hidden Monsters**

    To exit the Caption Editor,

6. Press [F7]

To return to the document window,

7. Select **OK**

    ✓ Press Enter

Editing a Graphics Image

If you retrieve either a bitmap image or vector image into a graphics box, the Image Editor allows you to edit the image. You can rotate, crop, scale, or adjust the color of an image. The fill type of a vector image can also be changed.

The first step to editing a graphics image is to specify the graphics box—either by using the mouse (double-click inside the graphics box with the Graphics or Page mode active) or by using the keyboard (select Graphics ⇒ Graphics Boxes ⇒ Edit and enter the appropriate graphics box number). When the Edit Graphics Box appears, select the Image Editor.

The Image Editor generally gives you four methods with which to execute a command—using the Button Bar, the menu bar, keystrokes, or the status bar located at the bottom of the screen. (Remember, you can only access the Button Bar using the mouse.) If changes are made using the Button Bar, the menu, or keystrokes, the changes are reflected in the status bar. For example, if you choose to rotate an image using the menu, the specified changes reflect on the status bar.

The Increment option, shown in the status bar displayed at the bottom of the screen, dictates the percent of change. The increment options are 1%, 5%, 10%, and 25%. For example, if you press Page Down to reduce the size of the image and the increment is set at 25%, the image will be reduced by one-fourth of its original size.

HANDS-ON ACTIVITY

In this exercise, you will work with the "PenPush" graphics and learn to scale, move, rotate, and flip the graphics; change its fill attribute; and reset it to its original state.

1. Select the "PenPush" graphics

    The Edit Graphics Box dialog box appears.

2. Select **Image Editor**

    The Image Editor window appears, as shown in Figure 13-21.

    Notice that the Increment option button at the bottom of the screen displays 10%, which indicates that whatever changes you make will be in 10-percent increments.

Enlarging or Reducing a Graphics Image

The default scale (proportionally changing the size) when a graphics appears in the Image editor is 100%. To change the scaling, press Page Up to enlarge the graphics or Page Down to decrease the size, or choose Edit ⇒ Position and select either Enlarge or Reduce. The enlargement or reduction

Figure 13-21

will be adjusted according to the increment chosen. If you have a mouse attached to your system, you can access options using the Button Bar along the top edge of the screen. If you click on Enlarge %, the graphics will be enlarged according to the increment chosen in the status bar. Conversely, if you click on Reduce %, the graphics will be reduced the percentage shown in the status bar.

To change the graphics image back to its original size and position, in the Image Editor choose Reset All in the Button Bar or Edit ⇒ Reset All.

▌ HANDS-ON ACTIVITY

First, you are going to change the Increment option to 25% and then you are going to reduce the size of your image.

1. Select **Increment** (until the Increment button in the status bar at the bottom of the screen appears as 25%)

2. Press [Page Down] 2 times

    The graphics image has been reduced by 50%.

3. From the pull-down menu, select **Edit** ⇒ **Position** ⇒ **Enlarge %**

    The graphics image has been enlarged by 25%.

4. Select **Edit** ⇒ **Position** ⇒ **Reduce %**

    The graphics image has been reduced by 25%.

    Compare your Image Editor to Figure 13-22.

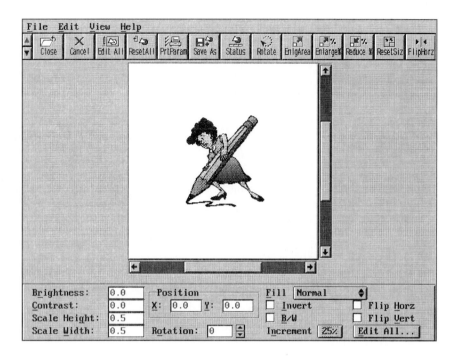

Figure 13-22

Notice that your graphics has been reduced by 50%.

5. On your own, increase the graphics 25%

Moving a Graphics Image in the Box

To move a graphics within the box, press either ⬆, ⬇, ⬅, or ➡ to move the image in a specific direction. The image will be moved according to the increment set in the status bar. An alternative method is to position the mouse pointer on either the vertical or horizontal scroll bars to adjust the position of the graphics.

▍HANDS-ON ACTIVITY

In this exercise you are going to move the image using the arrow keys. First, you need to change the increment.

1. Select **In**crement (until the button indicates 10%)

2. Press ➡ twice

3. Press ⬆ once

    Compare your image to the one shown in Figure 13-23.

Restoring the Default Setting of a Graphics Image

If you have made changes to your graphics image and wish to reinstate the original settings, choose either Reset All in the Button Bar or <u>E</u>dit ⇒ <u>R</u>eset All (*Shortcut keys:* Ctrl + Home).

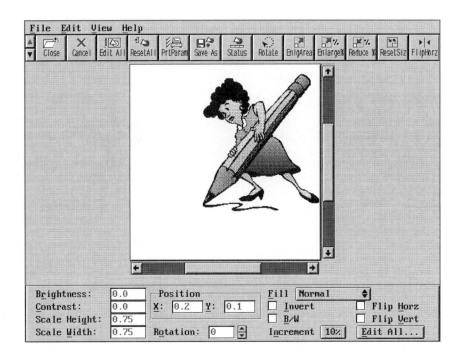

Figure 13-23

HANDS-ON ACTIVITY

In this exercise, you are going to return the graphics image to its original size and position.

1. Select **Edit** ⇒ **Reset All** or click on **Reset All** in the Button Bar

   ✓ Press Ctrl + Home

Rotating a Graphics Image

A graphics image can be rotated any number of degrees. Pressing + (plus key) rotates the image clockwise, and − (minus) rotates it counterclockwise according to the increment set in the status bar. An alternative method is to select the Rotation option in the status bar and enter the number of degrees to be rotated.

To use the *mouse* to rotate a graphics image, choose either Rotate in the Button Bar or Edit ⇒ Position ⇒ Rotate to display the rotation axis, then drag a vertical or horizontal axis line to rotate the image any number of degrees. The status bar displays the degree of rotation as you drag the axis line.

HANDS-ON ACTIVITY

In this exercise, you are going to rotate the graphics image 90 and 180 degrees.

Make sure the increment is set to 10%.

1. Press + (plus sign) 5 times

Notice that the status bar at the bottom of the Image Editor is displaying a Rotation of 180 degrees. Compare your graphics image to the one shown in Figure 13-24.

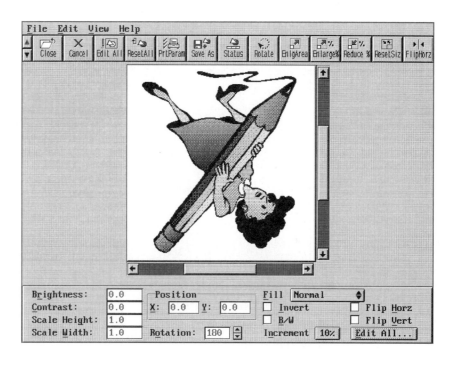

Figure 13-24

To reset your graphics image back to its original location,

2. Select **E**dit ⇒ **Reset A**ll or click on **Reset All** in the Button Bar

    ✓ Press Ctrl + Home

    Now you are going to rotate the graphics image 90 degrees. Make sure the **I**ncrement option is set to 5%.

3. Press – (minus sign) 5 times

    The status bar is now showing that the graphics image is rotated 90 degrees. Compare your Image Editor screen to the one shown in Figure 13-25.

4. On your own, reset the graphics image back to its original location

    TIP: If you have a mouse attached to your system, select the Rotate button on the Button Bar and experiment using the axis line to rotate the image.

Reversing a Graphics Image

The **E**dit ⇒ **A**ttributes menu allows you to flip or reverse an image on its horizontal or vertical axis. These options can also be accessed from the Button Bar.

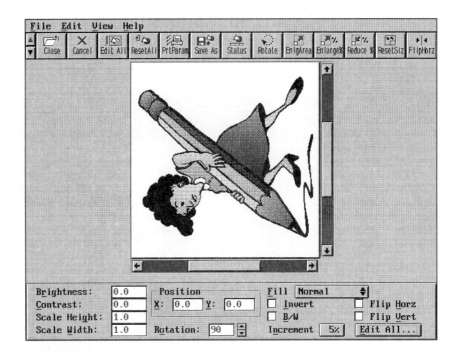

Figure 13-25

■ HANDS-ON ACTIVITY

In this exercise, you are going to reverse the graphics image on both its vertical and horizontal axis.

1. Select <u>E</u>dit ⇒ <u>A</u>ttributes ⇒ Flip <u>H</u>orizontal or click on **Flip Horz** in the Button Bar

   Compare your screen to the one shown in Figure 13-26.

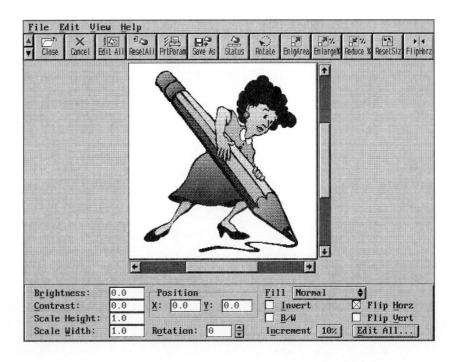

Figure 13-26

To reset your graphics image back to its original location,

2. Select **E**dit ⇒ **R**eset All or click on **Reset All** in the Button Bar

   ✓ Press Ctrl + Home

3. Select **E**dit ⇒ **A**ttributes ⇒ Flip **V**ertical or click on Flip **V**ert in the dialog box at the lower portion of the screen. You can see Flip Horz in the Button Bar; the Flip Vert button is also available if you press the up or down arrows on the left side of the Button Bar to view more buttons

Compare your screen to the one shown in Figure 13-27.

Figure 13-27

4. On your own, reset your graphics image back to its original orientation and location

■ **Changing the Fill Attributes of a Graphics Image**

The **F**ill option in the status bar allows you to make the graphics image transparent, or you may use the menu by selecting **E**dit ⇒ **F**ill ⇒ **T**ransparent or clicking on the Trnsprnt button in the Button Bar.

■ **HANDS-ON ACTIVITY**

In this exercise, you are going to change the Fill option setting for the graphics image to transparent.

1. Select **E**dit ⇒ **F**ill ⇒ **T**ransparent or click on **Trnsprnt** in the Button Bar

Compare your image to the one shown in Figure 13-28.

Figure 13-28

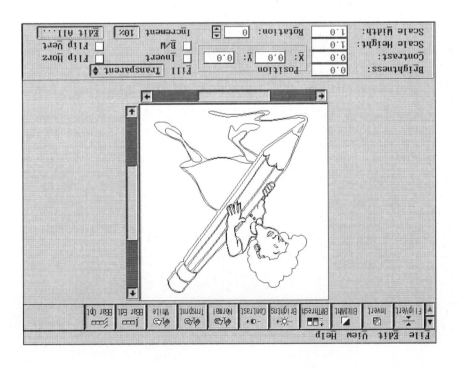

To restore the graphics image to its default settings,

2. Select Edit ⇒ Reset All or click on Reset All in the Button Bar

✓ Press Ctrl + Home

To exit and close the Image Editor,

3. Select File ⇒ Close or click on Close in the Button Bar

✓ Press F7

Creating a Shadow Border for a Graphics Box

To create a shadow effect for the currently selected graphics box, select the Edit Border/Fill option in the Edit Graphics Box dialog box. When the Edit Graphics Box Border/Fills dialog box appears, select Shadow. The Shadow dialog box displays, allowing you to choose shadow positions of Upper Left, Lower Left, Upper Right, Lower Right, or None. Make the desired selection and choose OK.

▌ HANDS-ON ACTIVITY

In this exercise you are going to create a shadow border for the figure box that contains the "PenPush" graphics.

1. On your own, select the PENPUSH graphics box

The Edit Graphics Box dialog box is displayed.

2. Select Edit Border/Fill

The Edit Graphics Box Border/Fill dialog box appears, as shown in Figure 13-29.

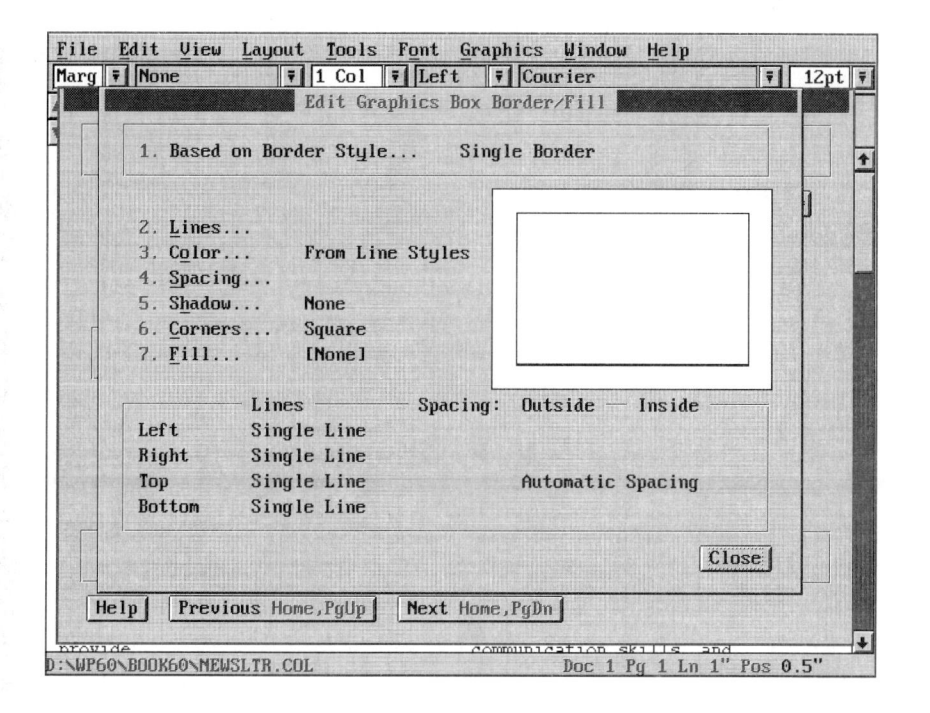

Figure 13-29

3. Select **Sh**adow

    The Shadow dialog box appears, as shown in Figure 13-30.

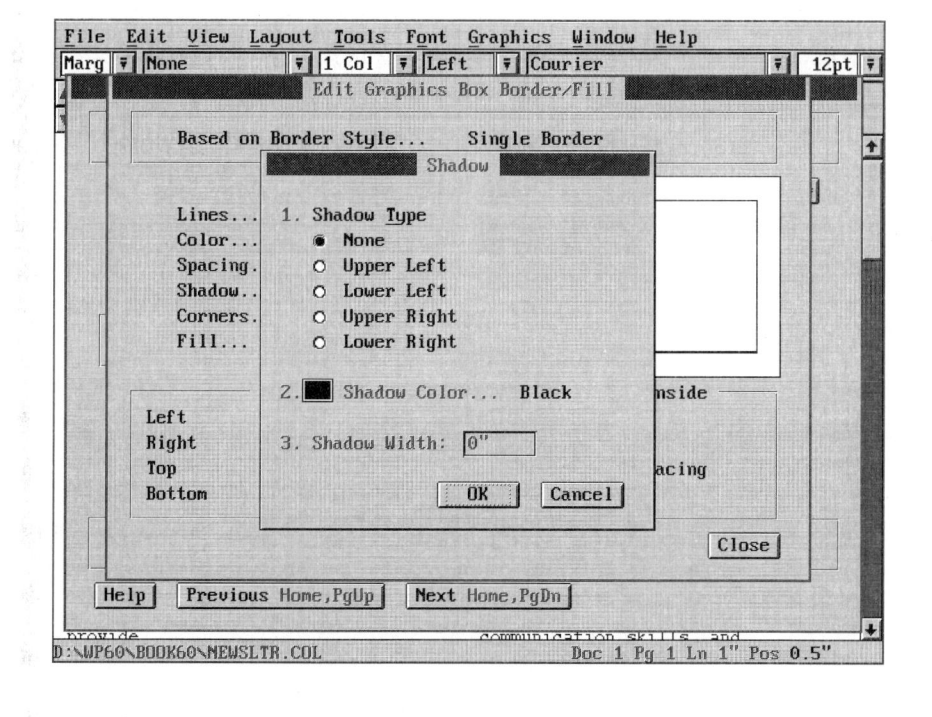

Figure 13-30

4. Select **Shadow T**ype

5. Select **L**o**wer Right**

    The default color for the shadow box is black and the shadow width is
    .125". To exit the dialog box,

6. Select OK

✓ Press Enter

7. Select Close

✓ Press F7

8. Select OK

✓ Press Enter

Compare your document to the one shown in Figure 13-31.

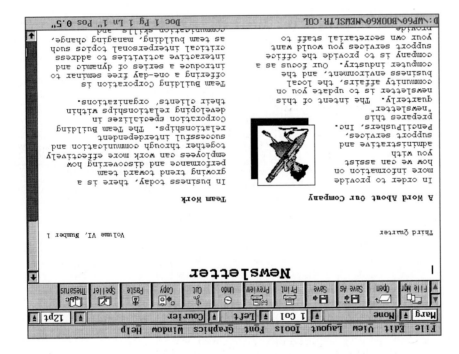

Figure 13-31

■ **Creating Graphics Lines**

The **Graphics Line** feature allows you to insert horizontal and vertical lines in a document. Graphics lines enhance headlines, create borders at the top and bottom of a page, and separate columns. The lines can be shaded or blank and can vary in thickness. A Graphics Line code—either [Graph Line:*n*; Horiz] (for Horizontal) or [Graph Line:*n*;Vert] (for Vertical)—is inserted at the cursor. The *n* represents the number that WordPerfect automatically assigns to each graphics line. Every graphics line is consecutively numbered, so you can easily select a specific line.

To create either a horizontal or vertical line, position the cursor where the line is to appear, then choose Graphics ⇒ Graphics Lines ⇒ Create (*Shortcut keys:* Alt + F9, 2, 1). The Create Graphics Line dialog box appears in which you can choose a horizontal or a vertical line and can change the thickness, the percent of gray shading, and the vertical and horizontal positions. To save your settings and close the dialog box, choose OK.

■ **HANDS-ON ACTIVITY**

You are going to create two horizontal graphics lines to enhance the headline of your newsletter. Before you begin, display the Reveal Codes screen.

1. Turn on Reveal Codes and position the cursor on the third [HRt] code after the heading "Newsletter"

   Compare your screen to the one shown in Figure 13-32.

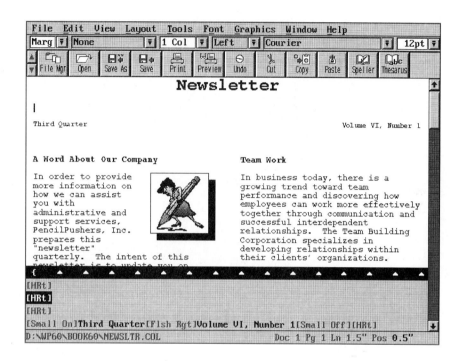

Figure 13-32

2. Select <u>G</u>raphics ⇒ Graphics <u>L</u>ines ⇒ <u>C</u>reate

   ✓ Press (Alt) + (F9), **2, 1**

   The Create Graphics Line dialog box appears, as shown in Figure 13-33.

   Notice that the Line <u>O</u>rientation is set to Horizontal. Your options are either Horizontal or Vertical. The <u>H</u>orizontal Position is set to Full, which means the graphics line will extend between the left and right margins. The <u>V</u>ertical Position option is Baseline, which instructs Word-Perfect to place the line at the position of the cursor. To change the thickness of the line,

3. Select <u>T</u>hickness

4. Select <u>S</u>et

   The cursor moves to the Set text box.

5. Type **.13** (for 0.13 inches)

6. Press (Enter)

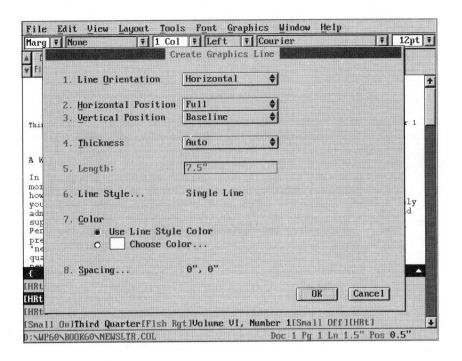

Figure 13-33

To close the dialog box,

7. Select **OK**

   ✓ Press [Enter]

8. Position the cursor on the blank line below the line that reads "Third Quarter"

9. Select **Graphics** ⇒ **Graphics Lines** ⇒ **Create**

   ✓ Press [Alt] + [F9], **2**, **1**

   The Create Graphics Line dialog box appears.

10. Select **Thickness**

11. Select **Set**

    The cursor moves to the Set text box.

12. Type **.03**

13. Press [Enter]

    To close the dialog box,

14. Select **OK**

    Compare your newsletter to the one shown in Figure 13-34.

▌ Editing a Graphics Line

Using the *mouse* is the easiest way to change the width, the length, and the position of a graphics line. Before a line can be edited, it must first be selected. To select a graphics line, position the mouse pointer someplace on

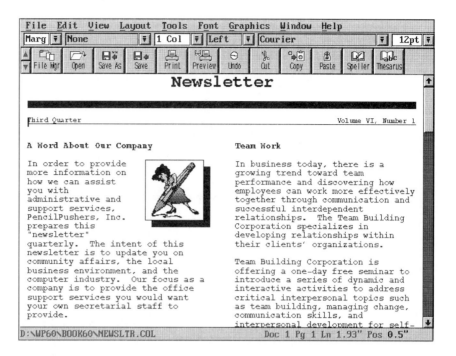

Figure 13-34

the line and click the left mouse button once. To indicate that the line is selected, WordPerfect places a dashed line and eight black sizing handles around the perimeter of the line.

To select and edit a graphics line using the keyboard, select Graphics ⇒ Graphics Lines ⇒ Edit (*Keyboard shortcut:* Alt + F9, 2, 2). The Select Graphic Line to Edit dialog box appears. Select Graphics Line Number and type the desired number and press Enter, then select Edit Line. (Remember, WordPerfect automatically numbers each graphics line, indicating it in the [Graph Line] code that is inserted when the line is created.)

Changing the Thickness and Length of a Graphics Line

To use the *mouse* to change the thickness of a line, position the mouse pointer on one of the sizing handles in the middle of the line, click and drag the sizing handle to the desired thickness, and release the mouse button. To change the length of a line, position the mouse pointer on one of the sizing handles at the end of the line, click and drag to the desired length and release the mouse button.

To use the *keyboard* to change the thickness of a line, in the Edit Graphics Line dialog box choose Thickness ⇒ Set, type the desired dimension of the line, and press Enter. To change the length of the line, select Horizontal Position ⇒ Set, type the desired length, and press Enter. Select OK to exit the dialog box.

▌ HANDS-ON ACTIVITY

In this exercise, you are going to increase the thickness of the top graphics line in your newsletter. If you do not have a mouse attached to your system, move to the "Using the Keyboard" portion of this activity.

Using the Mouse

1. Select the first graphics line

    Compare your graphics line to the one shown in Figure 13-35.

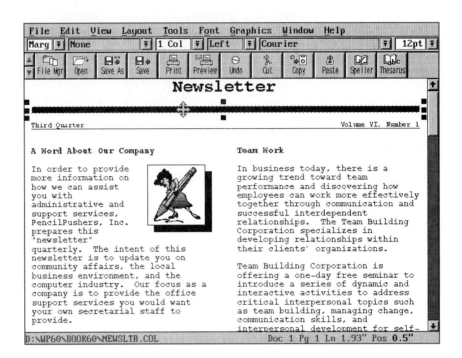

Figure 13-35

2. Position the mouse pointer on the bottom-center sizing handle, as shown in Figure 13-36

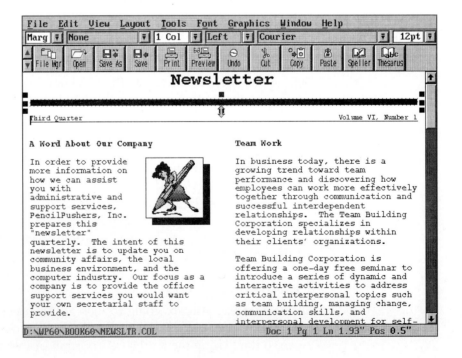

Figure 13-36

Notice that the mouse changes to a double-headed arrow.

3. Click and drag the mouse downward about ⅛ inch (if you were to look at Graphics ⇒ Line ⇒ Edit Horizontal, the thickness should be about .2")

4. Release the mouse button

Using the Keyboard

1. Select the top graphics line

    The Edit Graphics Line dialog box appears.

2. Select <u>T</u>hickness ⇒ <u>S</u>et

3. Type **.2**

4. Press Enter

5. Select **OK**

Moving a Graphics Line

To use the *mouse* to move a graphics line, select the line and position the mouse pointer someplace in the line (not on a sizing handle). The mouse changes to a four-headed arrow. Click and drag the line to the desired location and release the mouse button.

To use the *keyboard* to move a graphics line, at the Edit Graphics Line dialog box, choose <u>V</u>ertical Position ⇒ <u>S</u>et. Type the dimension relative to the top edge of the page and press Enter.

▌ HANDS-ON ACTIVITY

Now move the bottom graphics line downward. If you do not have a mouse attached to your system, go to the "Using the Keyboard" portion of this activity.

Using the Mouse

1. Select the bottom graphics line

2. Position the mouse pointer someplace in the graphics line

    The mouse changes to a four-headed arrow.

3. Click and drag the mouse downward about ⅛"

4. On your own, move the top graphics line to your liking

Using the Keyboard

1. Select the top graphics line

    The Edit Graphics Line dialog box appears.

2. Select <u>V</u>ertical Position ⇒ <u>S</u>et

3. Type `1.55`

4. Press Enter

5. Select **OK**

▌ **HANDS-ON ACTIVITY**

To finish your newsletter,

1. Save your document as `NEWS.COL`

2. Print your newsletter

   Compare your newsletter to the one shown in Figure 13-37.

3. Close your newsletter

▌ Creating a Letterhead

Since you now have some experience working with graphics boxes and graphics, you believe it is time to create a letterhead for PencilPushers, Inc. The letterhead you will create is shown in Figure 13-38 (page 364). Make sure you have a clear document window.

1. Select **Graphics** ⇒ **Graphics Boxes** ⇒ **Create**

2. Enter the following setings in the Create Graphics dialog box:

   1. Filename: PENPUSH.WPG

   7. Attach to: Page

   8. Edit Position: Horiz. Left (Margin)

   9. Edit Size: Width 1", Height 1"

   Y. Based on Box Style: User Box

   To position the cursor on the right margin,

3. Press Alt + F6

4. Select **Font** ⇒ **Font**

5. Select the font of your choice, select a font size of 24 points, and turn on Shadow and Bold attributes

6. Type `PencilPushers, Inc.`

7. Press Enter

8. Press Alt + F6

9. Select **Font** ⇒ **Font**

10. Select a font size of 10 points and turn on Shadow, Bold, and Italic attributes

11. Type `Administrative Support Services`

Newsletter

Third Quarter   Volume VI, Number 1

A Word About Our Company

In order to provide more information on how we can assist you with administrative and support services, PencilPushers, Inc. prepares this "newsletter" quarterly.  The intent of this newsletter is to update you on community affairs, the local business environment, and the computer industry. Our focus as a company is to provide the office support services you would want your own secretarial staff to provide.

Inside This Issue:

Team Work

In business today, there is a growing trend toward team performance and discovering how employees can work more effectively together through communication and successful interdependent relationships. The Team Building Corporation specializes in developing relationships within their clients' organizations.

Team Building Corporation is offering a one-day free seminar to introduce a series of dynamic and interactive activities to address critical interpersonal topics such as team building, managing change, communication skills, and interpersonal development for self-directed work teams.

Environmentally Aware

The Boulder Chamber is forming an Environmental Committee to focus on a broad range of interrelated environmental issues. A summer retreat has been scheduled to determine the committee's scope of work. To register for the Environmental Committee or to attend the planning retreat, call the Chamber at 444-2000.

Conducting New Business

A monthly networking and educational program for owners of businesses less than two years old. It features networking opportunities and a monthly topic of concern to newer businesses. New owners will gain support, have educational programs, networking opportunities, and

Figure 13-37 (page 1)

12. Press Enter twice

13. Press Alt + F6

14. Select **Font** ⇒ **Font**

15. Select a font size of 12 points and turn on Shadow and Bold attributes

16. Type `1200 Willow, Suite 300`

17. Press Enter

help in growing their businesses. Next session is September 20. Call Catherine Pyle at 422-3000 to make a reservation.

Sept 20	Hilton Inn	7:30 a.m.
Oct 23	The Regency	7:00 a.m.
Nov 16	Rodeway Inn	7:15 a.m.
Dec 15	The Westin	7:30 a.m.

Fall Conference

Take Note! Here is a quick way to update yourself on the latest trends and developments in the computer and communications industry. The 10th Annual Computer Conference will be held October 9 - 13th at the Mile-Hi Convention Center, Denver, Colorado. Presenters are highly skilled and knowledgeable in today's fastest changing industry. For your convenience, sessions are broken down into half day and all day sessions. To register, call the Conference Registration Office at 444-1212.

Targeting New Products

WordPerfect Corporation announces WordPerfect 6.0 for DOS to be released this month. Among the new and enhanced features are additional spreadsheet functionality, the ability to fax directly within WordPerfect, WYSIWYG editing, scalable fonts, selectable merge, and the DOS version of QuickFinder. This version is touted to be the best yet and beta test sites agree.

The Corporate Network

Probably no one needs to be convinced that computers empower individuals to do their jobs better and more efficiently. But what about individuals working together that need to share information and files? Individuals working on standalone computers need to share information and work together. However, sharing information in this type of network is called "Sneaker Net"--put your sneakers on and walk the information down the hall. A local area network (LAN) is made up of computers and shared devices that are physically connected by cables. LANs allow entire buildings and campuses to share expensive resources, such as laser printers, scanners, CD-ROM players, large capacity disk drives, software programs, etc. The cost of providing and maintaining a network is large, but the cost of not providing it is even larger.

The Darker Side of Computing

If someone mentions they have a virus, it may not be a physical illness. Computers

Beware of Hidden Monsters seem to also occasionally have an illness called a virus. A virus is no more than a small program written so as to "hide itself" on diskettes and transfer to any PCs/disks it comes in contact with, directly or via a computer network. The program code is "triggered" by some event (such as a particular date) and then activates some pre-programmed code to, for example, display a message on your screen, corrupt data or erase files. The

Figure 13-37 (page 2)

18. Press Alt + F6

19. Type **Boulder, CO 80302**

20. Press Enter

21. Press Alt + F6

22. Type **(303) 555-3000**

23. Turn off the Shadow and Bold attributes

danger is that viruses can replicate themselves on many disks without being noticed so they can spread widely before being triggered.

Our suggestion is be a "Wise Owl" and follow the four tips below for "safer-computing":

1. If your software allows, apply write-protect tabs on all program disks before installing the software.

2. Do not install software if you do not know where it's been.

3. Keep backups of your important files, especially corporate financial statements.

4. Bring your disks to the computer lab and use the virus detection software on the machines to check for viruses.

Awards

Ms. Priscilla Singer of Basin Enterprises was awarded the prestigious honor as "Business Person of the Year." Ms. Singer founded Basin Enterprises ten years ago and has successfully built a reputable company. Ms. Singer's business is located in the Spruce Building.

Figure 13-37 (page 3)

24. Press Enter twice

25. Create a graphics line with the following specifications:

    Thickness: .04"

    Horizontal Position: Full

    Vertical Position: Baseline

26. Press Enter

PencilPushers, Inc.
Administrative Support Services

1200 Willow, Suite 300
Boulder, CO 80302
(303) 555-3000

Figure 13-38

27. Select **F**o**nt** ⇒ **F**o**nt** and select Courier 10 cpi or 12 points

28. Save your letterhead as `LTRHD`

29. Print your letterhead and close the file

Using Watermark Images

A **watermark image** is a drawing, logo, clip art image, or headline that is printed behind the text of a document. Two different watermarks can appear on each page, or you can create two watermarks and have them print on alternating pages. Watermarks are not visible on-screen until the Graphics or Page mode is turned on.

To create a watermark, position the cursor on the page where the watermark is to begin, and select <u>L</u>ayout ⇒ <u>H</u>eader/Footer/Watermark (*Shortcut keys:* ⌈Shift⌉ + ⌈F8⌉, *5*). The Header/Footer/Watermark dialog box appears. Select <u>W</u>atermarks and then choose either Watermark <u>A</u> or Watermark <u>B</u>. Another dialog box appears in which you can choose All Pages, Even Pages, or Odd Pages. You also have the choice of either creating, editing, or turning off watermarks. If you choose either Create or Edit, the Watermark Editor appears. To add a graphics image, select <u>G</u>raphics ⇒ Graphics <u>B</u>oxes ⇒ <u>C</u>reate. Select <u>F</u>ilename and type the path and file name of the graphics image, then press ⌈Enter⌉. If you wish to edit the graphics image, choose Image Editor.

▌ HANDS-ON ACTIVITY

In this exercise, you are going to add a watermark image to the flyer you created in Lesson 11.

1. Open the file named SERVICES.COL

2. Select <u>L</u>ayout ⇒ <u>H</u>eader/Footer/Watermark

    ✓ Press ⌈Shift⌉ + ⌈F8⌉, **5**

    The Header/Footer/Watermark dialog box appears.

3. Select <u>W</u>atermarks

4. Select Watermark <u>A</u>

    The Watermark A dialog box appears, as shown in Figure 13-39.

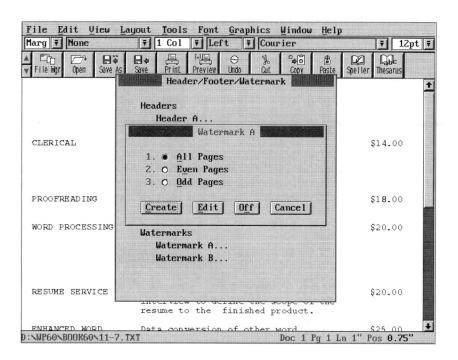

Figure 13-39

5. Select **A**ll Pages

6. Select **C**reate

The Watermark Editor appears, as shown in Figure 13-40.

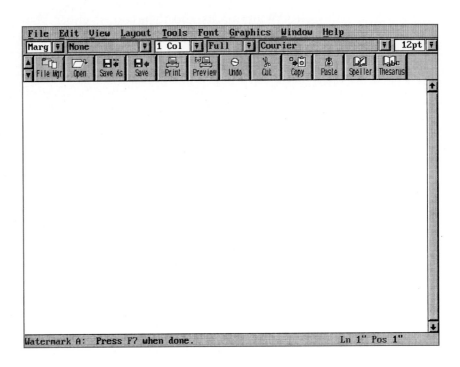

Figure 13-40

Now, to apply a graphics image,

7. Select **G**raphics ⇒ Graphics **B**oxes ⇒ **C**reate

The Create Graphics Box dialog box appears. Notice that the Based on Box St**y**le parameter is automatically set to Watermark Image Box and the **A**ttach To is anchored to a Page. The Edit **P**osition is also set to full margins, both vertically and horizontally.

8. Select **F**ilename

The Retrieve Filename dialog box appears.

9. Type **HOTAIR.WPG**

10. Press ⏎Enter

To exit the Create Graphics box,

11. Select **OK**

✓ Press ⏎Enter

The Watermark Editor redisplays. To exit and return to the document window,

12. Press F7

13. Save and print your document

Compare your printed document to the one shown in Figure 13-41.

PencilPushers, Inc.

Scope of Services

CLERICAL	Mailings, small or bulk (sorting & physical mailing only); typing miscellaneous labels, envelopes; filing; copying; miscellaneous small tasks.	$14.00
PROOFREADING	Available for all general text, excluding highly technical text.	$18.00
WORD PROCESSING	Manuscript text, business letters, personalized letters, contracts, proposals, mailing lists (typing and maintenance), bulk mailings, statistical typing, reports, special projects, etc.	$20.00
RESUME SERVICE	Complete services from initial interview to defining the scope of the resume to the finished product.	$20.00
ENHANCED WORD PROCESSING	Data conversion of other word processing files; text which incorporates some desktop publishing features (i.e. columns, tables) without using a desktop publishing program.	$25.00
DESKTOP PUBLISHING	Newsletters, Promotions, Layouts, Flyers, Corporate Reports, etc.	$35.00
BOOKKEEPING AND BILLING	Checkbook reconciliations, full-charge bookkeeping, payroll, financial reporting, financial statements, client billing, etc. Areas of billing expertise - service companies, real estate and therapy services.	$25.00
CONSULTING	Available in the areas of office procedures, office efficiencies, staffing, bookkeeping	$40.00

(All services are quoted on a per hour basis)

Figure 13-41

14. Close the document and exit WordPerfect

On Your Own

Review of Commands

Description	Menu Commands	Function Keys
Create a graphics box		
Resize a graphics box		
Move a graphics box		
Add a caption		
Edit a graphics image		
Enlarge or reduce a graphics image		
Rotate a graphics image		
Move a graphics image		
Restore the default setting of an image		
Reverse a graphics image		
Change fill attributes of a graphics image		
Create a shadow border		
Create a graphics line		
Edit a graphics line		
Change the thickness of a graphics line		
Move a graphics line		
Create a watermark image		

Lesson Review

1. What are the three basic steps when working with graphics boxes?

2. List the manipulations that can be performed on images.

3. List the eight graphics box types available in WordPerfect.

4. What is the difference between a user and a table graphics box?

5. How are the boxes numbered?

6. What graphics box type would you select to create a 3-D appearance?

7. How do you select a box using the mouse, and how does it appear after it is selected?

8. Using the mouse, how do you move the box once it has been selected, and what does the pointer change to?

9. What is the most expedient method to create a graphics box?

10. When using the most expedient method to creating a graphics box, what are the disadvantages?

11. How do you put a caption on a graphics box?

12. What types of lines can be inserted?

13. When selecting the Attach to parameter, what options are available?

14. Describe a watermark image.

15. What is the keystroke shortcut to create dot leaders with the Flush Right feature?

16. List the steps to select a graphics, using the keyboard.

17. Define a sizing handle and explain its purpose.

18. When you need to edit a bitmap image, what editor is available for this purpose?

19. How can you eliminate a caption from automatically being numbered by WordPerfect?

▮ Assignments

13.1 Directions

1. Retrieve your CONFER.COL document.
2. Delete the heading "Call for Papers."
3. Center and type the title CELEBRATE in very large and bold type.
4. Create 3 blank lines.
5. Center and type 10th Anniversary Annual National Conference in bold, italic, large, and create 2 blank lines below the heading.
6. Insert a horizontal line .1" thick. Press Enter twice.
7. At the left margin, in small size, type Paris, France.
8. On the same line, flush with the right margin, type August 4-7, 1994.
9. One line below, insert a horizontal line .01" thick.
10. On the second page, force the paragraph that reads "In addition to. . ." to the second column.
11. Save again and print the document.

13.2 Directions

1. Save the CONFER.COL document as NEWSCONF.SD (in case you make a mistake, the original will still be intact).

2. In the upper-left-hand corner of column 1 (just after "Call content") insert the LIGHTHS.WPG image.

3. Edit the <u>S</u>ize option and change the width to 1.5" and the height to 1.35". Change the Position to Left.

4. Put a caption beside the Figure number entitled "Conference in France."

5. Save NEWSCONF.SD, print, and exit.

13.3 Directions

1. Open NEWSCONF.SD.

2. Flip the image horizontally in the figure box.

3. Select the graphics line under "10th Anniversary Annual. . ." and move it down about $^{1}/_{8}$".

5. Add a lower-right shadow border to the figure box.

6. Make any other changes you think will improve the appearance of your newsletter.

7. Save, print, and exit.

14

Creating Merge Documents

Objectives

Upon completion of this lesson, you will be able to do the following:

- Define fields and records
- Define form and data files
- Create form and data files
- Suppress printing of empty fields
- Merge form and data files
- Stop a merge process
- Merge to an envelope
- Merge to a label
- Merge to a table

This lesson introduces you to the Merge feature, which is designed to enable users to combine a form document with a variable document to create "personalized" letters, labels, envelopes, and forms. For example, if you need to send the same letter to several people, as well as print a label for each individual, the Merge feature will save you time.

Starting Point

Before beginning the lesson, start WordPerfect 6.0. The document window should be blank. Make sure the Train Button Bar and the Ribbon are displayed. Locate your sample disk and insert it into the appropriate drive.

Using Merge

To use the **Merge** feature, you must create two files: a form file and a data file. The form document (such as a form letter, envelope, label, and so on) is called the **form file**. The **data file** is the source document that provides text or information to be merged into the form file. The data file is either a list or a table that contains the **variable** information (for instance, names, addresses, and phone numbers of different individuals). When Merge is executed, the specified variables in the data file are combined with the form file (form document or standardized letter), thereby producing an original document for each individual in the data file.

A word processing program's merge feature is somewhat similar to a database, in that it uses records and fields. All the information pertaining to one individual or entity is called a **record**. Each record can contain as much information (divided into **fields**) as needed. Each field would hold one piece of information—a person's last name or phone number, for instance. Also, as in a database, it is possible to sort and select the information contained in the files. (The sort feature is explained fully in Lesson 15.)

The data file can hold as many records as required. You are limited only by how much disk space and memory is available on your computer or network.

Creating a Data File

Before you create your data file, you first need to determine what information should be included, such as addresses, employee information, inventory lists, and so on. You may want to consider including information for future use that is not pertinent to the immediate project. For example, if you were creating a telephone list, you might not need the individuals' addresses, although at a later time you may want to use the same data file to create letters, at which time you would need that information.

Next, you need to consider how you want the information broken down. Should you put an individual's full name in one field, or split the name into separate fields for first name, middle initial, and last name? You may split the fields any way you choose, but try to find the most consistent approach to keeping all the varying types of information you work with.

Two records, for Mr. David Morgan and Dr. Stephanie Ross, are shown in Figure 14-1.

Notice that in order to separate records you must insert an END-RECORD merge command, which then automatically inserts a hard page break, as shown in the figure. Also notice that the information in each record is divided into fields with ENDFIELD merge commands.

The first field in the records is the individual's full name. Therefore, "Mr. David Morgan" and "Dr. Stephanie Ross" are the first fields in each record. The second field is all the address lines, the third field is the phone number, and the fourth field is the greeting name. WordPerfect numbers fields from top to bottom. Each record in Figure 14-1 has four fields, numbered accordingly.

In addition, notice that the address field (field 2) contains more than one line. The ENDFIELD merge command at the end of the last line only tells WordPerfect to count all lines as one field. Be aware that the number of lines or words in a given field does not have to be the same in all records. The address field for one record might take only two lines, but for another, five lines might be needed.

If a field is blank or empty, you still must place an ENDFIELD merge command in it. For example, field 3 in record 2 (Dr. Ross's record) has no phone number. Even though the field is empty, it still requires an END-FIELD merge command in order to keep the number of fields consistent.

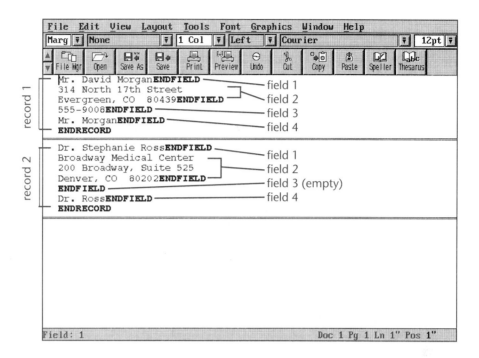

Figure 14-1

You create a data file the same way you do other documents. Begin with a blank screen, and don't be concerned with formatting features such as margins, since they will not take effect in a data file. You then follow these general steps:

- Type the first field, beginning on line 1.

- At the end of the first field, choose <u>T</u>ools ⇒ <u>Me</u>rge ⇒ <u>D</u>efine (*Shortcut keys:* Shift + F9) to select the type of merge document you are creating. Select <u>D</u>ata [Text] for typical mailing lists to be merged with letters, mailing labels, and the like. Then select End <u>F</u>ield. An ENDFIELD code and a hard return are inserted at the end of the field, and the message on the status bar will read "Field: 2" to indicate that you can go ahead with the second field.

- When you have entered all the fields for one record, choose <u>T</u>ools ⇒ <u>Me</u>rge ⇒ <u>D</u>efine ⇒ <u>E</u>nd Record (*Shortcut keys:* Shift + F9, 2). An ENDRECORD merge command and a hard page break are inserted to end the record.

- To save the data file, choose <u>F</u>ile ⇒ <u>S</u>ave, enter the file name, and choose OK.

Naming Fields in the Data File

As previously mentioned, the first field in each record is referred to as Field 1, the second as Field 2, and so on. As you type, the status line indicates the field currently being typed. However, if the records in the data file are lengthy, it is sometimes difficult to remember which field contains which information. Consequently, WordPerfect allows you to give the fields descriptive names. For example, you can call field 1 name and field 2 address.

As you enter information, the status line shows the field name in lieu of the field number.

To name the fields in a data file, you position the cursor at the top of the data file. Next, you choose <u>T</u>ools ⇒ <u>M</u>erge ⇒ <u>D</u>efine ⇒ <u>D</u>ata [Text] ⇒ Field <u>N</u>ames. The Field Names dialog box appears with the Field Names text box, prompting you for the name of the first field. Type the name of the first field (up to 37 characters are allowed) and press Enter. To add the next field name, type in the Field Na<u>m</u>e text box and press Enter. Choose OK to close the Merge Field Name(s) dialog box.

NOTE: Field names are not case-sensitive. A field name can be uppercase in the form file and lowercase in the data file.

▌ HANDS-ON ACTIVITY

In this exercise, you are going to create a data merge file that contains the list of speakers invited to participate in the Campus Computer Fair that you have been working on. The file will contain the following information:

field 1	name of the speaker
field 2	affiliation (organization or school)
field 3	address
field 4	phone number
field 5	salutation (Mr., Ms., Dr.)
field 6	seminar title
field 7	day of the seminar (day of week)
field 8	date of the seminar
field 9	time of the seminar

The first step in this exercise is to assign names to each field number. Remember, this is not a mandatory step, but doing so will make it easier to type the data merge file. Be sure you begin from a blank document window.

1. Select <u>T</u>ools ⇒ <u>M</u>erge ⇒ <u>D</u>efine

    ✓ Press Shift + F9

    The Merge Codes dialog box shown in Figure 14-2 appears for you to define what kind of merge form you are creating.

    This example file is a data list in text form.

2. Select <u>D</u>ata [Text]

    The Merge Codes (Text Data File) dialog box appears as shown in Figure 14-3.

    To begin the data file using names for field identification,

3. Select Field <u>N</u>ames

    The Field Names dialog box appears as shown in Figure 14-4.

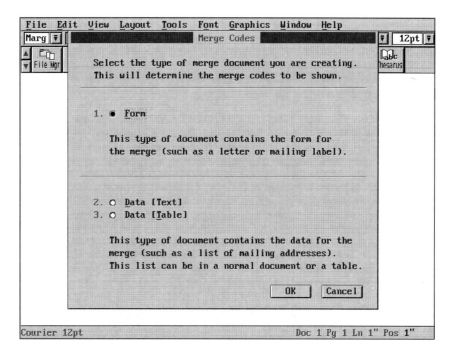

Figure 14-2

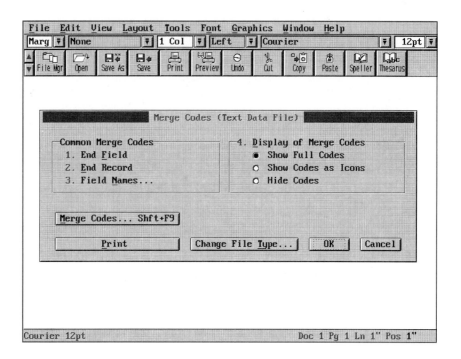

Figure 14-3

With the cursor blinking in the Field Name box, assign a name to Field 1:

4. Type **name**

5. Press Enter

The field "name" is stored as field 1. Now add another field name.

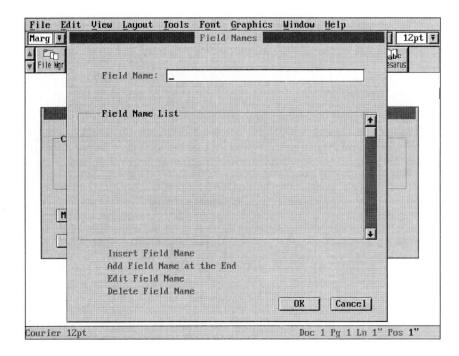

Figure 14-4

6. Type **affiliation**

7. Press (Enter)

8. Add the remaining field names in the order listed below, pressing (Enter) after each entry

   address
   phone number
   salutation
   seminar title
   day
   date
   time

   Compare your Field Names dialog box to the one in Figure 14-5.

   To close the Field Names dialog box,

9. Select **OK**

   The field names are listed at the top of the blank document screen followed by the merge code ENDRECORD and a hard page break, as shown in Figure 14-6.

▮ HANDS-ON ACTIVITY

Now you are ready to begin creating the data merge file. The file you are going to create is shown in Figure 14-7. Notice that the status line in the previous figure, Figure 14-6, is prompting "Field: name," indicating that the text for the name field is to be entered.

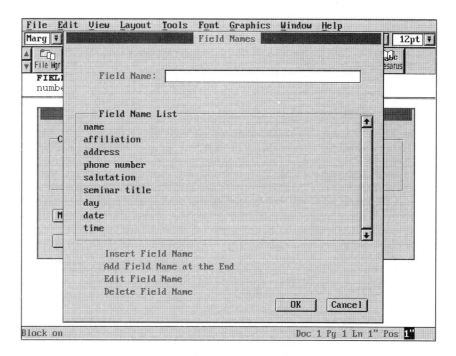

Figure 14-5

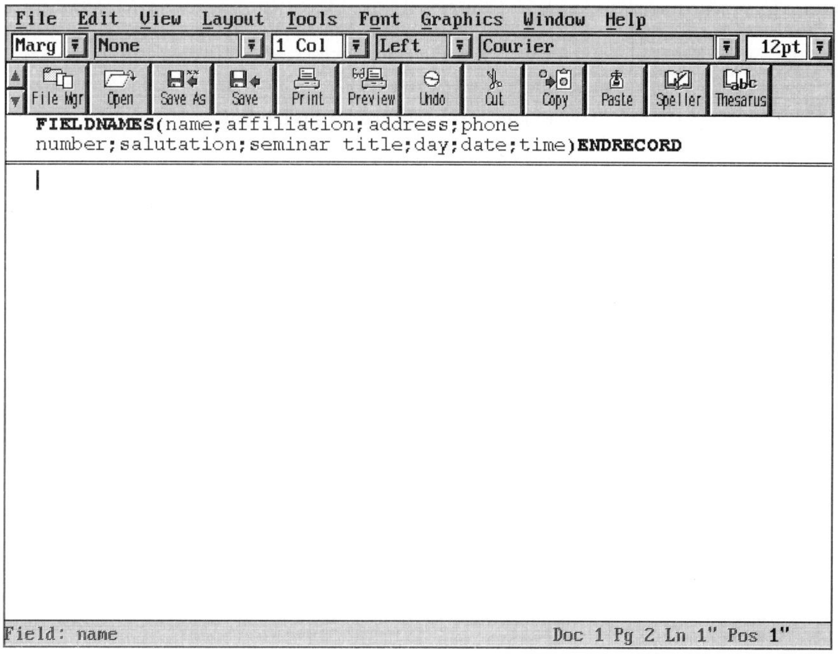

Figure 14-6

1. Type **Dr. Donna Cohen**

2. Select <u>T</u>ools ⇒ <u>M</u>erge ⇒ <u>D</u>efine ⇒ End Field

    ✓ Press F9

    An ENDFIELD code and a hard return are inserted at the end of the first field. The message on the status bar reads "Field Affiliation." Now let's enter the company name.

FIELDNAMES(name;affiliation;address;phone number;salutation;seminar title;day;date;time)**ENDRECORD**

Dr. Donna Cohen**ENDFIELD**
The Computer Learning Center**ENDFIELD**
4900 Lake Shore Drive
Boulder, CO 80304**ENDFIELD**
(303)555-8900**ENDFIELD**
Dr. Cohen**ENDFIELD**
WordPerfect for Windows**ENDFIELD**
Monday**ENDFIELD**
October 9**ENDFIELD**
9:00 a.m. - 10:30 a.m.**ENDFIELD**
ENDRECORD

Mr. Conley Adams**ENDFIELD**
ENDFIELD
111 South Hampton
Broomfield, CO 80038**ENDFIELD**
(303)555-0200**ENDFIELD**
Mr. Conley**ENDFIELD**
Customizing Windows**ENDFIELD**
Tuesday**ENDFIELD**
October 10**ENDFIELD**
8:30 a.m. - 10:00 a.m.**ENDFIELD**
ENDFIELD

Ms. Rebecca Joseph**ENDFIELD**
AAA Technology Institute**ENDFIELD**
900 River Bend Circle
Boulder, CO   80302**ENDFIELD**
(303)555-2000**ENDFIELD**
Rebecca**ENDFIELD**
DOS 6.0**ENDFIELD**
Wednesday**ENDFIELD**
October 11**ENDFIELD**
9:00 a.m. - Noon**ENDFIELD**
ENDRECORD

Mr. George Blum**ENDFIELD**
American Computer Training Institute**ENDFIELD**
55 Charlotte
Boulder, CO 80302**ENDFIELD**
(303)555-5000**ENDFIELD**
Mr. Blum**ENDFIELD**
Memory Management**ENDFIELD**
Wednesday**ENDFIELD**
October 11**ENDFIELD**
1:00 p.m. - 3:00 p.m.**ENDFIELD**
ENDRECORD

Figure 14-7

Mr. Mark Spence**ENDFIELD**
Northern Colorado Technical University**ENDFIELD**
500 Broadway
Denver, CO 80202**ENDFIELD**
(303)555-1233**ENDFIELD**
Mr. Spence**ENDFIELD**
Networking**ENDFIELD**
Tuesday**ENDFIELD**
October 10**ENDFIELD**
1:00 p.m. - 3:00 p.m.**ENDFIELD**
ENDRECORD

Dr. Patricia Davis**ENDFIELD**
Boulder Business College**ENDFIELD**
700 Post Road
Boulder, CO 80302**ENDFIELD**
(303)555-1000**ENDFIELD**
Dr. Davis**ENDFIELD**
OS/2**ENDFIELD**
Monday**ENDFIELD**
October 9**ENDFIELD**
1:00 p.m. - 3:00 p.m.**ENDFIELD**
ENDRECORD

Figure 14-7 (continued)

3. Type `The Computer Learning Center`

4. Select <u>T</u>ools ⇒ M<u>e</u>rge ⇒ <u>D</u>efine ⇒ End <u>F</u>ield

   ✓ Press F9

   Enter a two-line address:

5. Type `4900 Lake Shore Drive`

6. Press Enter

7. Type `Boulder, CO 80304`

8. Select <u>T</u>ools ⇒ M<u>e</u>rge ⇒ <u>D</u>efine ⇒ End <u>F</u>ield

   ✓ Press F9

9. Type `(303)555-8900`

10. Select <u>T</u>ools ⇒ M<u>e</u>rge ⇒ <u>D</u>efine ⇒ End <u>F</u>ield

    ✓ Press F9

11. Type `Dr. Cohen`

12. Select <u>T</u>ools ⇒ M<u>e</u>rge ⇒ <u>D</u>efine ⇒ End <u>F</u>ield

    ✓ Press F9

13. Type `WordPerfect for Windows`

14. Select <u>T</u>ools ⇒ M<u>e</u>rge ⇒ <u>D</u>efine ⇒ End <u>F</u>ield

    ✓ Press `F9`

15. Type `Monday`

16. Select <u>T</u>ools ⇒ M<u>e</u>rge ⇒ <u>D</u>efine ⇒ End <u>F</u>ield

    ✓ Press `F9`

17. Type `October 9`

18. Select <u>T</u>ools ⇒ M<u>e</u>rge ⇒ <u>D</u>efine ⇒ End <u>F</u>ield

    ✓ Press `F9`

19. Type `9:00 a.m. - 10:30 a.m.`

20. Select <u>T</u>ools ⇒ M<u>e</u>rge ⇒ <u>D</u>efine ⇒ End <u>F</u>ield

    ✓ Press `F9`

    To notify WordPerfect that you have typed all the information for Dr. Cohen and that this is the end of the first record,

21. Select <u>T</u>ools ⇒ M<u>e</u>rge ⇒ <u>D</u>efine ⇒ <u>E</u>nd Record

    ✓ Press `Shift` + `F9`, `2`

    An ENDRECORD merge command and a hard page break ([HPg]) are inserted to end the record.

22. On your own, continue typing the remainder of the records as shown in the figure above; in the second record (Mr. Conley Adams), the affiliation field is blank—therefore, be sure to insert an EndField code

    When you're finished, carefully compare your document to the one in Figure 14-7.

23. Select <u>F</u>ile ⇒ <u>S</u>ave

    ✓ Press `F10`

    TIP: We recommend that you use the same file extension for all your data files (for example, .LST), so that you can easily distinguish these files from others listed in your directory.

24. Name the file `A:SPEAKER.LST`

    NOTE: This book assumes that you are using a sample disk in drive A for your practice files. Substitute a different drive letter if necessary.

25. Close the file

▌ Creating a Form File

The format of the form file can be any you choose: a letter, a memo, a preprinted form, a contract, a label, or an envelope. However, your choice of format is important since it determines what the final document(s) will be.

To start the form, insert the desired format codes in the usual manner. Next, you use the menu <u>T</u>ools ⇒ M<u>e</u>rge ⇒ <u>D</u>efine ⇒ <u>F</u>orm to define what type of merge file you are creating. When you are ready to input the text for the form file, you simply begin typing the document. When you come to a place that requires a personalized insert from the data merge file, you use the menu <u>T</u>ools ⇒ Merge ⇒ <u>D</u>efine ⇒ <u>F</u>ield to insert a field code, which designates a particular number/name field from a data merge file. The code appears as FIELD(*n*). The *n* represents either the specified field number or field name from the data document. For example, when you merge the form file with the data file, FIELD(1) would instruct WordPerfect to insert the contents of field 1 of each record into that location in the form file.

You can use a field number or name as many times as necessary in the document (for example, you might repeat the name of the addressee in the final paragraph). You don't have to use all the field numbers or names in the form file.

To prevent blank lines (fields for which no information is entered) from appearing in the resulting merged document, you type a question mark at the end of the FIELD code in the form document; FIELD(*n?*). You type the question mark after the field number.

You create a form file much as you do other documents:

- Start with a blank screen and make any formatting changes you desire. Remember that the formatting changes made in the form file are reflected in the final merged document.

- Begin typing the document.

- When you reach a point where a variable needs to be inserted from the data document, choose <u>T</u>ools ⇒ M<u>e</u>rge ⇒ <u>D</u>efine.

- The Merge Codes dialog box appears. To define the type of merge document, select <u>F</u>orm.

- The Merge Codes (Form File) dialog box appears. To tie the data from field 1 in the data file to the form file, select <u>F</u>ield. Then type either the appropriate field number or the field name. For example, if the first field in the data merge file is called "name," you can type either **1** or **name**. Remember, field names are not case-sensitive.

- Choose OK.

- Continue this procedure each time you need a variable inserted until you have completed the document.

- Close and save the form file.

We recommend that you use the same file extension for all your form files (for example, .FRM), so that you can easily distinguish these files from others listed in your directory.

▌HANDS-ON ACTIVITY

In this exercise, you are going to create a form file consisting of a form letter inviting guest speakers to the Campus Computer Fair. For clarity, you will use field names when specifying a particular field, in lieu of field numbers. The letter you will create is shown in Figure 14-8.

Make sure you have a clear document window displayed. The first step is to open your letterhead that you created in Lesson 13. (There is a completed copy of the letterhead file provided for you on the student sample disk, called LTRHD.)

PencilPushers, Inc.
Administrative Support Services

1200 Willow, Suite 300
Boulder, CO 80302
(303) 555-3000

_____

(today's date)

FIELD(name)
FIELD(affiliation)
FIELD(address)

Dear **FIELD**(salutation):

PencilPushers, Inc. is again proud to be the lead sponsor of the Campus Computer Fair, an annual educational event. This 3-day fair will take place October 9-11 at the university field house. "Latest and Greatest" is the theme this year; for vendors to show off the hottest hardware and slickest software on the market.

In addition to the hands-on demos, free lectures will be presented by local professionals stressing the impact of computers in business today. Since you have had numerous years of experience in the computer technology field and are a long-standing member of the Boulder Business Council, we are inviting you to be one of our speakers.

The lecture topic we have selected for you is "**FIELD**(seminar title)" to be presented on **FIELD**(day), **FIELD**(date), from **FIELD**(time) in the main meeting hall. In appreciation for your participating as a speaker you will receive a $300 gift certificate at Software Plus.

Your immediate reply to this invitation is appreciated.

Sincerely yours,

(your name)
President
PencilPushers, Inc.

Figure 14-8

1.   Select **File** ⇒ **Open** the file named A:LTRHD

To position the cursor at the end of the document,

2.   Press Home , Home , ↓

3.   Press Enter twice

Now you are going to use the DATE Code feature, which ensures that the letter will always reflect the current date.

4. Select <u>T</u>ools ⇒ <u>D</u>ate ⇒ <u>C</u>ode

    ✓ Press Shift + F5 , **2**

5. Press Enter 3 times

    To instruct WordPerfect that this new document is a merge form and to insert the contents of field 1 or the field name at this position,

6. Select <u>T</u>ools ⇒ <u>M</u>erge ⇒ <u>D</u>efine

    ✓ Press Shift + F9

    The Merge Codes dialog box appears.

7. Select <u>F</u>orm

    The Merge Codes (Form File) dialog box appears, as shown in Figure 14-9, with a list of possible merge codes.

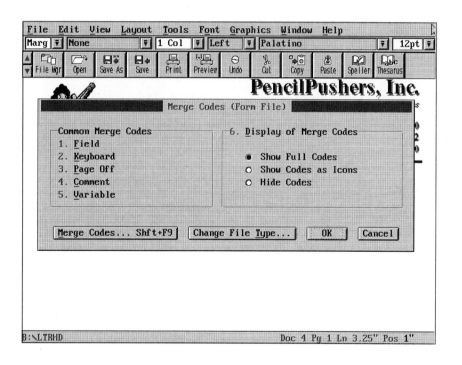

Figure 14-9

8. Select <u>F</u>ield

    Another dialog box titled Parameter Entry appears. A text box is prompting you to enter the field number or name, as shown in Figure 14-10.

    At this point you can type either **1** or **name** to designate Field 1.

9. Type **name** (either upper or lower case)

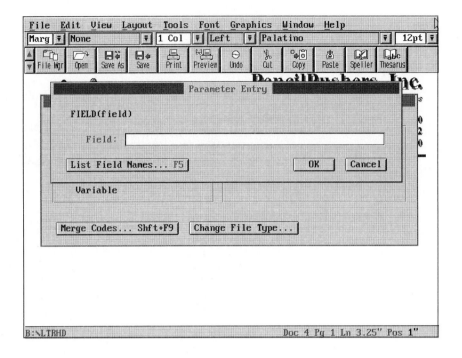

Figure 14-10

10. Select **OK**

✓ Press (Enter)

To move to the next line,

11. Press (Enter)

Insert the next field:

12. Select **Tools** ⇒ **Merge** ⇒ **Define**

✓ Press (Shift) + (F9)

The Merge Codes (Form File) dialog box appears.

13. Select **Field**

At the Parameter Entry screen, instead of typing the name of the field, let's display a list of the field names so that we will be certain of the spelling.

14. Select **List Field Names**

✓ Press (F5)

The first time you use the List Field Names feature, it asks you to type the name of the data merge file you are using.

15. Type **A:SPEAKER.LST**

16. Select **OK**

✓ Press (Enter)

The List Field Names dialog box appears, as shown in Figure 14-11, displaying all the field names from the file SPEAKER.LST in alphabetical order.

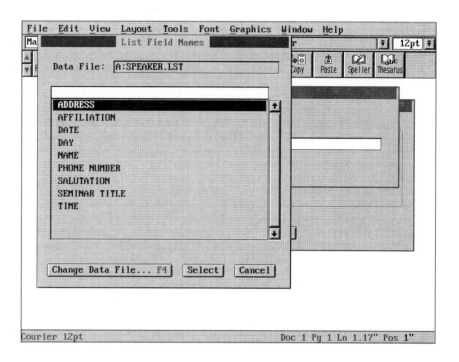

Figure 14-11

17. Select **AFFILIATION**

18. Choose **Select**

    ✓ Press Enter

    The FIELD(AFFILIATION) code is placed in the form letter.

    In Record 2 of the data merge file (Mr. Conley Adams), the affiliation field is blank. You need to ensure that Mr. Adams' letter does not appear with a blank line between his name and address.

19. Position the cursor in front of the ending parenthesis [)] in the line that reads **FIELD(AFFILIATION)**

20. Type **?** (question mark)

    The field should appear as FIELD(AFFILIATION?).

21. Press End to position the cursor at the end of the line

22. Press Enter

23. On your own, continue typing the letter as shown in Figure 14-12, inserting the FIELD code where indicated

24. Use your SIG macro to insert the signature block

25. Close and save the file, naming it **A:SEMINAR.FRM**

FIELD(address)

Dear **FIELD**(salutation):

PencilPushers, Inc. is again proud to be the lead sponsor of the Campus Computer Fair, an annual educational event. This 3-day fair will take place October 9-11at the university field house. "Latest and Greatest" is the theme this year; for vendors to show off the hottest hardware and slickest software on the market.

In addition to the hands-on demos, free lectures will be presented by local professionals stressing the impact of computers in business today. Since you have had numerous years of experience in the computer technology field and are a long-standing member of the Boulder Business Council, we are inviting you to be one of our speakers.

The lecture topic we have selected for you is "**FIELD**(seminar title)" to be presented on **FIELD**(day), **FIELD**(date), from **FIELD**(time) in the main meeting hall. In appreciation for your participating as a speaker you will receive a $300 gift certificate at Software Plus.

Your immediate reply to this invitation is appreciated.

Sincerely yours,

(your name)
President
PencilPushers, Inc.

Figure 14-12

Merging the Form and Data File

To merge the form and data files to create personalized letters, always start from a blank document screen. Then choose Tools ⇒ Merge ⇒ Run. The Run Merge dialog box appears. In the Form File text box, type the name of the form file, and in the Data File text box type the name of the data document and choose Merge.

During the merging process, the status bar will prompt "Merging." When Merge is completed, the resulting finished merge document is displayed with the cursor positioned at the bottom. Browse through all the pages to check to see that the merge correctly placed the variable information in each letter. You can now print the document. It is recommended that you do not save the resulting merge document, since it will take valuable disk space and can be re-created by performing Merge again.

▌ HANDS-ON ACTIVITY

In this exercise, you are going to merge the form file (SEMINAR. FRM) and the data file (SPEAKER.LST) you just created. Be sure you begin with a blank document window.

1. Select <u>T</u>ools ⇒ M<u>e</u>rge ⇒ <u>R</u>un

    ✓ Press Ctrl + F9 , 1

    The Run Merge dialog box appears, as shown in Figure 14-13.

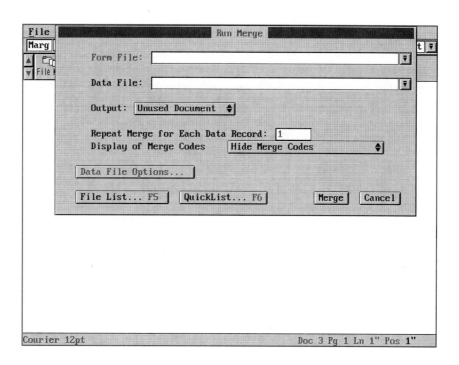

Figure 14-13

The cursor is blinking in the Form File text box.

2. Type **A:SEMINAR.FRM**

3. Press Tab

    The cursor is now positioned in the Data File text box.

4. Type **A:SPEAKER.LST**

5. Select **Merge**

    ✓ Press Enter

    When Merge is finished, the resulting merge document displays in your document window, and the cursor is positioned at the bottom of the document.

6. Using either the scroll bar or the cursor movement keys, browse through your document to make sure your merge was successful. If it was not, scrutinize your form and data files to make sure they were typed correctly and repeat the merge process. Good luck!

7. Print your resulting merge document

8. Close the document, but do not save it

Stopping Merge

Should you need to stop the Merge process, press [Esc]. If that does not work, a CANCELOFF merge command may be embedded in the Form or Data file. This CANCELOFF command disables the [Esc] function and obstructs you from stopping merge. If this occurs, press [Ctrl] + [Break] as an alternative.

Merging to an Envelope

You may merge your data file containing a list of names and addresses with a form file that has been set up as an envelope. You will use the same steps learned in previous lessons to create the envelope settings, then insert the field codes to make it into a merge form file.

HANDS-ON ACTIVITY

In this exercise, you are going to create a form file that contains the formatting for an envelope and the necessary field names. Be sure you have a clear document screen.

The first step is to create the envelope.

1. Select Layout ⇒ Envelope

   ✓ Press [Alt] + [F12]

   The Envelope dialog box appears.

2. Select Mailing Address

   Now you are ready to define this document as a merge form and enter the field names. You want the name, affiliation, and address.

3. Select Tools ⇒ Merge ⇒ Define ⇒ Form

   ✓ Press [Shift] + [F9], 1

   The Merge Codes (Form File) dialog box appears.

4. Select Field

5. Type name

6. Select OK

   ✓ Press [Enter]

7. On your own, insert the affiliation and address fields. Be sure to place the question mark in the affiliation field, so that records without an affiliation will not have a blank line between name and address.

   To complete the insertion of field names,

8. Press [F7]

   Compare your screen to Figure 14-14.

   Close the Envelope dialog box and insert the envelope into a document screen.

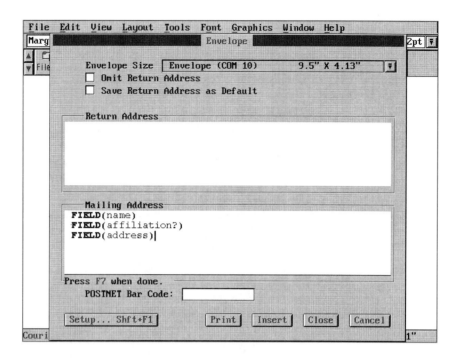

Figure 14-14

9. Select **I**nsert

   ✓ Press Enter

   *TIP: You may want to view your page, using **F**ile ⇒ Print Pre**v**iew, to verify that you have created an envelope form.*

10. Close and save the file using the name `A:ENV.FRM`

    Now, merge the envelope form with the speaker mailing list. Make sure you begin from a blank document screen.

11. Select **T**ools ⇒ M**e**rge ⇒ **R**un

    ✓ Press Ctrl + F9 , 1

    The Run Merge dialog box displays with the file names from your previous merge operation still displayed for Form File and Data File.

12. Select **Form File**

13. Type `A:ENV.FRM`

14. Press Tab

    The cursor is now positioned in the Data File text box. If the file name A:SPEAKER.LST is not listed, enter it as the data file.

15. Select **Merge**

16. On your own, use the **F**ile ⇒ **Print Pre**v**iew** feature to view your envelopes, pressing Page Up or Page Down to move from one to another

17. Close the file, but do not save

▌Merging to Labels

WordPerfect has a built-in labels feature that enables you to select from pre-defined label settings to create mailing labels, file folder labels, disk labels, and many more. You can type the labels individually or merge them with a mailing list.

When you create labels, WordPerfect creates many **logical pages** on one **physical page**. The physical page is the entire piece of paper and the logical pages are smaller defined areas (labels) on one physical page. For example, many label forms are sold with 30 labels on one sheet.

Before you can merge to a label, you must create a merge form and select one of the label definitions that best matches the label forms you have purchased. Once the label form is defined, you then use the same steps to embed the field codes in your Label Form file as you did when creating the Envelope Form file.

Defining Three-Across Labels

Let's imagine that you purchased labels on $8\frac{1}{2}$" x 11" sheets with 3 columns across and 11 rows down. That means that each sheet holds 33 labels that measure 2.83" in width and 1" in height. This is a standard label, sold by the 3M Company and described as No. 7733.

To choose a label form definition for three-across labels, choose Layout ⇒ Page ⇒ Labels. The Labels dialog box appears. The cursor is located at the top of a list box filled with predefined label descriptions for the standard label forms available from most office supply stores. Move with either the directional arrows or the scroll bar to find the type of label forms you have purchased. Notice that as you move through the list, the section at the bottom left-hand corner of the screen shows you the details, with the exact dimensions for each particular type of label in the list. When you have located the correct label definition and it is highlighted, choose Select from the menu.

The Labels dialog box then appears so that you may enter any special instructions about paper feeders or margins. When your printer settings are complete, select OK to return to the Page Format dialog box with the label description you selected listed in the Labels text box. Choose OK.

▌HANDS-ON ACTIVITY

Before beginning this section, if you have more than one printer available, you may wish to define which printer will be used for printing mailing labels. Choose File ⇒ Print/Fax and look at the Current Printer name to see which printer driver is active. If the printer listed under Current Printer is not the printer on which you will be printing labels, choose Select to pick a different printer from the Select Printer list. Close the Print dialog boxes.

In this exercise you are going to create a three-across label paper definition. Three-across labels come on $8\frac{1}{2}$" x 11" sheets containing three columns and 11 rows. Each individual label measures 1" x 2.83". The labels do not start precisely at the top and left edge of the paper—there is a small margin before the labels begin.

1. Select Layout ⇒ Page ⇒ Labels

    ✓ Press Shift + F8 , **3, 5**

The Labels dialog box appears.

Move the cursor to the correct label description in the list of predefined label forms.

2.   Highlight **3M 7733**

Notice the Label Details section, showing the measurements of each label. Compare your screen to Figure 14-15.

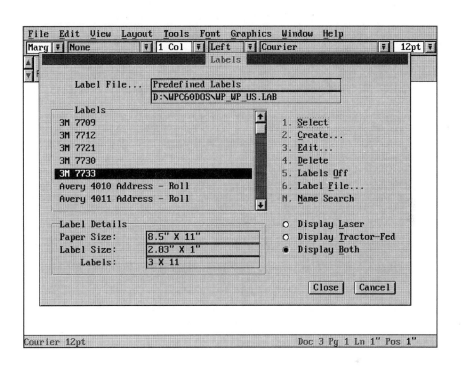

Figure 14-15

3.   Choose **S**elect

If this is the first time you have used that particular label definition on your computer, the Labels Printer Info dialog box appears.

To accept these settings,

4.   Select **OK**

✓ Press [Enter]

The label definition has been stored and your screen returns to the Page Format dialog box. You can see that the name of the labels that you selected is now placed in both the Paper Size/Type and the **L**abels selections in the Paper Sizes section of this menu, as shown in Figure 14-16.

To continue,

5.   Select **OK**

✓ Press [Enter]

If you are working in the Graphic mode, the size of the document screen has been reduced to the width of one label. The right-hand side of the screen is not accessible.

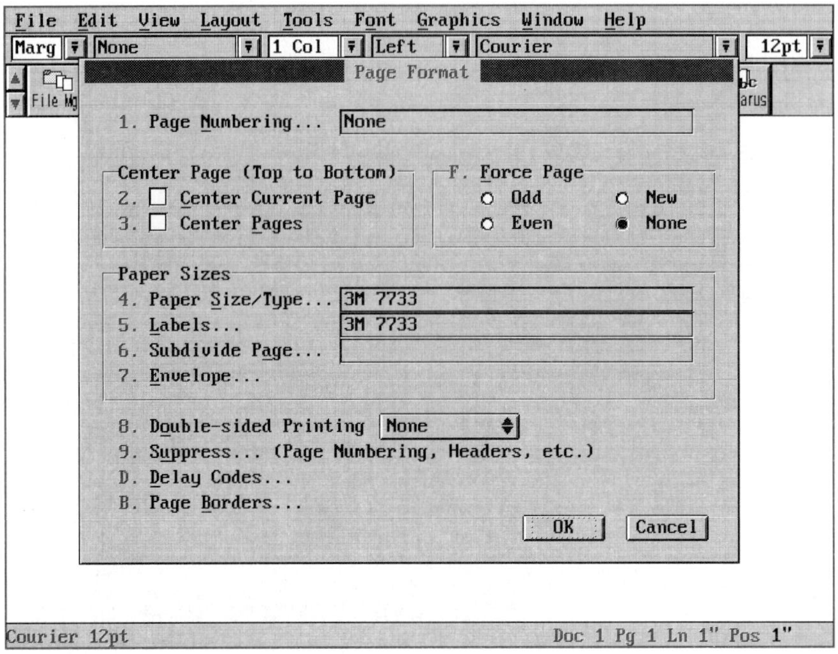

Figure 14-16

Next, you need to define this sheet of labels as a merge form file and embed the field codes to connect it to the data file A:SPEAKER.LST.

6. Select <u>T</u>ools ⇒ <u>M</u>erge ⇒ <u>D</u>efine

   ✓ Press Shift + F9

7. Select <u>F</u>orm

8. Select <u>F</u>ield

9. Type **name**

10. Select **OK**

    ✓ Press Enter

11. On your own, using <u>T</u>ools ⇒ <u>M</u>erge ⇒ <u>D</u>efine, insert the affiliation field (with a question mark in case of blanks) and address field.

    NOTE: The label form will contain the same field information as the envelope form. Refer back to Figure 14-14 to compare your work.

12. Close the file and name it **A:LABEL.FRM**

13. On your own, merge A:LABEL.FRM and A:SPEAKER.LST

    When the merge is complete, your document screen displays a single row of labels—not three across. It appears that the labels did not generate in a three-across format, *until* you view the text as it will actually print using the Print Preview feature.

14. Select <u>F</u>ile ⇒ Print Pre<u>v</u>iew

    Compare your Print Preview window to the one shown in Figure 14-17.

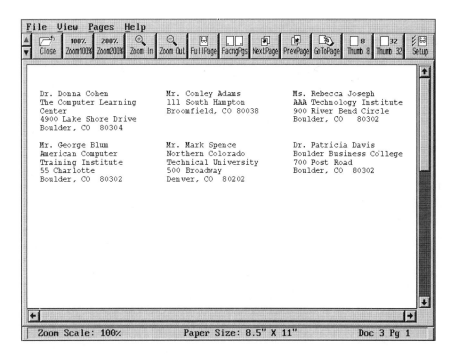

```
 File  View  Pages  Help
 ▲  ┌──┐  100%   200%    ⊕       ⊖      🔳     🔲      📄      📄      📄     □ 8   □ 32  📄
 ▼  Close  Zoom100%  Zoom200%  Zoom In  Zoom Out  FullPage  FacngPgs  NextPage  PrevPage  GoToPage  Thumb 8  Thumb 32  Setup
┌──────────────────────────────────────────────────────────────────────┐ ▲
│                                                                        │█
│                                                                        │█
│    Dr. Donna Cohen          Mr. Conley Adams         Ms. Rebecca Joseph│█
│    The Computer Learning    111 South Hampton        AAA Technology Institute│█
│    Center                   Broomfield, CO 80038     900 River Bend Circle│█
│    4900 Lake Shore Drive                             Boulder, CO   80302│█
│    Boulder, CO  80304                                                   │█
│                                                                        │
│    Mr. George Blum          Mr. Mark Spence          Dr. Patricia Davis │
│    American Computer        Northern Colorado        Boulder Business College│
│    Training Institute       Technical University     700 Post Road      │
│    55 Charlotte             500 Broadway             Boulder, CO   80302│
│    Boulder, CO  80302       Denver, CO  80202                           │
│                                                                        │
│                                                                        │
│                                                                        │
│                                                                        │
│                                                                        │
│                                                                        │
│                                                                        │ ▼
├──────────────────────────────────────────────────────────────────────┤
│ ◄                                                                    ► │
├──────────────────────────────────────────────────────────────────────┤
│  Zoom Scale: 100%         Paper Size: 8.5" X 11"         Doc 3 Pg 1     │
└──────────────────────────────────────────────────────────────────────┘
```

Figure 14-17

15. On your own, exit the Print Preview screen and close the file without saving the changes

Merging to a Table

To merge to a table, you must first create the table with columns, headings, and enhancements, by using the Table menu. You will then edit the table, defining it as a merge form file. Up to this point, when you performed the Merge process, each record was placed on a separate "page." But in the case of a table, all the records need to appear on the same page, so you instruct Merge not to create a new table for each record nor to repeat the headings for each record. There are three new merge codes that you must use.

The LABEL and GO merge commands control the path of Merge. The LABEL command, followed by a label name, is used to mark a specific location in the file. The GO command is used to point Merge to the named location. This creates a "loop" so that the headings are not included. The third merge command is called NEXT RECORD. It instructs WordPerfect to move to the next record after processing the current one.

HANDS-ON ACTIVITY

In this exercise you are going to create a table listing your guest speakers for the Campus Computer Fair. Begin with a blank document screen.

1. Change the left and right margins to ½ inch

2. Create a table with 3 columns and 4 rows

3. Block the first row and join the cells

   With the first row still blocked and the table menu displayed, add bold, large, and center.

4. Select <u>C</u>ell ⇒ <u>A</u>ppearance ⇒ <u>B</u>old ⇒ <u>S</u>ize ⇒ <u>L</u>arge ⇒ <u>J</u>ustification ⇒ <u>C</u>enter ⇒ OK

   With the first row still blocked and the table menu displayed, add background shading.

5. Select <u>L</u>ines/Fill ⇒ <u>F</u>ill ⇒ Fill St<u>y</u>le ⇒ 10% Shaded Fill ⇒ <u>S</u>elect ⇒ OK ⇒ Close

   With the Table menu displayed, block the second row and add bold and center.

6. Block the second row and select <u>C</u>ell ⇒ <u>A</u>ppearance ⇒ <u>B</u>old ⇒ <u>J</u>ustification ⇒ <u>C</u>enter ⇒ OK

7. Exit the Table menu and type the headings as shown in Figure 14-18

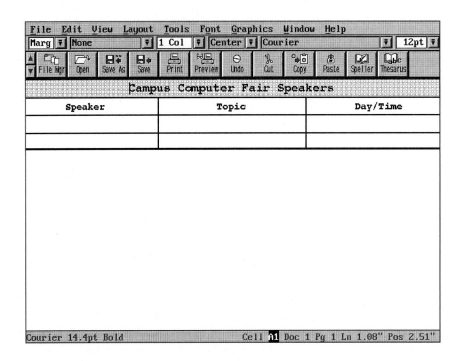

Figure 14-18

8. Save the document as **A:TABLE.FRM**

   Now, you are going to define the document as a merge form and insert the LABEL merge command, which points to a specific position in the document.

9. Position the cursor in cell A3

10. Select <u>T</u>ools ⇒ <u>M</u>erge ⇒ <u>D</u>efine ⇒ <u>F</u>orm ⇒ Merge Codes

    ✓ Press (Shift) + (F9), **1**, (Shift) + (F9)

    The All Merge Codes dialog box appears, as shown in Figure 14-19.

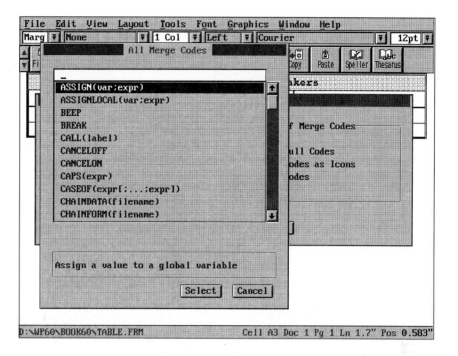

Figure 14-19

Use the directional arrows or the scroll bar to move within the list of merge codes.

11. Highlight **LABEL**(label)

12. Choose **Select**

The Parameter Entry dialog box appears, as shown in Figure 14-20.

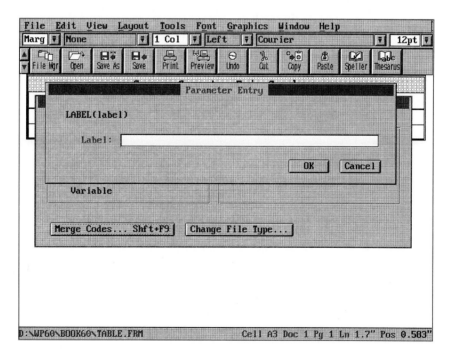

Figure 14-20

13. Type `Loop`

14. Select **OK**

    ✓ Press Enter

15. Select Tools ⇒ Merge ⇒ Define ⇒ Field

    ✓ Press Shift + F9 , 1

16. Type `name`

17. Select **OK**

    Position the cursor in cell B3.

18. Select Tools ⇒ Merge ⇒ Define ⇒ Field

    ✓ Press Shift + F9 , 1

19. Type `seminar title`

20. Select **OK**

    Position the cursor in cell C3.

21. Select Tools ⇒ Merge ⇒ Define ⇒ Field

    ✓ Press Shift + F9 , 1

22. Type `day`

23. Select **OK**

24. Press Enter

25. Select Tools ⇒ Merge ⇒ Define ⇒ Field

    ✓ Press Shift + F9 , 1

26. Type `time`

27. Select **OK**

28. Select Tools ⇒ Merge ⇒ Define ⇒ Merge Codes

    ✓ Press Shift + F9 , Shift + F9

29. Highlight **NEXTRECORD**

30. Choose **Select**

31. Position the cursor in cell A4

32. Select Tools ⇒ Merge ⇒ Define ⇒ Merge Codes

    ✓ Press Shift + F9 , Shift + F9

33. Highlight **GO(label)**

34. Choose **Select**

    The Parameter Entry dialog box appears.

35. Type `Loop`

    This instructs WordPerfect to go back to the specific place in the document designated as "Loop" and not to repeat any text before this position.

36. Select **OK**

    Compare your document to the one shown in Figure 14-21.

Campus Computer Fair Speakers		
Speaker	**Topic**	**Day/Time**
LABEL(Loop)**FIELD**(name)	**FIELD**(seminar title)	**FIELD**(day) **FIELD**(time)**NEXTRECORD**
GO(Loop)		

Figure 14-21

37. Close the file and save the file (its name is still A:TABLE.FRM)

38. On your own, merge A:TABLE.FRM and A:SPEAKER.LST

    Compare your resulting merge document to the one shown in Figure 14-22.

Campus Computer Fair Speakers		
Speaker	**Topic**	**Day/Time**
Dr. Donna Cohen	WordPerfect for Windows	Monday 9:00 a.m. - 10:30 a.m.
Mr. Conley Adams	Customizing Windows	Tuesday 8:30 a.m. - 10:00 a.m.
Ms. Rebecca Joseph	DOS 6.0	Wednesday 9:00 a.m. - Noon
Mr. George Blum	Memory Management	Wednesday 1:00 p.m. - 3:00 p.m.
Mr. Mark Spence	Networking	Tuesday 1:00 p.m. - 3:00 p.m.
Dr. Patricia Davis	OS/2	Monday 1:00 p.m. - 3:00 p.m.

Figure 14-22

39. Either print the document or use the Print Preview feature

40. Exit WordPerfect

On Your Own

Review of Commands

Description	Menu Commands	Function Keys
End field	_____	_____
End record	_____	_____
Name fields	_____	_____
Start Merge	_____	_____
Define a merge form	_____	_____
Insert a field code	_____	_____
Access merge codes	_____	_____

Lesson Review

1. Name and describe the two files necessary for merge functions.

2. Describe a record.

3. Describe a field.

4. What are two examples of form files you might create?

5. Why is it not recommended to save the document resulting from a merge?

6. How do you prevent blank lines from appearing when there is no information in a field?

7. What is the LABEL command used for?

8. What is the GO command used for?

Assignments

14.1 Directions

1. Use the following information to create a form letter in a standard letter format with corresponding fields. You may either use the field numbers or field names to line the form letter to the data file:

Date / Field 1(name) / Field 2(address) / **Dear** Field 3 (salutation): / **Thank you for agreeing to teach** Field 4(course number), Field 5(course name), **for the CMS Department this fall. Your class meets on** Field 6(day), **from** Field 7(time). / **Classes start August 24, and we will have an orientation meeting sometime during the last week of August. / Let me know if you have any questions. / Sincerely yours, Anne Rickard, Class Coordinator, CMS Department** (Save the file as **CLASSES.FRM**)

2. Create the fields shown as follows for a merge letter: name, address, salutation, course no., course name, day, time. Entries for the fields are:

Record 1:

John M. Hunter
135 Broadway
Denver, CO 80222
John
CMS 201
Principles of Information
Systems
Monday, Wednesday, and Friday
9:30 to 11:45

Record 2:

Mary Schaub
600 Locust
Littleton, CO 90122
Mary
CMS 211
COBOL
Tuesday and Thursday
13:00 to 13:50

Record 3:

Lois Hardin
1200 Logan
Lakewood, CO 89000
Lois
CMS 323
Data Communications
Monday and Wednesday
14:00 to 15:15

Record 4:

Marc Lord
3444 Pine
Aurora, CO 89001
Marc
CMS 223
Word Processing
Monday, Wednesday, and Friday
8:00 to 8:50

3. Save the file as PARTIME.LST.

4. Merge the two files, and print the letters.

14.2 Directions

1. Create a three-across label form document using 3M 7753 for the names and addresses in PARTIME.LST, name it PARTLAB.FRM, and merge the files.

2. Print the merged file, simulating the labels with ordinary paper.

14.3 Directions

1. Create an envelope form document with name and address fields, name it PARTENV.FRM, and merge the PARTIME.LST document with it.

2. Print, again simulating envelopes with ordinary paper.

14.4 Directions

1. Create a three-column table as a form document, with the title CMS CLASS SCHEDULE bold, large, and centered.

2. Type column headings, boldface and centered, as follows: Instructors/Course No. & Name/Day & Time.

3. Use these fields in the PARTIME.LST data file to fill in the table: Name(1), Course No.(4), Course Name(5), Day(6), and Time(7). Be sure to use the LABEL, GO, and NEXTRECORD codes. Name the file PARTABLE.FRM.

4. Merge the new form file PARTABLE.FRM with the data file PARTIME.LST and print the table.

15

Sorting and Selecting

Objectives

Upon completion of this lesson, you will be able to do the following:

- Identify fields, lines, words, and keys in the Sort feature
- Sort lines, paragraphs, and merge-records
- Sort within a table
- Set up text correctly for Sort to work
- Select text based on specific criteria

When you are using WordPerfect's variety of features, you may want, for example, to alphabetize a list of names or to sort zip codes in numerical order. In this lesson you will become familiar with how to sort such text. You will also learn how to select specific items that meet specific criteria. For example, you could list only those individuals who live in a certain zip code area.

Starting Point

Before beginning the lesson, start WordPerfect 6.0. The document window should be blank. Make sure the Train Button Bar and Ribbon are displayed. Locate your sample disk and insert it into the appropriate drive.

Sort

You can use the **Sort** feature to sort lines, paragraphs, merge-records, and the items in a table. To do so, you must have the file open. However, when the sort procedure is complete, the file on the screen is replaced with the sorted one. If you wish to keep the original, unsorted file intact, you need to use File ⇒ Save As to save the sorted file under a new name.

You may find it helpful to review the following definitions before proceeding with the Sort exercises:

Records As you learned in Lesson 14, a record is a body of information relating to one individual or entity. Assume you are working with an address list. All the information (name, address, city, state, zip, and so on) about one individual—Mr. Jones, for example—is considered a record. All the information about another person, say Mrs. Smith, is considered another record. In a sort (or selection) procedure, records are the units that are sorted (or selected).

Four types of records can be used in these procedures: **merge records, line records, paragraph records,** and **table records.** In a line sort, each line constitutes a record. Likewise, in a paragraph sort, each paragraph constitutes a record. In a merge record, as you recall, the variables separated by the ENDRECORD merge code are records. In a table, each row comprises a record.

Fields As you remember from Lesson 14, each record is divided into fields. A particular field will have the same information in one record as in the next. For example, a city in an address list is considered a field. You can have any number of fields in a record.

In doing a sort, you will need to specify the field number to sort on. Fields are numbered sequentially in WordPerfect. In lines or paragraphs, fields are separated by tabs or indents. In merge records, fields are separated by ENDFIELD merge codes in the secondary file.

Lines In a line sort, each line is a record, lines are counted from top to bottom, and fields are separated by tabs or indents. However, merge records and paragraph records can have multiple lines, each of which is *not* a record. So, for these types of sorts, a line number must be specified.

Words Words are separated by spaces within a line or field and are usually counted from left to right. Words can, however, be counted from right to left by using negative numbers. Since a field may contain several words, the number of the word must be specified.

Keys Keys are the items (word or number) on which you want to sort (or select) records. You can sort records in a file on up to nine keys. Key 1 has the first priority, key 2 has second priority, and so on. For example, if you have a list of names, and you want to sort them primarily by the last name and then (if duplicate last names are found) sort by the first name, key 1 is assigned to the last name and key 2 is assigned to the first name.

Using Sort

To perform a sort, choose Tools ⇒ Sort (*Shortcut keys:* Ctrl + F9, 2). The Sort (Source and Destination) dialog box appears. The **Source** can either be "from" the text currently displayed on the screen or from a data file on disk. The **Destination** is the location where WordPerfect should place the result of the sort and can either send the sorted text back "to" the screen or to a new file on disk. Document on Screen is the default; select OK.

Now the Sort dialog box appears. The type of data file is automatically recognized by WordPerfect and placed in the Record Type section of the dialog box. If the automatic Record Type is not correct, you may open the drop-down list box and choose the correct type of source document (Line, Paragraph, Merge Record). In the Key Definitions section, specify the key, type, field, line, and word. Choose OK.

Next, select Sort <u>K</u>eys and enter information about each key, such as type, order, field, line, word. Then choose Close.

To define the sort keys, first choose whether the field is alpha (alphanumeric) or numeric. In an alphanumeric sort, characters are evaluated from left to right, and each numeral is treated as a separate character. In a numeric sort, numbers are sorted as numeric values instead of as a string of characters. The table below illustrates the difference:

Alpha	Numeric
1	1
10	2
11	3
12	10
13	11
2	12
20	13
3	20

If the key consists of both numbers and letters, choose <u>A</u>lpha. If the key consists of numbers the same length (such as account numbers, zip codes, Social Security numbers), either Alpha or Numeric can be chosen. If the numbers are uneven in length, always choose Numeric.

When you want to perform a line sort, be sure that only *one* tab stop is entered between columns in the file you are sorting and that each line ends with a hard return. If more than one tab stop is present or the hard return is missing, the sort will be unsuccessful.

CAUTION: If the file contains text that is not to be included in the sort procedure (such as a title or heading), be sure to block only the text that is to be sorted. Otherwise your heading will be sorted into the data.

▌ HANDS-ON ACTIVITY

In this exercise you will use the sample file DOORPRIZ.DOC. This file contains a list of merchants donating door prizes to the Campus Computer Fair, the name of the item donated, the quantity, and the retail price of each item. You will practice sorting by several different combinations of columns.

NOTE: As in other lessons, the example files are provided for you on the sample disk that is available from your instructor.

1. Open the file DOORPRIZ.DOC

   This sample file is a typical line file, meaning that it is designed like a list. It contains four tabbed columns that make up the fields and consists of seven rows composing the records. Compare your file to Figure 15-1.

   If you look at the codes in the DOORPRIZ.DOC file with Reveal Codes, you will notice that each field is defined by a tab and each line

Golden Bear	Key chains	10	8.50
Sounds, Inc.	CD's	5	14.00
Treasure Chest	Certificates	3	25.75
Yogurt Express	Certificates	7	2.59
Adam's Apple	Mouse Pads	10	4.99
Software Plus	Disk Storage Box	5	12.99
Angelo's Pizza	Certificates	10	7.50

Figure 15-1

ends with a hard return. The tabs in the first two fields are left tabs, the quantity tab is a right tab, and the retail price tab is a decimal tab.

First, you are going to sort the list by item name and merchant. Key 1 will be the item name (field 2, word 1) and key 2 will be the merchant name (field 1, word 1). There will be exact duplicates found in key 1, so the sort will go on to process key 2.

2. Select <u>T</u>ools ⇒ So<u>r</u>t

   ✓ Press Ctrl + F9 , **2**

The Sort (Source and Destination) dialog box appears, as shown in Figure 15-2.

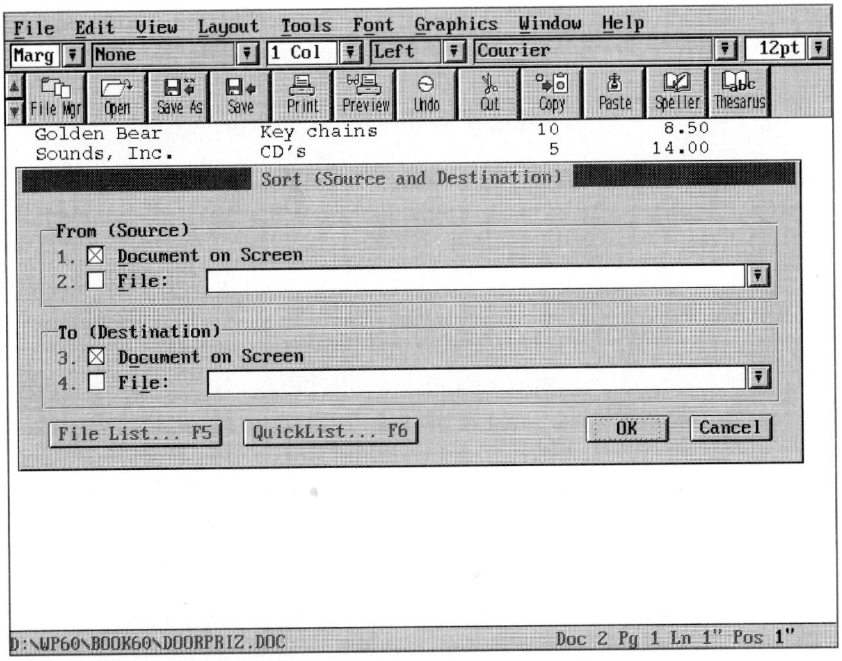

Figure 15-2

Document on Screen is selected as the default for both Source and Destination.

3. Select **OK**

   ✓ Press Enter

The Sort dialog box appears at the bottom of your screen, as shown in Figure 15-3. Make sure Line is selected in the Record Type section.

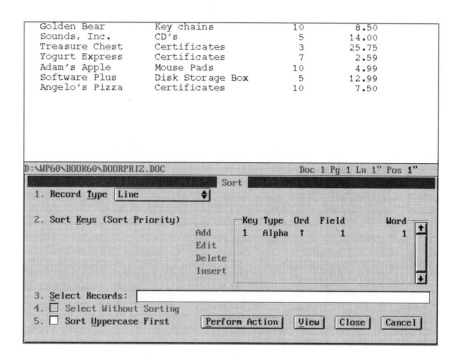

Figure 15-3

Now, you are going to set the two sort keys.

4. Select **Sort Keys**

    Key 1 is already listed in the Sort Keys (Sort Priority) list, shown with the default settings (Type Alpha, Field 1, Order ascending, Word 1). We need to edit this key in order to sort by item name in field 2.

5. Select **Edit**

    The Edit Sort Key dialog box opens to allow you to define your sort key instructions, as shown in Figure 15-4.

    In the Edit Sort Key dialog box, make sure the Type is Alpha for key 1, the Order is Ascending, Field is 1, and Word is 1. All the current settings for key 1 are correct except Field should be changed to 2. Even though some of the items in field 2 have more than one word, we will sort by the first word of field 2.

6. Select **Field**

7. Type **2**

8. Select **OK**

    ✓ Press [Enter] twice

    The main Sort dialog box returns and your key 1 description is listed in the Key List box. To define another sort level, add key 2 to sort by merchant name.

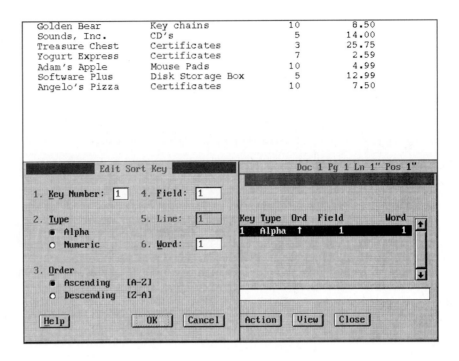

Figure 15-4

9. Select **Add**

   The new key is already numbered Key 2, Type is Alpha, Order is Ascending, Field is 1, and Word is 1. The defaults are correct.

10. Select **OK**

    Compare your Sort dialog box to Figure 15-5.

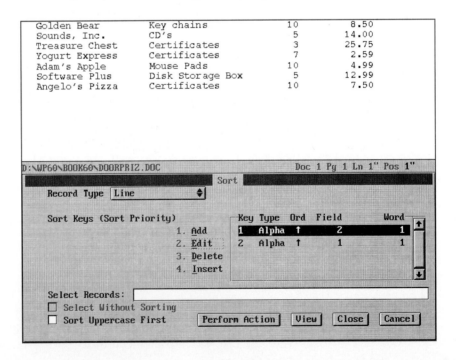

Figure 15-5

Begin the sort:

11. Select <u>P</u>erform Action

    Your file is now in order of item name. The three stores giving gift certificates are listed in alphabetical order by merchant name.

▌ HANDS-ON ACTIVITY

Now, you are going to sort the list in descending order by the retail price of the door prize (field 4). In other words, the highest priced door prize will be listed first.

The file DOORPRIZ.DOC should still be open.

1. Select <u>T</u>ools ⇒ So<u>r</u>t

   ✓ Press ⌈Ctrl⌉ + ⌈F9⌉, **2**

   To accept the source and destination as the screen,

2. Select **OK**

   The Sort dialog box appears. Make sure the <u>L</u>ine is still the Record Type.

3. Select Sort <u>K</u>eys

   Now let's create a sort key to sort by retail price (field 4) in descending order.

4. Select <u>A</u>dd

   The Edit Sort Key dialog box appears. The Key number should be 3.

5. Make the following necessary settings:

<u>T</u>ype:	**Numeric**
<u>O</u>rder:	**Descending**
<u>F</u>ield:	4
<u>W</u>ord:	1

6. Select **OK**

   The sort key settings from the previous exercise still remain in the key list. You must delete the unwanted key settings.

7. Select the Key 1 setting

8. Select <u>D</u>elete

9. On your own, delete any other unnecessary keys

   Compare your dialog box to the one shown in Figure 15-6.

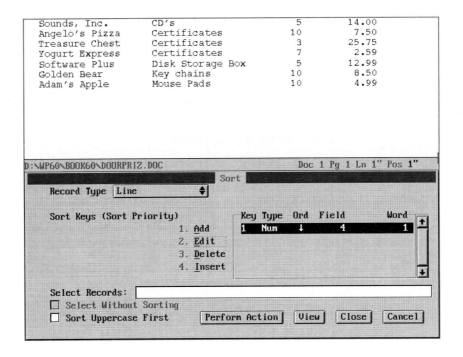

```
        Sounds, Inc.         CD's                   5      14.00
        Angelo's Pizza       Certificates          10       7.50
        Treasure Chest       Certificates           3      25.75
        Yogurt Express       Certificates           7       2.59
        Software Plus        Disk Storage Box       5      12.99
        Golden Bear          Key chains            10       8.50
        Adam's Apple         Mouse Pads            10       4.99




D:\WP60\BOOK60\DOORPRIZ.DOC                        Doc 1 Pg 1 Ln 1" Pos 1"
┌────────────────────────────────┤ Sort ├──────────────────────────────┐
│  Record Type  [Line          ▼]                                       │
│                                                                       │
│  Sort Keys (Sort Priority)      ┌Key Type  Ord   Field        Word┐   │
│                      1. Add     │1   Num    ↓      4              1│ ▲ │
│                      2. Edit    │                                 │   │
│                      3. Delete  │                                 │   │
│                      4. Insert  │                                 │   │
│                                 │                                 │ ▼ │
│  Select Records: [                                                  ]  │
│  ☐ Select Without Sorting                                             │
│  ☐ Sort Uppercase First    [Perform Action] [View] [Close] [Cancel]  │
└───────────────────────────────────────────────────────────────────────┘
```

Figure 15-6

10. Select **P**erform Action

    Your file is sorted. Compare your document to the one shown in Figure 15-7.

Treasure Chest	Gift Certificates	3	25.75
Sounds, Inc.	CD's	5	14.00
Software Plus	Disk Storage Box	5	12.99
Golden Bear	Key chains	10	8.50
Angelo's Pizza	Gift Certificates	10	7.50
Adam's Apple	Mouse Pads	10	4.99
Yogurt Express	Gift Certificates	7	2.59

Figure 15-7

11. Close the file without saving the changes

▌ HANDS-ON ACTIVITY

In this exercise, you are going to sort a merge data text file by zip code. If you recall, in Lesson 14 you created a data text file that consists of the invited guest speakers for the Campus Computer Fair. For your convenience, we have included a copy of this file on your example disk, called SPEAKER .SRT. Open this file.

For your reference, a copy of the first record is shown in Figure 15-8.

Up to now, you have always numbered the words of a field from left to right and the lines of a field from top to bottom. For instance in the example above, field 3 (address) looks like this:

```
Dr. Donna CohenENDFIELD
The Computer Learning CenterENDFIELD
4900 Lake Shore Drive
Boulder, CO 80304ENDFIELD
(303)555-8900ENDFIELD
Dr. CohenENDFIELD
WordPerfect for WindowsENDFIELD
MondayENDFIELD
October 9ENDFIELD
9:00 a.m. - 10:30 a.m.ENDFIELD
ENDRECORD
```

Figure 15-8

4900 Lake Shore Drive
Boulder, CO 80304

The line number for the city (Boulder) could be numbered as line 2, but what if the next record looks like this?

123 Broadway
Canyon Office Park
Colorado Springs, CO 80023

Now, the city should be numbered as line 3. Also, the state in the first example—if counted from left to right—would be word 2, whereas in the second example the state is word 3. If both these addresses were in the same data file, you would have inconsistency in your sort if you counted the lines from the top down and the words from left to right.

The correct way to sort these two addresses would be to count the lines from the bottom up. You know the city is always on the last line of the address, so instead of line 2 or line 3, using a negative number (line -1) would always sort by the last line of the field. Similarly, to locate the state in both examples, the word number would be word -2 (the second to the last word, counting from right to left).

The zip code is always located in the last word of the last line in field 3. In the sort keys menu, you want to specify the zip code field as the key: field 3, line -1, and word -1.

1. Select **T**ools ⇒ **So**r**t**

   ✓ Press Ctrl + F9 , **2**

   The Source and Destination are set for screen.

2. Select **OK**

   ✓ Press Enter

   The Sort dialog box appears. Make sure **Record** **T**ype is set for Merge Data File.

3. Select **Sort Keys**

4. Select **Edit**

    The Edit Sort Key dialog box appears. Make the following settings:

    <u>T</u>ype: **Numeric**
    <u>O</u>rder: **Ascending**
    <u>F</u>ield: **3**
    <u>L</u>ine: **-1**
    <u>W</u>ord: **-1**

5. Select **OK**

    ✓ Press ⎡Enter⎤

    Delete any unnecessary keys. Compare your dialog box to the one shown in Figure 15-9.

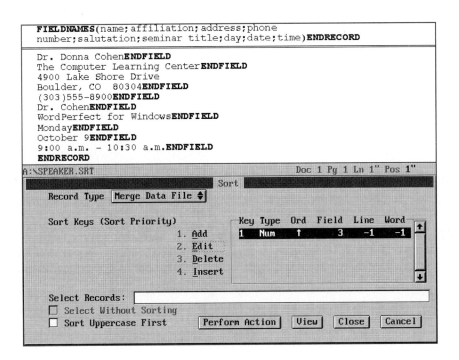

Figure 15-9

6. Select **Perform Action**

7. Verify that the file is now arranged in zip code order; close the file without saving the changes

▌ HANDS-ON ACTIVITY

In this exercise, you are going to sort the merge data file first by city and then by last name. The city will be specified as key 1, field 3, line -1, word 1, and the last name will be specified as key 2, field 1, line 1, word -1. Open SPEAKER.SRT.

1. Select <u>T</u>ools ⇒ So<u>r</u>t

   ✓ Press Ctrl + F9 , **2**

   The Source and Destination are set for screen.

2. Select **OK**

   ✓ Press Enter

   The Sort dialog box appears. Check to make sure the Record <u>T</u>ype is set for Merge Data File.

3. Select **Sort <u>K</u>eys**

4. Select <u>A</u>dd

5. Make the changes in your dialog box to reflect the following:

   Key 1

<u>T</u>ype:	**Alpha**
<u>O</u>rder:	**Ascending**
<u>F</u>ield:	**3**
<u>L</u>ine:	**-1**
<u>W</u>ord:	**1**

   Key 2

<u>T</u>ype:	**Alpha**
<u>O</u>rder:	**Ascending**
<u>F</u>ield:	**1**
<u>L</u>ine:	**1**
<u>W</u>ord:	**-1**

6. Select **OK**

   ✓ Press Enter

7. Delete any unnecessary keys

8. Select <u>P</u>erform Action

9. Check to make sure your sort is successful. Your records should be arranged first in order by city and then within duplicate cities arranged by last name

10. Close the file without saving the changes

▌ HANDS-ON ACTIVITY

In this exercise, you are going to perform a paragraph sort. The file you will need to open from your student sample disk is called PARA.SRT. The file is shown in Figure 15-10 for your reference.

Each paragraph of this document has a numbered section heading and a topic name; for example, Section 3 is Calendar software. If you view the file with reveal codes, you will see that there is one Tab between the section

SECTION 1   Word Processing is one of the most obvious time-savers for office automation. Instead of typing slowly and carefully to avoid mistakes, users can type at rough-draft speed. They can then correct errors; spell check, insert, delete, move, and copy blocks of text; and print the document in a few minutes.

SECTION 2   Electronic Mail allows the user to send a message via computers within the same room, within the same building, across a campus, or across the ocean. A software package is loaded on some type of computer, and every person using a workstation attached to that computer has the capability of sending a message to every other person at a workstation.

SECTION 3   Calendar software allows you to keep track of meetings and appointments made for one day, one week, or one month.

SECTION 4   Time Management software manages our most valuable resource—time. This software helps people manage by judicious planning, by prioritizing tasks, and then by working efficiently, effectively and creatively within the constraints of the calendar.

SECTION 5   Spreadsheets are probably the most widely used software packages by business people today. A spreadsheet is a tool for analyzing data. It is a problem solver, an instrument used to assemble data into a logical format. It is used to measure, analyze, and project.

Figure 15-10

number and the topic name. Therefore, the section number is field 1 (words 1 and 2), and the topic is field 2. The paragraphs are currently listed by section number, so let's sort by topic.

1. Select **T**ools ⇒ **So**rt

    ✓ Press Ctrl + F9 , **2**

    The Source and Destination are set for screen.

2. Select **OK**

    ✓ Press Enter

    The Sort dialog box appears. Make sure that the Record **T**ype is set for **Paragraph.**

3. Select **Sort K**eys

    *NOTE: The selections for the sort keys used in the previous sort may still remain in the Sort dialog box. Since you are only going to sort on one key, select **D**elete several times until only 1 key setting shows in the key list.*

4. Select **E**dit

    Enter the following settings in your Edit Sort Key dialog box:

    Key 1
    Type: **Alpha**
    Order: **Ascending**

Line: 1

Field: 2

Word: 1

*CAUTION: Notice that the order of Field, Line, and Word are in differ-
ent order when sorting a paragraph file than in previous screens when
sorting a line or a merge file. Check your keys carefully.*

5. Select **OK**

    ✓ Press [Enter]

6. Select **P**erform Action

    Compare your sorted file to the one shown in Figure 15-11.

SECTION 3   Calendar software allows you to keep track of meetings and appointments made for one day, one week, or one month.

SECTION 2   Electronic Mail allows the user to send a message via computers
within the same room, within the same building, across a campus, or across the
ocean. A software package is loaded on some type of computer, and every person
using a workstation attached to that computer has the capabiity of sending a message to every other person at a workstation.

SECTION 5   Spreadsheets are probably the most widely used software packages
by business people today. A spreadsheet is a tool for analyzing data. It is a problem solver, an instrument used to assemble data into a logical format. It is used to
measure, analyze, and project.

SECTION 4   Time Management software manages our most valuable resource—
time. This software helps people manage, by judicious planning, by prioritizing
tasks, and then by working efficiently, effectively and creatively within the constraints of the calendar.

SECTION 1   Word Processing is one of the most obvious time-savers for office automation. Instead of typing slowly and carefully to avoid mistakes, users can type
at rough-draft speed. They can then correct errors; spell check, insert, delete,
move, and copy blocks of text; and print the document in a few minutes.

Figure 15-11

7. Close the file without saving the changes

▍ HANDS-ON ACTIVITY

In this exercise, you are going to sort a table. Open the example file
SPEAKER.TBL from your sample disk. The document is shown in Figure
15-12 for your reference.

   You are going to sort the table by last name of the speaker, which you
will define as the last word of column 1. To sort only the data and *not* the
two heading rows, you will block the portion of the table to sort.

1. Position the cursor on the first word in cell A3

Campus Computer Fair Speakers		
Speaker	**Topic**	**Day/Time**
Dr. Donna Cohen	WordPerfect for Windows	Monday 9:00 a.m. - 10:30 a.m.
Mr. Conley Adams	Customizing Windows	Tuesday 8:30 a.m. - 10:00 a.m.
Ms. Rebecca Joseph	DOS 6.0	Wednesday 9:00 a.m. - Noon
Mr. George Blum	Memory Management	Wednesday 1:00 p.m. - 3:00 p.m.
Mr. Mark Spence	Networking	Tuesday 1:00 p.m. - 3:00 p.m.
Dr. Patricia Davis	OS/2	Monday 1:00 p.m. - 3:00 p.m.

Figure 15-12

2.   Block rows 3 through 8

3.   Select **T**ools ⇒ So**r**t

   ✓ Press Ctrl + F9 , **2**

   The Sort dialog box appears. The Record Type has already selected Table as the sort type. The Sort **K**eys are still showing the default settings. Since we only need one sort key for this exercise, edit key 1 to sort by last name.

4.   Select Sort **K**eys

5.   Select **E**dit

   Make the following changes to the Edit Sort Key section of the dialog box:

   Key 1:
   T**y**pe: Alpha
   Order: Ascending
   Cell: 1
   Line: 1
   Word: -1

6.   Select **OK**

   Compare your dialog box to the one shown in Figure 15-13.

7.   Select **P**erform Action

   The table will now appear in order of last name of speaker. Compare your sorted table to the one shown in Figure 15-14.

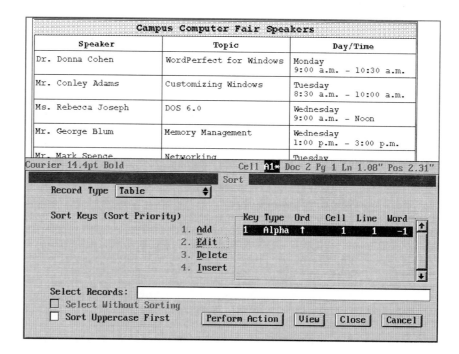

Figure 15-13

Campus Computer Fair Speakers		
Speaker	Topic	Day/Time
Mr. Conley Adams	Customizing Windows	Tuesday 8:30 a.m. - 10:00 a.m.
Mr. George Blum	Memory Management	Wednesday 1:00 p.m. - 3:00 p.m.
Dr. Donna Cohen	WordPerfect for Windows	Monday 9:00 a.m. - 10:30 a.m.
Dr. Patricia Davis	OS/2	Monday 1:00 p.m. - 3:00 p.m.
Ms. Rebecca Joseph	DOS 6.0	Wednesday 9:00 a.m. - Noon
Mr. Mark Spence	Networking	Tuesday 1:00 p.m. - 3:00 p.m.

Figure 15-14

8. Close your file without saving it

Using Select

There will be occasions when you do not want to use an entire list of records. You might instead want to have a sublist that contains records meeting a specific criterion—for example, a list of individuals who live in a specific zip code or who have an annual income of more than a specified amount.

To filter out certain records from a file is called **Select.** You can use any of the following **logical symbols** to set conditions on which to filter the records:

Operator	Function
=	Equal to
<>	Not equal to
>	Greater than
<	Less than
>=	Greater than or equal to
<=	Less than or equal to
&	And
¦	Or (the "pipe" symbol)

To use the Select feature, first specify the desired keys in the Sort Keys definition section of the Sort dialog box. Next, in the <u>S</u>elect Records text box, type the condition. For example, suppose you want to pull all the records for vendor donation = certificates. In that case, you would define key 1 as the donation column, and in the <u>S</u>elect Records text box you would type Key1=Certificates.

▎ HANDS-ON ACTIVITY

In this exercise, you are going to select all the vendors who are donating gift certificates. Key 1 will be the donation (field 2, word 1), and you will specify key 2 as the vendor name (field 1, word 1) so that the records will appear in alphabetical order by vendor.

1. Begin with a blank document window and open the DOORPRIZ.DOC file

2. Select <u>T</u>ools ⇒ So<u>r</u>t

   ✓ Press ⌨Ctrl + ⌨F9 , **2**

   The Source and Destination are set for screen.

3. Select **OK**

   ✓ Press ⌨Enter

   The Sort dialog box appears.

4. Select Sort <u>K</u>eys

   First, you need to edit key 1.

5. Select <u>E</u>dit

6. Make the following settings for key 1:

<u>T</u>ype:	**Alpha**
<u>O</u>rder:	**Ascending**
<u>F</u>ield:	**2**
<u>W</u>ord:	**1**

7. Select **OK**

   Since you are going to sort on two keys, add a second key.

8. Select **A**dd

9. Make the following settings for key 2:

   <u>T</u>ype: **Alpha**
   <u>O</u>rder: **Ascending**
   <u>F</u>ield: **1**
   <u>W</u>ord: **1**

10. Select **OK**

11. Select the **S**elect Records text box

    To set your filter condition, enter the following select statement to list only donations (key1) equal to certificates.

12. Type `Key1=Certificates`

    Compare your dialog box to the one shown in Figure 15-15.

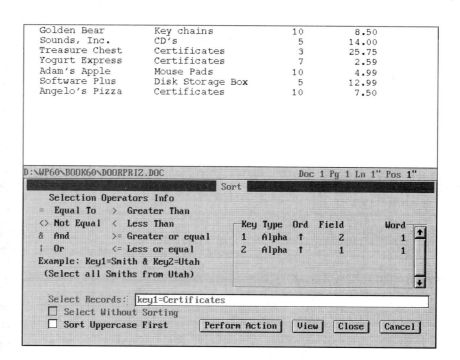

Figure 15-15

13. Select **P**erform Action

    The sublist appears on your screen, displaying the three matching records. There are only three vendors who are donating certificates and they are listed in alphabetical order by vendor name. Compare your screen to the list shown in Figure 15-16.

    To save this file without overwriting your original file, use the Save As feature.

Angelo's Pizza	Certificates	10	7.50
Treasure Chest	Certificates	3	25.75
Yogurt Express	Certificates	7	2.59

Figure 15-16

14. Select <u>F</u>ile ⇒ Save <u>A</u>s

15. Name the document `GIFTCERT.LST`

16. Close the file

▌ HANDS-ON ACTIVITY

In this exercise, you are going to create a sublist of all your high donors—vendors that are donating five or more gifts that have a retail value of at least $10.00.

1. Open DOORPRIZ.DOC

2. Select <u>T</u>ools ⇒ So<u>r</u>t

   ✓ Press Ctrl + F9 , **2**

   The Source and Destination are set for screen.

3. Select **OK**

   ✓ Press Enter

   The Sort dialog box appears. Make sure the Record <u>T</u>ype is set for Line.

4. Select **Sort <u>K</u>eys**

5. Select <u>E</u>dit

6. Make the following key settings:

   Key 1 (to set your first sort priority on the number of donations)
<u>T</u>ype:	**Numeric**
<u>O</u>rder:	**Ascending**
<u>F</u>ield:	**3**
<u>W</u>ord:	**1**

   Key 2 (to set your second sort priority on the amount of each donation)
<u>T</u>ype:	**Numeric**
<u>O</u>rder:	**Ascending**
<u>F</u>ield:	**4**
<u>W</u>ord:	**1**

   To return to sort the database,

7. Select **OK**

Move to the <u>S</u>elect Records text box. Enter the selection statement for quantity greater than or equal to 5 and the price greater than or equal to 10.

8. Type `key1>=5&key2>=10`

    Remember, the **&** specifies that both conditions must be met.

    Compare your dialog box to the one shown in Figure 15-17.

    NOTE: You may type the select statement either with or without spaces around the "&" sign. See the select statement example shown in Figure 15-17.

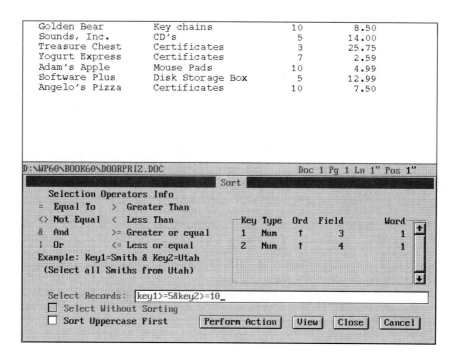

Figure 15-17

9. Select <u>P</u>erform Action

    The filtered list appears on your screen. There are two vendors that meet the criteria of donating five or more gifts that have a retail value of at least $10.00.

    Since you do not want to overwrite your original file, use the Save As feature.

10. Select <u>F</u>ile ⇒ Save <u>A</u>s

11. Name the document **DONATE.BIG**

12. Exit WordPerfect

On Your Own

Description	Menu Commands	Function Keys
Begin Sort or Selection	_____	_____

Review of Commands

Lesson Review

1. What are two of the four record types that can be sorted in WordPerfect?

2. What comprises a record in a merge record?

3. What denotes a record in a table?

4. How are words defined in a sort?

5. How are keys defined, and how many keys can be used in a sort?

6. What are the essential formatting criteria for a line sort?

7. How would you sort only on the state field in the following record? (Specify alpha or numeric, plus the field, line, and word numbers of the key.)

   NameENDFIELD
   StreetENDFIELD
   City/State/ZipENDFIELD

8. What logical symbol denotes "greater than or equal to"?

9. What symbol do you use when selecting more than one condition?

Assignments

15.1 Directions

1. Create the following line file with headings (type a three-line title, boldfaced and centered):

   THE UNIVERSITY OF LEARNING
   CMS Department
   Fall Semester

2. Set up headings for the following five columns (remember to use only one [Tab] between each column):

   Student Name/City & State/Age/GPA/Scholarship Amount

3. Enter the following information:

Cathy Ward/Denver, Colorado/24/3.2/1,000
Linda A. Werner/Arvada, Colorado/26/2.9/900
Boyd G. Rivera/Denver, Colorado/18/2.0/400
Charles Dysert/Aurora, Colorado/39/1.5/600
Wendy Pope/Arvada, Colorado/45/3.7/1,200
Laurie Wright/Arvada, Colorado/20/3.5/1,100

4. Save the file as STUDENTS.SCH.

15.2 Directions

1. Open the file STUDENTS.SCH.
2. Save the file as STUDENTS.LN.
3. Line sort the file on the students' last names, in ascending order.
4. Save the file, print it, and close it.
5. Open STUDENTS.SCH.
6. Save the file as STUDENTS.GPA.
7. Line sort on the students' GPA in ascending order.
8. Save the file again, and print and close it.

15.3 Directions

1. Open the file STUDENTS.SCH.
2. Save the file as STUDENTS.25.
3. Select all students older than 25 with a GPA greater than 3.0.
4. Save the file and print and close it.
5. Open STUDENTS.SCH.
6. Save it as STUDENTS.600.
7. Select students with a GPA above 3.0 and a scholarship amount greater than or equal to $600.
8. Save the file, and print it.
9. From the original file, create and print a list of all students who live in Arvada. Save it as STUDENTS.ARV.

16

Working with Lengthy Documents

Objectives

Upon completion of this lesson, you will be able to do the following:

- Use the conditional end of page feature
- Utilize the widow/orphan control feature
- Create, edit, and delete footnotes
- Add paragraph and page borders
- Use QuickMark to locate a position in your document
- Create and utilize a bookmark
- Enter comments
- Use the automatic paragraph numbering feature
- Mark text for a table of contents
- Define a table of contents
- Generate a table of contents

Working with a lengthy document can be cumbersome, even intimidating, and may mean that you need to create footnotes or generate a table of contents. This lesson introduces you to functions needed when working with longer documents. You will use two features that assist in determining a page break, such as a conditional end of page and widow/orphan protection. You will also learn to polish your documents by using paragraph numbering, adding borders, creating footnotes, and generating a table of contents.

▌ Starting Point

Before beginning the lesson, start WordPerfect 6.0. The document window should be blank. Make sure that the Train Button Bar and the Ribbon are displayed. Open a document on your sample disk called FEASIBLE.STE. This document is approximately five pages long, and we suggest you print this document so that you will have a reference available.

▓ Conditional End of Page

The **Conditional End of Page** feature protects a specified number of lines from being divided by a page break so that, for example, a heading will not appear by itself at the bottom of a page. WordPerfect will always keep the specified number of lines together, even if it has to place a page break before the lines to do so. To initiate this feature, position the cursor at the beginning of the first line to be affected and choose <u>L</u>ayout ⇒ <u>O</u>ther ⇒ <u>C</u>onditional End of Page (*Shortcut keys:* Shift + F8, 7, 2). The cursor moves to the Number of Lines to Keep Together text box. Type the number of lines to be kept together and press Enter, then choose OK. A [Cndl EOP:*n*] code is inserted. The *n* represents the number of lines to be kept together.

▌ HANDS-ON ACTIVITY

In this exercise, you will use the Conditional End of Page feature to keep the heading "Secretarial Support," located at the bottom of page 4, with at least two lines of the first paragraph associated with it, currently on page 5.

1. Using the scroll bar or the cursor, position your document window so that the bottom of page 4 and top of page 5 are visible

    Compare the document window to the one shown in Figure 16-1.

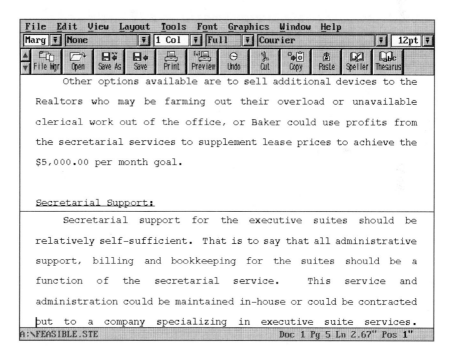

Figure 16-1

2. Position the cursor at the beginning of the line that reads "Secretarial Support"

3. Click on <u>L</u>ayout ⇒ <u>O</u>ther

    ✓ Press Shift + F8, **7**

The Other Format dialog box appears, as shown in Figure 16-2.

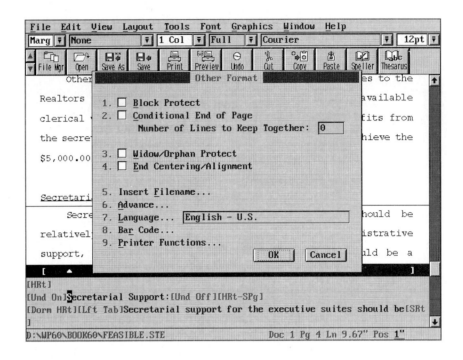

Figure 16-2

4. Select <u>C</u>onditional End of Page

   The cursor moves to the Number of Lines to Keep Together text box.

5. Type **4** (to keep four lines together)

6. Press (Enter)

7. Select **OK**

   The page break is now positioned above the heading. Compare your document to the one shown in Figure 16-3.

Widow/Orphan Control

If you have typed long reports and manuscripts before, you may know that it is frowned upon to have a page break separate the first or last line of a paragraph (widows/orphans) from the rest of the paragraph. WordPerfect has an option, called **Widow/Orphan**, that prevents widows and orphans from occurring. This option keeps at least two lines of a paragraph together by sacrificing the stipulated bottom margin. To activate the Widow/Orphan feature, position the cursor on the page where the feature is to take effect. If you want it to be active for your entire document, make sure your cursor is positioned at the top of the page (or the beginning of the document). Choose <u>L</u>ayout ⇒ <u>O</u>ther ⇒ <u>W</u>idow/Orphan (*Shortcut keys:* (Shift) + (F8), 7, 3). A [Wid/Orph:On] code is inserted at the cursor position.

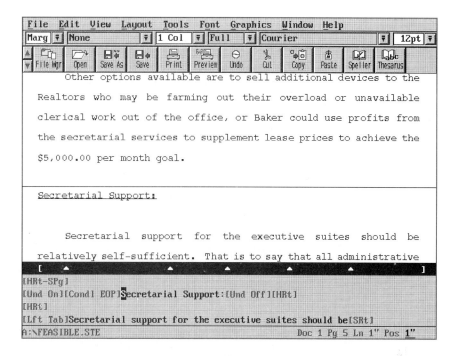

Figure 16-3

HANDS-ON ACTIVITY

In this exercise, you will activate the Widow/Orphan feature to ensure that at least two lines of all paragraphs remain on one page. The last paragraph on page 1 has the last line placed at the top of page 2. To view this,

1. Using the scroll bar or directional arrow keys, move the cursor to make the bottom of page 1 and the top of page 2 visible on your screen, as shown in Figure 16-4

    As you can see, because of the positioning of the page break, one short line from the last paragraph on page 1 will print by itself on the beginning of page 2. The text will read better and the printed page will look more presentable if at least two lines from the paragraph are together on page 2.

    To instruct WordPerfect to keep two lines of a paragraph together when encountering a page break throughout your entire document,

2. Position the cursor point at the top of the document

3. Select **Layout** ⇒ **Other** ⇒ **Widow/Orphan**

    ✓ Press Shift + F8 , **7**, **3**

4. Select **OK**

    ✓ Press Enter

5. On your own, use Reveal Codes to view the [Wid/Orph:On] code

    View the page break between pages 1 and 2 to see that two lines of the paragraph are carried to the top of page 2.

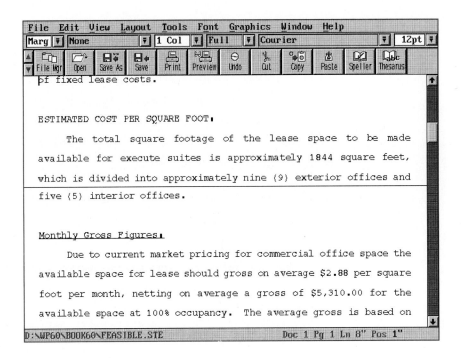

Figure 16-4

6. Press Page Down

7. On your own, position the cursor at the beginning of the document, turn on the page numbering feature, and instruct WordPerfect to print a page number at the bottom center of each page

Working with Footnotes and Endnotes

Footnotes and **endnotes** are used to give the source for material provided in a document (such as the name of a book or periodical, the author and publisher, the date of publication, and page references) or to give additional detailed information. Footnotes are placed at the bottom of the page in which the material is referenced, and their variant, endnotes, are placed at the end of the document on a separate page.

WordPerfect automatically numbers each footnote/endnote sequentially. Also, since footnotes are placed on the same page as their reference numbers, WordPerfect automatically subtracts the number of lines used by the footnotes and adjusts the text on the page accordingly.

Creating a Footnote

To create a footnote, position the insertion point where the footnote number is to be placed and choose Layout ⇒ Footnote ⇒ Create (*Shortcut keys:* Ctrl + F7, 1, 1). The Footnote window appears and the correct (sequential) footnote reference number displays. Type the footnote and press F7. The reference number appears in the body of the text, but the actual footnote cannot be seen, unless the Page mode is activated or until you either print or preview the document.

▌HANDS-ON ACTIVITY

In this exercise, you are going to create three footnotes.

1. Position the cursor after the phrase that reads "The support for this pricing" located on page 2

    Compare your screen to the one shown in Figure 16-5.

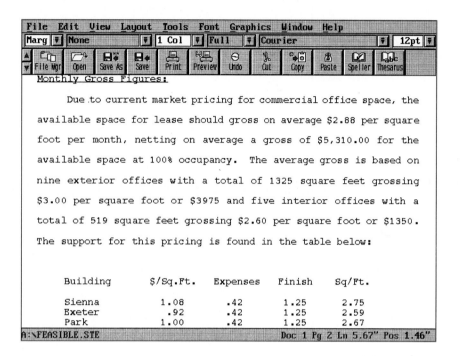

Figure 16-5

2. Select <u>L</u>ayout ⇒ <u>F</u>ootnote ⇒ <u>C</u>reate

    ✓ Press Ctrl + F7 , 1, 1

    The Footnote window appears, displaying a very small superscript number 1, as shown in Figure 16-6.

3. Type **These figures are based on lease space of approximately 500 square feet.**

    To close the footnote window and return to your document,

4. Press F7

5. Either turn on the Page mode or use the Print Preview feature to view your footnote. Compare your page to the one shown in Figure 16-7

    Now, you are going to add another footnote at the end of the phrase "independently could be purchased and/or leased" on page 3.

    TIP: Use Search F2 to locate the phrase.

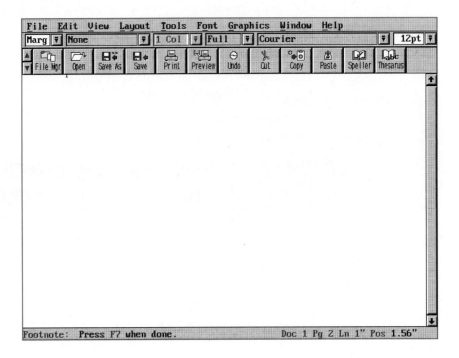

Figure 16-6

6. Position your cursor after "independently could be purchased and/or leased"

7. Select <u>L</u>ayout ⇒ <u>F</u>ootnote ⇒ <u>C</u>reate

   ✓ Press Ctrl + F7 , 1, 1

   The Footnote window appears and displays a "2," indicating that the next footnote reference number is in the proper sequential order.

8. Type `Estimated cost of leased equipment per month is $3,800.00`

9. Press F7

10. On your own, move the cursor to the next sentence, "Secretarial support should be offered at the executive suites on a per usage basis." Create a third footnote that reads "Unit prices available upon request."

Editing a Footnote

To edit a footnote, choose <u>L</u>ayout ⇒ <u>F</u>ootnote ⇒ <u>E</u>dit (*Shortcut keys:* Ctrl + F7 , 1, 2). The Footnote Number dialog box appears. Type the footnote number to be edited and choose OK. Make the desired changes and press F7 .

▌HANDS-ON ACTIVITY

In this exercise, you are going to change the first footnote, since the figures are based on 650 square feet. Your cursor may be located anywhere in the document.

which is divided into approximately nine (9) exterior offices and five (5) interior offices.

<u>Monthly Gross Figures:</u>

Due to current market pricing for commercial office space, the available space for lease should gross on average $2.88 per square foot per month, netting on average a gross of $5,310.00 for the available space at 100% occupancy. The average gross is based on nine exterior offices with a total of 1325 square feet grossing $3.00 per square foot or $3975 and five interior offices with a total of 519 square feet grossing $2.60 per square foot or $1350. The support for this pricing[1] is found in the table below:

Building	$/Sq.Ft.	Expenses	Finish	Sq/Ft.
Sienna	1.08	.42	1.25	2.75
Exeter	.92	.42	1.25	2.59
Park	1.00	.42	1.25	2.67
Meadow	1.13	.42	1.25	2.80

<u>Existing Leases:</u>

Let it be understood that there are existing executive suite leases available in the range of $1.85 to $3.00 per square foot. However, consideration for building and office location, cost of parking, and available services should be made. Buildings with superior service and location are maintaining higher than average lease and occupancy rates.

[1]These figures are based on lease space of approximately 500 square feet.

Figure 16-7

1. Select **L**ayout ⇒ **F**ootnote ⇒ **E**dit

    ✓ Press Ctrl + F7 , 1, 2

    The Footnote Number dialog box appears, similar to the one shown in Figure 16-8.

    To specify the first footnote for edits,

2. Type 1

3. Select **OK**

    The Footnote window appears.

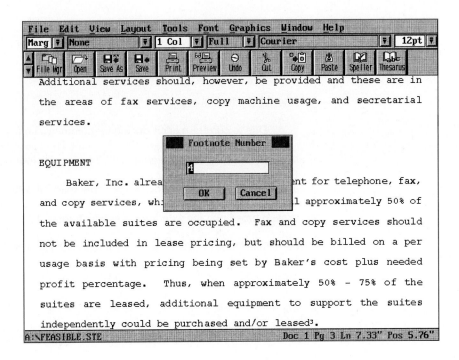

Figure 16-8

4. On your own, change 500 to **650**

5. Press `F7`

6. On your own, use the Page mode or the Print Preview feature to view the change to your footnote

Deleting a Footnote

To delete a footnote, position the cursor in the document either just before or just after the footnote reference number. If the cursor is before the reference number, press `Delete`, or if it is after the reference number, press `Backspace`. Remember, if you accidentally delete a footnote, immediately use the Undo feature to restore the footnote.

█ HANDS-ON ACTIVITY

In this exercise, you are going to delete the second footnote.

1. Position the cursor before the second footnote reference number, as shown in Figure 16-9

2. Press `Delete`

    The footnote is deleted.

3. On your own, move to the next paragraph and notice that footnote 3 is automatically renumbered to 2

█ Adding Borders to Paragraphs

The **Paragraph Borders** feature allows you to create a border around a paragraph, or even to block any amount of text and then surround it with a border. A variety of border and fill styles can be selected, or you can customize

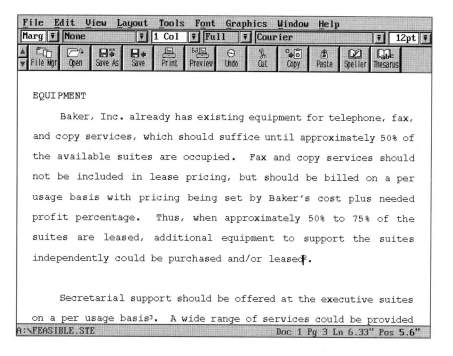

File   Edit   View   Layout   Tools   Font   Graphics   Window   Help

Marg ▼ | None   ▼ | 1 Col ▼ | Full ▼ | Courier   ▼ | 12pt ▼

File Mgr   Open   Save As   Save   Print   Preview   Undo   Cut   Copy   Paste   Speller   Thesarus

EQUIPMENT

Baker, Inc. already has existing equipment for telephone, fax, and copy services, which should suffice until approximately 50% of the available suites are occupied. Fax and copy services should not be included in lease pricing, but should be billed on a per usage basis with pricing being set by Baker's cost plus needed profit percentage. Thus, when approximately 50% to 75% of the suites are leased, additional equipment to support the suites independently could be purchased and/or leased.

Secretarial support should be offered at the executive suites on a per usage basis³. A wide range of services could be provided

A:\FEASIBLE.STE   Doc 1 Pg 3 Ln 6.33" Pos 5.6"

Figure 16-9

your own. To add a paragraph border, select Layout ⇒ Lines ⇒ Paragraph Borders (*Shortcut keys:* Shift + F8, 1, 5). The Create Paragraph Border dialog box appears. To add or change the style, select the Border Style option, and to add or change the shading, select Fill Style option. To close the dialog box, choose OK.

▌ HANDS-ON ACTIVITY

In this exercise, you are going to add a border to the columnar table located on page 2. Since you want more than one paragraph to be surrounded with the border, the first step is to block the heading and the columns.

1. Position the cursor in front of the word "Building" in the heading of the columnar table

2. Select Edit ⇒ Block

   ✓ Press F12

3. Press ↓ 6 times

4. Select Layout ⇒ Line ⇒ Paragraph Borders

   ✓ Press Shift + F8, 1, 5

   The Create Paragraph Border dialog box appears, as shown in Figure 16-10.

   To place a single-line border (the default) around the blocked text,

5. Select OK twice

   ✓ Press Enter twice

   Compare your table to the one shown in Figure 16-11.

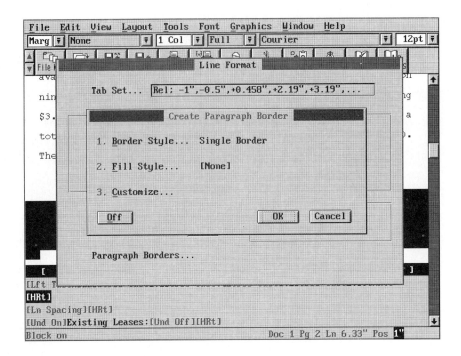

Figure 16-10

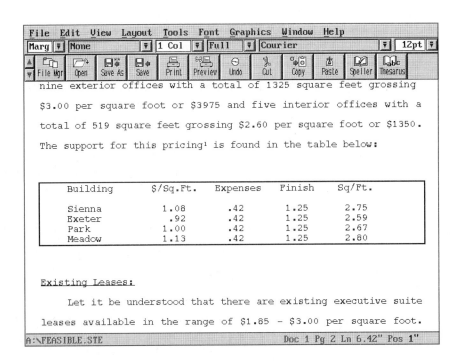

Figure 16-11

Using Bookmarks

The **Bookmark** feature allows you to mark one or many places in a document so that you can quickly return to that position the next time you open that document for edits. For example, if you were editing a lengthy document and need to close the file and return to it later, you can use the

Bookmark to mark the particular location where you stopped working. The next time you retrieve the file, using the Bookmark feature will quickly move the cursor to the place you marked.

A **QuickMark** is a generic bookmark and there can only be one Quick-Mark in a document at any time. If a second QuickMark is placed in a document, the first one is deleted. To create a QuickMark, position the cursor at the location to be marked. Select E̲dit ⇒ Boo̲kmark and then choose Set QuickMark (*Shortcut keys:* Ctrl + Q). To find the QuickMark, the cursor can be located anyplace in the document. Select E̲dit ⇒ Boo̲kmark ⇒ F̲indMark (*Shortcut keys:* Ctrl + F) and then choose F̲ind QuickMark (*Shortcut keys:* Ctrl + Q). WordPerfect automatically places a QuickMark at the cursor whenever you save a document.

▌HANDS-ON ACTIVITY

In this exercise, you are going to save your document and then use the QuickMark to locate the position of the cursor when the document was saved.

1. Position the cursor at the beginning of the columnar table on page 2

2. Save your document and name it **FEASIBLE.FIN**

    Remember, WordPerfect automatically places a QuickMark at the cursor position when a document is saved.

3. Display the Reveal Codes screen to view the [Bookmark] code

    Now, use the bookmark to find your place when you saved the file last.

4. Position your cursor at the top of the document

5. Select E̲dit ⇒ Boo̲kmark ⇒ F̲ind QuickMark

    ✓ Press Ctrl + **F**

    The cursor is instantly moved to the bookmark at the top of the table.

Creating and Locating a Bookmark

You can have several bookmarks in one document; however, each bookmark must have a unique name. To create a bookmark, position the cursor at the location to be marked and select E̲dit ⇒ Boo̲kmark ⇒ C̲reate (*Shortcut keys:* Shift + F12, 3). The Create Bookmark dialog appears. Type a unique name and press Enter. A [Bookmark:*name*] is placed at the cursor position. To find a specific bookmark, select E̲dit ⇒ Boo̲kmark ⇒ F̲ind (*Shortcut keys:* Shift + F12, 1), then type the bookmark name.

▌HANDS-ON ACTIVITY

In this exercise, you are going to create a bookmark, move the cursor, and then locate the bookmark.

1. Position the cursor at the top of page 3

2. Select <u>E</u>dit ⇒ Boo<u>k</u>mark ⇒ <u>C</u>reate

✓ Press (Shift) + (F12), **3**

The Create Bookmark dialog appears, with the first 40 characters of text from the document. To clear the text,

3. Press (Backspace)

Compare your screen with Figure 16-12.

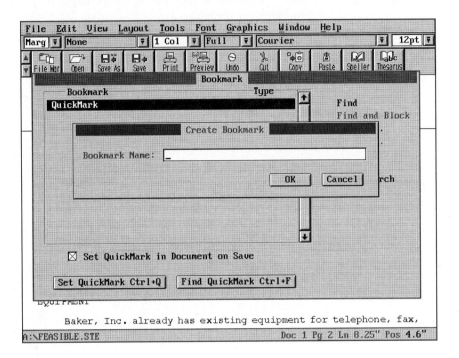

Figure 16-12

4. Type **BK1**

5. Press (Enter)

6. On your own, use the Reveal Codes screen to view the [Bookmark] code

   NOTE: When the [Bookmark] code is highlighted, it expands to [Bookmark:BK1], displaying the bookmark number.

7. Move the cursor to the bottom of the document

   To find the BK1 bookmark,

8. Select <u>E</u>dit ⇒ Boo<u>k</u>mark

   ✓ Press (Shift) + (F12)

   The Bookmark dialog box appears.

9. Highlight **BK1**

10. Select <u>F</u>ind

    The cursor is now moved back to the top of page 3.

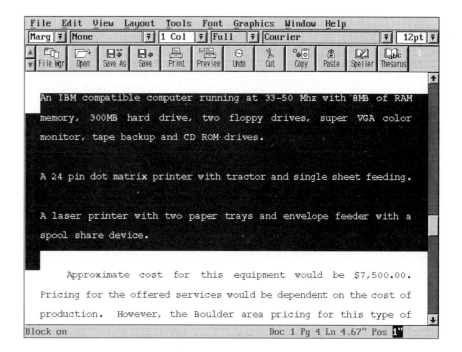

Figure 16-14

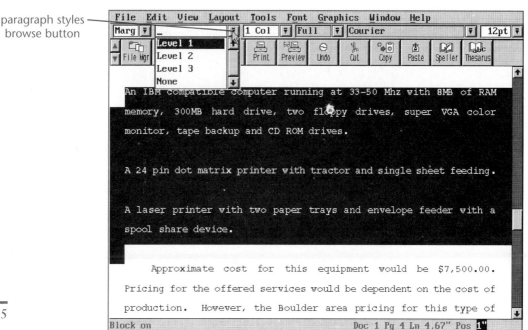

paragraph styles browse button

Figure 16-15

The three blocked paragraphs are automatically numbered and indented.

5.   Block the same three paragraphs again

   CAUTION: Be sure the blocking begins on the "1." of the first numbered paragraph.

6. Click on the **Paragraph Styles Browse** button

7. Double-click on the **Level 2** option

Each paragraph is now automatically indented to the next tab stop and the numbering style changes to lowercase alphabetical letters. To change from Level 2 to Level 1,

8. Block the same three paragraphs again

9. Click on the Paragraph Styles Browse button

10. Double click on the Level 1 option

Using the Keyboard

1. Locate the paragraph that begins "An IBM compatible computer running" at the top of page 4

2. Block the 3 paragraphs as shown previously in Figure 16-14

3. Select **Layout** ⇒ **Styles**

   ✓ Press Alt + F8

The Style List dialog box appears as shown in Figure 16-16.

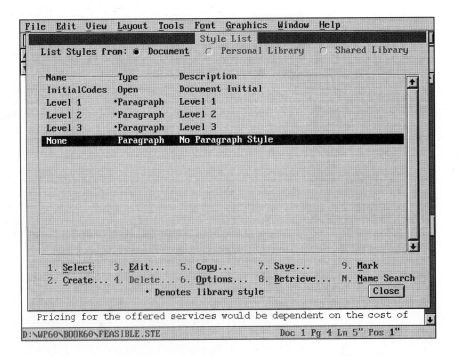

Figure 16-16

4. Highlight **Level 2 Paragraph**

5. Select **Select**

NOTE: *The blank lines between the paragraphs are also numbered.*

6. On your own, using Reveal Codes, remove the automatic paragraph numbering codes [Para Style:Level 1;;] from the blank lines between the three numbered paragraphs

7. Block the same three paragraphs again

8. Select <u>L</u>ayout ⇒ <u>S</u>tyles

   ✓ Press Alt + F8

9. Highlight **Level 3 Paragraph**

10. Select <u>S</u>elect

    Each paragraph is now automatically indented to the third tab stop and the numbering style changes to Roman numerals, including the blank lines.

11. On your own, block the paragraphs and apply the Level 1 Paragraph style. Delete the automatic paragraph numbering codes in the blank lines.

▍ Creating a Table of Contents

As a useful enhancement for lengthy documents, WordPerfect creates a **table of contents**, using text that you mark. Five levels of headings/subheadings can be specified. Generally, you mark the title page, headings, and subheadings of the document, plus any appendices, and the marked text is placed into the table of contents, showing the specified page of each entry. There are three basic steps to generate a table of contents:

- Marking the text to be used in the table of contents
- Defining the page numbering style of the table of contents
- Generating the table of contents

Marking the Text

To mark the text, block the text and choose <u>T</u>ools ⇒ Ta<u>b</u>le of Contents ⇒ <u>M</u>ark (*Shortcut keys:* Alt + F5 , 1). Type a number indicating the level for the heading and press Enter. To exit the dialog box, select OK. A [Mark Txt ToC Begin,*n*] code is inserted before the marked text and a [Mark Txt ToC End,*n*] code is placed at the end of the text. The *n* represents the level number.

▍ HANDS-ON ACTIVITY

In this exercise, you are going to mark the text that should appear in the table of contents. You will specify two levels.

1. Block **INTENT** on page 1 of your feasibility proposal document

2. Select <u>T</u>ools ⇒ Ta<u>b</u>le of Contents ⇒ <u>M</u>ark

   ✓ Press Alt + F5 , **1**

The Mark Table of Contents dialog box appears, as shown in Figure 16-17.

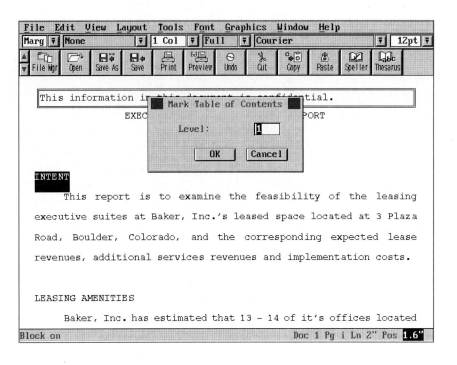

Figure 16-17

Level 1 is already indicated in the dialog box. To accept the level,

3. Select **OK**

   ✓ Press Enter

4. On your own, mark the following text as level 1 (Search F2 is a fast way to locate the text):

   LEASING AMENITIES
   OBJECTIVE
   ESTIMATED COST PER SQUARE FOOT
   SPECIAL SERVICES
   EQUIPMENT
   STAFFING
   SUMMARY

   Now, you are going to mark text as a second level.

5. Select **Monthly Gross Figures** (near the top of page 2)

6. Select **Tools** ⇒ **Table of Contents** ⇒ **Mark**

   ✓ Press Alt + F5 , 1

7. Type **2** (to specify Level 2)

8. Select **OK**

9. On your own, mark the following text as Level 2:

   Existing Leases
   Word Processor
   Secretarial Support

Defining the Table of Contents

The process of defining the table of contents tells WordPerfect how many levels you have marked in the text, the number style you prefer, and the location for the table of contents (ordinarily, after the title page). To define the table, position the insertion point where the table is to be generated, and choose Tools ⇒ Table of Contents ⇒ Define (*Shortcut keys:* [Alt] + [F5], 2, 1). The Define Table of Contents dialog box appears. Specify the number of levels and the numbering format, and choose OK.

▌ HANDS-ON ACTIVITY

In this exercise, you are going to instruct WordPerfect that you have two levels marked for the table of contents.

1. Position the insertion point at the top of the document

   To create a new page to be used for the table of contents,

2. Press [Ctrl] + [Enter]

   Notice that the status bar indicates Page 2.

   Now, define the table of contents.

3. Press [Page Up] to position the cursor at the beginning of the document.

4. Center, bold, and type **TABLE OF CONTENTS**

5. Press [Enter] 3 times

6. Select Tools ⇒ Table of Contents ⇒ Define

   ✓ Press [Alt] + [F5], **2**, **1**

   The Define Table of Contents dialog box appears as shown in Figure 16-18.

7. Select **Number of Levels**

   The cursor moves to the text box. To specify that you have two levels defined,

8. Type **2**

9. Press [Enter]

10. Select **Level Style # Mode**

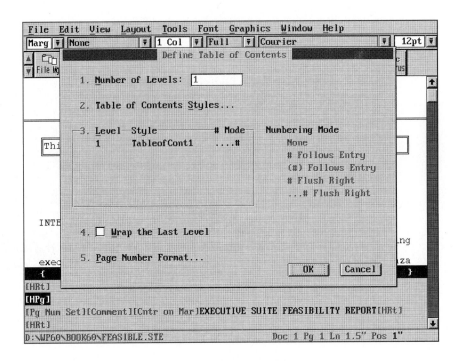

Figure 16-18

The default numbering style (as reflected in the dialog box) positions the page number on the right margin with dot leaders running from the topic to the number. The numbering style may be changed by selecting the desired style in the Numbering Mode list. To accept the parameters specified in the dialog box,

11. Select **OK**

Before you begin generating your table of contents, you are going to instruct WordPerfect to begin numbering page 2 as page 1 and specify the table of contents page to be numbered with lowercase Roman numerals.

12. Move your cursor to the top of the document immediately preceding "TABLE OF CONTENTS"

13. Select **Layout** ⇒ **Page** ⇒ **Page Numbering**

The Page Numbering dialog box appears. Notice that the Page Number Position specifies bottom center. The Page Number option is displaying an Arabic number. You want the table of contents number to be a lowercase Roman numeral.

14. Select **Page Number**

The Set Page Number dialog box appears, as shown in Figure 16-19.

15. Select **Numbering Method**

16. Select **Lower Roman**

17. Select **OK** 3 times

✓ Press Enter 3 times

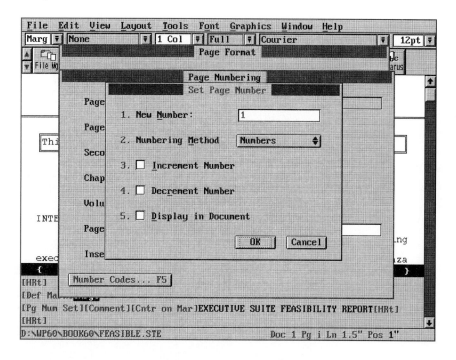

Figure 16-19

Notice that the status bar prompt reads "Page i."

The next step is to instruct WordPerfect to number page 2 as 1.

CAUTION: Be sure the cursor is at the beginning of page 2.

18. Select <u>L</u>ayout ⇒ <u>P</u>age ⇒ Page <u>N</u>umbering

19. Select Page <u>N</u>umber

    The Set Page Number dialog box appears.

20. Select New <u>N</u>umber

    The cursor moves to the text box.

21. Type **1**

22. Press Enter

    Now, you will need to specify the style as Arabic.

23. Select Numbering <u>M</u>ethod

24. Select <u>N</u>umbers

25. Select **OK** 3 times

    ✓ Press Enter 3 times

Generating the Table of Contents

The third and final step in creating the table of contents is the generation. Choose <u>T</u>ools ⇒ <u>G</u>enerate (*Shortcut keys:* Alt + F5 , 4). The Generate dialog box appears. To begin the generation, choose OK.

▍ **HANDS-ON ACTIVITY**

You are now ready to generate your table of contents. Position your cursor on the third [HRt] code following the "TABLE OF CONTENTS" heading.

1. Select <u>T</u>ools ⇒ <u>G</u>enerate

    ✓ Press `Alt` + `F5`, **4**

    The Generate dialog box appears, as shown in Figure 16-20.

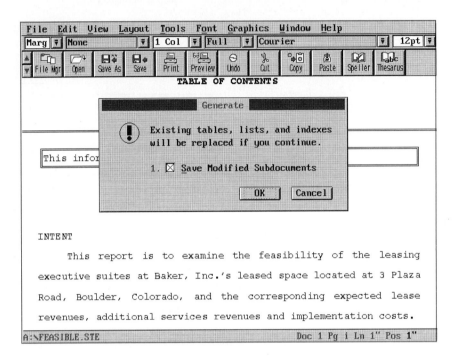

Figure 16-20

WordPerfect is warning that if you previously generated a table of contents, it will be replaced with the new one. To proceed with the generation of your table of contents,

2. Select **OK**

    ✓ Press `Enter`

    Compare your table of contents to the one shown in Figure 16-21.

▍ **Placing a Border Around a Page**

Earlier in this lesson you placed a border around a paragraph. You can also place a border around a page with the <u>L</u>ayout ⇒ <u>P</u>age ⇒ Page <u>B</u>orders feature. The **Page Border** feature will print on the current page and all subsequent pages, or you can block text on a particular page and surround it with a border. The Create Page Border dialog box allows you a variety of border and fill options. The <u>C</u>ustomize option allows you to change the corner styles and create shadow borders.

```
 File  Edit  View  Layout  Tools  Font  Graphics  Window  Help
Marg ▼ TableofCont1 ▼ 1 Col ▼ Full ▼ Courier                    ▼ 12pt ▼
```

```
                        TABLE OF CONTENTS

INTENT. . . . . . . . . . . . . . . . . . . . . . . . . . 1

LEASING AMENITIES . . . . . . . . . . . . . . . . . . . . 1

OBJECTIVE . . . . . . . . . . . . . . . . . . . . . . . . 1

ESTIMATED COST PER SQUARE FOOT. . . . . . . . . . . . . . 1
      Monthly Gross Figures. . . . . . . . . . . . . . . . 2
      Existing Leases. . . . . . . . . . . . . . . . . . . 2

SPECIAL SERVICES. . . . . . . . . . . . . . . . . . . . . 3

EQUIPMENT . . . . . . . . . . . . . . . . . . . . . . . . 3

STAFFING. . . . . . . . . . . . . . . . . . . . . . . . . 4
      Word Processor . . . . . . . . . . . . . . . . . . . 4
      Secretarial Support. . . . . . . . . . . . . . . . . 5

SUMMARY . . . . . . . . . . . . . . . . . . . . . . . . . 5
```

```
D:\WP60\BOOK60\FEASIBLE.STE              Doc 1 Pg i Ln 1.67" Pos 1"
```

Figure 16-21

HANDS-ON ACTIVITY

The final step in polishing your document is to add a title page.

1. Position the cursor at the beginning of the document

   To create a new page,

2. Press Ctrl + Enter

3. Position the cursor on the new page

   You are going to retrieve a title page that has already been created for you. Locate your sample disk. Once again, in the instructions below we specify drive A; however, if you are using a different drive, specify the appropriate drive letter.

4. Select File ⇒ Retrieve

   In the Retrieve Document dialog box,

5. Type A:TITLE.STE

6. Press Enter

   Now, to add a shadow border,

7. Block all the text on the title page

8. Select Layout ⇒ Page ⇒ Page Borders

   ✓ Press Shift + F8, 3, B

   The Create Page Border dialog box appears.

Notice that the border style is Single Border. Now, you are going to specify a shadow border.

9. Select **C**ustomize

The Customize Page Border dialog box appears, as shown in Figure 16-22.

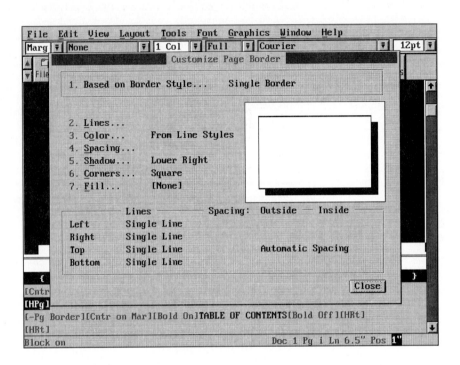

Figure 16-22

10. Select **Sh**adow

The Shadow dialog box appears, as shown in Figure 16-23.

11. Select **Shadow T**ype

12. Select **L**ower **Right**

To exit the dialog box and return to the document window,

13. Select **OK**

14. Select **Close**

15. Select **OK** 2 times

16. On your own, use the Center Current Page feature to center the title page and utilize the Suppress feature so that the page number will not print on the title page. Also, since you added a page, you will need to change the starting page number for the table of contents page. Finally, locate the (your name) text, delete it, and type your name

17. Save and print the document

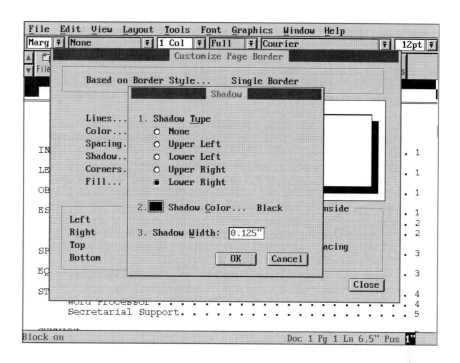

Figure 16-23

Compare your document to the one shown in Figure 16-24 beginning on page 451.

18. Exit WordPerfect

On Your Own

Review of Commands

Description	Menu Commands	Function Keys
Mark a conditional end of page	_____	_____
Apply widow/ orphan protection	_____	_____
Create a footnote	_____	_____
Edit a footnote	_____	_____
Create a paragraph border	_____	_____
Create a QuickMark	_____	_____
Find a QuickMark	_____	_____
Create a bookmark	_____	_____
Locate a bookmark	_____	_____
Create a comment	_____	_____

Apply paragraph numbering	_____	_____
Mark text for a table of contents	_____	_____
Define a table of contents	_____	_____
Generate a table of contents	_____	_____
Create a page border	_____	_____

▌ Lesson Review

1. What is the purpose of the Conditional End of Page feature?

2. What is a widow/orphan in WordPerfect?

3. What distinguishes footnotes from endnotes?

4. After inserting a footnote, can you see it on your document screen?

5. What happens to remaining footnotes when new ones are added or others are deleted?

6. List the three steps to take in creating a table of contents.

7. What is the purpose of a comment?

8. How can you place one border around three paragraphs?

9. What does the Bookmark feature allow you to do?

10. Define a QuickMark.

11. What happens if a second QuickMark is added to a document?

12. How many levels of automatic paragraph numbering are available?

13. List the numbering styles for each level of automatic paragraph numbering.

14. When the Page Border feature is activated on a page, where is the border printed?

▌ Assignments

16.1 Directions

1. Retrieve the document called DOWNSIZE.SD from your sample disk, and save it as DOWNSIZE.NEW to keep the original intact.

2. Create a title page with a border and the following information in bold, attractively spaced:

MOVING INFORMATION SYSTEMS APPLICATIONS FROM LARGE SYSTEMS TO NETWORKED MICROCOMPUTERS/ (DOWNSIZING)/The Association of Management/Conference Paris, France, 1994

3. In the Literature Review section there are four citations by Eckerson, Bulkeley, Horwitt, and Sheier. Remove the last name and date, enter a footnote number in its place, and use the following information for the footnote for each of the citations:

Bulkeley, William M., "PC Networks Begin to Oust Mainframes in Some Companies." The Wall Street Journal, May 23, 1990.

Eckerson, Wayne, "Hospital to Replace Minis with Microcomputer LANS." Network World, October 8, 1990.

Scheier, Robert L., "Local Area Networks Pull End Run on the Mainframe." P C Week, September 10, 1990.

Horwitt, Daniel S., "Turn of the Century Tactics for Mainframes." Mainframe Management, August 4, 1990.

4. At the end of the Research Design section, add the following, and number the paragraphs using WordPerfect's automatic paragraph numbering feature:

The questions asked of each of the companies were as follows:

Please describe the hardware in the company's information system at present.

What hardware was added to the above list in the last five years?

What hardware was eliminated, downgraded, upgraded, or used in a different manner in the last five years?

How many networks do you have?

5. To prevent any widows or orphans from occurring, at the beginning of your document implement the Widow/Orphan feature.

6. Save, print, and exit the document.

16.2 Directions

1. Open the DOWNSIZE.NEW document, and save as DOWN-SIZE.TWO.

2. Following the title page, put in a header entitled "Downsizing" with an attractive horizontal line and page numbering.

3. Protect the table with conditional end of page.

4. Mark the following headings for a table of contents: Abstract, Introduction, Review of Literature, Research Design, Research Findings, and Conclusions.

5. Create a new page after the title page for the table of contents. (Be sure your pointer is after the Header code.)

6. Define the table of contents for one level.

7. Change the page number on the table of contents page to a lower-case Roman numeral (i).

8. Change the page number of the first page of text to an Arabic 1.

9. Generate the table of contents.

10. Save again, print, and exit.

EXECUTIVE SUITE FEASIBILITY REPORT

For

Baker, Inc.

(today's date)

Submitted by

PencilPushers, Inc.
(your name)

Figure 16-24

TABLE OF CONTENTS

i

Figure 16-24 *(continued)*

EXECUTIVE SUITE FEASIBILITY REPORT

Quote Valid through 3/31

INTENT

This report is to examine the feasibility of the leasing executive suites at Baker, Inc.'s leased space located at 3 Plaza Road, Colorado, and the corresponding expected lease revenues, additional services revenues and implementation costs.

LEASING AMENITIES

Baker, Inc. has estimated that 13 - 14 of its offices located at 3 Plaza Road, Suite 200, Boulder, Colorado could be made available for executive suite leasing (see Attachment A).

Executive suites are medium to small office spaces in which the lease price includes, in this instance, telephone equipment and answering services, reception services, and conference room usage.

OBJECTIVE

The objective of making these offices available for executive suite leasing would be to cover Five Thousand Dollars ($5,000.00) of fixed lease costs.

ESTIMATED COST PER SQUARE FOOT

The total square footage of the lease space to be made available for executive suites is approximately 1844 square feet, which is

Figure 16-24 *(continued)*

1

divided into approximately nine (9) exterior offices and five (5) interior offices.

Monthly Gross Figures:

Due to current market pricing for commercial office space, the available space for lease should gross on average $2.88 per square foot per month, netting on average a gross of $5,310.00 for the available space at 100% occupancy. The average gross is based on nine exterior offices with a total of 1325 square feet grossing $3.00 per square foot or $3975 and five interior offices with a total of 519 square feet grossing $2.60 per square foot or $1350. The support for this pricing[1] is found in the table below:

Building	$/Sq.Ft.	Expenses	Finish	Sq/Ft.
Sienna	1.08	.42	1.25	2.75
Exeter	.92	.42	1.25	2.59
Park	1.00	.42	1.25	2.67
Meadow	1.13	.42	1.25	2.80

Existing Leases:

Let it be understood that there are existing executive suite leases available in the range of $1.85 - $3.00 per square foot. However, consideration for building and office location, cost of parking, and available services should be

---

1 These figures are based on lease space of approximately 650 square feet.

2

Figure 16-24 *(continued)*

made. Superior service and location buildings are maintaining higher than average lease and occupancy rates.

SPECIAL SERVICES

As previously mentioned, the executive suites offered by Baker, Inc. would include the services of telephone equipment and answering services, reception services, and conference room usage. Additional services should, however, be provided and these are in the areas of fax services, copy machine usage, and secretarial services.

EQUIPMENT

Baker, Inc. already has existing equipment for telephone, fax, and copy services, which should suffice until approximately 50% of the available suites are occupied. Fax and copy services should not be included in lease pricing, but should be billed on a per usage basis with pricing being set by Baker's cost plus needed profit percentage. Thus, when approximately 50% - 75% of the suites are leased, additional equipment to support the suites independently could be purchased and/or leased .

Secretarial support should be offered at the executive suites on a per usage basis[2]. A wide range of services could be provided such as word processing, clerical, desktop publishing, bookkeeping/billing, etc. with a minimum offer of

---

2 Unit prices available upon request.

Figure 16-24 *(continued)*

computerized word processing and clerical functions. The equipment necessary to operate such secretarial services effectively would be:

1.   An IBM compatible computer running at 33-50 Mhz with 8MB of RAM memory, 300MB hard drive, two floppy drives, super VGA color monitor, tape backup and CD ROM drives.

2.   A 24 pin dot matrix printer with tractor and single sheet feeding.

3.   A laser printer with two paper trays and envelope feeder with a spool share device.

Approximate cost for this equipment would be $7,500.00. Pricing for the offered services would be dependent on the cost of production. However, the Boulder area pricing for this type of word processing service does range from $16.00 - $20.00 per hour for word processing with Denver being as high as $25.00 per hour. Industry Production Standards are also available to assist in the billing process to insure clientele are being charged a fair time for the work produced.

STAFFING

Word Processor:

The cost of a full-time word processor to provide secretarial services may be prohibitive at the onset (see Attachment B). Baker, Inc. does have the ability

4

Figure 16-24 *(continued)*

to utilize the services of Uptown Realty Consultants secretaries until the work volume is adequate to support the full-time position.

Other options available are to sell additional devices to the Realtors who may be farming out their overload or unavailable clerical work out of the office, or Baker could use profits from the secretarial services to supplement lease prices to achieve the $5,000.00 per month goal.

Secretarial Support:

Secretarial support for the executive suites should be relatively self-sufficient. That is to say that all administrative support, billing and bookkeeping for the suites should be a function of the secretarial service. This service and administration could be maintained in-house or could be contracted out to a company specializing in executive suite services. Contracting out the secretarial services could potentially save training costs, but limit flexibility of revenues.

SUMMARY

In review, to achieve the $5,000.00 per month goal, Baker, Inc. would need to lease 14 offices for an average of $2.88 per square foot per month. The costs involved at the onset of this endeavor would be in the areas of computer equipment and secretarial costs. Additional costs acquired once service demands

Figure 16-24 *(continued)*

5

exceeded current equipment capacity would be in the areas of a fax machine, an additional copier and additional telephone equipment (figures unavailable).

The revenues to offset these additional expenses would be realized from charges to the executive suite tenants on a per usage basis. A projected Income Statement for the first 12 months of this endeavor is attached for clarification.

Figure 16-24 *(continued)*

6

COMMAND SUMMARY

Feature	Menu Selection	Shortcut
Add Markings	File ⇒ Compare Documents ⇒ Add Markings	Alt + F5, 8
Advance	Layout ⇒ Other ⇒ Advance	Shift + F8, 7, 6
Alignment	Layout ⇒ Alignment	Shift + F8, 1, 2
Appearance	Font ⇒ Font ⇒ Appearance	Ctrl + F8, 3
Append Block (Block on)	Edit ⇒ Append	Ctrl + F4, 4
Backup Options	File ⇒ Setup ⇒ Environment ⇒ Backup	Shift + F1, 3, 1
Beep Options	File ⇒ Setup ⇒ Environment ⇒ Beep	Shift + F1, 3, 2
Block	Edit ⇒ Block	Alt + F4 or F12
Bold	Font ⇒ Bold	F6 or Ctrl + B
Borders	Graphics ⇒ Borders	Alt + F9, 3
Box (Graphics Create)	Graphics ⇒ Graphic Boxes ⇒ Create	Alt + F9, 1, 1
Box (Graphics Edit)	Graphics ⇒ Graphic Boxes ⇒ Edit	Alt + F9, 1, 2
Button Bar	View ⇒ Button Bar	
Button Bar Setup	View ⇒ Button Bar Setup	
Cancel		F1
Cancel Print Jobs	File ⇒ Print/Fax ⇒ Control Printer ⇒ Cancel	Shift + F7, 6, 1
Cascade Window	Window ⇒ Cascade	Ctrl + F3, 1, 5
Case Conversion	Edit ⇒ Convert Case	Shift + F3
Center All Pages (Top to Bottom)	Layout ⇒ Page ⇒ Center Pages	Shift + F8, 3, 3
Center Page (Top/Bottom)	Layout ⇒ Page ⇒ Center Current Page	Shift + F8, 3, 2
Center Text	Layout ⇒ Alignment ⇒ Center	Shift + F6
Change Default Directory	File ⇒ File Manager ⇒ Change Default Dir	F5, H
Character Format	Layout ⇒ Character	Shift + F8, 6
Close File	File ⇒ Close	F7

Feature	Menu Selection	Shortcut
Color (Printer)	Font ⇒ Print Color	Ctrl + F8, C
Color (Display)	File ⇒ Setup ⇒ Display ⇒ Graphics ⇒ Color	Shift + F1, 2, 1, 2
Color (Font)	Font ⇒ Font Color	Ctrl + F8, C
Columns	Layout ⇒ Columns	Alt + F7, 1
Comment	Layout ⇒ Comment	Ctrl + F7, 2
Compare Document	File ⇒ Compare Document	Alt + F5
Compose Character	Font ⇒ WP Characters	Ctrl + W
Conditional End of Page	Layout ⇒ Other ⇒ Conditional End of Page	Shift + F8, 7, 2
Control Printer	File ⇒ Print/Fax ⇒ Control Printer	Shift + F7, 6
Convert Case (Block on)	Edit ⇒ Convert Case	Shift + F3
Copy Block (Block On)	Edit ⇒ Copy	Ctrl + F4, 2
Copy	Edit ⇒ Copy	Ctrl + C
Copy File	File ⇒ File Manager ⇒ Copy	F5, 4
Copy and Paste (Block on)	Edit ⇒ Copy and Paste	Ctrl + F4, 2 or Ctrl + Ins
Counters	Layout ⇒ Character ⇒ Counters	Shift + F8, 6, 4
Cross Reference	Tools ⇒ Cross Reference	Alt + F5, 1, 4
Cross Reference, Generate	Tools ⇒ Generate	Alt + F5, 4
Create Directory	File ⇒ File Manager ⇒ Change Default Dir	F5, H
Current Directory	File ⇒ File Manager ⇒ Current Dir	F5, U
Cut (Block on)	Edit ⇒ Cut	Ctrl + X
Cut and Paste (Block on)	Edit ⇒ Cut and Paste	Ctrl + F4, 1
Date, Code	Tools ⇒ Date ⇒ Code	Shift + F5, 2
Date, Format	Tools ⇒ Date ⇒ Format	Shift + F5, 3
Date, Text	Tools ⇒ Date ⇒ Text	Shift + F5, 1
Decimal Align	Layout ⇒ Character ⇒ Decimal Align	Shift + F8, 6, 1
Delay Codes	Layout ⇒ Page ⇒ Delay Codes	Shift + F8, 3, D
Delete (Block On)	Edit ⇒ Cut	Ctrl + F4, 3
Delete File/Directory	File ⇒ File Manager ⇒ Delete	F5, 6
Directory Tree	File ⇒ File Manager ⇒ Directory Tree	F5, F8
Document Comments	Layout ⇒ Comment	Ctrl + F7, 2
Document Compare	File ⇒ Compare Documents	Alt + F5, 8 or 9
Document Format	Layout ⇒ Document	Shift + F8, 4
Document Initial Codes	Layout ⇒ Document ⇒ Document Initial Codes	Shift + F8, 4, 1
Document Summary	Layout ⇒ Document ⇒ Summary	Shift + F8, 4, 4
DOS Shell	File ⇒ Go to Shell	Ctrl + F1, 1
Dot Leaders	Layout ⇒ Character ⇒ Dot Leader Character	Shift + F8, 6, 3
Double Sided Printing	Layout ⇒ Page ⇒ Double Sided Printing	Shift + F8, 3, 8
Double Underline	Font ⇒ Double Underline	Ctrl + F8, 3, 3
Endnote	Layout ⇒ Endnote	Ctrl + F7, 3
Enter (or Return)		Enter
Envelope	Layout ⇒ Envelope	Alt + F12
Equation	Graphics ⇒ Graphics Boxes ⇒ Create	Alt + F9, 1, 1

Feature	Menu Selection	Shortcut
Exit	File ⇒ Exit	[F7]
Exit WordPerfect	File ⇒ Exit WP	[Home], [F7]
Export File	File ⇒ Save As ⇒ Format	[F10], 2
Extra Large Font	Font ⇒ Size/Position ⇒ Extra Large	[Ctrl] + [F8], 4, 6
File Manager	File ⇒ File Manager	[F5]
Fill Styles	Graphics ⇒ Fill Styles	[Alt] + [F9], 4
Fine Font	Font ⇒ Size/Position ⇒ Fine	[Ctrl] + [F8], 4, 2
Flush Right	Layout ⇒ Alignment ⇒ Flush Right	[Alt] + [F6]
Font	Font ⇒ Font ⇒ Font	[Ctrl] + [F8], 1
Font Appearance	Font ⇒ Font ⇒ Appearance	[Ctrl] + [F8], 3
Font Size (relative)	Font ⇒ Font ⇒ Relative Size	[Ctrl] + [F8], 4
Font Size (points)	Font ⇒ Font ⇒ Size	[Ctrl] + [F8], 2
Font Position	Font ⇒ Font ⇒ Position	[Ctrl] + [F8], 5
Footers	Layout ⇒ Header/Footer/Watermark ⇒ Footers	[Shift] + [F8], 5, 2
Footnotes	Layout ⇒ Footnote	[Ctrl] + [F7], 1
Force Page	Layout ⇒ Page ⇒ Force Page	[Shift] + [F8], 3, F
Format	Layout	[Shift] + [F8]
Frame Window	Window ⇒ Frame	[Ctrl] + [F3], 1, 2
Generate	Tools ⇒ Generate	[Alt] + [F5], 4
Go to Character/Page	Edit ⇒ Go to	[Ctrl] + [Home]
Go to Shell	File ⇒ Go to Shell	[Ctrl] + [F1], 1
Grammatik	Tools ⇒ Writing Tools ⇒ Grammatik	[Alt] + [F1], 3
Graphics	Graphics	[Alt] + [F9]
Graphics Boxes	Graphics ⇒ Graphics Boxes	[Alt] + [F9], 1
Graphics Image Retrieve	Graphics ⇒ Retrieve Image	[Alt] + [F9], R
Graphics Lines	Graphics ⇒ Graphics Lines	[Alt] + [F9], 2
Graphics Print Quality	File ⇒ Print/Fax ⇒ Graphics Quality	[Shift] + [F7], G
Graphics Mode	View ⇒ Graphics Mode	[Ctrl] + [F3], 3
Hard Hyphen	Layout ⇒ Special Codes ⇒ Hyphen	-
Hard Page	Layout ⇒ Alignment ⇒ Hard Page	[Ctrl] + [Enter]
Hard Return		[Enter]
Hard Space	Layout ⇒ Special Codes ⇒ Hard Space	[Home] + [Spacebar]
Hard Tab (left)	Layout ⇒ Special Codes ⇒ Left	[Home], [Tab]
Hard Tab (center)	Layout ⇒ Special Codes ⇒ Center	[Home], [Shift] + [F6]
Hard Tab (right)	Layout ⇒ Special Codes ⇒ Right	[Home], [Alt] + [F6]
Hard Tab (decimal)	Layout ⇒ Special Codes ⇒ Decimal	[Ctrl] + [F6]
Headers	Layout ⇒ Header/Footer/Watermark ⇒ Headers	[Shift] + [F8], 5, 1
Help	Help	[F1]
Hidden Text	Font ⇒ Hidden Text	
Home		[Home]
Horizontal Line	Graphics ⇒ Graphics Lines ⇒ Create	[Alt] + [F9], 2, 1

Feature	Menu Selection	Shortcut
Horizontal Scroll Bar	View ⇒ Horizontal Scroll Bar	
Hypertext	Tools ⇒ Hypertext	`Alt` + `F5`, 6
Hyphenation (on/off)	Layout ⇒ Line ⇒ Hyphenation	`Shift` + `F8`, 1, 6
Hyphenation (zone)	Layout ⇒ Line ⇒ Hyphenation Zone	`Shift` + `F8`, 1, 7
Indent (left)	Layout ⇒ Alignment ⇒ Indent ->	`F4`
Indent (left/right)	Layout ⇒ Alignment ⇒ Indent -><-	`Shift` + `F4`
Index Define	Tools ⇒ Index ⇒ Define	`Alt` + `F5`, 2, 4
Index Generate	Tools ⇒ Index ⇒ Generate	`Alt` + `F5`, 4
Index Mark	Tools ⇒ Index ⇒ Mark	`Alt` + `F5`, 1, 1
Initial Codes	Layout ⇒ Document ⇒ Document Initial Codes	`Shift` + `F8`, 4, 1
Initial Codes Setup	Layout ⇒ Document ⇒ Initial Codes Setup	`Shift` + `F8`, 4, 2
Initial Font	Layout ⇒ Document ⇒ Initial Font	`Shift` + `F8`, 4, 3
Initialize Printer	File ⇒ Print/Fax ⇒ Initialize Printer	`Shift` + `F7`, 8
Insert		`Ins`
Italics	Font ⇒ Italics	`Ctrl` + `F8`, 3, 4 or `Ctrl` + I
Justification	Layout ⇒ Justification	`Shift` + `F8`, 1, 2
Keyboard Layout	File ⇒ Setup ⇒ Keyboard Layout	`Shift` + `F1`, 4
Labels	Layout ⇒ Page ⇒ Labels	`Shift` + `F8`, 3, 5
Language	Layout ⇒ Other ⇒ Language	`Shift` + `F8`, 7, 7
Large Font	Font ⇒ Size/Position ⇒ Large	`Ctrl` + `F8`, 4, 4
Line Draw	Graphics ⇒ Line Draw	`Ctrl` + `F3`, 5
Line Format	Layout ⇒ Line	`Shift` + `F8`, 1
Line, Graphic	Graphics ⇒ Graphics Lines ⇒ Create	`Alt` + `F9`, 2, 1
Line Height	Layout ⇒ Line ⇒ Line Height	`Shift` + `F8`, 1, 8
Line Numbering	Layout ⇒ Line ⇒ Line Numbering	`Shift` + `F8`, 1, 4
Line Spacing	Layout ⇒ Line ⇒ Line Spacing	`Shift` + `F8`, 1, 3
List Define	Tools ⇒ List ⇒ Define	`Alt` + `F5`, 2, 2
List Generate	Tools ⇒ Generate	`Alt` + `F5`, 4
List Mark	Tools ⇒ List ⇒ Mark	`Alt` + `F5`, 2
List Files	File ⇒ File Manager	`F5`
Location of Files	File ⇒ Setup ⇒ Location of Files	`Shift` + `F1`, 5
Look (at files)	File ⇒ File Manager ⇒ Look	`F5`, 3
Macro Record	Tools ⇒ Macro ⇒ Record	`Ctrl` + `F10`
Macro Control	Tools ⇒ Macro ⇒ Control	`Ctrl` + `Pg Up`
Macro Play	Tools ⇒ Macro ⇒ Play	`Alt` + `F10`
Margin Release	Layout ⇒ Alignment ⇒ Back Tab	`Shift` + `Tab`
Margins	Layout ⇒ Margins	`Shift` + `F8`, 2
Mark Text		`Alt` + `F5`
Master Document	File ⇒ Master Document	`Alt` + `F5`, 3

Feature	Menu Selection	Shortcut
Math	Tools ⇒ Math	`Alt` + `F7`, 3
Maximize Window	Window ⇒ Maximize	`Ctrl` + `F3`, 1, 3
Merge Define	Tools ⇒ Merge ⇒ Define	`Shift` + `F9`
Merge Run	Tools ⇒ Merge ⇒ Run	`Ctrl` + `F9`, 1
Minimize Window	Window ⇒ Minimize	`Ctrl` + `F3`, 1, 1
Mouse	File ⇒ Setup ⇒ Mouse	`Shift` + `F1`, 1
Move Block (Block on)	Edit ⇒ Cut and Paste	`Ctrl` + `F4`, 1
Move Page	Edit ⇒ Select ⇒ Page	`Ctrl` + `F4`, 3, 1
Move Paragraph	Edit ⇒ Select ⇒ Paragraph	`Ctrl` + `F4`, 2, 1
Move Rectangle (Block on)	Edit ⇒ Select ⇒ Rectangle	`Ctrl` + `F4`, 1
Move Sentence	Edit ⇒ Select ⇒ Sentence	`Ctrl` + `F4`, 1
Move Tabular Column (Block)	Edit ⇒ Select ⇒ Tabular Column	`Ctrl` + `F4`, 1
Name Search	File ⇒ File Manager ⇒ Name Search	`F5`, N
New Page Number	Layout ⇒ Page ⇒ Page Numbering ⇒ Page Number ⇒ New Number	`Shift` + `F8`, 3, 1, 2, 1
New Endnote Number	Layout ⇒ Endnote ⇒ New Number	`Ctrl` + `F7`, 3, 3, 1
New Footnote Number	Layout ⇒ Footnote ⇒ New Number	`Ctrl` + `F7`, 1, 3, 1
New File	File ⇒ New	
Next Window	Window ⇒ Next	`Ctrl` + `F3`, 1, 6 or `Ctrl` +Y
Normal Font	Font ⇒ Normal	`Ctrl` + N
Number of Copies	File ⇒ Print/Fax ⇒ Number of Copies	`Shift` + `F7`, N
Open File	File ⇒ Open	`Shift` + `F10`
Other Format	Layout ⇒ Other	`Shift` + `F8`, 7
Outline	Tools ⇒ Outline	`Ctrl` + `F5`
Outline Bar	View ⇒ Outline Bar	
Overstrike Create	Layout ⇒ Character ⇒ Create Overstrike	`Shift` + `F8`, 6, 5
Overstrike Edit	Layout ⇒ Character ⇒ Edit Overstrike	`Shift` + `F8`, 6, 6
Page Borders	Layout ⇒ Page ⇒ Page Borders	`Shift` + `F8`, 3, B
Page Break	Layout ⇒ Alignment ⇒ Hard Page	`Ctrl` + `Enter`
Page Format	Layout ⇒ Page	`Shift` + `F8`, 3
Page Mode	View ⇒ Page Mode	`Ctrl` + `F3`, 4
Page Numbering	Layout ⇒ Page ⇒ Page Numbering	`Shift` + `F8`, 3, 1
Paper Size/Type	Layout ⇒ Page ⇒ Size/Type	`Shift` + `F8`, 3, 4
Paragraph Borders	Layout ⇒ Line ⇒ Paragraph Borders	`Shift` + `F8`, 1, 5
Paragraph Numbering	Layout ⇒ Styles	`Alt` + `F8`
Password Protection	File ⇒ Save As ⇒ Password	`F10`, `F8`
Paste Block	Edit ⇒ Paste	`Ctrl` + `F4`, P or `Ctrl` + V
Position	Font ⇒ Size/Position	`Ctrl` + `F8`, 5
Previous Window	Window ⇒ Previous	`Ctrl` + `F3`, 1, 7
Print Block (Block on)	File ⇒ Print/Fax ⇒ Blocked Text	`Shift` + `F7`, 5

Feature	Menu Selection	Shortcut
Print Color	Font ⇒ Print Color	Ctrl + F8, C
Print Document on Disk	File ⇒ Print/Fax ⇒ Document on Disk	Shift + F7, 3
Print Full Document	File ⇒ Print/Fax ⇒ Full Document	Shift + F7, 1
Print Multiple Copies	File ⇒ Print/Fax ⇒ Number of Copies	Shift + F7, N
Print Multiple Pages	File ⇒ Print/Fax ⇒ Multiple Pages	Shift + F7, 4
Print Preview	File ⇒ Print Preview	Shift + F7, 7
Printer Control	File ⇒ Print/Fax ⇒ Control Printer	Shift + F7, 6
Printer Functions	Layout ⇒ Other ⇒ Printer Functions	Shift + F8, 7, 9
Printer Initialize	File ⇒ Print/Fax ⇒ Initialize Printer	Shift + F7, 8
Printer Select	File ⇒ Print/Fax ⇒ Select	Shift + F7, S
Protect Block	Layout ⇒ Other ⇒ Block Protect	Shift + F8, 7, 1
Pull-Down Menus	View ⇒ Pull-Down Menus	
QuickFinder	File ⇒ File Manager ⇒ Use QuickFinder	F5, F4
QuickList	File ⇒ File Manager ⇒ QuickList	F5, F6
QuickMark Find	Edit ⇒ Bookmark ⇒ Find QuickMark	Ctrl + F
QuickMark Set	Edit ⇒ Bookmark ⇒ Set QuickMark	Ctrl + Q
Redline	Font ⇒ Redline	Ctrl + F8, 3, 8
Redo (List Files)	File ⇒ File Manager ⇒ Redo	F5, F5
Remove Redline/Strikeout	File ⇒ Compare Documents ⇒ Remove Markings	Alt + F5, 9
Rename File	File ⇒ File Manager ⇒ Move/Rename	F5, 5
Repeat	Edit ⇒ Repeat	Ctrl + R
Replace Text	Edit ⇒ Replace	Alt + F2
Retrieve Block	Edit ⇒ Paste	Ctrl + F4, P or Ctrl + V
Retrieve Document	File ⇒ Retrieve	Shift + F10
Retrieve Image	Graphics ⇒ Retrieve Image	
Reveal Codes	View ⇒ Reveal Codes	Alt + F3 or F11
Ribbon	View ⇒ Ribbon	
Save	File ⇒ Save	Ctrl + F12
Save As, File or Block	File ⇒ Save As	F10
Screen Setup	View ⇒ Screen Setup	Ctrl + F3
Scroll Bar - Horizontal	View ⇒ Horizontal Scroll Bar	
Scroll Bar - Vertical	View ⇒ Vertical Scroll Bar	
Search Backward	Edit ⇒ Search ⇒ Backward Search ⇒ Search	Shift + F2
Search Forward	Edit ⇒ Search ⇒ Search	F2
Select	Edit ⇒ Select	Ctrl + F4
Select Printer	File ⇒ Print/Fax ⇒ Select	Shift + F7, S
SetUp	File ⇒ Setup	Shift + F1
Shading	Graphics ⇒ Fill Styles	Alt + F9, 4
Shadow (font)	Font ⇒ Shadow	Ctrl + F8, 3, 6
Shell	File ⇒ Go to Shell	Ctrl + F1, 1
Size/Position Text	Font ⇒ Size/Position	Ctrl + F8

Feature	Menu Selection	Shortcut
Small Size Font	Font ⇒ Size/Position ⇒ Small	`Ctrl` + `F8`, 4, 3
Smallcaps	Font ⇒ Small Caps	`Ctrl` + `F8`, 3, 7
Sort	Tools ⇒ Sort	`Ctrl` + `F9`, 2
Sort (Files)	File ⇒ File Manager ⇒ Sort by	`F5`, 9
Sound Clip	Tools ⇒ Sound Clip	`Ctrl` + `F7`, 5
Spacing	Layout ⇒ Line ⇒ Line Spacing	`Shift` + `F8`, 1, 3
Special Characters	Font ⇒ WP Characters	`Ctrl` + W
Special Codes	Layout ⇒ Character ⇒ Special Codes	`Shift` + `F8`, 6, 7
Spell Check	Tools ⇒ Writing Tools ⇒ Speller	`Ctrl` + `F2`
Spreadsheet	Tools ⇒ Spreadsheet	`Alt` + `F7`, 5
Stop Printing	Files ⇒ Print/Fax ⇒ Control Printer ⇒ Stop	`Shift` + `F7`, 6, S
Strikeout	Font ⇒ Strikeout	`Ctrl` + `F8`, 3, 9
Styles	Layout ⇒ Styles	`Alt` + `F8`
Subdivide Page	Layout ⇒ Page ⇒ Subdivide Page	`Shift` + `F8`, 3, 6
Subscript	Font ⇒ Size/Position ⇒ Subscript	`Ctrl` + `F8`, 5, 3
Summary (document)	Layout ⇒ Document ⇒ Summary	`Shift` + `F8`, 4, 4
Superscript	Font ⇒ Size/Position ⇒ Superscript	`Ctrl` + `F8`, 5, 2
Suppress Page#/Hdrs/Ftrs	Layout ⇒ Page ⇒ Suppress	`Shift` + `F8`, 3, 9
Switch to Next Window	Window ⇒ Switch	`Shift` + `F3`
Switch to Specific Window	Window ⇒ Switch To	`Ctrl` + `F3`, 1, 8 or `F3`
Tab Set	Layout ⇒ Tab Set	`Ctrl` + `F11`
Table Create	Layout ⇒ Tables ⇒ Create	`Alt` + `F7`, 2, 1
Table Edit	Layout ⇒ Tables ⇒ Edit	`Alt` + `F11`
Table of Authorities	Tools ⇒ Table of Authorities	`Alt` + `F5`, 2, 3
Table of Contents, Define	Tools ⇒ Table of Contents ⇒ Define	`Alt` + `F5`, 2, 1
Table of Contents, Generate	Tools ⇒ Generate	`Alt` + `F5`, 4
Table of Contents, Mark	Tools ⇒ Table of Contents ⇒ Mark	`Alt` + `F5`, 1
Text Mode	View ⇒ Text Mode	`Ctrl` + `F3`, 2
Text Print Quality	Files ⇒ Print/Fax ⇒ Text Quality	`Shift` + `F7`, T
Thesaurus	Tools ⇒ Writing Tools ⇒ Thesaurus	`Alt` + `F1`, 2
Thousands Separator	Layout ⇒ Character ⇒ Thousands Separator	`Shift` + `F8`, 6, 2
Tile Window	Window ⇒ Tile	`Ctrl` + `F3`, 1, 4
Typeover		`Ins`
Undelete	Edit ⇒ Undelete	`Esc`
Underline	Font ⇒ Underline	`F8` or `Ctrl` + U
Undo	Edit ⇒ Undo	`Ctrl` + Z
Vertical Line (graphics)	Graphics ⇒ Graphics Lines ⇒ Create	`Alt` + `F9`, 2, 1
Vertical Scroll Bar	View ⇒ Vertical Scroll Bar	
Very Large Size Font	Font ⇒ Size/Position ⇒ Very Large	`Ctrl` + `F8`, 4, 5
View Graphics Mode	View ⇒ Graphics Mode	`Ctrl` + `F3`, 3
View Page Mode	View ⇒ Page	`Ctrl` + `F3`, 4

Feature	**Menu Selection**	**Shortcut**
Watermark	Layout ⇒ Header/Footer/Watermark ⇒ Watermarks	Shift + F8 , 5, 3
Widow/Orphan	Layout ⇒ Other ⇒ Widow/Orphan	Shift + F8 , 7, 3
Window	Window	Ctrl + F3 , 1
Window Cascade	Window ⇒ Cascade	Ctrl + F3 , 1, 5
Window Frame	Window ⇒ Frame	Ctrl + F3 , 1, 2
Window Maximize	Window ⇒ Maximize	Ctrl + F3 , 1, 3
Window Minimize	Window ⇒ Minimize	Ctrl + F3 , 1, 1
Window Next	Window ⇒ Next	Ctrl + F3 , 1, 6 or Ctrl + X
Window Previous	Window ⇒ Previous	Ctrl + F3 , 1, 7
Window Switch	Window ⇒ Switch	Shift + F3
Window Switch To	Window ⇒ Switch To	Ctrl + F3 , 1, 8 or F3
Window Tile	Window ⇒ Tile	Ctrl + F3 , 1, 4
WordPerfect Characters	Font ⇒ WP Characters	Ctrl + W
Word Search	File ⇒ File Manager ⇒ Search	F5 , E
Writing Tools	Tools ⇒ Writing Tools	Alt + F1
Zoom	View ⇒ Zoom	Ctrl + F3 , 7

B

CODES

APPENDIX

Code	Description
-	Hard Hyphen (Character)
[-Hyphen]	Hyphen
[-Soft Hyphen]	Soft Hyphen
[-Soft Hyphen EOL]	Soft Hyphen at End of Line
A [Auto Hyphen EOL]	Automatic Hyphen at End of Line
B [Back Tab]	Back Tab (Margin Release)
[Bar Code]	Bar Code
[Begin Gen Txt]	Beginning of Generated Text
[Binding Width]	Binding Width
[Block]	Block
[Block Pro Off]	Block Protect Off
[Block Pro On]	Block Protect On
[Bold Off]	Bold Off
[Bold On]	Bold On
[Bookmark]	Bookmark
[Bot Mar]	Bottom Margin
[Box Num Dec]	Box Number Decrement
[Box Num Disp]	Box Number Display
[Box Num Inc]	Box Number Increment
[Box Num Meth]	Box Number Method
[Box Num Set]	Box Number Set

	Code	Description
C	[Calc Col]	Calculation Column (Math)
	[Cancel Hyph]	Cancel Hyphenation of Word
	[Cell]	Table Cell
	[Change BOL Char]	Change Beginning of Line Character
	[Change EOL Char]	Change End of Line Character
	[Chap Num Dec]	Chapter Number Decrement
	[Chap Num Disp]	Chapter Number Display
	[Chap Num Inc]	Chapter Number Increment
	[Chap Num Meth]	Chapter Number Method
	[Chap Num Set]	Chapter Number Set
	[Char Box]	Character Box
	[Char Shade Change]	Character Shade Change
	[Char Style Off]	Character Style Off
	[Char Style On]	Character Style On
	[Cntr Cur Pg]	Center Current Page (Top to Bottom)
	[Cntr on Cur Pos]	Center on Cursor Position
	[Cntr on Mar]	Center on Margins
	[Cntr on Mar (Dot)]	Center on Margins with Dot Leaders
	[Cntr Pgs]	Center Pages (Top to Bottom)
	[CNTR TAB]	Hard Centered Tab
	[Cntr Tab]	Centered Tab
	[CNTR TAB (DOT)]	Hard Centered Tab with Dot Leaders
	[Cntr Tab (Dot)]	Centered Tab with Dot Leaders
	[Col Border]	Column Border
	[Col Def]	Column Definition
	[Color]	Text Color
	[Comment]	Document Comment
	[Condl EOP]	Conditional End of Page
	[Count Dec]	Counter Decrement
	[Count Disp]	Counter Display
	[Count Inc]	Counter Increment
	[Count Meth]	Counter Method
	[Count Set]	Counter Set
D	[Date]	Date/Time Function
	[Date Fmt]	Date/Time Format
	[Dbl Und Off]	Double Underline Off
	[Dbl Und On]	Double Underline On
	[Dbl-Sided Print]	Double-Sided Printing
	[DEC TAB]	Hard Decimal-Aligned Tab
	[Dec Tab]	Decimal-Aligned Tab
	[DEC TAB (DOT)]	Hard Decimal-Aligned Tab with Dot Leaders
	[Dec Tab (Dot)]	Decimal-Aligned Tab with Dot Leaders
	[Dec/Align Char]	Decimal-Aligned Character

Code	**Description**
[Def Mark]	Definition Marker for Index, List, Table of Authorities, or Table of Contents
[Delay]	Delay
[Delay Off]	Delay Off
[Delay On]	Delay On
[Do Grand Tot]	Calculate Grand Total (Math)
[Do Subtot]	Calculate Subtotal (Math)
[Do Total]	Calculate Total (Math)
[Dorm HRt]	Dormant Hard Return
[Dot Lead Char]	Dot Leader Character

E

[End Cntr/Align]	End of Centering/Alignment
[End Gen Txt]	End of Generated Text
[Endnote]	Endnote
[Endnote Min]	Endnote Minimum Amount
[Endnote Num Dec]	Endnote Number Decrement
[Endnote Num Disp]	Endnote Number Display
[Endnote Num Inc]	Endnote Number Increment
[Endnote Num Meth]	Endnote Number Method
[Endnote Num Set]	Endnote Number Set
[Endnote Placement]	Endnote Placement
[Endnote Space]	Endnote Spacing
[Ext Large Off]	Extra Large Font Size Off
[Ext Large On]	Extra Large Font Size On

F

[Filename]	Filename
[Fine Off]	Fine Font Size Off
[Fine On]	Fine Font On
[First Ln Ind]	First Line Indent
[Flsh Rgt]	Flush Right
[Flsh Rgt (Dot)]	Flush Right with Dot Leaders
[Flt Cell Begin]	Floating Cell Begin
[Flt Cell End]	Floating Cell End
[Font]	Font
[Font Size]	Font Size
[Footer A]	Footer A
[Footer B]	Footer B
[Footer Sep]	Footer Separator Space
[Footnote]	Footnote
[Footnote Cont Msg]	Footnote Continued Message
[Footnote Min]	Footnote Minimum Amount
[Footnote Num Dec]	Footnote Number Decrement
[Footnote Num Disp]	Footnote Number Display
[Footnote Num Each Pg]	Restart Footnote Numbers Each Page

Code	Description
[Footnote Num Inc]	Footnote Number Increment
[Footnote Num Meth]	Footnote Number Method
[Footnote Num Set]	Footnote Number Set
[Footnote Sep Ln]	Footnote Separator Line
[Footnote Space]	Footnote Spacing
[Footnote Txt Pos]	Footnote Text Position
[Force]	Force Odd/Even Page
[Formatted Pg Num]	Formatted Page Number

G

Code	Description
[Graph Line]	Graphics Line

H

Code	Description
[HAdv]	Horizontal Advance
[HCol]	Hard Column Break
[HCol-SPg]	Hard Column Break-Soft Page Break
[Header A]	Header A
[Header B]	Header B
[Header Sep]	Header Separator Space
[Hidden Off]	Hidden Text Off
[Hidden On]	Hidden Text On
[Hidden Txt]	Hidden Body Text (Outline)
[HPg]	Hard Page Break
[HRow-HCol]	Hard Table Row-Hard Column Break
[HRow-HCol-SPg]	Hard Table Row-Hard Column Break-Soft Page Break
[HRow-HPg]	Hard Table Row-Hard Page Break
[HRt]	Hard Return
[HRt-SCol]	Hard Return-Soft Column Break
[HRt-SPg]	Hard Return-Soft Page Break
[HSpace]	Hard Space
[Hypertext Begin]	Hypertext Begin
[Hypertext End]	Hypertext End
[Hyph]	Hyphenation State
[Hyph SRt]	Hyphenation Soft Return

I

Code	Description
[Index]	Index Entry
[Italic Off]	Italics Off
[Italic On]	Italics On

J

Code	Description
[Just]	Justification
[Just Lim]	Word Spacing Justification Limits

K

Code	Description
[Kern]	Kerning

	Code	**Description**
L	[Labels Form]	Labels Form
	[Lang]	Language
	[Large Off]	Large Font Size Off
	[Large On]	Large Font Size On
	[Leading Adj]	Leading Adjustment
	[Lft HZone]	Left Edge of Hyphenation Zone
	[Lft Indent]	Left Indent
	[Lft Mar]	Left Margin
	[Lft Mar Adj]	Left Margin Adjustment
	[LFT TAB]	Hard Left-Aligned Tab
	[Lft Tab]	Left-Aligned Tab
	[LFT TAB (DOT)]	Hard Left-Aligned Tab with Dot Leaders
	[Lft Tab (Dot)]	Left-Aligned Tab with Dot Leaders
	[Lft/Rgt Indent]	Left and Right (Double) Indent
	[Link]	Spreadsheet Link
	[Link End]	Spreadsheet Link End
	[Ln Height]	Line Height
	[Ln Num]	Line Numbering
	[Ln Num Meth]	Line Numbering Method
	[Ln Num Set]	Line Number Set
	[Ln Spacing]	Line Spacing
M	[Macro Func]	Macro Function
	[Math]	Math State
	[Math Def]	Definition of Math Columns
	[Math Neg]	Math Negate
	[MRG:command]	Merge Programming Command
	[Mrk Txt List Begin]	Beginning of List Entry
	[Mrk Txt List End]	End of List Entry
	[Mrk Txt ToC Begin]	Beginning of Table of Contents Entry
	[Mrk Txt ToC End]	End of Table of Contents Entry
O	[Open Style]	Open Style
	[Outline]	Outline
	[Outln Off]	Outline Off (Font Attribute)
	[Outln On]	Outline On (Font Attribute)
	[Ovrsrk]	Overstrike
P	[Paper Sz/Typ]	Paper Size and Type
	[Para Border]	Paragraph Border
	[Para Box]	Paragraph Box
	[Para Num]	Paragraph Number
	[Para Num Set]	Paragraph Number Set
	[Para Spacing]	Paragraph Spacing

Code	Description
[Para Style]	Paragraph Style
[Para Style End]	Paragraph Style End
[Pause Ptr]	Pause Printer
[Pg Border]	Page Border
[Pg Box]	Page Box
[Pg Num Dec]	Page Number Decrement
[Pg Num Disp]	Page Number Display
[Pg Num Fmt]	Page Number Format
[Pg Num Inc]	Page Number Increment
[Pg Num Meth]	Page Numbering Method
[Pg Num Pos]	Page Number Position
[Pg Num Set]	Page Number Set
[Ptr Cmnd]	Printer Command

R

Code	Description
[Redln Off]	Redline Off
[Redln On]	Redline On
[Ref Box]	Reference to Graphics Box
[Ref Chap]	Reference to Chapter
[Ref Count]	Reference to Counter
[Ref Endnote]	Reference to Endnote
[Ref Footnote]	Reference to Footnote
[Ref Para]	Reference to Paragraph
[Ref Pg]	Reference to Page
[Ref Sec Pg]	Reference to Secondary Page
[Ref Vol]	Reference to Volume
[Rgt HZone]	Right Edge of Hyphenation Zone
[Rgt Mar]	Right Margin
[Rgt Mar Adj]	Right Margin Adjustment
[RGT TAB]	Hard Right-Aligned Tab
[Rgt Tab]	Right-Aligned Tab
[RGT TAB (DOT)]	Hard Right-Aligned Tab with Dot Leaders
[Rgt Tab (Dot)]	Right-Aligned Tab with Dot Leaders
[Row]	Table Row
[Row-SCol]	Table Row-Soft Column Break
[Row-SPg]	Table Row-Soft Page Break

S

Code	Description
[Sec Pg Num Dec]	Secondary Page Number Decrement
[Sec Pg Num Disp]	Secondary Page Number Display
[Sec Pg Num Inc]	Secondary Page Number Increment
[Sec Pg Num Meth]	Secondary Page Number Method
[Sec Pg Num Set]	Secondary Page Number Set
[Shadow Off]	Shadow Off
[Shadow On]	Shadow On
[Sm Cap Off]	Small Caps Off

Code	Description
[Sm Cap On]	Small Caps On
[Small Off]	Small Font Size Off
[Small On]	Small Font Size On
[Sound]	Sound Clip
[Speller/Grammatik]	Speller/Grammatik State
[SRt]	Soft Return
[SRt-SCol]	Soft Return-Soft Column Break
[SRt-SPg]	Soft Return-Soft Page Break
[StkOut Off]	Strikeout Off
[StkOut On]	Strikeout On
[Subdivided Pg]	Subdivided Page
[Subdoc]	Subdocument (Master Document)
[Subdoc Begin]	Beginning of Subdocument
[Subdoc End]	End of Subdocument
[Subscpt Off]	Subscript Off
[Subscpt On]	Subscript On
[Subtot Entry]	Subtotal Entry (Math)
[Suppress]	Suppress Header, Footer, Watermark, or Page Number
[Suprscpt Off]	Superscript Off
[Suprscpt On]	Superscript On

T

Code	Description
[Tab Set]	Tab Set
[Target]	Target (Cross-Reference)
[Tbl Dec Tab]	Table Decimal Tab
[Tbl Def]	Table Definition
[Tbl Off]	Table Off
[Tbl Off-SCol]	Table Off-Soft Column Break
[Tbl Off-SPg]	Table Off-Soft Page Break
[Tbl Tab]	Table Tab
[THCol]	Temporary Hard Column Break
[THCol-SPg]	Temporary Hard Column Break-Soft Page Break
[Third Party]	Third Party (Non-WordPerfect Corporation) Code
[Thousands Char]	Thousands Character
[THPg]	Temporary Hard Page Break
[THRt]	Temporary Hard Return
[THRt-SCol]	Temporary Hard Return-Soft Column Break
[THRt-SPg]	Temporary Hard Return-Soft Page Break
[ToA]	Table of Authorities Entry
[Top Mar]	Top Margin
[Total Entry]	Total Entry (Math)
[TSRt]	Temporary Soft Return

Code	Description
[TSRt-SCol]	Temporary Soft Return-Soft Column Break
[TSRt-SPg]	Temporary Soft Return-Soft Page Break

U

Code	Description
[Und Off]	Underline Off
[Und On]	Underline On
[Undrln Space]	Underline Spaces
[Undrln Tab]	Underline Tab
[Unknown]	Unknown Code

V

Code	Description
[VAdv]	Vertical Advance
[Very Large Off]	Very Large Font Size Off
[Very Large On]	Very Large Font Size On
[Vol Num Dec]	Volume Number Decrement
[Vol Num Disp]	Volume Number Display
[Vol Num Inc]	Volume Number Increment
[Vol Num Meth]	Volume Numbering Method
[Vol Num Set]	Volume Number Set

W

Code	Description
[Watermark A]	Watermark A
[Watermark B]	Watermark B
[Wid/Orph]	Widow/Orphan Protect State
[Wrd/Ltr Spacing]	Word Spacing and Letter Spacing

INDEX